# Emmaus
# and the Abbé Pierre

# Emmaus and the Abbé Pierre

## An Alternative Model of Enterprise, Charity and Society

*Axelle Brodiez-Dolino*

*Translated from the French by Alexandra Harwood*

*Introductory preface by Selwyn Image CBE JP, Founder and Vice-President of Emmaus UK*

SciencesPo. Les Presses

*Emmaus and the Abbé Pierre. An Alternative Model of Enterprise, Charity and Society* was first published in French in 2008 *by* Presses de Sciences Po under the title *Emmaüs et l'abbé Pierre* – Presses de Sciences Po, 117 bd Saint-Germain, 75006 Paris, France
www.pressesdesciencespo.fr


The translation of the book was made possible thanks to the generous contribution of Emmaus UK and Emmaus International.
Translated from the French by Alexandra Harwood, a translator and conference interpreter accredited by the European Union and the United States.

ISBN print 978-2-7246-1391-9
ISBN pdf web 978-2-7246-1392-6
ISBN epub 978-2-7246-1393-3
ISBN xml 978-2-7246-1394-0

Cover photo:
"Abbé Pierre and the ragpickers, founders of Emmaus, repair site, Pomponne forest, 1953-1955" © Emmaüs International


Printed and bound in France by BSRepro.

*"I have suffered more in my life for the anger that I haven't had the courage to enact than for that which I have been able to overcome."*

*Abbé Pierre*

*"In the face of any human suffering, as far as you can, work not only to provide relief without delay but to destroy its causes. Work not only to destroy its causes, but to provide relief without delay."*

*The Rule of Emmaus*

# CONTENTS

## II – THE 1960s & 1970s: THE MOVEMENT QUIETLY BEGINS TO THRIVE



## III – 1980–2000: EMMAUS RETURNS TO THE MEDIA AND THE POLITICAL ARENA

# Preface

## An Alternative Model of Enterprise, Charity and Society

When Abbé Pierre set up the first Emmaus Community in 1949, in post-war Paris, he had no idea he was founding either a major social enterprise or an international movement. So far as he was concerned, he was simply responding to a shocking and unacceptable situation and doing what he felt was right and necessary. His experience as priest, resistance hero and parliamentarian had moulded him to fight injustice, and his activist nature was such that it had to be something practical. The level of homelessness and unemployment in the capital was, for him, a scandal that demanded dynamic action.

In this case, and with crucial input from the first twenty homeless and unemployed people he took into his own life and home, he began collecting donations of furniture, clothing and household goods for resale in a large wooden shed erected in what had formerly been the garden. Other collected items, like metal, rags and paper, were bundled and recycled. The aim was to provide a home and living for the "Companions", as the twenty were called, and to use any proceeds thereafter to help house those worse off than themselves.

This kind of thinking was so much a part of his nature and training, I think, that the originality of creating a charity that worked, restoring self-respect to those who had lost it by providing a supportive home and meaningful work, and in the process turning grudging receivers into motivated givers, barely occurred to him. Similarly, when successfully marshalling the entire population of France to address the scandal of homelessness, he seemed to regard the response as normal and to be expected. Injustice was intolerable and had to be fought. Even the name he chose for the first Community – Emmaus – taken from one of his favourite stories in the New Testament, where two disciples regained hope and purpose through an encounter with the risen Christ on the road to a small village called Emmaus, was intrinsic to his character and thinking.

Today, the Movement he created is one of the largest NGOs in France, second only in size to the Red Cross. Worldwide, across thirty-seven countries in 2012, there are 327 self-supporting Communities and more than 440 partnership organisations. Most are non-English-speaking.

My first encounter with Emmaus was in 1960, as a modern languages student at Cambridge. Abbé Pierre was a fervent internationalist who believed that by enabling students to travel and work together he could do something practical to assist reconciliation in post-Second-World-War Europe. To this end, he sought to use the Emmaus Communities established in Paris by inviting university students from around Europe to spend their summer vacation working there alongside Companions.

For three summer months I salvaged coal from cellars, cleared houses and apartments, tore paper and bundled rags. We were a motley crew. With me were two other students, as well as around twenty French Companions, a Benedictine worker-priest, and the Community leader. The Companions came from every walk of life and level of society. Many were alcoholics, nearly all ex-servicemen; a number had been in prison; one or two were redundant executives fallen on hard times. Nearly all had significant problems or trauma to overcome. We ate well, and were paid about £5 and two packets of Gauloises cigarettes a week. As the Abbé Pierre himself was always travelling, the administration of our Community (the first, as it happens) was handled by the much admired (and equally feared) Lucie Coutaz, a lay sister and his long-time assistant both in the Resistance and in parliament. He always referred to her as "the co-founder of the Emmaus Movement" and from the little I saw of her, and what I read later in her excellent book, *Quarante ans avec l'Abbé Pierre*, she was a beacon for him as well as for the integrity of the secular Movement he had created.

We worked in groups of three: a (not always totally sober) driver and two Companions. Despite occasional lapses, for which poor management was generally responsible, there was a sense of striving and purpose and that what we were doing – no one thought of it then as social enterprise – was both right and a meaningful path to changed lives and renewed purpose. Even we students were proud to be known as Companions. After three months I returned to my studies, speaking a form of French that raised some eyebrows and suppressed smiles at my university oral examination. Thereafter, for the next thirty years, I got on with my career as an international marketing consultant and forgot about Emmaus...

... Until late 1989, when homeless people began to appear on the streets of Cambridge. There was no local night shelter then, and I was asked by the founder of a charity set up to address this scandal to try and raise money for one. My business background was in market research so it was natural for me to meet the people living on the street and in the makeshift camp they had set up by the river, and to ask them what they wanted and how they felt about night shelters.

Not good. Night shelters were dreaded as places where you would be robbed while sleeping, if indeed you were able to do so surrounded by sickness, drunkenness and violence.

A few days later I was talking to a very lucid but angry man in the soup and sandwich shelter we had set up in the base of the city-centre car park. Every idea I had he shot down in flames. Eventually, I became so frustrated I asked him what on earth he did want. His answer changed my life. "I would have thought it was obvious to someone of your so-called intelligence," he said. "I want somewhere where I can work, where I feel I belong and where I can recover my self-respect."

His last two words took me back those thirty years. I tried to buy time and said that he reminded me of a French organisation called Emmaus that did just that, but that I had no idea whether it still existed or not. His next remark put the seal on my fate. "And what the **** are you going to do about it?" he asked. Emmaus UK was born.

The next day I looked in the Paris phone book, contacted Abbé Pierre, enlisted his instant and enthusiastic support and set about trying to set up an Emmaus Community in the UK.

Abbé Pierre still spoke not a word of English and most of the local friends and colleagues I was able to involve scarcely a word of French. But we visited Communities in France, wrote a business plan, and started seeking funds through our networks relying on what we had seen, what we were told by mostly highly sceptical counterparts in France and drawing on our own business and administrative experience.

In 2012, twenty-two years later, we have twenty-four Emmaus Communities up and running in the UK with a further twelve active development projects. Each costs in the order of £1.5 million to set up and fund until economic self-sufficiency is achieved. Our focus is primarily on Communities rather than housing provision. Nevertheless, the UK is now the largest and fastest-growing Emmaus Movement outside France, and external research shows that, taking all start-up and running costs into account, the net social value of the average Community over twenty years is £9.3 million. For the business-minded, this level of saving to the public purse is enough to quicken the pulse of any venture capitalist.

Shortly after its publication, Laurent Desmard gave me a copy of the French version of this history. Laurent had been Abbé Pierre's private secretary for over twenty years and told me that he thought this book was the best thing that had been written about the Movement. On reading it, I was struck by the similarity in the growing pains of this significant multi-national enterprise with our own experience in the UK, as well as that of other countries I knew.

As a result, I became convinced that if colleagues in Emmaus, as well as informed or interested readers in management and government, were able to read what really happened, as opposed to the sentimental and partial accounts available in English, and relate this to their own practical experience and expertise, the Movement's relevance to the social problems to our own time might be better appreciated; and with that, I dared to hope that our own growth in the UK and the English-speaking world might be encouraged and accelerated.

When I first proposed the publication of this history in English some concern was expressed that it was insufficiently respectful of the Founder, Abbé Pierre. He himself would, of course, have kicked that one rapidly into touch, as he was eminently aware of and quite open about his gifts and deficiencies. Indeed, in one memorable conversation a couple of years before his death about the Movement's survival when he was no longer there, he said to me: "Listen! I am the worst manager I know. If Emmaus can grow as it has while I am there, it will have no problem when I am gone."

Be all that as it may, a general consensus was rapidly achieved of the international value of a true and objective account, in English, of how the Movement grew and the conviction that this work was fit for such a purpose.

We may of course all turn out to be completely wrong. After all, history shows us that the world is filled with examples of those who have failed to learn its lessons. But even if we do not succeed fully in our primary purpose – and in social enterprise, where head and heart are often equally challenged, this is quite possible – the chronicle of Emmaus is to many of us as important an account of a social and moral enterprise as significant in the twentieth century as General Booth's seminal work *In Darkest England and the Way Out* was in the nineteenth century. On that count alone, we know it deserves to be widely read.

No project like this can succeed without teamwork, and we have been fortunate in the talents that came together to realise this with the limited funds at our disposal. Support from the (original) publishers, as well as friends and supporters of Emmaus UK, has been fantastic.

Special thanks also to Alex Harwood, our gifted translator, and our friends in Brussels, Chris Guichot de Fortis and Julia Poger, for finding and supporting her. Emma Rose, our volunteer editor in chief and the Communications team and all at Emmaus UK – fantastic work! Lastly, but critically, heartfelt thanks to two particular long-term supporters who donated the seed-corn funding that encouraged contributions from Companions and Communities of Emmaus UK and ensured that the scope and reach of this particular piece of post-war social history has been extended.

Selwyn D. Image CBE, JP
*Founder and Vice-President of Emmaus UK*
October 2012

# Introduction

Val-de-Grâce, Monday 22 January 2007, 5:25am. In prayer, at ninety-four years of age, Abbé Pierre is at last called upon to set out on that "great holiday" for which he said he had been waiting since the age of eight. His death saw the political class united in their tributes. Jacques Chirac, French President at the time, was the first to react to the news: "The very heart of the French nation has been wounded. It has lost a great man, a conscience and an embodiment of kindness." Dominique de Villepin, the Prime Minister of early 2007, described Abbé Pierre as "a force of indignation, able to move hearts and minds." The Mayor of Paris bemoaned the loss of "one of the most outstanding figures in modern France," the herald of "an unremitting battle to see each and every man enjoy their right to dignity and a roof." Speaking on behalf of a communist party, which had not always looked upon Abbé Pierre with the greatest warmth, Marie-George Buffet praised his "determination to take a stand against the unacceptable, to fight against poverty in all its forms." Former French President Valéry Giscard d'Estaing called for a state funeral – although a period of national mourning was instead observed at the family's request – and Laurent Fabius suggested his remains be placed in the Panthéon, a symbolic gesture, but one that went against Abbé Pierre's wish to be laid to rest in Esteville, alongside the first Companions. Unable to obtain the *santo subito* canonisation, Jean-Louis Borloo, the Minister for Employment, Work and Social Cohesion, announced that by way of tribute to Abbé Pierre's lifelong struggle, the forthcoming law protecting vulnerable citizens' rights to go through the courts if the state failed to provide them with housing would be named after him.[1]

A prophet for the modern age; a sage and irrepressible troublemaker; France's most popular man, seventeen times at number one in France's Top Fifty best-loved figures list; Abbé Pierre embodied an all-consuming commitment to the cause and an astonishing capacity to rise up in the face of poverty and injustice, dealing them one blow after another. His erudite persona as a religious figure – he was a Franciscan friar who became a priest, celebrated Mass every day and never removed his cassock or cape – as a critic of the Church, and as a man who refused to proselytise, placed him somewhere between the ancient and the modern, between religious devotee and champion of the secular cause, between St Vincent de Paul and *Médecins sans frontières* or *Les Enfants de Don Quichotte*. Forever moving between being a provider of traditional charity and a politician attacking the system, he was able to both defend the night soup runs in the 1980s and, in the 1990s, use his fame to promote the DAL, an association working to protect a person's right to housing. In doing so, he came across as far more modern a figure than Mother Teresa, the icon of the international solidarity movement of the time.

## Beyond the Founder, the Emmaus Movement

The journey, the character and convictions of this great man are crucial in understanding Emmaus. Indeed, this book investigates all three in detail. But it was even more vital to focus on the role of Abbé Pierre, due to the fact that despite the large number of works written about him, including autobiographies and books from journalists and activists, no academic work had been devoted to him.[2] It was thus important to emphasise new or previously unanalysed areas that had come to light during our research and that we deemed to be important from an investigative point of view, particularly in understanding his relationship with politics and the Church. Pieces had been written conducting a moral analysis of events in Abbé Pierre's private life that had impacted on the general public, which were known about at the time, and were useful in understanding the major crises that rocked the Emmaus movement. We chose to pitch our work somewhere between the two, to touch on these private events without going into the details.

However, Abbé Pierre is also the tip of an iceberg: Emmaus. Little is known about this iceberg, despite the fact that the organisation is, in many ways, a pioneer in the "charity-solidarity" movement. It made revolutionary use of the media; provided civil society with a new form of expression; adopted an innovative approach to poverty and the poor; and emphasised the relationship between the economic system and social conditions. Yet few are aware that the organisation exists. In a 1990 survey conducted by market researcher *Sofres*, Emmaus did not appear on the list of the ten most frequently mentioned NGOs.[3] In 1992, while 80% of people surveyed knew who Abbé Pierre was, only 20% knew of his organisation. However, despite being born of the work of a few rubbish-dump scavengers – Ragpickers – who had themselves been thrown onto society's scrapheap, today [2008] Emmaus has the second largest budget of any French NGO and is the largest French parastatal organisation after the French Red Cross.[4] The fact is Emmaus lived for a long time in the shadow of its founder. It was at worst unknown and at best thought of as a group of rag-and-bone men, the forgotten relics of a bygone age. At the same time, constantly in the media spotlight, Abbé Pierre was seen to be the hero and herald, even the very embodiment, of international solidarity. This ignorance of the organisation is also the result of its diverse range of viewpoints and internal divisions. The French movement gradually developed into a series of bodies that varied greatly in size and in the goals they sought to achieve. Their causes included social housing; establishing Communities; the fight to stop families getting into debt and the fight against acute social exclusion; as well as monitoring the problem of inadequate housing and trying out new ways to curb it. These different organisations were further divided by their relationship to their founder and the political sphere, and by their views on involving professionals in their work. As a result, there were no fewer than seven "families" of Communities, created through internal divisions.[5] This means that although for a number of years the Emmaus organisation chart has been growing steadily simpler, with a reduction in the number of its constituent bodies, it still remains utterly indecipherable to the layman, the media and, worse still, a significant number of activists. This book aims to remedy this ignorance of the organisation by piecing together the different, and in fact very lucid, reasoning that has over time seen this complex, tree-like diagram grow and develop.[6]

We have had unrestricted access to all of the movement's archives, many of which had not yet been deposited[7] and could be consulted at the various associations' headquarters. This is an important point: despite the divisions within the movement and the archives' private status, each association did everything it could to help us in our work. We combed through archives at the Central Union of Communities (UCC), the Union of the Friends and Companions of Emmaus (UACE), Association Emmaus, Emmaus-Habitat, the National Committee of the Friends of Emmaus, *SOS-Familles*, the Abbé Pierre Foundation for the housing of the poor, Emmaus France and Emmaus International. In addition, formal and informal interviews allowed us to complete our picture of Emmaus, particularly where the smallest and/or newest organisations were concerned, and allowed us to further investigate certain areas.

## At the Centre of the History of Poverty and Humanitarian Aid

Emmaus is part of that new generation of associations that blossomed in the post-war period. Today these associations represent the lion's share of the French solidarity movement and receive the most media coverage. The traditional Christian associations (for example, *Conférences, Dames et Sœurs de Saint-Vincent-de-Paul, Petites Sœurs des pauvres* and the Salvation Army) began their decline in the inter-war period. In 1945–6 they were joined by *Secours catholique, Secours populaire* and *Petits Frères des pauvres.* The first of these aimed to unite the Catholic sector of the solidarity movement; the second was created as a vehicle for communist efforts and the third to provide assistance to the large number of elderly people living in poverty. Emmaus was born some years later in 1949 and focused on the social exclusion that resulted from inadequate housing. The organisation ATD, which became ATD Fourth-World in 1968, was created in 1961 after breaking away from Emmaus. It specialised in tackling the most acute forms of exclusion.

Like many of poverty's facets, a great deal remains unknown about the historical development of these organisations. This is due, in part, to the lack of freely accessible archives,[8] but also to the lack of interest in the subject amongst historians. A great deal of research has focused on poverty and the poor from the Middle Ages to the nineteenth century,[9] while those claiming to also investigate the twentieth century have, in reality, often paid it negligible attention.[10] There is only one piece of historical research on the subject that defies this general rule,[11] together with a few significant works from sociologists, political scientists, philosophers and theologians that are more of an historical nature,[12] and a few rare pieces written by historians on the organisations themselves.[13]

This phenomenon is the result of the near-universalisation of social protection in the post-war period that, together with the subsequent prosperity of the *Trente Glorieuses*,[14] appears to have sounded the death knell for poverty. Significantly, in his 1974 book, *The Excluded: One French Man Out of Ten*, René Lenoir looks at a heterogeneous group of the "socially ill-adapted", the handicapped, young offenders, drug-addicts, those who are suicidal or mentally ill, but rarely discusses the poorest members of society.[15] Yet research into ATD Fourth-World demonstrated how at that time abject poverty continued to exist in the form of residual pockets that were almost built into the very fabric of society.[16] It is also known that the elderly were equally affected until the *minima vieillesse*, the French welfare payment for the elderly poor, was increased in 1975. At the same time, Emmaus allowed the spotlight to be thrown on some of the most silent forms of exclusion, such as the emergence of shanty towns and inadequate housing, relocation and poverty.

Next came the 1980s and a radical turning point: the economic crisis plunged the "new poor" into poverty and destitution. These were people "who believed they'd never fall on hard times, who thought poverty couldn't touch them. People who were seen as comfortably off."[17] From then on, winter saw the homeless hit the headlines. The Emmaus crusade, which in the 1950s had waged war to a larger extent against the lack of housing, now began to focus on poverty. Targeted initiatives were developed to fight against acute exclusion, Communities significantly increased the number of places available, and housing associations tried out new ways of managing social housing. The work continued in the 1990s with the focus being placed on finding lasting solutions to the problem. The Abbé Pierre Foundation was created to house the socially disadvantaged, and organisations were set up to facilitate the social integration of women and the youngest and most ill-adjusted people.

In presenting a whole host of responses to the problem (responses that were withdrawn between 1960 and 1970 and then rolled out again from the 1980s onwards), Emmaus was from the outset able to take the multi-faceted, ever-changing nature of poverty into account, and the words of sociologist Jean Labbens remain relevant to this day: "The concept is a simple one, but one which appears to directly avoid those who look at things from a purely economic perspective: a poor man is not a rich man with less money, he is another man entirely."[18] Through the figure of Abbé Pierre, the organisation was also largely instrumental in bringing the poor out of the shadows and giving them a new place in French society. This standpoint, which inextricably linked the charitable and the political, was also a scientific theory. "To read between the lines of charitable speeches and policies, rooted in the ways in which the causes and effects of poverty are represented, is to consider through one lens the social ideologies of society's elites."[19] Social historian Bronislaw Geremeke has taken this concept to another level: "If societies let themselves be defined and understood by the way they punish or accept otherness, [one] could even go as far as to say that societies may rightfully be judged on the basis of those they exclude."[20]

Less is known about the fact that Emmaus is also an international movement that, from the spring of 1954 onwards, became sensitive to the issue of global hunger and inequalities. The organisation fostered greater understanding of the fact that "domestic" and "international" humanitarian efforts are two sides of the same coin and raised the profile of Christian initiatives to support development and the Third World. With things being made difficult for him in his own French organisations between 1956 and 1958, Abbé Pierre decided upon an "exit strategy" and, with requests for his assistance flooding in from abroad, he devoted the next two decades to making the movement an international one and Emmaus thus took root in all four corners of the globe. It is today [2008] present in thirty-nine countries, through 327 of its organisations and 442 partner organisations.

This international dimension is significant for three reasons. First it throws light on an area of Abbé Pierre's life which is rarely studied: his work as a missionary – work he dreamed of even as a teenager. Furthermore, it brings to light new information on the restructuring of the Catholic humanitarian aid movement working in the Third World and on the fight against global hunger being waged by advocates of alter-globalisation. Finally, as we have shown to be the case with *Secours populaire*, it is largely by looking at the international work of major NGOs that their relationship to politics, or in Emmaus' case to religion, can be understood. Theories on the decline of the major ideologies and meta-narratives, which no doubt hold true at least in part for metropolitan France, must also be heavily qualified. The Emmaus example demonstrates to what extent politics and religion, which were slowly dismissed in the West in the 1980s and stifled by organisations' increasing dependency on the State, largely continued to colour the work of groups in the Southern hemisphere. The message these groups sought to convey had been resonating since the 1960s. Politics and religion then made a comeback; politics first, bursting back on the scene in the 1990s in the form of new social movements and globalised utopia.

## From Charity to Solidarity

Despite the fact that elsewhere Emmaus rightly declared itself to be a non-confessional movement that did not seek to proselytise, until the 1980s in France and the mid-1990s internationally, it had been a very religious movement. Religion has left an indelible mark on Emmaus' approach to the poor.

In Christian teaching, the poor man is an ambiguous figure based largely on the parallels between the material and the spiritual. He is at once the embodiment of asceticism and, by extension, the embodiment of the humility required before God. Indeed, one must be poor to receive God's grace and, on several occasions, Jesus asked those he loved to leave everything behind; their hands "must be empty in order to receive."[21] As a result, the poor are the first to arrive at God's kingdom, whether specific figures such as Lazarus,[22] or an indeterminate group. The Beatitudes read "Blessed are the poor, for theirs is the Kingdom of heaven."[23] Finally, the poor are Christ incarnate. Christ himself chose to live among the poor, having disposed of material wealth. And so, at the bottom of the social scale but at the top of the spiritual one, they impose obligations upon the rich, stemming from the commandment, "Love thy neighbour as thyself."[24] Numerous references are made to the poor throughout the Scriptures. It is clear, therefore, that the hope of salvation through work, central to the Catholic faith,[25] is also one of the beliefs that have traditionally underpinned Emmaus' work.

Abbé Pierre saw himself as deeply rooted in the Church – although the Church perhaps was not always of the same view. If he wanted to bring about reform, it was from the inside; if he wanted to shake things up, it was to return to original ways of thinking. He was, in essence, a modern-day Luther. A Luther with a focus on the poor, who was more concerned with practical work than with religious dogma and who had never contemplated leaving the Church. The son of bourgeois parents, he gave up his possessions and inheritance to become a monk. He aspired to a life of poverty and asceticism, and constantly recalled his "discovery of the link between God and poverty... which must be at our very core if we are to find Him."[26] He admired Saint Francis, who "entered into universal communion more than anyone. He did so out of love for Jesus, love which saw him strive to imitate Jesus' asceticism in the most literal way possible. You see, Saint Francis had discovered, embodied in Jesus, the link which could not be ignored: the link between poverty and Love of the Almighty."[27] To him, the poor man was a sacred being and he believed that "when, throughout the course of his life, a man has held out his hand to the poor, he can be sure that when he dies, God will be holding his other hand."[28]

Like his contemporary Abbé Rodhain,[29] in expressing his religious beliefs as concrete social initiatives, Abbé Pierre displayed anthropological optimism.[30] Like Rodhain too, he believed that in practice the theological order ought to be turned on its head and that charity led to faith far more often than the other way round. And again, like Rodhain, he benefited from being revered as "the social face of charity."[31] However, unlike Rodhain, who sought to revive charity and strived to demonstrate that Catholicism could provide the answer to all of mankind's questions,[32] Abbé Pierre was a disciple of the social Catholic movements that rejected charity to espouse secular values, seek social justice and successfully complete the "political modernisation test."[33]

He then began to develop a unique appreciation of the interplay between charity and politics, perfectly expressed in Emmaus' original precept: "In the face of all human suffering, strive, as far as you can, not only to relieve it without delay, but also to destroy its cause. Strive not only to destroy its cause, but to relieve it without delay." It was this precept which, in 1954, saw waste-collection and soup runs for the "street sleepers" go hand in hand with efforts to pressure the state into adopting new laws to protect them. It was this precept which saw humanitarian aid workers in the development sector declare: "In seeking to attack the causes of poverty, Emmaus should not forget to directly tackle its effects, in particular in the countries where men are not yet able to take their fate into their own hands."[34] It is this precept which, since the 1980s, has triggered the launch of a whole host of initiatives to tackle the problem, ranging from those easing suffering, to those stamping out its root causes. Finally, one of the things that makes Emmaus' work truly unique is how it breaks up the "giver receiver" partnership by adding a third giver: the poor man himself. This poor man is the socially and/or economically excluded Companion who, in showing solidarity towards his neighbour, rediscovers hope and a *raison d'être*. "Where this attitude differs from charity is where Emmaus' entire purpose can be found: to save those who suffer by making them the saviours of those who suffer most."[35]

The organisation's media coverage, its open-mindedness, unique characteristics and the increasing secularisation of society later combined to make one viewpoint within Emmaus emerge and to water down its original identity. This phenomenon is by no means unusual. The same thing happened with *Secours catholique*, at its roots a

Catholic organisation, and with *Secours populaire*, originally a communist organisation. Today's typical Emmaus activist is no longer religious. Many are atheist, both at the bottom and at the top of the organisation's hierarchy, and those who are religious no longer declare their beliefs. Emmaus is also not a member of Catholic institutional networks such as the *Conseil national de solidarité*.[36] Nevertheless, religion continues to quietly influence Emmaus' work. In France, it does so very quietly indeed, even if it emerges when going through the archives that both *SOS-Familles* and the committees of friends agreed at their general assemblies to hold Sunday morning Mass. In the committees of friends, this practice continued into the 1990s. Priests were also key figures in the movement at national level up until the 1980s. Religion's influence has been less subtle abroad. Up until the 1990s, in a significant number of countries, Emmaus was led by priests. Once again, this phenomenon is in no way new. With its very name, *Secours catholique* continues to openly declare its religious identity, and the higher up you go in the hierarchy of *Secours populaire*, the more Communists you find. The old major ideologies, both political and religious, which underpinned these organisations, are most certainly in crisis, but they are not dead. Rather, they are simply changing shape.

## From the Rag-and-Bone Trade to a Social Economy Where Solidarity is Key

Emmaus has for a long time occupied a unique position in the aid-work sector, in refusing (or minimising) cash donations and subsidies and in making a dogma of its independence through work. It was *through* the communities, committees of friends and business initiatives working towards the reintegration of the socially excluded that this work came to form part of the environmental, salvaging and, by extension, sustainable development movements that were still in their embryonic stages. In the same way, it was also an integral part of a social economy where solidarity was fundamental; two concepts that Emmaus had put into practice long before they had been recognised as such.

Salvaging is first of all symbolic, because it works by analogy. Individuals discarded by society work on the objects discarded by society. In doing so, they give back to these objects a social purpose, while reclaiming their own. Men seen as worthless and on the edge of society work in places seen as worthless and on the outskirts of town; they work first of all on the rubbish dumps and then in the communities, which are built away from villages to give them the space to burn the rubbish. The shame and stigma that, until the 1970s, were attached to being a Companion, reflected the taboo surrounding waste at the time. Conversely, since the 1980s, the enhanced socio-economic prestige of salvaging has gone hand in hand with the rising status of Companions. But, more than anything, salvaging has an economic purpose – it allows companions to live independently of aid, organise themselves, and even turn a profit, enabling them to also help society's poorest people.

In becoming rag-and-bone men in January 1952, the Emmaus companions revived a profession in decline (it had enjoyed its heyday in the nineteenth century). In the 1830s, a distinction was made between rag-and-bone collection in the street and the purchasing of second-hand goods for resale. The rag-and-bone men specialised in salvaging items thrown out in the streets.[37] Their trade had a hierarchy. At the top was the runner, with three tools: a basket he carried on his back, a lantern and a hook, or *biffe*, as it was known colloquially in France at the time. Up there with him was the magpie, who worked at night to salvage the best items. At the bottom of the pile there was the ordinary rag-and-bone man who worked at night without any equipment, the seconder who went through the rubbish after the magpie and the sifter who went through the rubbish dumps. Finally, the mid-nineteenth century saw the emergence of a less nomadic group of rag-and-bone men who turned a few streets into their personal hunting ground. They were committed to starting work every day at dawn and could sell on their patch to another rag-and-bone man. A number of middlemen working between the ordinary rag-and-bone men and their superiors also began to appear. These included wholesalers – traders and men who repaired the salvaged goods.

But, at the turn of the century, pressure from the Paris prefect Eugène Poubelle and research from Louis Pasteur combined to change the face of the profession, when the use of "refuse boxes" was made mandatory. The mixing of different types of waste in these boxes altered the quality of the waste to such an extent that box covers were later introduced to allow it to ferment. At the same time, there were increasing demands from manufacturers and competition from other professions for this useful waste. These professions included the sellers and bric-à-brac traders who went from door to door requesting the items that had previously been discarded in the street. Furthermore, new manufacturing processes for wood pulp were being developed and rubbish tips were moving further and further away from the cities. As a result, the rag-and-bone trade was in crisis. It was then branded as an insanitary practice, and the rag-and-bone men themselves were driven out of the cities. This was particularly the case in Paris. While until the 1860s, the rag-and-bone men lived in the poor and insalubrious areas of the city, the health and sanitation services moved them on to the old city fortress area, and then out into the suburbs in 1941. In crisis and a victim of bad press, the profession was officially outlawed in 1950. The Emmaus Companions' decision to become rag-and-bone men was therefore a last resort to ensure their survival. Their disputes with those rag-and-bone men who worked on their own individual hunting ground, which forced them to abandon the bins in favour of salvaging unwanted items from people's attics, became socially and economically a blessing in disguise.

From that point on, the Emmaus Communities flourished in a niche that was somewhat neglected, where there was little competition and no regulation. It was, in a way, a niche outside the market given that until the 1970s waste was in abundant supply, but in no real demand.[38] However, since the 1980s, the situation has changed dramatically. Increasing concern for the environment in the 1970s, which was heightened by major natural disasters,[39] gradually spread to the whole population. The consumer culture of the *Trente Glorieuses* saw an increase in waste at the end of the supply chain. Technological developments produced new synthetic materials and more sophisticated packaging. The 1975 law on waste disposal and salvaging laid the foundations for further, hard-line regulation, later consolidated by the 1992 EU law. The salvaging market became increasingly competitive, with vast sums of money at stake. The early rag-and-bone men were forced to turn themselves into professional salvagers, despite the fact that they had vastly different goals and a much smaller budget than the major firms. In France, as elsewhere, community life began to feel the full force of the market economy and has yet to find a way to survive.

# I – THE 1950s: FROM THE CATACOMBS TO COLLAPSE

# *Chapter 1* / A UTOPIAN COMMUNITY (1949–1954)

While 1954 is often hailed as the beginning of Emmaus, the movement had begun to take root in 1949. Furthermore, the Great Campaign of the winter of 1954 can only be understood within the context of what Abbé Pierre and his Companions had already created: a new, community-based utopia, a fight for access to housing and a unique blend of charity, pressure on state authorities and initiatives sometimes bordering on the illegal. The three mystical emanations of the Abbé – that of priest, former Resistance fighter and Member of Parliament – also made an indelible mark on Emmaus.

First came the meeting, then the Community. It was a Community that allowed desperate men to live and work side by side, choosing to use what little they had left to help homeless families. It was established against the backdrop of an acute housing crisis and born of Abbé Pierre's basic belief that without housing there could be no salvation for the poor, as those without a home were deprived of privacy, independence and any basic form of protection. With this belief in mind, Emmaus needed to collect money with which the Community could survive and also to fund the building materials and site, and the construction of the Community for those most disadvantaged members of society. It was these needs that triggered "the Uprising of Kindness", a campaign as spontaneous as it was exceptional. With the benefit of hindsight, however, it became clear that over time, parts of the campaign were too loftily revered.

## Abbé Pierre Before Emmaus

*"It is never I at the helm of the ship, who decides which course to steer. I can only follow the captain. I have always aspired to a life of contemplation, isolation; a life alone with God. But my steps, the steps I have taken freely along this path towards my heart's desires, have always taken me elsewhere."*[1]

This is an odd comment for a man so well known for his work helping people across the globe and a comment that conveys, as his life was drawing to a close, just how greatly Abbé Pierre would have liked to live a life of seclusion in a strict Capuchin monastery. It explains how, time and time again, a "captain" threw him into the thick of political and social action, forcing him to follow a path that lead him in the opposite direction to the one he had carved out for himself. This is, of course, a very Christian interpretation of events, depicting a believer placing himself entirely in the hands of God. However, it is an historical interpretation too, of a journey rich in experiences and struggles that were motivated by his empathy with human crises and tragedy. It becomes a philosophical evaluation of life when the Abbé affirms that "life's true greatness lies in the fact that we are given consent rather than a choice. We enjoy the freedom which makes us responsible for answering calls for help."[2]

Born in Lyons on 5 August 1912 to an upper-middle-class Catholic family, Henri Grouès, to use his real name, was the fifth of eight children. He took pleasure in recalling certain defining moments from his childhood. Around the age of seven, he was once denied permission to attend a party as punishment for lying. When his brothers returned home, he refused to join them in reliving the delights of an event from which he had been absent. In recalling this particular memory, Abbé Pierre explained how "half an hour later, my father called me and led me in to his office. He didn't shout at me, but I could see he was very unhappy. 'Henri, how is it possible for you not to be happy when the others are happy?' he asked me. I will never forget that moment: the expression of suffering on my father's face. He was unhappy because I was unhappy. It was at that moment that I stopped looking to simply satisfy myself and myself alone. Up until then, I'd taken great pleasure in doing just that."[3] There is no doubt that this is a somewhat teleological and hagiographical recollection of events; one that is believed to have prompted him to abandon selfishness in favour of kindness and altruism despite having not long reached the age of reason.

Another defining moment came at the age of eleven. His father, a director of the Foundries of the Rhône, worked every Sunday at the

*Hospitaliers veilleurs*, a Catholic association in Lyons.[4] One Sunday, after Mass, he took Henri and one of his brothers along with him. The Abbé recalled watching his father: "There he was, sleeves rolled up in the middle of about fifty beggars. [He and his friend] were shaving them, cutting their hair, ridding them of vermin and serving up breakfast."[5] In discovering this unknown side of his father, the Abbé discovered charity in action. For Catholics this is the key to Salvation: "For I was hungry and you gave me food, I was thirsty and you gave me something to drink, I was a stranger and you welcomed me, I was naked and you gave me clothing, I was sick and you took care of me, I was in prison and you visited me."[6] In demonstrating what it was to humbly assist those in need without a hint of condescension, the episode with his father also showcased the Sunday reversal of roles, where the rich man becomes the poor man's servant. Such role reversal, central to the Gospels, harks back to the parable of "The Rich Young Man", which reads, "But many who are first will be last, and the last will be first."[7] More generally, it evokes the Bible's teachings on God's kingdom, where, for example in Beatitudes, the social pyramid is inverted: "Blessed are you who are poor, for yours is the Kingdom of God. Blessed are you who are hungry now, for you will be filled... But woe to you who are rich, for you have received your consolation. Woe to you who are full now, for you will be hungry."[8] Lastly, according to Abbé Pierre's interpretation of the key events in his life, his father's attitude to the poor heralded that which he would himself later adopt within Emmaus, no longer on Sundays alone, but on a daily basis.

Despite the fact that little is known about this period, we should nevertheless briefly mention the Abbé's time as a boy scout. While he often referred to receiving the totem of contemplative beaver, which suited him so well,[9] the crucial role that his scouting days played in his later work with the poor cannot be denied: they equipped him with vital social skills and allowed him to develop new talents. As a boy scout he was taught about the practicalities of providing assistance; about how to live with others and cope with risk; he grew acclimatised to difficult environments; and learnt how to get projects off the ground.

It is more difficult to analyse the Abbé's long revelation, which Bernard Violet discusses at great length; his meeting with Yves. Here, we will simply recall that while in church at Christmas 1926, Henri heard Yves sing. His voice was the veritable "voice at of an angel".[10] Listening to him sing awoke feelings within Henri that would run deep for a long time: a mixture of impossible friendship, platonic love and mystical discovery. Given that the Abbé never subsequently experienced homosexual desires, the episode's significance lies more in the fact that the feelings it sparked grew so intense over the next few years that Henri began to spell his name with a "y" so that he could merge it with Yves to form "Henryves".

One final defining moment was the inspiration of Assisi. As a teenager on pilgrimage to Rome, he discovered the beauty of Assisi in a moment of "violent" and "indescribable emotion".[11] He went on to discover more about St Francis, his first followers and their life in Carceri; those caves tucked away in the mountains. The Abbé said of the episode, "it was the first time that I sensed that solitude and asceticism could be filled with more of the meetings with the Almighty that I wished for, and which all my studies and discussions up until that point had been unable to generate [...] You ask me who I am. If I neglected to recount that episode, the picture you would take away would be one of a different man, another man entirely, and there's no doubt that everything which later filled my life would make no sense at all."[12]

Henri Grouès had fragile health; he was often ill and confined to his bed. However he described how "almost all of these periods of illness remain hugely significant, both in my mind and in reality. They were periods of isolation, contemplation and Christian reading."[13] After a period of doubt, the inspiration of Assisi and his reading saw him once again firmly rooted in the Christian faith. Indeed, his faith was so strong that he sometimes went as far as to engage in mortification or self-flagellation.[14] In 1931, at the age of nineteen, he decided to enter the order of the Capuchins, the strictest and most austere branch of the Franciscans. It was, in the Abbé's eyes, the most eremitical and ascetic branch of them all; where living conditions were the harshest but also the closest to those of the people who suffered most. Having been named “brother Philippe”, he spent his first year in “radical worship”,[15] between nightly prayers and daily recitals of the Psalms. This “period of true inner happiness”[16] was nevertheless a period spent in the desert, and physically very gruelling. There were prayers between midnight and two in the morning, a wooden plank for a bed, a habit for pyjamas, and the friars went barefoot and had their heads shaved. He was ordained on 24 August 1938. However, ultimately, life as a Capuchin was less in line with his aspirations than he had first anticipated, and with his health no longer able to withstand the regime, he left the monastery in 1939. At his request, he was posted the following month to the diocese of Grenoble, which he viewed at the time as less bourgeois than Lyons.

The move, followed by a bout of pleurisy, forced him to take a brief detour en route to the diocese. He worked as a hospital chaplain in La Mûre (September 1940), and then as a priest in charge of religious instruction in a state-funded orphanage in Côte-Saint-André. In the summer of 1942, he was once again posted to Grenoble, this time to work as an assistant priest in the cathedral.

It was this new post which sparked his involvement in the Resistance.[17] He was first called upon, in July 1942, to hide and organise the evacuation of Jews to Switzerland, and he established teams to lead them through the Alps. In August, with the help of nuns from Notre-Dame de Sion, he set up a workshop at home to produce identity cards. As he said himself, this involvement in the Resistance was not the result of political will, but rather of a wish to protect the innocent. It stemmed from his profound acceptance of risk as part of Christian charity and from his involvement with those becoming aware of the Jews’ fate and with the efforts being made to protect them. In February 1943, he began to hide those seeking to avoid conscription into the Vichy regime’s *Service de travail obligatoire*, which provided forced labour for Germany.[18] In March, he created the first guerrilla band of the Resistance, or maquis, in Chartreuse; then in April, he founded a newspaper whose aim was to train and educate maquis leaders. It was called the *Union patriotique indépendante* (UPI) and, in the end, only three issues were produced. At the same time, he printed at home and distributed thousands of pamphlets entitled *Résistance*, which sought to raise awareness of the various spiritual beliefs within the Resistance movement. He also helped to organise the distribution of small books of Christian testimony, entitled *Témoignage chrétien*, and set up committees in Grenoble where members of the Resistance could provide each other with mutual support. In November, with the help of a group of young labourers, he stole a large quantity of military equipment from the Italian forces occupying Grenoble. According to the diocesan archives, "He hid these with a view to them being used by the secret army. Surrounded by the enemy in looted barracks, he managed to escape with one final load."[19] Lastly, right up until January 1944, he helped to supply the Maquis du Vercors.

It was during this period that he met Lucie Coutaz, who would remain his loyal secretary until her death in 1982. Looking for someone to help him produce the UPI, he sought advice from Father Henri de Lubac, a Jesuit theologian and professor at the Catholic University of Lyons. However, de Lubac was also a member of the Resistance and suggested Lucie Coutaz-Repland for the job. Born on 9 May 1899 in Savoie to an agricultural labourer, as a teenager she suffered from osseous tuberculosis and was left paralysed. She was forced to wear heavy corsets until, on 11 September 1921, she was miraculously cured at Lourdes.[20] In 1915 Coutaz began work at the French pasta manufacturer Lustucru and went on to manage the books of the Cartier-Millon family who owned the firm. After her disability forced her to take a career break, she completed her secretarial studies and became the secretary to Lustucru's Managing Director before taking up the same post at the Paper, Paste and Cardboard Union. Devoutly religious, she worked as a lay sister in the inter-war period. (She was a Consecrated Virgin but there is no evidence to suggest that she was affiliated to a particular order.) Coutaz was then called upon to help the management of the French Confederation of Christian Workers (CFTC). When the confederation was dissolved by the Vichy regime in November 1940, she was posted to Grenoble's *Office social de renseignements*, or intelligence bureau, which would become a vital cog in the Resistance machine. It was here that she met Henri Grouès in the spring of 1943, and became an invaluable source of support for him as he carried out his work.

Located and hounded in Grenoble in September 1943, Grouès was forced to hide in Lyons under the new pseudonym "Abbé Pierre". From November 1943 to January 1944, he provided assistance to the regional Chief of Staff and was responsible for communications. With the help of Captain Tixier, he also managed to smuggle into Switzerland Jacques de Gaulle, the paralytic brother of General Charles de Gaulle, and Jacques' wife, and provided those detained at the Montluc fort with fresh supplies.

He was later hunted down in Lyons too, forcing him to move on to Paris in February 1944, this time under the pseudonym "Abbé Houdin". Here he set up a new workshop to manufacture identity cards. On 19 May, upon his return from a trip to Spain where he had been sent to create a new smuggling route through the Pyrenees, he was arrested by the Gestapo but was able to make his escape during the night. He returned to Spain immediately and stayed there until mid-June 1944, in order to convey intelligence to fellow members of the Resistance. Under the pseudonym "Sir Henry Barlow", he was then sent to Algiers until the beginning of August 1944, to work for the Intelligence and the diplomatic corps. It was there that he met General de Gaulle and gave an address, which was broadcast on radio, using his earlier pseudonym of "Abbé Pierre". Finally, on 9 August, he was given permission to enlist and was subsequently posted to Morocco as a chaplain with the Navy. According to the diocesan archives of Grenoble, from August 1944 to January 1945, "he was pivotal in providing intelligence to the Moroccan authorities."[21] In January 1945, he was sent on a mission to the Naval Ministry in Paris and once again asked Lucie Coutaz to assist him. At the end of the war, Abbé Pierre was awarded the Croix de Guerre with palm and Lucie Coutaz received the Croix de Guerre with bronze star.

This involvement in the Resistance is crucial in understanding the aura which surrounded the Abbé's persona at the end of the war, but also in understanding the belief that would underpin Emmaus' work: the belief that if needs be, rights should be respected before the law, and that what is legitimate should be defended above what is legal. Abbé Pierre has remarked, "we must dare to think, and know how to look to an authority higher than those who are only human."[22] It is also from this period that he kept the pseudonym that is famous today and that evokes, for those who were aware of his activities, his "twenty-three months of living in the shadows",[23] the risks he managed to take, and the ideas for which he fought.

Upon his return from Africa, he was caught up in political action. While the Church appeared to have lost all credibility following its dealings with the Vichy government, he was called upon by Pierre-Henri Teitgen, Minister for the Navy and co-founder of the Christian Democrat party (MRP), to stand for election. His superiors in the Church approved his candidacy. He was elected in Nancy in October 1945 as an independent, his electoral list grouped with that of the MRP. Once again, he asked Lucie Coutaz to assist him. Coutaz, whose work as a lay sister was not entirely compatible with working as the secretary of a Member of Parliament, requested a private audience with Pope Pius XII who gave her his blessing.[24] Re-elected in the spring of 1946, this time as a member of the Christian Party, and appointed as the secretary of the *Commission de la défense nationale*, Abbé Pierre finally left the MRP, having spoken out repeatedly against the government's foreign policy in Indochina and in protest against their putting down of the Brest construction workers' strike in April 1950. Together with Paul Boulet and Charles d'Aragon, he founded an "independent left" group, and in doing so took a further step towards the left of the political spectrum. In 1951, he stood as an independent candidate in the legislative elections. However, the new *loi des apparentements*, which allowed electoral lists to be grouped in a bid to reduce the influence of the Communists and the Gaullists in government, went against him and he was not re-elected.

A defining feature of this period in parliament is the battle to see the status of conscientious objector officially recognised; a battle the Abbé waged alongside André Philip. However, the pair would not emerge victorious until the end of the Algerian war. Of further significance was the government's lack of concern for the issues of housing and poverty – it took a keener interest in financial matters – and the strong friendships Abbé Pierre formed with key political figures; from both the Communist Party (PCF) – Roger Garaudy – and the MRP – Senator Léo Hamon and future minister Robert Buron.

However, despite all this, he would later admit that "this was the least important period of [his] life."[25]

While he never really got involved in political action, from 1948 onwards he devoted time and energy to the *Mouvement universel pour une Confédération mondiale*, a pacifist umbrella organisation aiming to promote and guarantee world peace. He was elected president of the organisation in the summer of 1948 and travelled the world in this capacity for four years. During this time, he would famously meet Albert Einstein, who was also a member.

Abbé Pierre was thus anything but a small-time country priest when he founded Emmaus. A monk who had joined the diocesan clergy, a priest in the Resistance, and then a Member of Parliament, his journey was a rich and complex one, shaped in part by circumstance: his health being too poor to withstand the life of a Capuchin, he became a priest in Grenoble, at the heart of the Resistance. Then, following the Liberation, he was called upon to enter politics and restore the former glory of a Church whose reputation was in tatters. His career as a militant can be pieced together through the many interviews he gave, which seem to suggest that the depth of his faith, discovered in childhood, was the constant that allowed his career to develop in a linear fashion. However, reassembling his career in this way produces only one of the red threads that ran through the tapestry of the Abbé's life, and gives a retrospective sense of order and logic to a journey full of ups and downs where, by his own admission, he struggled as teenager to decide between becoming a sailor, a missionary or a bandit, and where he ultimately came to combine all three.

## The "Catacombs Period"

*"It all started because my house was too big."*[26]

### The mystique of the encounter

Obliged by his parliamentary duties to live for some of the time in Paris, and forced in October 1947 to leave an apartment he had rented in the Rue de Grenelle, Abbé Pierre signed the lease on 38 Avenue

Paul-Doumer, a large, run-down house in Neuilly-Plaisance, in the suburbs to the east of Paris.

From May 1948 onwards, as the building and repair works progressed (a kitchen and a dining hall were installed in the basement, along with bedrooms upstairs and a small chapel), the house became a place where various groups of people could meet and study in the winter. These included worker-priests and priests from the area, the Paris Mission, the MRP workers' movements and seminarians. In the summer it became a hostel for members of the Christian Workers' Youth movement (the JOC), members of the Catholic Students' Youth movement (the JEC)[27] and boy scouts. The diocesan buildings department in Versailles suggested to him that he make the premises available to the Christian Camping and Youth Hostel Association (OCCAJ). Official youth-hostel status was granted in the summer of 1949.[28] At the same time, a not-for-profit organisation called Emmaus-OCCAJ was set up to oversee the running of the hostel and raise money. The hostel was a success: 5,000 overnight stays in 1948 and 7,000 in 1949.

The name "Emmaus" is a reference to the episode in the Gospel of Luke (XXIV:13–35) where, on Easter Day, two frightened and desperate disciples who were fleeing Jerusalem met a passer-by on the road to the village of Emmaus. Having arrived at the inn, they invited the traveller to share their meal; when they blessed and broke the bread, they recognised the traveller as Jesus. Once more filled with hope, they returned home to announce the news. Abbé Pierre had been reflecting upon this passage since 1941, thinking of it as "a philosophy, a mystery, of invigorating disillusion": following the vision of a saviour of Israel chasing out the Roman occupier, Jesus explains to the disciples the error of their ways and gives them new hope.

The name "Emmaus" also evokes the inn, its proximity to the capital (Neuilly is on the outskirts of Paris, just as Emmaus is on the outskirts of Jerusalem) and the wish to "rediscover the good Lord" therein.[29] This notion of disillusion also related to the horrors of the concentration camps still raw in people's minds, which were a frequent subject of discussion and which prompted Abbé Pierre to write in the leaflet introducing Emmaus: "Emmaus: created so that even after days of darkness, hope may once again shine bright." But the name was also premonitory for an organisation that would look to welcome those who had lost all reason to hope and give them a place to stop and take stock before they continued along the path to new hope.

However, the real birth of Emmaus was not so much the creation of the hostel as the mythical meeting with "Georges". In October 1949,[30] the Abbé was called following a suicide attempt by Georges Legay. Looking back on the incident, Abbé Pierre remarked, "What was his life like? The man's entire youth had been lost to a divided home. Frail and weak at around the age of twenty years old, he discovered how his family had tricked him and destroyed his relationship with his fiancée for money, a relationship that thirty years later he continued to mourn like a child. In a fit of rage he murdered his father and was sentenced to life in a penal colony."[31] After twenty years in Cayenne, the capital of French Guiana, Legay returned to France, having been pardoned for heroic conduct during a fire. An alcoholic and suffering from malaria and tuberculosis, he found his wife had remarried and his daughter didn't recognise him. He decided to drown himself. When interviewed by Bernard Chevallier, Abbé Pierre recalled:

> "It was at that moment that Emmaus was born. I did what I did without a second thought, with no hidden agenda, [to go] against the very notion of charity. Instead of saying, 'you are unhappy, I will give you a home, a job and some money', the circumstances compelled me to say exactly the opposite. I could only tell him the truth: 'you are desperately unhappy, and I have nothing I can give you... but you, given that you want to die, you've nothing to lose. So, why don't you give me your help to help others?' If ever that principle were forgotten, Emmaus would cease to exist. That is, above all else, the very essence of Emmaus: saying to those who see themselves as a burden, who feel they no longer serve any purpose: 'I have nothing to give you except my friendship and my asking you to help me, so that together we may save others.'"[32]

Emmaus sought to offer this first Companion, and all the others who followed, not so much *the means* to live but *a reason* to live and in doing so, paradoxically, put those who had lost everything in a position to give.

This fortuitous meeting reached a very Christian conclusion when a family, having been evicted from their home three days before Christmas, became the first family to be taken in by Abbé Pierre. After trying in vain to find them shelter and with no room at the hostel, the Abbé put them in a room where he regularly celebrated Mass, "in the place of the good Lord. To the shocked youngsters who questioned what I was doing, I said that I believed that Jesus was present in the consecrated bread, but also that I was convinced that there, on that evening, Jesus was not feeling the cold in the host, but in the hands and feet of these children with no roof and no fire to keep them warm."[33] Abbé Pierre then took out a loan to buy a small plot of land in Neuilly-sur-Marne and built them a home in the spring of 1950, with the help of the first Companions and the young people from the hostel.

The news of Georges Legay's welcome spread immediately and others in distress also turned to the Abbé, becoming Companions too. News spread about the priest who was building for the homeless, and drew in many families searching for a home. Thus, in all pragmatism, the Emmaus Community was born.

## Financing the buildings

From then on, more and more plots of land were bought, sometimes without planning permission in order to keep costs down. First, there was the Maison du Pont in Neuilly-Plaisance, bought in spring 1950 using the expenses allowance that Abbé Pierre was given as a Member of Parliament. Seven families set up home there in September 1950, housed in old Nissen huts from Aubervilliers that had been bought, dismantled, sanded down, cleaned and rebuilt. Next, was Champs-Fleuris in October 1950, which was sold to Abbé Pierre by the mayor at a knockdown price in order to house homeless families. Here, large tents were put up, later followed by small chalets. In autumn 1951, temporary accommodation was built at Coquelicots in Neuilly-sur-Marne on a "build now, pay later" basis.

Work then began on more permanent accommodation. The first site, La Pépinière (an old abandoned plant nursery in Pontault-Combault), benefited from a payment plan under the *loi Loucheur*, a law under which the government subsidise housing for the masses. A financial support company was set up to grant and then oversee the repayment of thirty-three loans; each would build one house for one family.[34] The land was bought and the loan was to be paid back over five years.

In June 1953, Abbé Pierre poached the twenty-eight-year-old economist Henri Camus from the social secretariat of the Versailles diocese to manage the loans. Camus became the movement's first paid employee. The next two sites were granted the official status of home-buying cooperatives: le Bouquet (a group of quick-build "Phénix houses" in Pontault-Combault) and Torcy were built using a loan to be repaid in monthly instalments. This plan meant that families could gradually get a foot on the property ladder and eventually own their own home.

However, the constant stream of urgent requests for accommodation meant that makeshift housing was not forgotten. In March 1953 La Pomponnette was set up on a small piece of the Pomponne forest near Lagny. The land was bought and cleared, and a campsite was created consisting of canvas tents, caravans and the shells of old cars, which provided accommodation for around thirty families. Gérard Marin and Roland Bonnet have noted that "each family had nowhere to live except in these wrecks and rickety two-by-three shacks stuck in the mud, with no lighting and with an icy draught that was so cold it could have killed them."[35] However, living here was far better than returning to the horrors and lack of privacy they had previously endured.

Up until 1951, this small Community survived on Abbé Pierre's parliamentary expenses allowance, the small contributions made by the families themselves, and the donations made following Abbé Pierre's sporadic appeals for funds, with Lucie Coutaz keeping a tight grip on the purse strings. However, the loss of this expenses allowance made the situation untenable and Lucie Coutaz's part-time secretarial job far from covered the running costs of Emmaus' rapidly expanding network. Twice, at the end of December 1951,[36] Abbé Pierre had made up his mind to beg in secret in Paris, by distributing a small pamphlet, which a friend printed for him; the money to be repaid at a later date. Alerted to Abbé Pierre's predicament, a friend, who'd once been a Ragpicker, suggested he tried *la biffe* instead (salvaging useful waste from dustbins using a special hook). Such work began on 1 January 1952, but *la biffe* was the prerogative of the town dustmen and soon afterwards a dispute and subsequent agreement between the two sides saw the Companions instead focus their efforts on collecting second-hand goods; working in shifts to recover items from cellars or attics. From February 1952 onwards, this practice was supplemented with *la biffe* carried out on the spreading fields or the rubbish dumps in the Parisian suburbs. Here, ex-convicts who did not have the right to reside in the city itself were able to work. They collected any material which could be resold, including paper, cardboard, rags and tins. If the work was difficult in winter on frozen rubbish dumps, it was even more gruelling in the summer, when the spreading fields became a breeding ground for infectious diseases. Some of the men slept where they worked, in salvaged wagons. Consequently, 1952 was the date when the Companions became Ragpickers, as well as builders.

Money was also donated. In 1952, Abbé Pierre won "Double or Quits", the famous TV game show presented by Zappy Max. Organised in advance and rigged slightly in Abbé Pierre's favour, the show raised his profile with the audience and the press, prompted the bank to grant him a loan to buy the plot of land at Pontault-Combault, and earned him enough money to buy a second-hand lorry. In 1953, with the lease due to expire, a donation from Baron Empain with certain conditions attached allowed him to buy the house at Neuilly-Plaisance.[37] This loan was supplemented *in extremis* by a handful of loyal friends and generous patrons, including Gilbert Cesbron and Edmond de Rothschild.

## "The missionary and the bandits"

The number of Companions continued to increase: 5 in summer 1951, 18 by the end of 1951, 150 by the end of 1952 and 185 by the end of the following year. Of that 185, 140 were Ragpickers and 45 were builders – clearly, the tables had quickly turned and collecting second-hand goods was now the occupation of choice. The Companions were housed across seven Communities at the end of 1952, and eight by the beginning of 1954.

While Georges Legay appears to have remained a shy and retiring figure with no real role in the Movement other than being its first Companion, from the very beginning there were a number of pivotal figures in the Emmaus ranks who stood out from the Companions of the time.[38] Pierre Lunel has described these Companions: "There were single men, without ties, tough nuts from the Legion, old volunteers in the German army and even former members of the Waffen SS or the 'it wasn't our fault-ers' whom the Third Reich had forcefully enlisted. Then there was the usual bunch of drunkards and misfits, the down-and-outs unable to work and the eternal drop-outs who had lost everything and made a hash of every opportunity life had thrown their way."[39] On 9 December 1952, Jules Carpentier arrived at Emmaus. Born in Rouen during the First World War, his real name was Joffrin, but he was renamed Jules after the Jules Joffrin square and metro station. After two years of active service, followed by five as a prisoner of war, and having been recently laid off by the firm for which he was working, Carpentier arrived at Neuilly-Plaisance and was sent to work on the rubbish dumps in Pontault-Combault. In an information letter issued by Emmaus International, he remarked how "all of a sudden, working away on the dumps, I discovered something extraordinary [...] You could find bread, tins of food, just about anything, and we realised that what we were doing was really useful; with the money we made from selling the things we found, we could help the families living in the Communities."[40] He found himself a job with a scrap metal dealer, but soon returned to Emmaus for good, believing he was "more useful there than working for a boss."[41]

Paul Desort arrived a few months later, on Ash Wednesday, 1953. He was forty-five years old and had come to Emmaus on a religious retreat. Born to a family of Lille bankers, he was taught by the Jesuits and was a keen pianist and painter. A middle-class childhood and adolescence had been followed by travels in Morocco, service in the Foreign Legion, a marriage, turbulent times in occupied France, shady business deals, and criminal charges that earned him two years in prison. From the moment he arrived, he was Abbé Pierre's irreplaceable right-hand man. Finally, Carpentier and Desort were joined by Jean-Yves Olichon, also fresh out of prison. Having previously worked as the overseer of a building site, he was immediately appointed the head of new building projects at Emmaus.

Living conditions were not exactly luxurious. Desort remembers living in "a miserable-looking house with a small balcony that had seen better days and a filthy, dilapidated window front and back [...] There I was, at the wheel of a ridiculous old banger; a tray with an engine. It was a clapped out Citroen of five or six horse-power. First stop: Bois-l'Abbé. It was an absolutely enormous rubbish dump where a handful of men, taking orders from a bloke with a peg-leg, lived in huts made of sheet metal and corrugated iron."[42] Money was tight: Carpentier described how the men weren't paid. We were entitled to only five francs a week and they'd still forget to give it to us [...] We slaved away morning 'til night. The first year, we worked fifteen-, sixteen-hour days for little more than five francs a week. We were skint."[43] Alcohol wreaked havoc, he explained too: "three-quarters of the men were members of the Legion who'd been pensioned off. They didn't have enough money to get by in the outside world, but they had too much to live in the Community. There was no clear leadership, no rules. There was just Abbé Pierre, Lucie Coutaz and a few men with good intentions. Saturday and Sunday were hellish – the men drank at least seven or eight litres of wine a day. But put yourself in their shoes – we had almost nothing to eat, we needed something to help us get through the fifteen-hour days! [...] Fights broke out over the slightest thing."[44]

## No Ordinary Association

### A charity breaking the mould

Each new family who arrived off the streets was one more family to house. From the very beginning, Emmaus was a construction company building illegal accommodation. To meet demand, the association flouted the restrictions of building permits, and even built without them when necessary. Desperate times did indeed call for desperate measures. Abbé Pierre remembered a defining moment in the Movement's history:

> "They turned up demanding to see the building permits for the new houses we were working on. So I replied: 'The next time you come back demanding that these workers show you a permit, which they can't afford on their meagre wage, I'm telling you now, I'll call the papers, the radio and film crews. I'll put on my Member of Parliament hat with my priest's stole underneath, then I'll get a pot of paint, pin up their birth certificates and write "permission to live" right across them.' Then I said 'when the law is designed in such a way that these workers, with their legal salary, cannot afford a house in which they can create a home and bring up a child in decent conditions, what is illegal is not building a house without a permit, it is the law itself that is illegal. Men should not bow down before the law. It is the law that should continually evolve to protect people's rights, starting with the rights of society's smallest members."[45]

This belief in the need to protect rights rather than uphold the law, to defend what is legitimate over and above what is legal, no doubt stems from Abbé Pierre's involvement in the Resistance. It was one of the cornerstones of Emmaus' work, but also one of the principles that set it apart from other, deeply law-abiding associations. Emmaus was prepared, if necessary, to stand up to the law.

However, Emmaus' aim was, above all, to help those living in poverty and to blow the whistle on it, and the two goals were inextricably linked. The Movement wished to blow the whistle on poverty by bringing together its victims and making it plain for all to see.[46] In the words of Boris Simon, Emmaus sought "to bring people face to face with the thoroughly unpleasant spectacle of the unjust suffering and distress of all those who were in such serious trouble":[47] the makeshift camps of canvas tents that had been hurriedly set up, the tiny shacks with no water or electricity, which were nevertheless a more favourable alternative to living with sixteen other people in a two-bedroom house or to a life on the streets, promiscuity and a total lack of privacy. Emmaus also wanted to speak out against poverty, and make its voice heard. The role Abbé Pierre assigned to the journalists who came to visit the camps out of curiosity was a vital one. Marin and Bonnet quote Abbé Pierre as saying, "we must shout, yell, about this outrageous housing crisis from the rooftops. It must become a national scandal, a source of national shame, a state matter. In order to shake up the powerful, wake up the rich, and make people aware of what's going on, it is vital that we get the national media on side."[48]

Emmaus also differed greatly from other organisations in the solidarity movement in that the issue of housing was its major concern. Finally, the Movement revived an old utopian dream by working according to the community model.[49]

## A religious organisation?

The place of religion within Emmaus was also unique. At that time, the vast majority of charitable associations were of religious origin or persuasion, and Emmaus was no exception. The Communists were more concerned with revolution than with providing sticking plasters for society's ills, and when any initiatives were launched, they were rather at trade-union or local-authority level and designed to help workers and their families. The socialists did not have a specific organisation. As a result, what was considered as "charity" was left in the hands of the religious organisations, which had, in practice, long controlled the sector.

Indeed, since its very beginning Emmaus was, in part, a religious organisation. Created by a priest, it was initially a meeting place for believers; Mass was held there every Sunday and grace was said before each meal. To remedy the shortfall in volunteers and provide moral guidance to the ex-convicts and Legionnaires who were the Companions of the day, "Father", as Abbé Pierre has always been known within Emmaus, asked the Church to send in reinforcements.

Reinforcements arrived in dribs and drabs, the Church reluctant to lose its troops to a new poverty army. Among them were some seminarians and a small handful of priests. The Abbé received moral support from Father Épagneul, founder of the brotherhood *Les Frères missionaires des campagnes*, and from the Voillaume brothers of the *Petits Frères de Foucauld* order. Father Norbert provided day-to-day support on the ground. He was the Father General of the White Canons who, upon his retirement in 1953, devoted his time fully to the Neuilly-Plaisance house. These were all men from the pre-Conciliar church who were eager to make use of the experience of worker-priests and who saw Emmaus as a new way of reaching out and spreading the word to the poorest members of society.

However, the influence of religion ends there. Of course, like the vast majority of the population at the time, the Companions had been brought up as Catholics but were non-believers. Mass remained optional – the Companions attended simply to please "Father" – and the vast majority of the Movement's support workers were non-religious. Most importantly, from 1954 onwards, the whirlwind of activity meant there was no longer any room for retreats and seminars at the hostel, nor time left for meditation.

## Winter 1954: "The Uprising of Kindness"

### The February 1954 appeal

In the midst of the housing crisis, the winter of 1953–4 was particularly harsh – temperatures dropped to minus 15° C – and the Companions were flooded with requests for accommodation. Well acquainted with the inner workings of the legislative process from his time as a Member of Parliament, Abbé Pierre attempted to persuade his friend, MRP member Léo Hamon, to table an amendment during the debate on the buildings budget that would see one billion francs earmarked for emergency accommodation. And yet, on the night of 3 January 1954, the very same night that a baby froze to death at the Coquelicots site, the Parliament adjourned the amendment indefinitely. In response the Abbé wrote an open letter to the Minister for Housing. *Le Figaro*, having just written a series of reports on Emmaus,[50] agreed to publish the letter on their 7 January front page. Furthermore, against all expectations, the Minister attended the baby's funeral.

It was at this point that the media began to take an interest in the housing crisis. Every night in January 1954, the Abbé and his Ragpickers would walk through the streets to hand out bowls of soup, bread and cups of hot coffee to the hundreds of "street-sleepers". At the same time, the Home Affairs Minister was stepping up the enforcement of eviction orders. Occasionally accompanied by journalists, the Companions unveiled the extent of this human tragedy, in which, according to Abbé Pierre's biographer Pierre Lunel, "only a handful of the victims were 'proper tramps'." He wrote, "they were everywhere; from the Panthéon to the *Jardin des plantes*, from the *Grands Boulevards* to the town hall. Alone or in groups, they were old men and women, craftsmen or workers on pensions too meagre to pay rent; mothers and their children evicted from their homes [...] young, smartly dressed men without a job; young families searching for non-existent housing, destitute after having paid for exorbitantly-priced lodgings; families who had fled overcrowded slums and the lack of privacy suffered in garrets and backyards; agricultural labourers who had returned from the south at the end of the harvest season; and vulnerable North African immigrants."[51] Parallels were drawn between the Abbé and St Vincent de Paul, who also went through the streets at night, helping the homeless. As one article on homelessness went to print, Abbé Pierre took to the airwaves and launched what became known as "the hundred franc note" campaign. In a few days, he had raised more than 1 million old francs.[52] At the end of the month, Radio Luxembourg invited him on air and promised to rebroadcast the appeals he made on behalf of the homeless.

However, the hot-drink runs were nothing more than a painful stopgap measure. How could they possibly just give someone a hot coffee, make sure their health was still holding up and leave with nothing more than a "good evening?" The Abbé consequently put in an offer on a piece of wasteland on the corner of the Rue de la Montagne-Sainte-Geneviève and the Rue Laplace, but had no money to build on it. He rented some large tents from a local Jewish stockist in Neuilly: on 29 January 1954, in the heart of the Latin Quarter, he set up a large tent complete with catalytic stoves and straw on the ground. That same evening, the homeless flocked to the camp in droves. Once the space was full, they slept in the police stations around the Panthéon or in the offices of the local health-insurance service. On Saturday 30 January, Madame Larmier, owner of the Rochester Hotel in the Rue de la Boétie, offered to open up her empty rooms to the homeless. These two sites would become the epicentres of the Movement's campaign. On 31 January, the Abbé preached in Courbevoie at the request of *La Croix* journalist Georges Verpraet, who lived in the area. The parishioners immediately set up the first Emergency Aid Committee, opened a *centre fraternal de dépannage* that very evening to hand out emergency supplies to the homeless, and began trawling the streets at night to pick up the "street-sleepers".

In the early hours of 1 February, a woman froze to death on a Parisian street in the arms of Emmaus Companions. She had been evicted the night before for falling behind with her rent. Georges Verpraet knew the editor-in-chief of the talking newspaper at the broadcasting service Radiodiffusion Française and also had connections at Radio Luxembourg.[53] On his advice, Verpraet and Abbé Pierre hurriedly wrote a message, which they persuaded the service's one-o'clock newsreader to read on air. At the same time they went to Radio Luxembourg, where they had also been given a slot on air. The two men each read their part of the message[54] – it was a message that would later become the famous February 1954 appeal. Abbé Pierre spoke first:

> "My friends, your help is needed! In the early hours of this morning a woman froze to death on the pavement of the Boulevard Sébastopol. She died clutching the eviction order that had been used to turf her out onto the street the day before yesterday. This very night in Paris and its suburbs, more than 2,000 people will be huddled in a corner in the frost, with no roof, no bread, and more than one of them will be almost naked. In the face of such horror, even the emergency campsites we have created are no longer able to deal with this emergency. In the last three hours, two emergency aid centres have been set up; one under canvas at the foot of the Panthéon, the other at Courbevoie. They are already bursting at the seams; we must open more centres everywhere. Tonight, in every city in France, in every district in Paris there must be places with bedding, straw, soup and a lamp on the door lighting up a sign that reads *'Centre fraternel de Dépannage'*. And underneath, these simple words: 'If you are suffering, whoever you are, come in, eat, sleep and regain hope. Here, you are loved.' The

> weather forecast is predicting a month of bitter frosts. These centres must remain open for as long as winter lasts. Faced with their brothers dying of poverty, everyone must stand firm and work towards one common goal: to make it impossible for this situation to continue. I beg you, let us love one another enough to do this without delay. Let one, miraculous thing emerge from so much pain: the common soul of the French nation. Thank you!"[55]

Georges Verpraet continued:

> "Each and every one of us can help the homeless. By tonight, or at the latest by tomorrow, we need 5,000 blankets, 300 large tents and 200 catalytic stoves. Bring them quickly to the Rochester Hotel, 92 Rue de la Boétie. There will be a meeting tonight, at eleven o'clock in front of the Montagne-Sainte-Geneviève tent, for volunteers and vans wishing to help with picking up street sleepers.
> "With your help, not a single man or child will have to spend tonight sleeping on asphalt or on a Paris railway platform. Thank you!"

There are countless theories behind the appeal's immediate success. The use of radio played a vital role, as it allowed voices and emotions to be heard. The message played on the fact that the housing crisis was of personal concern to many, which also undoubtedly contributed to the success of the appeal: homelessness was a problem that directly or indirectly affected every French family. The biting cold chilled everyone to the bone; everyone was therefore able to directly empathise with and show compassion towards those who were suffering. The opposite holds true for "distance suffering", which, as Luc Boltanski has shown, is all the more difficult to ease, "given that the victim is further away, and therefore opportunities for the spectator to take action are not as readily available."[56] There was also powerful, concrete evidence of the urgent need for action: a dying woman huddled in a corner on the pavement, clutching her eviction order to her chest. Furthermore, the appeal, which in no way disguised the horror of the situation and referred to women and children, was based on providing simple, tangible and immediate solutions – opening up places where people could sleep and providing blankets. The appeal also owed its success to the profile of the man behind it. Abbé Pierre was a priest and a former MP and Resistance member who, having already featured in the press for the past month, was now calling upon "the common soul of the French nation." Finally, this former political figure remained politically neutral, speaking instead from a humanitarian perspective and invoking the need for urgent action. There is no doubt that it was the combination of all these factors that made the appeal a success. It was followed by the media's growing infatuation with a figure who crossed all political and religious divides. The PCF were the only exception; initially continuing to harbour serious misgivings about him. In 1961, eight years on, 98% of those surveyed by the French Public Opinion Institute (IFOP) knew of Abbé Pierre.

## An exceptional campaign

Flooded with donations, the Rochester Hotel became the new campaign headquarters, and new telephone lines were hastily installed. The tent at Montagne-Saint Geneviève stayed up for five weeks, emergency aid centres sprung up left, right and centre, and 500 beds were set up on the premises of the health-insurance service, who closed their offices for three weeks to support the campaign. The local authority made the disused Orsay railway station available as a storage warehouse – it would remain in use until early June. The army and the department store BHV[57] contributed freight trucks; and the Paris city council, the prefecture and the Parisian transport network (RATP) opened up four disused metro stations.[58] Students from the prestigious higher-education establishment, the *École polytechnique*, worked in shifts around the clock to answer the phones and open post. Volunteers flocked to help with the night rounds, picking up the homeless, with Robert Buron at the helm. Buron was Abbé Pierre's friend from his Parliament days and he had since been appointed Minister for the Overseas Territories.

When the prefecture ordered the closure of the emergency shelters at the end of February, the homeless were moved to other temporary accommodation at Paris' city gates, including Saint-Ouen, Briançon and Vanves, where ten tents were erected, on loan from EDF until mid-May. Some also slept between four solid walls, at Lafayette, the town hall of the seventeenth *arrondissement*, and Bolívar metro station. At the end of April 1954, these places were still home to 180 households, including 110 children, 400 single men and 60 single women.

The media and the entertainment business threw their full weight behind the campaign. The gala evening organised at the Gaîté Lyrique theatre on 8 February 1954 was a who's who of Paris showbiz. The media spearheaded "operation clear-out", which aimed to collect old pieces of furniture and items from Parisian servants' rooms and make unoccupied rooms available to the homeless – 200 rooms were opened up as a result of the media's efforts. Meanwhile, the Abbé organised more and more meetings outside the capital, where Emergency Aid Committees were being set up. From March onwards, meetings were also held abroad.

In the political sphere, on 4 February, Parliament, which one month earlier had adjourned the vote on an amendment in favour of emergency housing, adopted a programme which earmarked ten billion-francs[59] for the construction of 12,000 basic houses – half to be built in the Paris region and the other half outside the capital. The number of houses was ten times greater than that originally requested. On 9 February, the Abbé was invited to Matignon, the official residence of the French Prime Minister, by the president of the Council of State. However, government involvement was far from problem-free. The bill had been passed but the money did not arrive, and it was up to the Abbé to dip into recently collected funds and foot the bill for the first houses. The government then pressed him to guarantee a national interest-free loan that financiers and major investors were all the more careful to avoid, given that the state was launching other, more attractive loans at the same time.[60] Instead of the anticipated five billion, this loan ultimately brought in only 2.2 billion.[61] However, in the end, the money needed to bring the total up to the promised ten billion was stumped up by the Ministry of Finance. Other measures to solve the housing crisis included a competition launched on 23 February to find the architect who would build cheap, basic accommodation, otherwise known as LEPN. On 27 March, the decree on the allocation of social housing was also finally passed, in accordance with the law adopted on 24 May 1951. Furthermore, on 15 July 1954, a law was passed which made it easier for buildings to be requisitioned for public use. Mass support for such initiatives also pushed *Caisse des dépôts*, the state company responsible for the shrewd investment of public money, to set up a state construction company: the *Société centrale immobilière.* The company was launched on 11 June to "solve the housing crisis by building quick, low cost housing on a massive scale."[62]

Like the authorities, the Church was equivocal in its attitude towards the campaign but was keen to get on board. While Abbé Pierre was undoubtedly something of a free-thinking priest, he was in no way a dissident and following the success of the appeal, he asked the Church to inform him of their stance on what he was doing. A letter arrived on 29 May 1954, signed by Monseigneur Guerry, Archbishop of Cambrai. It read: "It would appear that our role as bishops is to grant you complete freedom to carry out the work you do that reaches sectors of society often greatly distanced from the Church. Any patronage of your work on our part, which sought to bolster the Church's influence or which appeared to do so, would alienate many of those whom you aim to help. But our not getting publicly involved should not prevent us from thanking you for your work and should not prevent me from personally pledging you my full support. I thank God for having chosen you as his tool in so cruel and urgent an apostolic mission as alleviating the housing crisis." The Abbé viewed the letter as "a miracle"; it was a blessing without a request to play a supervisory role. The letter came shortly after the abrupt termination of the worker-priest experiment, which had suggested the Church would sit on the sidelines and cease to dogmatically enforce its views while continuing to do precisely that. In light of this, viewed as tacit approval of Abbé Pierre's work, the letter can also be read as an expression of the Church's wish to remain close to the Movement; while at the same time not fully endorsing discourse that was at times politically inflammatory, unlike its classic, non-subversive charitable counterpart.

At the time, *l'Osservatore Romano*, the semi-official newspaper of the Vatican, published both photos of and eulogistic tales about Abbé Pierre in abundance.[63] The Church's charitable organisation, *Secours catholique*, also pledged its support. In addition, despite a difficult relationship with Abbé Pierre,[64] Emmaus' secretary general Monseigneur Rodhain had already attempted to spread word of the Movement prior to 1954 and to obtain funding from middle-class circles. In February 1954, the charitable organisation Centrale Catholique gave Emmaus use of its ambulance car and blankets for the Montagne-Sainte-Geneviève tent. They also offered the services of their volunteer doctors and, on 19 February, opened up a campsite of eighteen heated tents at the Orléans city gate.[65]

## The media and the world of politics pledge their almost unanimous support

As the symbol of this mass campaign to help society's most vulnerable, Abbé Pierre became an icon, first of all within Emmaus. "Father", as he was always known, was also the Son who surrounded himself with disciples: "All of a sudden, the Ragpickers' old lorry conks out and refuses to start up. So the Father gets his old friend Robert Buron whom he'd met on the Parliamentary benches, and sets him to work as a taxi-driver. The Abbé hired the minister on the spot, in much the same way as Christ called upon certain fishermen to become fishers of men."[66] More generally, inside Emmaus, Abbé Pierre was often compared with biblical figures and was the focus of religious veneration.

His image outside Emmaus, a veritable media construct, was broadly similar. With his picture splashed across newspaper front pages, he moved between being a prophet of the modern age, and the benevolent intermediary of the worker-priests, newly condemned by the Vatican. He won over hearts and minds with his persona as a man of the Church whose feet were on the ground; a man who was half-secular and whose activities were only half above board. The Abbé Pierre legend had one, vital asset at its disposal: the face of the man himself. It was a handsome face and one which bore all the signs of someone with apostolic responsibilities: an honest expression, a Franciscan haircut and a missionary's beard, all rounded off by the trademark *canadienne* of a worker-priest and a pilgrim's cane. "He combined the codes of myth and modernity."[67] In this sense, the Abbé was a veritable "forest of signs".[68] They were signs that he would continue to hold dear, actively cultivating his image,[69] until his death. It was often suggested that the Abbé be canonised – even *Le Canard enchaîné,* one of France's most anti-clerical newspapers, expressed this view. Indeed, the paper throwing its full weight behind the cause was symptomatic of the Abbé Pierre fever that had gripped the French nation and that saw a whole host of affectionate nicknames bestowed upon him. These included "St John the Builder", "St Vincent de Paul" and "Roofin' Hood".[70] The rallying cry, *"Au pouvoir, l'Abbé!"* was also heard.

The press's almost unanimous endorsement of Abbé Pierre remained remarkable. *Le Figaro* pledged him their support in January 1954, followed by *La Croix*, and in February, all the major newspapers rallied behind the cause. *L'Humanité* was the only exception, initially launching an unrestrained tirade against a charitable campaign that they saw as merely aimed to palliate the effects of poverty. Roland Barthes took up this critical, communist stance at the end of his article, *"Iconographie de l'abbé Pierre"*: "Clearly, the issue is not how this forest of *signs* has managed to cover Abbé Pierre [...] I'm simply interested in society's consumption of these signs on a massive scale [...] and I am concerned for a society that is so eager to consume this image of charity it forgets to reflect upon its consequences, its uses and its limits. I sometimes come to wonder whether Abbé Pierre's beautiful and endearing iconography is not in fact the alibi that a large part of the French nation uses to once more substitute reality and justice with the signs of charity, and get away with it."[71]

Unanimous support for Abbé Pierre emerged once again during the "housing awareness days", organised at the end of 1954. At Emmaus' request, these events notably brought together the government's National Centre for the Improvement of Housing, social housing organisations, the presidents of chambers of commerce and tradesmen and the Guild of Architects. However, it also welcomed the trade unions (CGC and CFTC), the then communist *Secours populaire français*, the French Protestant Federation and the *Consistoire israélite* – the institution responsible for administering Jewish worship in France. Even the French Students' Union (UNEF) was in attendance. As the minutes of these meetings proudly emphasised, "It is rare in France, even when dealing with very specific issues, to be able to sit public and para-statal bodies around the same table as bodies from the private sector, which often have diverging, if not diametrically opposed points of view."[72]

Lastly, the film industry came on board. In autumn 1954, Charlie Chaplin was passing through Paris. He visited Abbé Pierre in person to give him half of his Lenin Peace Prize money of 2 million old francs. The Peace Prize's Russian origins caused a great deal of ink to be spilled. Meanwhile, the director Robert Darène put pressure on a sick Abbé Pierre and obtained the rights for a film.[73]

In the five days following the winter appeal, 150 million old francs were collected,[74] along with hundreds of tonnes of clothes, food and heating equipment. By 21 February, the total had risen to more than 400 million francs[75] and 10 million tonnes of donations, either in the form of goods in kind or waste that could be resold. When the total was counted in mid March, goods in kind included, it finally exceeded the one billion mark.[76] Beyond meeting the urgent needs of the poor, "the Uprising of Kindness" ended the legal impasse surrounding legislation in favour of basic housing for those most in need and raised awareness nationwide of the seriousness of the problem.

It also saw Emmaus acquire newfound fame and achieve unprecedented levels of growth; both of which were difficult to manage. Abbé Pierre told Bernard Chevallier: "After only a few days, there I was, little old me, barely even an administrator and certainly not a businessman, without any experience or legal expertise, sitting on more than 500 million old francs and in front of a pile of 300,000 letters; hounded by the press and the diplomatic corps, dealing with ministers, flooded with enquiries from well-intentioned volunteers, and faced with cries for help from people in all kinds of distress... never had I been as acutely aware as I was then that I wasn't cut out to lead, but simply to rouse people to action."[77] Indeed, while doing his utmost to rehouse families and give the new Companions a reason to live once more, the Abbé did not feel comfortable as a manager or a leader, and even less so a CEO.

# *Chapter 2* / THE BLOSSOMING OF NEW ACTIVITIES (1954–1958)

The success of the 1954 appeal caused the organisation's funds and activities to increase sharply. To take up the botanical image of a tree used by Emmaus time and time again since its beginning, there was, what one might call, "the blossoming" of new activities. In the words of Yves Goussault, Professor of Sociology and active member of Emmaus: "This tree with many branches had a common sap that flowed from a single trunk. This trunk, with its roots in the earth and in the mud, was life in an Emmaus Community. The Community was where it all happened; where a handful of men, no better than any others, but determined to work together to save each other, united to help those less fortunate than themselves."[1] But Emmaus was "a tree that had grown too quickly", and in no time at all, waste produced by mismanagement, local potentates and "black sheep" had begun to gnaw at its bark. Meanwhile, unmanageable "factory-Communities", and other Communities too weak to survive, fell into rapid decline.[2] Between its central activities, such as working on housing and building up Communities, and newer ones including the newspaper, homeless committees, housing unions and campaigns abroad, the Emmaus tree was burgeoning out of control and needed to be pruned – branches cut back here and stakes put in there. Bringing the tree back under control with the help of a new generation of more reliable, committed activists was a two-phase process. First, activities were centralised. Then, one after another, the subsidiary bodies were granted independence, until only one minimal structure remained under Emmaus' direct control. The majority of the young shoots that sprouted at that time would become the branches of the future; branches which grew ever stronger during the next stage of the Movement's history.

## A New Organisation is Created

The significant increase in both the Emmaus budget and support base required a new, more rigid structure to be put into place. Consequently "Association Emmaus" was created in order to coordinate Emmaus' various activities; the statutes were registered at the prefecture on 12 March 1954, and appeared in the *Official Journal* five days later.

Up until that point, aside from Lucie Coutaz, Abbé Pierre had been heavily reliant on two former offenders, Paul Desort and Jean-Yves Olichon. The group was of course assisted by a handful of seminarians and well-intentioned Christians, prepared to devote some of their time to the experiment. However, from February 1954 onwards, Abbé Pierre managed to surround himself with a number of high-flyers, friends and acquaintances who had recently rallied behind the cause. As a result, the board of directors of the brand-new organisation was made up of journalists (Georges Verpraet, Robert Barrat), lawyers (Jean Budin, Maître Chaumié), public notaries (one of whom practised in La Marnière) and industry chiefs (Georges Lillaz, CEO of the department store BHV; André Bercher, the managing director of a clothing company; Jean Bouchy, consulting engineer and a protégé of Gustave Eiffel). Also present were financiers (Monsieur Mourral, head of the French central bank, *Banque des intérêts français*; Dominique Denis; Jacques Lazard, heir to the famous Lazard bank), a member of the Economic Council who championed many a social cause (Guy Houist),[3] members of the Council of the State (Pierre Join-Lambert, in charge of petitions) and retired officers from the armed forces (Captain Boulat, who was also the vice-president of a family-support association). In June 1954, they were joined by two members of the trade union CFTC, Maurice Bouladoux and Jean Villot. In breaking radically with its predecessor, the make-up of this board of directors produced a clash of viewpoints and methods – suddenly, two worlds divided by everything except their support for the cause were brought together and collided in a most dramatic fashion.

Work on (re)structuring Emmaus began quickly. In order to replace the organisation's headquarters at the Rochester Hotel and house rapidly growing services, Emmaus purchased 32 Rue des Bourdonnais,[4] a building in the Les Halles district, at the very heart of working-class Paris. In addition to the fact that the organisation was in dire need of new headquarter premises, the building's location was ideal; it was in a poor area and would also serve as a drop-in centre and hostel. These services were finally up and running in January 1955. On the ground floor of the building was a drop-in centre where the homeless could come for help and advice, and in the basement there was a canteen and beds. There were eighty-five places in the men's dormitory, twenty-two beds in the female dormitory, and around one hundred places for people to sit, eat their fill and warm up. A part of the drop-in centre would ultimately be closed in early 1957, as it was impeding the smooth running of the Emmaus offices and making the premises unhygienic for the employees.

Another reorganisation measure was the appointment of secretary-generals, who controlled the services that Emmaus provided. In June, the members of the board divided responsibility for the various sectors between themselves. Jean Bouchy took charge of Communities; Georges Verpraet took over the newspaper; Maître Chaumié and Robert Barrat were responsible for emergency aid in Paris and the provinces, respectively; and Dominique Denis handled building projects. An invaluable source of support, Georges Lillaz, CEO of BHV, walked along the Rue du Rivoli every evening to stop by the headquarters and lend a hand. He also brought an engineer, Jacques Robine, on board. Robine worked for the movement from November 1954 to June 1956, and was tasked with creating an accounting service and ironing out the organisation's management problems.

From 1954 onwards, Emmaus' nascent sub-organisations were given formal structure and made official. Its social housing service became a limited company whose application to register its statutes, submitted on 25 January 1954, went noticeably to the top of the pile – it was approved by ministerial decree on 19 February.

Emmaus' activities in Paris, which provided emergency support to the homeless, received the same treatment. The drop-in centres, the social services, the housing services and house-clearing operations were all brought together under a not-for-profit umbrella organisation called ASLAP which worked to help the homeless in Paris and its suburbs. Its national counterpart, UNASL, was officially created in January 1955. For both internal and external communication, the newspaper *Faim et Soif des hommes* was founded in May 1954. Its circulation was promising right from the start – the 100,000 copies printed as a first run quickly ran out. By July, 14,700 subscriptions to the paper had been sold. A further 3,000 were taken out in October, and they peaked at 65,000 in the years 1955–6. In the spring of 1957, the newspaper would go from being a private limited company to a public limited company, but the number of subscriptions dropped to 40,000. The second half of 1954 marked the start of a gradual process that saw an umbrella association put into place, which brought together Emmaus' property companies. And finally, in September 1954, the Institute of Research and Action Against Global Poverty (IRAMM) was born to take charge of international activities and research. However, ties between these sub-organisations and Association Emmaus remained strong: in this first phase "the association's various activities [were] both consolidated within their internal structures and linked back to Emmaus as the central secretariat."[5]

During the second phase (1955–6) these organisations were made truly independent. The benefits of such independence were twofold. On the one hand, it fulfilled Abbé Pierre's desire to grant each organisation more freedom and flexibility; this was a project that had matured during his recovery from illness at the end of 1954. While a policy of "maximum centralisation and authoritarianism" may have initially appeared necessary, the time had come to enter a phase "of decentralisation and coordination" which was more flexible and more in line with the Abbé's own vision of the Movement. Furthermore, and for varying reasons, enabling each organisation to have a greater degree of independence satisfied the Association's board of directors. At the time, the board were eager to make Emmaus a viable and coherent entity and to balance finances that were as lacking in clarity as they were in profit. The organisation's shortfalls were the result of investments in building projects and new activities, but were also due to the blatant waste of resources and the odd case of embezzlement.

In addition, this second phase saw the Communities achieve independence.[6] The deterioration of internal relations and certain difficulties with Abbé Pierre[7] also led to the Association being stripped of the majority of its organisations, for fear it would implode. In 1958, it controlled only two insignificant activities: the problematic camp at Noisy and the Bourdonnais hostel. However, even after becoming independent the majority of these new organisations kept their headquarters at the Emmaus building in Paris, which allowed long-lasting, informal relations to be maintained.

## Housing: A Desperate Situation

### The housing crisis in France

Both the work carried out by the Ragpicker-builders since the early fifties and the 1954 appeal began as responses to the housing crisis. During the "catacombs period" the Abbé and his Ragpickers were flooded with requests for help, each more tragic than the last: a young worker whose wife had recently gone mad after three years of life in communal quarters and a total lack of privacy; three families and two babies in one room in Montreuil; families of twelve in muddy, makeshift huts; and parents on the brink of suicide on the eve of eviction from their home. In 1954 in the Paris region, 40% of houses were overcrowded and a fifth of all families lived in a hotel or hostel. This crisis was the result of a belief, which had long been at the heart of liberal politics, that property was an almost sacred economic and political cornerstone; it was a private possession that could not be subject to socialist state intervention.[8] Rooted in this minimal intervention strategy, the crisis was fuelled by years of inactivity – the property sector had been lagging behind other areas of the economy since the end of the nineteenth century, and this growth gap widened significantly with First-World-War inflation and a rent freeze that was subsequently extended. Other factors behind the crisis included the buoyant stock markets of the 1920s, which meant people were hardly inclined to put their money into property; an acute economic recession in the 1930s, which destroyed the initial effects of the 1928 Loi Loucheur in favour of social housing and seriously affected the amount of new building taking place;[9] and finally, the devastation of the Second World War, during which 1.4 million homes were damaged and 500,000 were destroyed.[10] The rental sector, which had not turned a profit since 1914, was neglected, incapable of meeting demand and increasingly run-down and overcrowded. However, the crisis, both quantitative and qualitative, affected the entire housing stock. In 1946, 20% of homes outside the French capital and 25% of the homes in Paris itself were more than one hundred years old; 450,000 homes were unsanitary; and a further 300,000 bedsits were uninhabitable. In towns with a population greater than 300,000, only 5% of homes were equipped with all the necessary utilities – running water, electricity, mains drainage and central heating.[11] After 1945, a handful of people did admittedly stand up and speak out against the housing situation, including demographer Alfred Sauvy (in 1946) and the Minister for Reconstruction and Town Planning, Eugène Claudius-Petit (in 1949). Employers were also growing concerned about a housing situation which saw their employees housed in substandard accommodation. Despite the fact that some measures were taken to remedy the problem, the housing issue was quickly buried beneath others – the fight to bolster economic growth and get France back on its feet, the French Union and the constitutional regime. The situation further worsened with the baby boom and the rural exodus.

Nevertheless, from September 1948 onwards, more proactive measures were taken under housing minister Claudius-Petit. The law passed on 1 September 1948 attempted to ensure that people received a return on their investments in the housing sector by removing the rent caps on new-builds and substantially increasing the rent on other houses. It also introduced tax relief to stimulate growth in the construction sector. The law adopted on 21 July 1950 laid the foundations for a housing programme that looked to the private sector for funds and saw the HBM (*habitations à bon marché*) officially renamed HLM (*habitations à loyers modérés*). However, the 1951–2 finance laws cut the housing budget in order to increase government arms spending.

A second offensive was launched under new housing minister Pierre Courant. From 1953 onwards, housing was one of the French authorities' social priorities and the government became heavily involved. Launched in January 1953, the ambitious Courant Plan provided for the construction of 240,000 houses a year. The plan aimed to grant various sectors of society a greater degree of financial solvency while at the same time slashing the cost price of construction, which remained unaffordable for many French people. Its key features were the launch of attractive savings rates, the creation of *"logécos"* (cheap family homes) and a modernisation plan for the construction sector. In addition, in August 1953, a ministerial decree made it obligatory for firms with over ten employees to contribute 1% of all salaries to the housing sector.[12] On 8 August 1953, a law was passed that made it possible for local authorities to expropriate land needed for the construction of residential areas.

However, French housing policy continued to be based on tax incentives designed to encourage economic agents to invest in the sector. In essence, the government had opted for "minimal intervention based on the principle that the sector would have a spill-over effect",[13] and the insignificant amount of funding provided meant that this spill-over effect was insufficient. Most importantly, the urgent need for housing remained. Indeed, it was in order to meet this need, while at the same time putting pressure on the government to continue with their own proactive measures, that Abbé Pierre took action in early 1954. The scale of the campaign, which served to consolidate the public's awareness of the problem, succeeded in obtaining a more sincere commitment from the government. Indeed, between 1954 and 1975, the effectiveness of state intervention in the construction sector was such that the housing stock grew by 50% and, at the same time, housing conditions were significantly improved.[14]

## Buying and building

As we have seen, from the end of January 1954 – in other words *before* 1 February – Emmaus had its own public limited social housing company. The most urgent task at the time was the construction of houses and, right from the word go, Emmaus became involved in the government programme launched in early February, which promised to create 12,000 "emergency or transit housing sites", comprising cheap, basic homes (LEPN). It was a humanitarian relief initiative that aimed to respond to tragedies on a day-by-day basis and was accepted as such. Nevertheless, the measure was a controversial one. It went against the philosophy that underpinned social housing insofar as it could only produce poor-quality housing for poor people, lead to social and spatial segregation which would be difficult to manage and create "new slums", adding to all those, already in place, which urgently needed to be demolished.[15]

To begin with, Emmaus' public limited social housing company bought up land as if it was going out of fashion. On 30 January, the board of directors approved the purchase of plots in Plessis-Trévise, then Argenteuil on 14 April, Argenteuil et Bezons on 9 May and Argenteuil et Sartrouville on 12 June. More land was purchased in Argenteuil on 20 June, in Bezons on 21 July and in Aulnay-sous-Bois on 30 July, and so it went on. This phase lasted until 1957.

At the same time, houses were being built as quickly as possible. On 8 February 1954, just one week after Abbé Pierre's call to action, Emmaus put up the money for and began work on the first emergency accommodation site in Plessis-Trévise – forty-eight LEPN houses and 200 emergency houses were to be built on forty hectares of land. Building was completed in record time and the first section of the site was opened on 30 April, with the housing minister in attendance. However, the consequence of such speed was imperfection – the builders had rushed their work and the ministerial services responsible for overseeing the project had not done their job properly. Emmaus-Habitat later declared: "it was regrettable that despite the fact that one-floor houses had been around for a hundred years, the craftsmen, who we trusted entirely, and the experienced technicians from the Ministry for Reconstruction and Housing, had not considered the fact that such houses could not be built without the traditional crawl space." It was also regrettable that the experts had neglected to comply with the requirement that external walls be insulated.[16] A few months later, the beams collapsed and mould covered the walls. Cracked sheets of fibre-cement had been put in the walls; the chimneys leaked and the houses were flooded. With damp walls and mud everywhere, in winter, even spending every last penny they had on heating the rooms, the families remained unable to warm the houses to above thirteen degrees. The housing site was some way outside the village and there was no public transport or common facilities. Furthermore, although originally designed to provide temporary accommodation, the site became a place where people stayed long-term, due to the lack of permanent housing available. Emmaus' social housing company, Emmaus HLM, was bitterly disappointed with the outcome of the project, but retained a clear sense of perspective, writing in *Faim et Soif*, "if we'd intended these housing sites to act as nothing more than shelters in the winter and campsites in the summer, then we had (just about) achieved our goal. The houses had enough floor space, four walls, a roof, a toilet, running water and even a chimney. People could survive in them, which was something in itself. But as they were, these houses had to be seen as temporary shelters and not as long-term accommodation, as we would understand it – they weren't homes, where families could thrive with everything they needed around them to live in freedom and happiness."[17] Nevertheless, the construction of the Le Plessis site meant the camp at la Pomponnette could be evacuated, and a large-scale operation to dry out the site and in turn solve its problems finally got under way.

Aulnay was the next construction project and 240 houses were built on the chosen site. This time, Emmaus was directly responsible for the project and solid foundations were used. Nevertheless, despite the fact that the building contracts had been issued following a competition to find architect-entrepreneurs, and an entirely legitimate call for tender, and despite the fact the plans had been approved by senior technicians at the Housing Ministry, the houses were still damp – albeit to a lesser extent. Some local councils also entrusted Emmaus with the task of building houses as part of the government's plan to erect 6,000 LEPN homes in the Paris region: forty were built in Chaville, fifty in Pontoise, fifty in Saint-Ouen-l'Aumône, 110 in Conflans-Sainte-Honorine, 150 in Aunay-sous-Bois, and so it went on. Improvements had to be carried out on these houses too as the roofs were not watertight.

Emmaus not only built emergency accommodation. In 1954, in Bezons and Argenteuil, work began on blocks of *logécos*. However, due to the way the project was financed, its cost price was very high indeed, and this was reflected in the rent the tenants were later charged. Much of the rent owed remained unpaid for many years and this eroded the budget. As part of the government's "operation-million", houses were also built in Aulnay. These were affordable, comfortable homes – they boasted a modern crawl space and good soundproofing – but lacked heating and were very damp. Finally, in 1956, work began on "non-social, category A" houses. These were houses built to comply with simplified standards and rent was minimal. At the request of some local councils, Emmaus also built "non-social, category B" houses, designed for the middle classes and executives. The revenue from this non-social housing meant that the social housing deficit could be financed, albeit with some difficulty.

Gathering together the initial funds required for these projects involved taking out a multitude of loans. Credit was obtained from *la Caisse des dépôts, la Caisse d'épargne* and the *Crédit foncier de France*, amongst others. The 1% of all salaries, which firms with over ten employees contributed to social housing, provided valuable extra funds. This was paid by bosses in the form of a repayable loan or as company shares. In fact, such funding increased from 5 million francs in 1954 to 60 million three years later.[18] Up until the late 1960s, while Abbé Pierre and the first activist-shareholders had lost their own majority, Association Emmaus remained the largest shareholder. Finally, a number of local councils also gave Emmaus land on which social housing could be built.

In its early years, the Emmaus social housing company worked on a whole host of different projects. In the space of three years, 1,500 houses were built, in addition to the 400 houses built in cooperatives with the aim of helping people get a foot on the property ladder. These were built under the aegis of the *Emmaus Société des cités*, which was set up in 1956 with Henri Camus at the helm. Construction began at breakneck speed but the pace then began to slow, allowing quality to take precedence over quantity. The archives of Association Emmaus read, "As far as housing is concerned, Abbé Pierre believes that our task is to provide emergency housing to the homeless, whether they be tramps or financially perfectly stable. Our role should be to encourage people to build housing and to help them to do so, but we should not automatically do everything ourselves. That would, incidentally, be impossible. If in 1954 we wished to do the building ourselves and devote the lion's share of our budget to it, it was because in fact we needed to do so to give ourselves the authority to speak, to be able to say 'we've done it – don't go telling us it's not possible.' It was a vital tool for our work inciting people to build housing."[19]

## A policy with social welfare in mind?

Emmaus was a limited social housing company unlike any other. As a company under private law it enjoyed a certain degree of freedom; as the offshoot of an organisation wholly committed to improving social welfare, it was obliged to balance the books, but not to make a profit. There was therefore something of a tug-of-war between two potentially contradictory principles: charity and sound management.

During 1954–5, the wish to see social institutions built as part of Emmaus housing sites emerged. Ideally, housing sites would include a teaching centre, a nursery, launderettes, meeting rooms, a library, social workers and even a church.[20] Nevertheless, the dream and the reality were some way apart. According to the archives of Emmaus-Habitat, in 1958, the social infrastructure in Emmaus housing sites was judged to be "clearly insufficient, even inexistent" as a result of financial constraints.[21] The company was seriously in the red. (In 1955, it had a debt of 21.5 million francs. By 1959, this debt had increased by 6.8 million.[22]) This debt was largely the result of administrative costs and the astronomical costs of certain activities. Emmaus was therefore sadly unable to invest in social infrastructure and relied on local councils to compensate for its own lack of means.

Emmaus was also forced to wage war against unpaid rent, particularly in Bezons and Argenteuil. These two sites alone accounted for two-thirds of the unpaid rent in 1958 and the amount left unpaid reached record highs (in 1960, 24% of rent remained unpaid, compared to 3.7% at other sites). From 1956 onwards, coercive measures were taken to remedy the problem: those who failed to pay were brought before the courts and links with the sub-prefect and the local police chief were strengthened so that they could assist with evictions and if necessary, with rehousing those driven out of their homes... in the ice-cold "igloos" of Noisy. The evictions unnerved some leaders, who were torn between the need to protect the poor and balance the books, but who were also aware of the social and educational purposes that evictions served (getting people used to paying rent) and of the ill will of some who failed to pay their rent. Emmaus-Habitat archives noted that such people were often "professionally unemployed or obstinate individuals, whom it was very difficult to track down on site during normal working hours."[23] In 1957, the decision was taken to hire a member of staff who would be specifically responsible for tackling the issue of unpaid rent. This person would have "the necessary qualifications and the required tact to deal with the people in question", but would also ensure that the background and paperwork of potential new tenants were more closely examined before they signed a contract.[24]

## The Communities: Planting the Roots

Together with housing, the Communities made up the nucleus of Emmaus' activity. However, considered by Abbé Pierre to be the "roots of the tree", they enjoyed a unique status: while housing or development aid were causes to be championed, while the newspaper was a tool, the Communities could adapt to any of Emmaus' battles. They were cocoons which provided warmth, and organisational structures which gave back hope to people. They were places where people could live and work to improve the lives of others, and they developed following the 1954 appeal.

### The development of the Communities

The February 1954 appeal led to the indisputable growth of the movement: there were 200 men on board in January 1954 and 1,000 a year later. In early 1957, there were already eighteen Communities up and running. However, these Communities were forced first of all to "withstand the wave of the Uprising of Kindness itself, all the false enthusiasm it whipped up, and its later decline. They were then forced to resist their own expansion, which was far too quick, and to cope with the lack of qualified leaders."[25]

The first new Community to take root was the women's Community in Plessis-Trévise, managed by Madame Renard. Born to a rich family, the widow of a naval officer who fought for de Gaulle and who was killed in the Italy campaign, Suzanne née Bourboulon lived in Morocco during the war. Called upon to train and manage the heads of women's services in the Marines and founder of the armed forces' orphanage, she met Abbé Pierre in 1944 when he travelled through Casablanca. On her return to civilian life, she remained in contact with Abbé Pierre and in 1953, devoted herself fully to the newly created organisation Friends of Emmaus. The Le Plessis Women's Community was opened on 1 May 1954. The nature and running of the women's Communities differed from those for men. This was not only because many of the women had been broken by a life of prostitution, but also because many brought their children with them and, as a general rule, lacked the physical strength of their male counterparts. This meant they were less suited to the usual Emmaus activities of collecting waste and construction work. As a result, the female Companions focused their efforts on repairing items and working with fabrics: sorting and washing rags, sewing, repairing mattresses, making rugs, lampshades and wooden toys, and working with rattan and other materials. Lastly, the women's Community was also unique in that serious violence and jealousy reigned, meaning the Le Plessis Women's Community was for a long time the only female or mixed Community able to survive.

The Bougival Community was the second new Community to open its doors, and was situated in the west of the Paris region: fifty men converted a run-down factory into a warehouse where old household goods, which the Companions had collected, could be sorted and sold. In 1955, the Community was breaking even and managed to turn a profit of 1 million francs a month. In addition to funding Emmaus' work with the poor, this profit funded the speedy installation of showers, electricity and four-bed rooms. Using the Community in Neuilly-Plaisance, La Réserve, as a model, more showers, hot water and individual bedrooms were then installed.

Communities were also opened across the rest of France. On 1 October 1954, "Captain Jean" founded a "Community of Hope" in

Lille. A northern industrialist and captain in the reserve, Jean Deroubaix was passing through Paris on 1 February 1954. He responded to the appeal and was appointed leader of the work being undertaken at Orsay railway station, which had been requisitioned for the storage of donated goods and renamed "the Station of Hope". He then returned to the north, decided to liquidate his businesses and devoted himself fully to Emmaus, opening a Community at the military fort of Wambrechies. In January 1955 a "Hope Commando" was founded under the leadership of Charles Caillaux, a former alcoholic who beat his addiction with the help of the association *Croix d'or.* The Community had a branch in La Rochelle and in one month it took in forty-five Companions.

In Alsace, Abbé Pierre's work had struck a chord with the young curate Abbé Landwerlin, who had close ties with the JOC and Catholic trade unionists. He used money put up by the Mulhouse homeless committee to open a Community and convinced the town hall to give him the site of the municipal rubbish dump. The Community set up home in a disused bus, initially with the help of Paul (of Normandy). In 1955, it was handed over to Henri Dobigies, who arrived at Emmaus in 1954 following Abbé Pierre's appeal and the closure of his factory.[26] Local residents were made aware of the Movement through Abbé Pierre's conferences and showings of the film *Les Chiffonniers d'Emmaüs.* Its beginnings were dramatic, as was always the case. Eight Companions lived in the bus and nine under canvas. However, as Dobigies wrote in his note to Jacques Robine, "given the fact that some of these tents [were] swept away by the wind, and that for four weeks, temperatures [fluctuated] between – 20 °C and – 26 °C, there [was] an urgent need to find four solid walls which could house the Community."[27] Consequently, a shack was purchased along with a diesel lorry and a large tent where items could be stored. Water mains and a telephone line were finally installed in 1956, and electricity followed in September. After eighteen months, Dobigies left Cernay and returned to Bourdonnais. Interviewed in *Faim etSoif,* he admitted, "Weariness also drove me to return, because we were living in very uncomfortable conditions. There was a language barrier, too. All the members of the Community spoke the Alsatian dialect and me, I only spoke French..."[28]

In Brest, the local homeless support committee also set up a Community, headed up by Paul le Roch; by the end of 1956 it boasted around forty Companions. As was often the case, the profits were first and foremost ploughed back into Emmaus' work with the poor and the Companions lived for a long time without either running water or electricity. However, the Brest Community was one of the first to ban alcohol. It gradually spread across Brittany thanks to the efforts of one Bernard Rigaud. He was twenty-six years old in 1957 when he took over Morlaix's travelling Emmaus team and went on to fill the same post in Quimper (1958), Crozon (1959), Plouescat (1961), Chateauneuf-du-Faou (1962) and Carhaix (1963), before finally moving to Quimperlé and creating an independent Community there in 1964. Other Communities sprung up in Rouen (January 1956), Marseilles (February 1956), Rennes, Évreux, Limoges and Nice, to name but a few.

However at that time, few of Emmaus' leaders had come to the Movement out of a sense of vocation. The majority were unreliable and/or dishonest and this produced local scandals and a staff turnover that hindered the smooth running of the organisation and tarnished its image. At the Cernay Community, between March 1957 and March 1960, there were no fewer than nine leaders. These were for the most part former Companions who had risen up through the ranks, and several of them lasted less than a month. There were also concerns about authoritarian, even military practices within Communities. Such concerns were first raised about the leadership of Jean-Yves Olichonat La Réserve, then later at Pontault-Combault. In response to these concerns, the management set about doing all it could to remedy and stabilise the situation. Opened in 1954, the Rennes Community was forced to close in 1956. The Nice Community came under scrutiny in June 1954 as a result of its dubious accounts. The Communities in Hazebrouck, Toulouse and Évreux were also shut down. The problems experienced at the Nîmes Community were nipped in the bud before they got out of hand. Lastly, the Pontault Community was split into three separate bodies and Jean-Yves was sent to develop Emmaus in Austria, then in Brazil. In spring 1956, the muddy, makeshift huts at Les Bordes were closed and the site merged with La Réserve. Problems at the Dunkirk and Lille Communities were ironed out and they got back on their feet.

## A few basic ground rules

More than anything else, the difficulties and scandals made Emmaus acutely aware of the need for rules. The first of these rules was laid down by Abbé Pierre in February 1955. He declared: "Within three months, the Companions must have succeeded in housing a family with the fruits of their labour. If they fail to do so, they will be cut off from Emmaus."[29] Faced with a shortage of executives, a balance had to be struck between trust ("off you go, do as you think best") and control ("we need to constantly ensure that men are put to the test time and time again in order to bring the capable men to the fore"). A centre was created for future leaders: the training programme comprised a two-week introduction to life as a simple member of an Emmaus Community, becoming familiar with the various activities (sorting, picking up unwanted household goods, waste-collection, resale, etc.) and a week of lessons in psychology and humanist studies. This was followed by six weeks' immersion in a Community.[30]

Discussion also focused on the place of religion within the movement. In summer 1954, Abbé Pierre, Father Norbert and Abbé Barral looked into creating a small congregation of priests and laymen within Emmaus itself. The congregation's spirituality would be akin to that of Father Foucault's *Petits Frères*, but would be focused on the presence of Christ within the poor, rather than at Communion.[31] The project was shelved, owing to the shortage of candidates. The Abbé-went back to the drawing board and in early 1955 he returned with the idea of *"fraternitaires"*. These were priests or seminarians who would agree "to act as facilitators rather than as leaders handing out orders".[32] These religious coordinators, who were a type of chaplain, protector of the spirit and of religion's place within Emmaus, were to be mere figures of moral authority: their job was to listen to the Companions without punishing them, and to advise the leader without making decisions on his behalf. Once again, the desired new order did not come to fruition. This was due to the lack of candidates put forward by a Church which, following the prohibition of worker-priests, was even more reluctant to support this experiment as it was wary of an Abbé who could not be easily kept in line.

However, Paul Beaudoin was one such maverick seminarian who came to assist Emmaus. Twenty-two years old in 1953, he was denied entry to the priesthood as he was deemed to be too likely to rock the boat. Posted to a middle-class parish in the Parisian suburbs, he made his escape and went to Lyons where he heard the 1954 appeal and decided to return to Paris once more. Abbé Pierre sent him to Orsay station, then to the muddy shacks of Les Bordes. Pierre Lunel has described Les Bordes as "the infamous Emmaus bog, a spreading field on to which, every morning, waste from Champigny and the surrounding villages was dumped by the tonne. It was a 200-hectare site in the east of Paris, where fermenting rubbish stretched as far as the eye could see. There were small groups of sad, grey huts, which stood in the bitter cold, awaiting the blistering heat, the swarms of mosquitoes, the foul stench..."[33] He stayed there for two years, until the site closed down, and then worked for a year at La Réserve before leaving Emmaus to get married.

Finally, 1956 saw the increased formalisation of the Emmaus system and its rules. In May, it became mandatory for each Community to have a four-man team, comprising a head "Companion" at the helm, a *"fraternitaire"* (priest) and two "Friends" (volunteers), who managed the Community and kept tabs on its activities. From then on, for any new Community to get the go-ahead it had to adhere to this structure. It was also made compulsory for each Community to submit a weekly report on its accounts and its staff. October brought with it the next stage of the process. The next stage, in October, saw each Community become independent following Abbé Pierre's observation that "centralisation was stifling Emmaus and ultimately hindering efforts to keep a close eye on the various different accounts".[34] Legally, from that point forward, each Community had to become a Not-for-Profit organisation; an "Association of Friends ofthe Ragpickers-Builders", placed in the hands of a board of directors of Friends. A Union was created to bring together the local associations. It was christened "The National Union of Associations of Friends and Communities of the Ragpicker-builders", and André Bercher was elected president.[35]

## The adventure of Normandy's travelling Communities

Following Abbé Pierre's repeated periods of absence and a latent conflict with the Paris management, Paul Desort, who was the Abbé's right-hand man and worked on the ground, left to take the Emmaus adventure to Normandy – a move which would later earn him the nickname "Paul of Normandy". The opportunity arose following the closure of the Rennes Community, which meant its Companions had to be placed elsewhere. Paul's adventure was also the result of an appeal for help made by Abbé Esnault, the priest of Alençon who, after finding an abandoned child in his confessional and placing her in the care of a young girl, found himself entrusted with four new-borns under similar circumstances and was at a loss as to what to do. At Abbé Pierre's instigation, Paul left for Alençon and the adventure began once more on 18 November 1956.

Paul, along with five Rennes Companions and six from an Emmaus refuge, made a group of twelve – a Christian symbol which Paul's story was quick to flag up. Together, they embarked upon a series of waste-collection operations in Orne, northwest France. Sleeping in barns and using old handcarts, in two weeks they had collected enough to support the abandoned children, but they also discovered the extent of the region's poverty and saw just how acute the need for housing was.[36] Having left Orne, they combed the whole of Normandy for useful waste. They did not, however, cross over into Brittany – this was the fiefdom of Paul le Roch and was thus enemy territory. One of the Companions, Jules, told Emmaus International of their experiences in Normandy:

> "We stayed in each village for three months, no longer. We worked to help the homeless and children living in poverty [...] We then worked to help the Third World. Abbé Pierre had been summoned by Indian Prime Minister Pandit Nehru who said to him: 'Abbé, you have worked in your country for those who had nowhere to live, but our problem is not that we are homeless, it is that we are dying of hunger' [...] Being a travelling Community was extraordinary. For example, every evening we would go and hold a meeting in a village asking them if they wanted to collect the useful waste from their village

themselves, and bring their old papers, rags... At times, there were 150, 200, even 300 vehicles. We unloaded them, sorted the waste, put aside half for the Community in the town and the other half for Emmaus' work throughout the world. [...] In Caen, on the same day, more than 2,000 vehicles arrived. It was amazing to be able to summon more than 2,000 vehicles in one day and to convince farmers to come with their tractors and their trailers to bring old papers and rags. It had to be something extraordinary for them to bother, for them to break with their routine."[37]

Life collecting waste on the road was monastic and disciplined, and the work was thankless and exhausting. The members of the team had to remain dirt-free, clean-shaven and abstinent in order to preserve the image of Emmaus; often, Companions requested board and lodgings. The travelling Communities retained the austerity and harshness of the Movement's beginnings, "the *desperado* style and spirit, the almost total deprivation" and the commando side of things.[38] By trawling through villages and sticking up posters, speaking in churches, gathering together local residents eager to help, and organising mammoth waste-collection operations, the travelling teams always tried to leave behind a structure, which was entrusted to a few friends of the Movement, or even a Community.

The adventure came to an end eight years later, in 1964 in Rouen, a city where teams had spent a total of two years. The troop appeared on television and sparked a number of reports; in a single day 3,600 vehicles arrived from 120 surrounding villages. Initially comprising eleven Companions, by that time Paul's entourage had swelled to 200; and in eight years profits had soared with 2.2 million francs collected.[39]

Just like Abbé Pierre, Paul of Normandy had adopted a persona. Lunel has remarked, "like Abbé Pierre, his [Paul of Normandy's] image remained etched in people's minds. Wherever he went, his image remained the same: he wore proletariat blue, black pilgrims' buskins, an activist's country hat and, slung over his shoulder, a railway worker's satchel. His image remained unchanged throughout the whole of his career at Emmaus, which spanned more than twenty years. He dressed the same way for everyone and everything: in ministerial offices, at Rotary Club drinks receptions and for official openings, and in squats, on muddy, makeshift housing sites and on the scrapheaps. The Father was seen to possess the qualities of an apostolate working for the poor, and Paul, the qualities of the poor man himself."[40] But, unlike the Movement's founder, "he did not discuss Emmaus at a national or global level. He was more concerned with activities at village or canton level."[41]

On the one hand, Paul Desort was one of the guiding lights in the history of Emmaus. A veritable organisational genius and charismatic "guru",[42] he was also a highly skilled orator who was, like Abbé Pierre, able to move the masses. Pierre Lunel allowed himself to succumb to Desort's charm and became his staunch defender and wrote: "Organised on the hoof as a one-off initiative for winter in order to save a few kids' lives, [the Normandy adventure] became a business that alone was the very embodiment of Emmaus. It gave life to that 'Great Emmaus' of Abbé Pierre's dreams, that missionary Emmaus, triumphant Emmaus, Movement of the people, which gave short shrift to the rigid structure of the Paris leaders who were at the time wholly occupied with rebuilding Communities."[43] A diehard supporter of Emmaus, through both the good times and the bad, he would later step into his master's shoes to promote "the ethic of conviction".[44]

However, underneath it all, Paul was also a troubled figure. Arriving at the Movement in 1953 with several convictions and spells in prison under his belt, outside Emmaus he would, until the mid-1970s, lead a double life, which was considerably less monastic and of which almost everybody, except most likely Abbé Pierre, was entirely unaware. A keen gambler with a penchant for women and fast cars, he exploited his group within Emmaus and used accounting methods that were far from rigorous, to say the least. Asked about Desort's activities in an interview, Yves Godard said, "What I didn't know at the time, what I would discover after a few years, was that he was using me, just as he was using Emmaus, to lead a double life. Very quickly, he gave me responsibilities; at twenty years old I was the leader of a Community, which, however good you are, is still a bit on the young side... After that, he would often ask for cash, so I'd hand over the proceeds from the bric-à-brac sales. Big wads of notes would change hands just like that, and I wouldn't bat an eyelid. So there you go, I was his unwitting accomplice, acting always in good faith. He'd say to me: 'Yves, mate, I've got to go to Bayonne, there's a family in trouble,' or 'there's an association being set up...'."

## The Running Sore at Noisy-le-Grand

While the majority of Emmaus' organisations were made independent from 1956 onwards, a tiny minority were still too weak to go it alone and stayed in the bosom of the Association. This was largely the case with the camp at Noisy-le-Grand, a huge site which stretched over thirteen acres. Part field once used for muck-spreading, part marshland, at the end of 1954 it became home to the poorest families from the Porte d'Orléans and la Pomponnette in Lagny, when the shelters set up at the main entry point to Paris were taken down. 1,100 people, or 247 families, with no education, job or qualifications, along with a handful of people who had failed to pay their rent to Emmaus' social housing company, were placed at the Noisy camp. What made this camp unique was that it almost exclusively welcomed French families living in poverty, unlike the camps for migrant workers who had jobs and therefore an income.

The families were initially placed in large, family-sized tents. With Abbé Pierre adamant that the families be rehoused before winter, factory workers gave up hours of their time to ensure that 200 small, fibre-cement houses were completed on time. These houses came to be known as "igloos", the name inspired by their shape. The plans stated that the houses "should be spread out across the site, with enough space between each one to ensure that families enjoyed the necessary privacy. We will build 500 small houses from fibre-cement and plaster tiles, which, under normal circumstances, will be able to house 500 families [...] Noisy will not be the camp of desolation – there will be water, electricity and proper plumbing. People will live in decent conditions."[45] In practice, the camp became known, first and foremost, as "the hamlet of distress"; a muddy, frozen cesspit in the winter, with no roads, waste-collection facilities, businesses, shops or schools within a two-kilometre radius. Not designed to last, these igloos were built without insulation and were thus freezing cold in the winter and scorching hot in the summer. The floors were made of trodden earth and there was neither a toilet nor electricity.

Managed until late 1954 by Paul, Jules and Abbé Duvallet, the camp was then placed in the hands of new leaders who struggled to organise it. As a result, relations between Emmaus and the residents became increasingly tense. The arrival of Father Joseph Wresinski on 11 November 1956 was a turning point. A thirty-nine year-old Abbé sent to manage the camp by his diocese, Wresinski himself came from a poor, Catholic family whose four children had been raised single-handedly by his mother. A pastry chef's apprentice and a member of the JOC, at the age of nineteen he began studying to become a priest in order to "give the poor back to the Church and the Church back to the poor."[46] Independently minded and critical of the state of the camp, he entered into a trial of strength with Emmaus. In her book on the Noisy camp, Francine de la Gorce wrote: "In order to get water fountains installed or an extra layer of hardboard put on the walls of the igloos, which were home to newborn babies, [Wresinski] had to negotiate with administrative officials who did not always understand what it was to live in the cold, with no water or electricity."[47] More money was paid out in mid-1957 in order to carry out emergency repairs on 150 igloos, build two new offices and three water pumps, lay roads through the camp, carry out camp-wide pest control, and build a children's garden. Nevertheless, the camp remained "atrocious" overall. When interviewed about the site, Henri Camus remarked:

> "You see, EDF, France's national electricity company, or their apprentices, put in the electricity. There were boy-scout types all over the place doing all sorts of jobs, but whatever they were doing, they hadn't bothered to build any roads through the site, so there were no roads... There were pavements but no roads. That was an absolutely appalling oversight on their part. There were no sewers – we were too far out; so they'd put in latrines instead. They'd been well installed, there were between five and ten of them, and the pits had to be regularly emptied. They'd piped water to where the latrines were, and there were taps, drinking fountains, available on a fairly regular basis. But what was serious was the fact that the site had no roads. It wouldn't have been

all that expensive to build some. These people were walking around in mud. And on top of it all, they'd built igloos for these people to live in. The igloos were made of a few bits of corrugated iron, nailed together. That's fine for a summer, but they remained there for I don't know how long. The camp was horrific; things quickly became impossible to endure. People were truly miserable in that place. It was awful [...] Wresinski used to say to us that Emmaus wasn't up to the job and, between you and me, he was absolutely right. What we'd done at the site up to that point was nothing: there were people who donated clothes, a bloke who cooked the meals, a place to eat them in; there were also a number of individual initiatives that were good in themselves, but there was no real thought behind them, no coherent plan being put into action."

Father Wresinski took the organisation in hand. In 1957, he built a block of changing rooms, a children's garden, and a library; he organised lessons in catechism for the residents, and fought to ensure that the children in the camp received an education. Gradually, the roofs of the igloos housing families with newborns were insulated with a layer of hardboard and the trodden-earth floors were covered in cement; the repulsive, muddy swamp, next to the camp, was dried out, and the areas around the water fountains were cleaned up. The Abbé celebrated Mass every morning, meaning baptisms, communions and funerals could take place. His top priority was building a chapel and Jean Bazaine agreed to make the stained-glass windows.

Wresinski's vision of the organisation centred on encouraging families to take responsibility for their own lives and ensuring they could live in dignity. In 1957, a cooperative was set up for the purchasing of clothes and shoes, and the following year a multi-purpose cultural centre was opened, which was unfortunately burned down as quickly as it had been built. Then, in 1959, a Community cultural centre was opened and, with the aim to "promote family life and social welfare", the centre became the heart of the camp. Wresinski focused first of all on organising the camp's women by creating a centre specifically for them. This centre was to become the lynchpin of Community life, offering courses in domestic skills and sewing, and providing modern laundry facilities and a children's play area. Holiday camps were set up along with summer play schemes. The camp refused to follow the Emmaus example and open a winter soup kitchen, dismissing them as "charity".[48] This decision was symptomatic of the camp's new approach, which was based not on providing handouts but instead on working with the families themselves, and taking their aspirations into account.[49]

At the end of 1958, the camp's closure was clearly on the cards. The authorities were looking to take back the land and in November 1959 the camp was declared a health hazard. This triggered a policy change within Association Emmaus. Despite the fact that in 1957 Emmaus had created the association "Friends of the Hamlet" in order to develop the camp's social services and provide it with more money, from then on the idea of closing it grew ever more appealing as it became clear it was a drain on resources.

However, the clash between Emmaus and the Noisy camp brought a misunderstanding to light. Since early 1959, Emmaus' social housing company had committed to rehousing families by building small groups of fifty houses in various villages across the Seine-et-Oise département, a region encompassing the western, northern and southern parts of Metropolitan Paris. As was the case with Le Plessis, the company intended each new housing site to have a warden "responsible for establishing order and discipline", its own sporting facilities, a social worker, and a nursery to educate the children "who were unable to find within their own families the examples and advice that they ought to have had."[50] The camp itself, however, was convinced that Emmaus was only able to offer housing to children while sending their parents to homeless shelters. In other words, that what it was "offering" was essentially to separate families, something which the camp found it simply impossible to endorse.[51]

The tempestuous relationship between Emmaus and the camp, and the growing disagreements between Wresinski and the camp's residents on the one hand, and the leaders of Emmaus on the other, caused things to break down completely. In spring 1959, the publication of an interview with Wresinski, significantly entitled "Abbé Pierre minus the legend", sent sparks flying once more: "[Abbé Pierre] dreams, talks, goes on and on about his big ideas while we're still stuck here with no running water. He thinks he's in the Middle Ages, St Vincent de Paul or something [...] Look at what he's actually achieved. He received almost one billion in 1954 and here, we've got no water or electricity. It's an absolute scandal."[52] In spring 1960, management of the camp was placed entirely in the hands of Friends of the Hamlet and Emmaus withdrew its own teams of workers. However, these steps failed to remedy the situation and Emmaus, still a member of the local landowner association's board of directors, was legally responsible for dealing with it.

## New Emmaus Organisations are Born

Finally, two large organisations, created as part of the Emmaus family in 1954, were quickly made independent.

### From homeless committees to the unionisation of housing

In his 1954 appeal, Abbé Pierre called upon the people of France to set up Emergency Aid Committees for the homeless, similar to that which had been set up the night before the appeal in Courbevoie. In the space of only a few days, committees had been set up across the country: in Nantes, Bordeaux, Montargis, Caen, Marseilles, Aix-en-Provence and elsewhere. On 10 May of that year, Emmaus registered the provisional statutes for a homeless association, and 6 July saw the birth of ASLAP, an association for the homeless in Paris and the surrounding area. Significantly, in 1956 the organisation changed its name to become an association *of* the homeless, reflecting the fact that Emmaus wished to move away from charity and see the homeless help themselves. Then on 13 November its national counterpart, UNASL, was created with Antoine d'Argent as president and Roger Dauphin as secretary-general. Initially these organisations were purely charitable and aimed to merely ease the effects of homelessness by housing families and those living on the streets. The organisations' achievements in their first year were far from insignificant: 144 associations or committees, twenty-six homeless shelters (1,400 beds) and 5,000 families rehoused.

Very quickly, however, housing the homeless became only one part of Emmaus' work. In December 1954, the decision was taken to adopt both a bottom-up and top-down approach and to "tackle the problem on a political level". Legal aid was created, the allocation of social housing became more efficient, and information campaigns were launched. At the same time, the authorities were lobbied and Emmaus battled to enforce the "right to housing", thirty-five years before it became law.[53] As part of this battle, in late 1954, UNASL recommended that the requisition of land by the state become a more widespread practice, that all available housing be used, that no one be evicted without alternative accommodation being found, that construction be accelerated, and that specific benefits be given to families.

A third initiative was also developed: squatting. An illegal practice, squatting was considered to be a vital tool in maintaining the pressure on the authorities following the 1954 appeal. At the same time, squats provided emergency accommodation for the homeless. When he left for Normandy in 1954, Paul returned to and stepped up the use of this old practice.[54] He sought legal protection in the law of 19 October 1945, which enshrined the right to requisition empty or unoccupied housing for use by the homeless. With the help of his emergency-aid team, Paul honed his technique: he gathered together a group of around thirty people in the small hours of the morning – thirty was the legal minimum needed to avoid being evacuated by the army and having the land requisitioned by the authorities. The group were placed in empty buildings which had been picked out in advance. Women and children went in first to curb the police violence.[55] In April 1954, fifty-six people were placed in an unoccupied building near the Gare de l'Est railway station. Then, in October, ten families went into a squat in Rue Max-Dormoy; in February 1955, sixty-two homeless people set up home in Rue Tiphaine; thirty-three families went to Rue Montmartre, and so it went on.

While these squats existed in the shadows, Rue Bourdonnais was at the centre of a media storm. It was the focus of a mammoth open-air operation designed to raise awareness about the summer closure of the homeless shelters and the subsequent influx of requests for housing. At the suggestion of Paul and his troops, and with Abbé

Pierre's support, it was decided that a large site in Paris should be occupied. The prefect gave the initiative the green light and was called upon to select the site – Sully Bridge was the final choice.[56] And so, between 30 July and 21 October 1955, 400 people, including 77 families and 139 children, set up home under canvas in the heart of Paris. With this campaign, Emmaus was just as intent on providing homeless families with the means to survive as it was on stirring up public opinion by gathering together a large number of tents in a move reminiscent of the early "catacomb camps".[57]

In the meantime, however, at the end of September, a court decision ordered the immediate evacuation of four Parisian squats. From that moment on, Association Emmaus began to shy away from using a technique viewed as deliberately provocative and as an attempt to square up to the authorities without any prior negotiation.[58] Paul continued to build squats regardless, including at the emergency housing sites in Orly in November 1955 and at the Midi site in December. On 25 January 1956, the Association's quiet misgivings about the squats became open disapproval when the Auteuil viaduct was occupied. It was a much smaller operation, involving only two families, and was short-lived – the police evacuated the squat the following morning. The failure of this squat prompted the others to fold. The end of the authorities' indulgence and Paul's departure were also to blame.[59]

Just like the 1954 appeal, which was somewhere between a charitable movement and a political campaign, Emmaus' work on behalf of the homeless was not intended to be either one or the other, but rather, as Abbé Pierre stated in his closing address at a UNASL congress in 1955, "a force to stir up the national civil consciousness". He declared: "faced with a national tragedy, a campaign [is] needed. Individual initiatives and government action [must] go hand in glove. It is through educating the public that we will succeed in educating those in government."[60] With this belief in mind, UNASL sought to directly influence electoral campaigns, for example the campaign of January 1956, by asking candidates to sign up to a fourteen-point charter, aware that "the real problem is political. Only the authorities can provide the solution."[61] The charter was signed by members of the socialist SFIO, the MRP, and the academic association, *Jeune*

*République*. This widespread support saw UNASL win the battle to push through the law banning winter evictions where no alternative accommodation had been found, and to enshrine the right to requisition professional and business premises to house the homeless. At the same time, Emmaus also sought to organise its service users. The Movement expressed its view that "the homeless and those in below-standard housing must appreciate the role they can play in public life; that their civic spirit can exert as much pressure on members of government as those who defend private interests as harmful, for example, alcohol."[62] Action thus began to move towards "the unionisation of housing".[63] During its 1956 conference, UNASL became the General Housing Confederation (CGL) and, in 1957, ASLAP renamed itself the Paris Region Housing Federation.

This move towards unionisation was a sign of new visions and rationale. UNASL "wished to become to housing what unionisation is to the workers' movement." Calls for the use of squats were louder than ever; squats being "to the unionisation of housing what striking is to the unionisation of labour." The squats "had been and remained the revolutionary form of emergency aid. They pitted the tragedy of the homeless against both the failings of government and the selfishness and mercenary behaviour of those who monopolised housing and speculated. This taking possession, illegally but legitimately, of an empty building was a statement declaring that in the hierarchy of values, the government must protect men over and above guaranteeing possession of an asset which no longer served its social purpose. Squatting challenged the principle of property ownership, seen as the right to abuse and to exploit."[64]

This new zeal for unionisation appeared – to put it mildly – "to have ruffled a few feathers within a group that some tended to see as a charitable organisation."[65] The development caused some to leave Emmaus' ranks, but it also attracted newcomers, particularly "worker activists" from the Christian left. Action then began to focus once more on squats, getting the homeless on the property ladder, and creating new networks of tenants. These initiatives gave the organisation a new identity. It became increasingly independent from Emmaus, right down to its name, but nevertheless remained close to the mother ship through its history, its activists and some of its fundamental values.

## IRAMM and development aid

Another organisation also flew the nest: the Institute for Research and Action Against World Poverty (IRAMM). IRAMM began to develop within Emmaus from October 1954 onwards, initially as an unofficial body. It became an official, Not-for-Profit organisation in September 1955, following Abbé Pierre's first visits abroad.

Applying the core principle of Emmaus – "serve first he who suffers most" – on a global scale, IRAMM also resolved to tackle other issues in addition to housing. They saw the need "to spark similar initiatives all the other areas where poverty causes devastation: disease, unemployment, hunger, illiteracy, etc. Action must be taken in all countries where it is urgently needed."[66] Before taking action, the association aimed to "study, support and raise awareness of global initiatives that are a testament to what man can achieve without a great deal of material wealth."[67] On the ground, it planned projects which were adapted to local needs and Emmaus' working methods, and recruited and trained volunteers. The organisation was placed in the hands of the young Yves Goussault. Born in 1923, he had just completed his novitiate with the Jesuits and was introduced to Emmaus by Henri Camus. He asked his diocese for permission to complete his training placement with the Movement, and developed a passion for emergency accommodation sites, workers' cooperatives and global issues, before finally leaving the Jesuits to marry and devote his attentions to issues affecting the developing world.

As far as housing was concerned, the Movement initially focused on France alone, conducting an extensive survey into substandard housing and urban slums. Carried out by the local committees, the survey produced a series of reports.[68] It is possible that the survey drew its inspiration from the major surveys carried out ten years earlier by the (Dominican) Father Lebret and his association Economy and Humanism. These surveys were conducted at the government's request, as part of the rebuilding projects under way nationwide.[69]

Abroad, the first projects were set up in Morocco. In spring 1956, the eldest son of Mohammed V, Prince Moulay Hassan (who would later become King Hassan II), came to France and asked to visit Emmaus' emergency accommodation sites in Le Plessis. Interested by what he saw, he requested that a mission be sent to Morocco to assess their shantytown problem. An Emmaus delegation travelled to Morocco and issued a series of recommendations; a training programme was drawn up at village level. The initiative was gradually rolled out across eighty villages and then, at the Moroccan government's request, across the whole country. Volunteer groups were set up in Tunisia, Senegal and Togo.

Through IRAMM, Emmaus quickly set about addressing the issue of world hunger. The early 1950s saw the Catholic world tentatively begin to rise up and speak out about the issue; two main organisations took action. There was *Pax Christi*, a Catholic organisation founded in 1950. Created to oppose the communist stance on world peace, the reports it published analysing the issue from 1951–2 onwards gradually began to take account of the uneven distribution of wealth on an international level – even if countries beset by famine, such as Greece in 1951, continued to be seen as needing protection against the sirens of communist propaganda more than anything else.[70] In 1953, *Pax Christi* established links with *Secours catholique* and the UN Food and Agricultural Organisation. However, until 1954, the matter was seen more as a development issue than one of foreign aid. It was only in 1955 that the organisation launched a campaign on "technical aid for under-developed nations",[71] and *Secours catholique* also began to tackle the issue.

Another important place where debate was conducted and where initiatives were tried and tested was within the movement "Economy and Humanism". Born in Brittany in 1897, Louis-Joseph Lebret was an officer in the navy before entering the Dominican order in 1923.[72] He joined the Vichy regime and then gradually distanced himself from the Pétain government, but stopped short of joining the Resistance. In 1941 he founded Economy and Humanism, which was granted the status of an official Dominican organisation two years later. Despite being the black sheep of the MRP, Lebret sided more closely with the Christian democrats. This affiliation did not stop him from engaging his movement in constructive dialogue with the Marxist school of thought, in particular through Father Henri Desroches, also a Dominican and one of Lebret's closest colleagues. The organisation began as a place for debate on the concept of Community, both as a utopian vision and a practical reality, before founding its own Community in 1944 – more an intellectual exercise than a working model – and attempting, in vain, to bring together a team that could penetrate the world of the working class. When in 1949–50, Rome put an end to dialogue with the Communists and ordered that Desroches cease his activities, Father Lebret refocused his attentions on the developing world.

Lebret was eager to breathe new life into the Church's social doctrine by incorporating into it the fruits of scientific research on the political economy. He had been taken on as a researcher at CNRS, France's National Centre for Scientific Research, and was appointed director of research in 1952. Latin America became the focus of his studies and a testing ground for his theories and ideas. In spring 1947, he gave lectures on the human economy in Rio and São Paulo, and took advantage of his time in Brazil to visit Uruguay, Argentina and Chile. These trips made him acutely aware of the need to combat under-development. On his travels, he made the acquaintance of two key Brazilian figures who would also leave a lasting impression on Abbé Pierre. The two men were Dom Helder Camara, who had been recently appointed the auxiliary bishop of Rio; and Josué de Castro, a philosopher, sociologist and nutritionist who worked closely with the FAO. In the early 1950s, Father Lebret became a recognised specialist in sociology and the role of economic policy in development.

Emmaus' approach to development was just as much characterised by the fact it was ahead of its time, as by its proximity to this second movement. While the issue slowly began to capture the attention of French Catholics, *Faim et Soif* dealt with it in its very first issue, in May 1954, with a report bearing the straight-talking title: "Two Men Out of Three Are Going Hungry". The report was written by Josué de Castro, who had since been appointed president of the FAO. He was assisted by Father Lebret, who had recently celebrated the publication of his book, *The Geopolitics of Hunger.* In August 1954, a new special report looked at illiteracy across the world and the fight to eliminate this scourge.

Following the Bandung conference in April 1955, the issue took on a more political dimension. Symbolic of the process that saw the Third World make its own voice heard and the political existence of formerly colonised peoples recognised, the Bandung conference also tackled the issue of development head-on and proposed a system whereby Southern countries would provide each other with mutual assistance, along with agreements with Northern countries, and the creation of a special fund, which would pool UN contributions and investments from the IBRD.[73] The conference was relayed in *Faim et Soif,* in a comment column penned by Daniel Rops of the *Académie Française.*

Aside from its awareness-raising activities, Emmaus also turned words into action. It did so initially through IRAMM, which was spearheading its own initiatives, but also through its membership of a new international organisation, ASCOFAM, created to tackle world hunger. In 1956, on the advice of Father Lebret, Josué de Castro, still the president of the FAO, visited Abbé Pierre in hospital. Castro suggested that together they form "a people's movement, [working] parallel to the FAO and along the same lines as the internationalist movement; a movement able to influence authorities at all levels." He told Abbé Pierre, "Lebret will be responsible for research, inspiring the masses, and putting things in to practice on the ground. I can bring my experience of international politics to the table, and you, you can help us. You can be the 'voice of the voiceless' and speak for the multitude of victims."[74] Founded in March 1957, ASCOFAM split into a series of subsections. "Informing and educating public opinion" was managed by IRAMM, and "documentation, research and training" was placed under the aegis of Economy and Humanism. ASCOFAM aimed to develop "an initiative whose spirit and working methods would mean that we were able, if not to tackle all the problems facing us, to at least open up a few new lines of action; lines of action that were modest in their desired outcome, but serious and exemplary enough to trigger larger-scale initiatives better adapted to the gravity of the situation."[75] In other words, ASCOFAM aimed to be an organisation whose aims were broadly similar to those of IRAMM and Economy and Humanism, and which, from the outset, would bear the hallmark of an internationalist movement.

However, together with Economy and Humanism, IRAMM moved further and further away from Emmaus for reasons which were both ideological (Emmaus branded IRAMM a merely intellectual exercise) and personal. In January 1957, the association moved its headquarters to Geneva. It renamed itself IRAM (Institute for Research and Action in Aid of Human Development) and in June set up a central board and a general secretariat. In 1961, the organisation removed all references to both Abbé Pierre and Emmaus from its founding charter. Conversely, Emmaus ceased to refer to IRAM, but spoke instead of the new French section of ASCOFAM, founded in 1962.

The unique nature of this Emmaus–FAO–Economy and Humanism alliance should here be underscored, even if its three members did not always see eye to eye. At the time, *Pax Christi* was primarily motivated by the desire to eradicate the communist threat, in order to ensure that the formerly colonised peoples now gaining independence did not fall victim to Marxism. Conversely, the Communists had lost interest in development long before this point, opting instead to provide direct aid by sending money and arms to the national liberation movements fighting across the globe. Against this backdrop, the Emmaus–FAO–Economy and Humanism alliance adopted a third strategy: the provision of fraternal aid. Development aid essentially took the form of a Christian charity that had taken on global proportions. The alliance also aspired to be political, calling on "rich nations to treat their brothers as equals, rather than looking to ruthlessly safeguard undeserved privileges."[76] While this stance was not revolutionary, in the sense that it in no way advocated the reversal of the status quo, it did reject any attempt to simply relieve the effects of poverty. Instead, the alliance aimed to challenge economic liberalism and neocolonialism, to change the system from within, and to find grass-roots development solutions in order to put an end to colonial-style exploitation and enter into a new era of fairer trade.

Consequently, in the years following “the Uprising of Kindness”, the organisation’s output was prolific and its activities diversified considerably. After a period of centralisation, granting independence to its subsidiary bodies became the order of the day. Some of those able to survive on their own became independent from the parent association, but remained deeply rooted in Emmaus as a movement. Emmaus HLM, the Communities and the newspaper, are three such examples. Others (action in aid of the homeless, the unionisation of housing, development aid) followed their own path, while those unable to stand on their own two feet stayed safely ensconced in the Emmaus nest. However, during this period many cracks also began to show. Some sources of tension, such as IRAMM or the Noisy camp, were ultimately resolved through what Albert O. Hirschmann has termed “exit”.[77] Other sources of tension, however, were profoundly internal, bringing to light different but related misgivings about the Emmaus system. These would only be eradicated following major, open crisis.

# *Chapter 3* / IMPLOSION (1954–1958)

*"From the very first stages in Emmaus' development I was terrified and thus constantly on the lookout for someone who could take hold of the reins. On countless occasions, I dared to hope I had found someone who could step into my shoes and do the things I was unable to do." (Abbé Pierre)*[1]

Seen from the outside as a charismatic leader of his movement, there is no doubt whatsoever that within Emmaus, Abbé Pierre was an icon and protector but, increasingly, not a leader. Initially, he felt neither prepared for nor capable of managing the growth of the Movement. He appeared increasingly weak: dosed up on amphetamines to keep up with the 1954 campaign[2] and sleeping very little indeed in the early months, he would come to suffer extreme exhaustion and, between 1954 and 1958, he was in and out of hospital, spending a total of twenty-two months in a hospital bed, and undergoing six operations. Furthermore, he put in only rare appearances at Emmaus itself, travelling all over France and the world to deliver his message. When he finally returned to Emmaus, he was reluctant to arbitrate the conflicts, diverging trends and rival camps within the Movement – prophetic advocates of "the ethic of conviction" on the one hand and managers who championed "the ethic of responsibility" on the other.[3]

Two other factors are also important in understanding why the years that followed the "Uprising of Kindness" was a period of darkness and taboo, plagued by aggravated conflicts, unspoken truths and internal disagreements over the identity of Emmaus, when it could have been, on the contrary, a time of prosperity and recognition of the Movement. First, Abbé Pierre would prove to be easily tempted by the pleasures of the flesh, a weakness which has only recently been publicly acknowledged, but which at the time fuelled the fears of those in the know. Added to the mix was an increasingly complex relationship with the Church, which would ultimately attempt to regain control of the Movement by forcing its founder into retirement.

And so, while the years 1954–8 saw a veritable plethora of new Emmaus activities take seed and flourish, they also saw the collapse of the Movement. This collapse was caused by the acute fears and conflicts within, by the decision to empty the Association in order to limit the damage as far as possible should a scandal come to light, and by the Movement being placed, once again, under the control of the Church hierarchy which, after several failed attempts, managed to establish itself as the guardian of Emmaus.

## In the Black Box of the Dark Years

### "Ethic of conviction" *vs* "ethic of responsibility"

Behind the united façade and the blossoming of activities far and wide, which tended to create the impression that each of the Movement's members enjoyed a degree of independence acceptable to one and all, proponents from two opposing schools of thought were locking horns. To use Weberian terminology, "the ethic of conviction" was pitted against "the ethic of responsibility". By 1955, the conflict between the two had become palpable and was acknowledged by Abbé Pierre. He declared, "the main difficulty we face is the need to pull the cart with two completely different breeds of horse: on the one hand there are the Communities, and on the other the administrators at the Rue des Bourdonnais."[4] Indeed, on the one hand, there were Paul and Jean-Yves who wished to preserve the adventurous spirit of the Movement's beginnings, who displayed real charisma, and who enjoyed a legitimacy that was based both on their seniority within the Movement and on the fact that they were Abbé Pierre's personal favourites. On the other hand, there were those figures who were newer to the Movement, but who were high flyers with a sharp mind for business and all things legal and economic, who were crucial to the Movement's survival. The veterans accused the newcomers of being soulless managers, while the newcomers accused the veterans of being crooks, responsible for plunging Emmaus into financial ruin. Somewhere between the two camps stood Abbé Pierre, far from a natural manager and anxious to protect his protégés, but also acutely aware of the need to shore up an organisation on the brink of collapse.

The Movement was also divided over its relationship to the political sphere and to the action undertaken by the State. For Paul, the key to preserving Emmaus' identity as a political and prophetic movement was building squats, just as it had been the building of illegal dwellings in the early days of Emmaus. These squats were often discreet, to ensure their survival, but sufficiently spectacular to provoke a reaction. Conversely, the board of directors, with their more scrupulous regard for the law, preferred to bypass squats in favour of a diplomatic, less dramatic phase whereby members pulled together to strengthen the Movement from within, before laying it open to criticism.

To conclude, Emmaus was a battleground for two rival viewpoints. One, "the ethic of conviction" and centrifugal forces, was the chosen philosophy of Emmaus' great orators and ex-convicts from the outset, without whom Emmaus would never have been able to get off the ground. It advocated a return to the organisation's roots as a prophetic movement with a sense of adventure. The other, "the ethic of responsibility" and centripetal force, was defended by the management and emphasised the need to consolidate the Movement's foundations, to prune non-viable branches from the Emmaus tree, put in stakes to support those in need, and plant new cuttings from those that were thriving. Two viewpoints, each embodying one side of Emmaus, but seemingly irreconcilable.

## The church tightens its grip

Initially, despite keeping a close eye on Emmaus, the Church only guided the Movement from afar, unable to take control. Long before 1954, the Catholic hierarchy was concerned about this embryonic initiative. In 1953, "seizing the opportunity provided by a sizeable donation [from Baron Empain], the secretary to the Cardinal [Feltin], Monseigneur Touvet, asked *Secours catholique* to infiltrate the Emmaus board of directors in order that he might inform the episcopal commission of the Movement's activities. The men working under Jean Rodhain [Secretary-General of *Secours catholique*] discovered that Emmaus had neither official association status nor a board of directors. They attempted to help shed further light on the situation, but

Abbé Grouès and his assistants repeatedly sidestepped meetings and visits."[5] On 26 January 1954, Monseigneur Rodhain threw in the towel and informed the cardinal that he was unable to carry out his mission.

The resounding success of the 1954 appeal took both the Church and its charitable organisation, *Secours catholique*, by surprise. At the time, *Secours catholique* had been working for months towards opening a night shelter in Paris and had also been appealing for donations. Rodhain provided Emmaus with a team of workers whose job it was to introduce a more rigorous accounting system, but these efforts were in vain. Even in 1954, "Abbé Pierre continued to resist the slightest attempt made by the Church to exercise any influence whatsoever over the Movement."[6]

To keep a watchful eye on proceedings and ensure that Emmaus adhered to at least basic organisational standards, the Church appeared at last to play its trump card –it allowed Abbé Pierre to make use of key figures he had requested from its ranks in order to cement religion's place within his Movement. In January 1955, on Henri Camus' request, the Bishop of Versailles granted Abbé Jean Duvallet permission to go to Emmaus. Duvallet was a young priest with a social conscience who, newly ordained, had founded a Community for homeless children in Conflans. From February onwards he attended the meetings of the board of directors. It was also in 1955 that Cardinal Liénart, Bishop of Lille, sent Abbé Leurent on a mission to Emmaus. Abbé Leurent had been acquainted with the Movement since the creation of the Wambrechies Community (Nord département) in 1954 and "was posted to Emmaus to assist Abbé Pierre with his duties as a minister."[7] He divided his time between administrative tasks and the promotion of spiritual activities within the Communities in the Paris region. It would seem likely that, following ordinary procedure, these two priests consulted their superiors on such matters.

The Church's attitude remained ambiguous. On the one hand, it benefited from being able to preserve a fledgling organisation that, although unquestionably out of the ordinary, was headed up by a priest, which served to restore the Church's prestige. On the other hand, it did not seem desirable for Emmaus, an uncontrollable, disorganised and sometimes unorthodox organisation, to become overly legitimate while *Secours catholique* was in place to take charge of all charitable endeavours. The Church also benefited from establishing a system that allowed it to control Emmaus from within, and it would have been inconceivable for the Church to give the green light to a new religious order following the prohibition of the worker-priests. As far as Abbé Pierre was concerned, he wished to garner the Church's support while ensuring it was not able to play a supervisory role.

In 1955, statements made in public by Abbé Pierre fuelled the Church's fears. In April, the French icon was invited to the USA, first to the University of Princeton and then to give a series of conferences and sermons. He visited New York's homeless, met France's consulate-general in Los Angeles, and was introduced to President Eisenhower in Washington. At the request of Canada's church authorities, Abbé Pierre then travelled to Canada and spoke to an audience of 20,000, issuing violent diatribes against the opulent wealth of the institutional Churches, viewed as an insult to the poorest members of society and a misinterpretation of the Gospels. This prophetic critique of effulgence, which went against the fundamental values of Christianity, ruffled a few feathers among the Catholic authorities who had invited him to speak. Abbé Pierre was impossible to control, sure of his values and prepared to defend them, and his speeches spawned a series of cabals within the Church who, it seems, appeared to bring out the big guns to bring him down, accusing him of doctrinal heresy. He was forced to answer the charges before his superiors at the Vatican. However, it is believed that they gave him their full support.[8]

Abbé Pierre was also increasingly frail. Exhausted by the pace of the life he had led since 1942, and dogged by poor health throughout childhood and adolescence, he fell seriously ill in both winter 1951 and January 1953. His health worsened again in autumn 1954, when abscesses forced him to go into hospital and then to take time out to rest on a retreat in southern France. He was out of action for a total of five months. In winter 1956–7, he was admitted to hospital once again and then ordered to go on retreat to a seminary in Alençon. He was hospitalised again in late 1957, when it appears that stomach pains which had plagued him on and off for years became almost impossible to endure. On this occasion he was admitted to a private

Swiss clinic chosen by his superior Monseigneur Fougerat, Bishop of Grenoble.[9] An operation on his diaphragmatic hernia took place in mid-December. Despite the fact the hernia was benign, the Abbé would emerge from the procedure weak, depressed, and in a state of nervous exhaustion. This prompted the Church to take action once again, formally appointing Father Monnier as Abbé Pierre's associate. Father Monnier was a Jesuit, already in his later years, who had been assisting Abbé Pierre on the Church's orders since October 1957.[10] The Church continued to be involved, appointing a new Emmaus coordinator in 1958: the Franciscan Father Jacques, born Jean Vreck.

## The fallibility of the icon

This new, proactive attempt by the Church to gain a hold over the Movement can be explained by a factor that undoubtedly came into play in the year 1954–5. It was a taboo subject, but one crucial to understanding the Church's actions: the fallibility of Abbé Pierre when it came to keeping the vow of chastity which he made to the Church. While it has only recently, and on the Abbé's initiative, become public knowledge that he faltered,[11] what today is seen as a confession of humanness at the time fuelled an intense fear of scandals which appeared morally unacceptable and liable to send Emmaus crashing to the ground. In reality, Abbé Pierre was difficult to keep under control where his private life was concerned and his entourage had to remain mindful of possible slip-ups, with Lucie Coutaz the first to shoulder such responsibilities. Abbé Pierre, so steadfast in his religious and political beliefs, struggled to keep his amorous desires in check. Consequently, the Catholic hierarchy and the Emmaus management agreed that together they would do all they could to nip potential scandals in the bud, protect the Abbé from himself and Emmaus from the Abbé.

This well-kept secret came to light only gradually, despite the fact that it is crucial in understanding the fears and attitudes of the time. Marin and Bonnet hinted at the issue in their 1969 book, when they wrote: "Abbé Pierre became the prey of the fanatics, the cranks and the zealots. Countless hands would touch him as if he were a totem with magic powers, a statue with miraculous properties [...] People tore strips from his clothes as if they were relics [...] Delirious virgins fainted in ecstasy at his feet, as they would at the feet of an icon. He was asked to heal the sick and the infirm [...] Despite fighting with every fibre of his being to 'keep a straight head', he found it increasingly difficult to resist the intoxicating whirlwind of excitement which was circling around him. Unsurprisingly, he succumbed to temptation. He [was] an exceptional man, but a man all the same!"[12] Nothing emerges more clearly from Bernard Chevalier's 1979 book. However, this work is nothing more than a compilation of interviews with Abbé Pierre and its primary aim is to construct a non-controversial image of the Abbé by which he could be remembered. In 1992, the issue resurfaced in a book penned by Pierre Lunel, with pages 210 to 219 peppered with frequent references to the "erratic behaviour of the Father", to "the obfuscation of the virtuous", to "the increasingly hard-line moral stance of Barrat", a member of the board of directors of Association Emmaus, and to Abbé Pierre's "misconduct". References to the problem become gradually more explicit. Lunel notes that from February 1954 onwards, "women pursued the Father relentlessly", and describes how "his friends wore themselves out trying to ensure that he was followed at all times, that he was accompanied everywhere he went to protect him against himself." Finally, Lunel includes an interview with the Abbé in which he explains how, out of the vows of obedience, poverty and chastity, which he promised to uphold, it was by far the third of the three which caused him to suffer most. In this interview it also becomes clear that the Abbé's weakness for the pleasures of the flesh was the world's worst-kept secret. Lunel writes: "Emmaus was also at risk of collapse if even the slightest detail of the Abbé's scandalous private life emerged, but the power of the Abbé Pierre legend meant that those outside Emmaus followed the example of those close to him and kept their lips sealed. The press had played too large a part in constructing the Abbé Pierre legend to now change their stance and shatter it to pieces."[13] However, the biography from journalist Bernard Violet, published in 2004, was, like the 1979 work, based almost entirely on sources from Abbé Pierre or those close to him and made no reference whatsoever to this past.

In the end, it was Abbé Pierre himself who openly revealed the secret in 2005. In *Mon Dieu... Pourquoi*, the book he co-wrote with Frédéric Lenoir, he states: "Speaking openly about my desires does nothing to weaken them and I have, on occasion, given into these desires for the briefest of moments. However, I have never enjoyed repeated sexual encounters because I have never let sexual desire take root. Doing so would have led me to embark upon a long-term relationship with a woman, which was against my chosen way of life. And so yes, I have experienced sexual desire and, on rare occasions, the satisfaction thereof, but this satisfaction was a real source of dissatisfaction, because I did not feel that I was being true to myself."[14] This confession had an important role to play as official discourse within – and for – the Catholic Church on the issue of the marriage of priests, and with these words a definitive, courageous stance was adopted in a theological and social debate. Moreover, it was of pivotal importance for Emmaus, in that it largely explained their fear of the "whiter-than-white" members of the original Emmaus 32,[15] and their desire to protect an organisation which they knew could collapse at any time.

## "The Murder of the Father?" (December 1957–March 1958)

The "murder of the Father", which those within Emmaus continue to this day to attribute to the Movement's later obsession with robust, no nonsense management, cannot be understood in isolation from its complex, painful backdrop. The frail icon, ill-balanced on his pedestal and often absent – either seriously ill and being nursed back to health, or travelling the world to answer the countless calls for help – left those at the head of the Movement living in fear that the many scandals would come to light. On a local level, there were the leaders who made off with the takings; and on a national level, there were the revelations about various indiscretions, which threatened to bring Emmaus crashing to the ground. And yet, in spite of it all, Emmaus remained bound to its founder, particularly as far as its finances were concerned. Indeed, many donors made their cheques payable to Abbé Pierre, rendering Emmaus dependent on the funds he agreed to manage. However, his use of the funds was often shrouded in secrecy and he was often free to spend them as he saw fit, without needing to account for every franc spent. On 23 July 1954, Association Emmaus acknowledged that "[Abbé Pierre] is obliged to keep back much of the money donated to deal with certain instances of acute suffering. Payments made to help these people cannot be officially recorded in the Emmaus accounts because the cases are too specific and require a level of discretion, which means the Council cannot be informed."[16] Yet just as these funds were needed to protect the Emmaus image, they were equally crucial in allowing the Movement to continue its activities on a permanent basis. Keeping Emmaus alive meant depersonalising it and rendering it independent from its founder.

## The 1958 split

By the end of 1957, Abbé Pierre was once again out of control and several of those closest to him decided, with the approval and under the watchful eye of the Church, to send him away from France for a time, in a bid to get him back on his feet. An operation on a diaphragmatic hernia was the official line: he had in fact been sent to a psychiatric clinic in Switzerland, which treated leading public figures, and would be committed for a total of six months.[17]

Lucie Coutaz was seldom on hand, having suffered an accident in October. As a result, Abbé Pierre was most often surrounded by the Abbés Leurent, Monnier and Zundel, who were friends, confidants and members of the Church. Having undergone an operation on his hernia on 18 December, he had bestowed power of attorney on both Abbé Leurent and Lucie Coutaz. A slow, difficult recovery process then followed and he received several letters from members of Emmaus asking him to stand down. On 30 December, Doctor Durand ruled out any plans Abbé Pierre had to return to Paris and ordered him to spend some in isolation, away from the action. He was to live with Lucie Coutaz and an "associate" appointed by the Church – Father Monnier was chosen to fill the post on a temporary basis – and from that moment on, the doctor officially became solely responsible for deciding the fate of Abbé Pierre.[18]

On 12 January 1958, Dr Durand agreed that Abbé Pierre could strip Abbé Leurent and Lucie Coutaz of their power of attorney and take back control over his own affairs. Furthermore, in order to help lift Abbé Pierre's depression, Durand recommended the Abbé gradually return to his work at Emmaus.[19] However, when Abbé Pierre expressed a wish to attend the Emmaus general assembly on 21 January, the doctor refused to grant him permission to do so. Consequently, the founder appointed Durand as his representative and ordered him to go to Paris on his behalf. In a meeting held prior to the assembly, the board of directors listened to Durand's account of Abbé Pierre's condition. The Doctor stated that the fragile state of the Abbé's health meant he needed time out to recover. He informed the board that the Abbé could be out of action for an extended period of time and asked them to take any decisions arising from this state of affairs. This was, in other words, an explicit request that the Bourdonnais leaders once again take the Movement in hand, and that the founder be granted an "extended" period of leave. However, the board remained hopeful that things would improve. Evidence from Father Monnier (the Church authority) was followed by the testimony of Dr Durand (the medical professional), and in light of both accounts it was "decided to extend the mandate of the outgoing directors until 1 March 1958". This was a move to buy them time so that, faced with such a complex situation, they could wait before making any major decisions.

On the day of the assembly, while Dr Durand was in Paris, Abbé Pierre decided to hand over his powers to Jean Bouchy, until he had been nursed back to health. Bouchy was the first of Emmaus' active "Friends"[20] or supporters to become a leader of the Movement and was the vice-president of Association Emmaus. The decision was formally adopted by the board during its meeting on 29 January and by the assembly on 1 March. Nevertheless, the Abbé would later take the view that his powers had been "extorted"[21] from him "at a time when the state of his health meant he was not in a position to defend himself."[22]

It does in fact appear that Abbé Pierre was subject to gruelling medical treatment. For Pierre Lunel, the programme was almost deadly: "It involved injections, sleep, isolation, and rest, with no room for anything else whatsoever [...] The conscientious little doctor was particularly proud of the shock treatment he administered. He was, as he assured his patient, the only practitioner of such treatment in the world, was he not? [...] For periods of up to seven days straight, he would plunge his patient into a state of 'hibernation', depriving him of all food or contact with the outside world. These were extended comas; it was almost as if he was being treated by being put to death rather than put to sleep, and each time, Pierre would emerge weak and numb."[23] However, research conducted by historians in psychiatric medicine suggests that the picture might not have been quite as dramatic as that painted by Lunel. At the time, sleep treatment was common practice and it was highly likely that while Abbé Pierre was not allowed to eat food orally, he would have been fed through an intravenous drip.

Whatever the truth, the extraordinary general assembly of 1 March made the following statement: "Your administrative office is deeply saddened by the fact that it now has no other option but to take account of the Abbé's state of exhaustion. It has also come to the conclusion that it ought to spare him all sources of worry and stress, particularly those related to administration. It is for this reason that you will not find his name on the list from which you are invited to choose. It is of course clearly understood that as soon as his health allows, the Friends who have taken on the burdensome task of helping him during his period of absence will call a meeting of the general assembly immediately and hand him their resignation, in order to allow him to return to his rightful place as apostle of the homeless. Likewise, the fact that Miss Coutaz is needed by the bedside of our sick friend means that she too is absent from the list. We, as the general assembly, are praying for his speedy recovery and ask Miss Coutaz to assure our sick friend that we are with him in his time of need."[24]

Paul viewed this process, which saw the Emmaus management isolate Abbé Pierre from the Movement and place him under the supervision of the Church, as a putsch. Conversely, for the members of the board, it was a painful decision taken "with great reluctance",[25] but one which the circumstances made necessary. To avoid the situation being entirely misread, it should again be made clear at this point that the decision was not so much one taken by the Abbé or the

Emmaus management as one taken "by the doctor and the [Church] hierarchy [...] Many of our friends outside the Movement were informed of the decision through an almost official statement [...] Abbé Pierre was no longer able to perform a managerial role within Emmaus and dealing with the Movement's practical difficulties became our responsibility now more than ever before. At the same time, a priest appointed by the Church had recently arrived to ensure that morality and spirituality were present in all our activities."[26]

Already depleted of all strength, in early April 1958, Abbé Pierre fell ill once more, struck down this time, it seemed, by viral hepatitis. In light of the fact that the Abbé's stay in hospital showed no signs of coming to an end, Abbé Maurice Zundel, a Swiss theologian whose diocese was near the clinic, encouraged Abbé Pierre to cut ties with Dr Durand, despite the fact that the doctor enjoyed the support of the Catholic church hierarchy. He recommended that Abbé Pierre seek the advice of Dr Pierre Bour, a French neuro-psychiatrist who was "horrified by Abbé Pierre's treatment" and a staunch advocate of gentler forms of therapy.[27] However, it was not until August that Abbé Pierre changed doctor. In the meantime, in July, Dr Durand granted the Abbé permission to spend time recuperating at Hauterive Abbey, near Fribourg.

As his strength returned, Abbé Pierre gradually began to take things in hand once more: he came to realise that those working at the Bourdonnais headquarters "had thought it appropriate not to send him, for months, (personal) correspondence, money orders, any meeting documents whatsoever and, of course, no minutes."[28] On the advice of Dr Durand and with the help of Lucie Coutaz, he decided to rebuild his own secretariat in Switzerland, and took back control of his bank account and mail, thereby breaking the terms of the agreement signed during the March assembly.[29] According to José Balista, despite the fact Dr Durand was no longer Abbé Pierre's personal doctor, "[he]exerted a hold over him for almost two years, interfering in his personal affairs and controlling everything he did."[30]

As a result of Abbé Pierre's actions, from August 1958 onwards, Emmaus found itself without any funds of its own, entirely dependent on the Abbé's willingness to transfer money from Switzerland. Relations between the two sides appeared to thaw when the Abbé promised "to return to the Association the sums of money that it was thought had been sent to him to help fund the activities carried out by Association Emmaus."[31] However, these payments would ultimately arrive "sporadically"[32] rather than on a regular basis. The situation finally reached a point of no return. In an interview, Henri Camus recalled: "At some point, Abbé Pierre took back control of his bank account and that was when things got really serious, because the directors no longer trusted us. It was at that point that he lost his position within Association Emmaus. They removed him from Association Emmaus [...] God's honest truth, the association no longer had a penny to its name. Abbé Pierre had all the money and the Association had all the financial obligations. And it's been like that ever since." The bond of trust was also broken on the other side – the private letter written by Yves Goussault and dated 20 September 1958 describes "the bitterness still evident in Abbé Pierre's letters and comments."

Committed to a psychiatric clinic in Switzerland for six months of treatment, Abbé Pierre came under pressure from all sides to keep his distance from Emmaus and relinquish his powers. He was under pressure from his doctor; and from the Church, which was undoubtedly eager to see the Movement thrive in the long term as long as it "towed the line", and offered its full support to Association Emmaus who had been charged with the task of keeping Emmaus alive. Lastly, Abbé Pierre was under pressure from the Association itself, which could only enjoy authority and legitimacy if it was handed clear powers once more. Under such pressure, he gave up his fight and agreed to the demands. However, as his recovery progressed, he began to rebel against those attempting to take control of his affairs and isolate him from his own organisation.

## (Mis)interpretations

These bitter conflicts between warring factions at the top of the Emmaus hierarchy, seen by some at worst as what "murdered" the Father, and at best as a betrayal, and by others as a crippling burden but one that had to be borne to ensure the Movement's survival, would wear on for several decades. The history of Emmaus, the way it later developed, its quirks, its clans and their varied relationships to the founder, are all a direct consequence of these dark years and the black myth they left behind.

Indeed, from 1958 to the 1980s, using either proven facts or fabricated information, each camp carved out its own myth, and forged an individual identity by defining itself in opposition to the other. To use vocabulary coined much later on, members of the Movement were either "Abbé-Pierrists" (from Paul's camp) or "Emmausian" (heirs to the Bourdonnais throne).[33] The former were accused of foolhardy risk-taking and rushing headlong into the unknown, and the latter of having murdered the Father. The conflict saw puerile adolescents pitted against the masterminds of sacrilegious parricide; bandits against self-righteous members of the Bourgeoisie. However, each side's contempt for the other ran so deep that the later Emmaus story was more one of cold, mutual ignorance than one of passionate crossfire.

The first attempt to relieve tensions came in the form of Bernard Chevalier's 1979 book, which was a collection of interviews with Abbé Pierre. Chevalier was a veteran of the Movement, a member of the camp that had which had remained "faithful" to the Abbé but moderate in its views and open to dialogue. One of the book's striking characteristics was its wish to conceal the disputes that had rocked Emmaus over the years, and to avoid ruffling feathers. The backdrop against which this book was published made this an extremely wise decision. A whole twenty years after the first seeds of conflict were sown, the two sides were just beginning to agree to sit down, talk to each other, and contemplate the possibility of establishing a common institutional authority in the long term. Abbé Pierre was delighted at the development and, in an attempt to heal old wounds, made a visible effort to avoid inflammatory comments.

By 1992, the backdrop had changed yet again. Emmaus France was back on track and those who had lived through the difficult times were slowly dying. It now seemed possible to resurrect the past and to examine it using a more detached, analytical approach. The book by Pierre Lunel, a university lecturer in Roman law, was also based on lengthy interviews with Abbé Pierre, along with other first-hand accounts from the period and evidence collected by combing through previously unpublished archives of the Abbé's personal papers. This research combined to produce a more comprehensive account of the Movement's early years. The book did not sell itself as a collection of interviews or as an academic work, but rather as a book with broad public appeal, comprising a series of reconstructed dialogues pieced together. However, charmed by Abbé Pierre's character, the author proved himself to be easily swayed by the Abbé's version of events. Consequently, in the book, the Emmaus management are at times dealt with unceremoniously and at other times are described with ambivalent compassion, as "honest people who got scared."[34]

The most recent of the major works on the subject was journalist Bernard Violet's interview with Abbé Pierre, which was published in 2004. Like its counterparts, this was a thorough, well-researched piece of work based on lengthy interviews and flaunted the fact that it provided access to two previously unseen sources. These were Abbé Pierre's will – which did not, in reality, provide any significant information – and the letters he wrote as an adolescent. These provided the inside scoop on his relationship with Yves from 1926. Violet also allowed himself to be swayed by the bitter, resentful remarks of an ageing man, going so far as to include fallacious statements about Jean Bouchy. Abbé Pierre is quoted in the book as saying: " 'The man to whom I had transferred all of my powers took advantage of my illness to cut me off from Emmaus. He was an honest man, but nevertheless one of the big fish to whom I had granted power of attorney. Believing that I was beyond help, he wanted to replace me.' [...] Bouchy's bizarre behaviour, which Abbé Pierre brought to light, was in fact more serious than he believed it to be. His actions were more than the misguided attempt of an ambitious man to get his way..."[35] And yet Jean Bouchy was in no way an execrable individual harbouring ruthless ambition. He only reluctantly accepted extremely burdensome responsibilities in a time of acute crisis. Furthermore, Georges Lillaz, who was undoubtedly the member of the Bourdonnais team closest to Abbé Pierre, would later declare that "his [Bouchy's] unwavering devotion to the Movement has been so valuable and been such a force for good that I will forever be moved by and deeply admire his work."[36] He also gave his health and his life to the Movement, when he died prematurely from a heart attack in 1961.

These changing viewpoints were in part due to the personalities of and editorial choices made by the books' authors. And yet, given that these three works were, more than anything, mere receptacles for interviews with the Abbé, it is clear that in terms of the memory of Emmaus, which he wished to leave behind, the founder himself was gradually becoming increasingly less forgiving. This was not without consequences for internal relations: the Movement would be unable to make peace with the past if old wounds were sporadically reopened by texts that insisted on unearthing old conflicts and, furthermore, that did so with very little hard evidence to support their version of events.

There is one final tale that belongs in this chapter; one that refuses to be buried and continues to poison internal relations to this day. It is the tale of a certain Lucie Coutaz who, at sixty years of age, was brutally thrown out of the Rue des Bourdonnais house and on to the street, suitcase in hand:[37] matricide had followed patricide.

The eviction of Lucie Coutaz, which no one can deny took place, was in reality a gradual process, and one executed using symbolic rather than physical violence. In order to justify the fact that she was temporarily absent from the list of elected representatives, the general assembly of 1 March reminded those present that "Miss Coutaz [was] needed in Geneva, by the bedside of our sick friend" since she had been his personal secretary since 1945. Yves Goussault's private letter provides one explanation as to why she was removed from the Movement in the autumn, this time for good: "[the task which had been entrusted to us] came with another painful condition attached: we were to remove Miss Coutaz from the Movement, refusing as she did to accept the reality of the situation with which we had been brutally confronted. As far as this matter is concerned, I speak in full knowledge of the facts, because I have tried long and hard, on several occasions, to make her understand that desperate times call for desperate measures. Initially, I thought I had succeeded in bringing her round to our way of thinking, but the conversations which she went on to hold with friends both inside and, alas, outside the Movement made it clear to me that on the contrary, she was determined to stand against us [...] She would tell those who visited her time and time again that people were doing nothing but lying and scheming, and that activities would soon resume under the leadership of 'the only boss God wished to see in place'. We showed her the patience of a saint and did everything we could to get her on side. However, she refused to budge and Mr Bouchy was forced to inform her that she would be leaving Emmaus, while assuring her that she would be given the financial guarantees she demanded."[38]

I will conclude this chapter by remarking upon the astounding emptiness of Church archives on Abbé Pierre. Whether this be in Paris, Cambrai (the archives of the French Assembly of Cardinals and Bishops), Issy-les-Moulineaux (the national archives centre for the Church of France), Grenoble (the site of the diocesan archives in view of the fact that the Bishop of Grenoble had always been Abbé Pierre's hierarchical superior) or Bourgoin-Jallieu (where the Little Sisters of Catholic Maternity Wards held the correspondence of Monseigneur Guerry), it is a constant source of debate. The lack of material in these archives makes it difficult to gauge the exact role played by the Church during this period, even if there is nevertheless no doubt that it was a crucial and decisive one. The Church was primarily concerned with ensuring the long-term survival of, and discreetly controlling, a project which restored its former glory, albeit indirectly. Later on, the conspiracies against Abbé Pierre, who was accused by some of doctrinal heresy and by others of destabilising the institutional Churches or of crypto-communism, are thought to have led to the matter being referred to the Vatican, who did, however, appear to offer its full support. Finally, the fear of moral scandal, the increasingly bitter disputes within Emmaus, and the physical weakness of an often ill Abbé Pierre, led those at the top of Emmaus France to intervene; a move endorsed by Association Emmaus. After the Jesuit Father Monnier, it was the Franciscan Father Jacques who was finally appointed as central leader and who managed to achieve the virtually impossible in maintaining the trust of both the Abbé and the Bourdonnais team at the same time.

As for the founder, he had been cast aside by everybody – the Association, the Church and the medical profession – within his own Movement in France. Consequently, he left to sow new seeds abroad.

Countless cries for help were flooding in from overseas, and trips to Belgium, Austria, Denmark and Sweden would confirm to him the importance of helping Emmaus take root across the globe – a mission to which he would devote himself fully for the next twenty years.

# II – THE 1960s & 1970s: THE MOVEMENT QUIETLY BEGINS TO THRIVE

In the early 1960s, after independence had been granted to many of Emmaus' subsidiary bodies, only four initiatives remained under the organisation's direct control: its social housing, the Communities, the Association (an old umbrella organisation which had been all but emptied), and the newspaper *Faim et Soif.* The housing cooperatives and the General Confederation of Housing, whose offices remained in the Rue des Bourdonnais, were independent, but retained "close ties" with the organisation.

The extent of the tensions that had marked the previous era and the media storm surrounding the issue of poverty during the *Trente Glorieuses* made the late 1950s to the late 1970s a period of quiet development for Emmaus. There was the tactful development of the organisation's limited social housing company, which was forced to remove a number of irksome thorns from its side (Noisy, and the emergency accommodation sites) and to consolidate its role as a business. The Communities, whose day-to-day running was underpinned by the modern Emmaus philosophy of robust management, also began to silently thrive. They too began to refocus their attention on strengthening their internal structures and launched large-scale initiatives to improve social welfare. Lastly, there was the prudent development of the Committees of Friends which, while they had been thriving previously in France, now exploded to such an extent that in the 1970s, no one at Emmaus was able to count them all.

In contrast, the organisations closest to Abbé Pierre remained as attached to making grandiose statements as they did to taking action. Paul and his entourage continued with their epic adventures, and in the summer, Emmaus launched huge summer camps for the young; while at the same time internal disagreements led new groups to break away and set up elsewhere. And thus, one maverick group after another, Emmaus gradually took root across the whole of France.

Furthermore, particularly noteworthy was the organisation's rapid expansion abroad: Abbé Pierre began to move beyond France's borders to travel the world, answer calls for help, spread the idea of Emmaus, and give the Movement concrete, structured form across the globe. Indeed, it was through his work in the Southern hemisphere that the old Emmaus model was given new life: the South was home to the world's poorest people and those who suffered most, the South was where development began to develop a human face, and it was in the South, too, where the Movement's political and religious identity, which had become less visible in metropolitan France, was once again expressed.

No one specific date marks the end of this period, which drew to a close in the late 1970s: 1975 for *SOS-Familles* (this was the start of development); 1977 for the organisation's social housing programme (the Barre Law was adopted, which reduced government expenditure on social housing and the department began to undergo wholesale restructuring) and for the Central Union of Emmaus Communities (UCC) (with the departure of Michel Lefebvre); 1978 for the Union of Friends and Companions of Emmaus (UACE) (the pinnacle of the organisation's efforts to give itself a rigid structure); or 1980 for the Committees of Friends (a creation of the National Committee of Friends of Emmaus, or CNAE), and so the list goes on. However, for all of these organisations, the real break with the past came with the end of the *Trente Glorieuses.* Indeed, the arrival of the economic crisis would profoundly alter the face of poverty in France and would force Emmaus to make wholesale changes in order to adapt to the new climate.

# *Chapter 4* / EMMAUS HLM AND THE RISE OF SOCIAL HOUSING

In the 1950s, a whole host of migratory and demographic phenomena combined to further increase the need for housing: the baby boom, an increased life expectancy, a reduced mortality rate, the quickening of the now mass exodus from the countryside to the towns, and the influx of French citizens returning to the Motherland from North Africa following decolonisation. The French government took action, adopting a policy of house-building on a massive scale, which was based on the industrialisation of the building industry and the construction of large housing estates. This policy remained in place until 1977, when an important housing reform bill entered into force. The bill constitutes something of a "before" and "after" so far as this chapter is concerned, but until then France played catch-up and endeavoured to meet its housing needs: 300,000 houses were built in 1958 and 550,000 in 1975. The Emmaus social housing company (Emmaus HLM) was equally quick to expand: with 250 houses at the end of 1954, it owned 7,500 in 1975. In 1959, the company's capital of 812,000 new francs was divided between 149 shareholders; by 1975, 440 shareholders owned a slice of a 7-million-new-franc pie. This growth had a direct impact on the organisation's total wage bill: 142 employees were on the books in 1964; by 1978 this number had swelled to over 200 – and the company was still only operating in the Paris region.[1]

While these figures suggest that the organisation was thriving, they should not conceal the difficulties encountered. With the first emergency housing sites rapidly falling into a state of disrepair and the "running sore" at Noisy refusing to disappear, the company had to settle the winter 1954 accounts and begin to build longer-lasting housing. However, the organisation was still faced with the difficult trade-off between providing quality housing and meeting the social needs of the homes' residents, between increasing and reducing costs. Furthermore, with other social housing companies on the ground,

Emmaus HLM found itself in the difficult position of being a small firm operating in a saturated market. It succeeded, nevertheless, in developing an effective social policy, some aspects of which were truly original.

## Balancing the Accounts of Winter 1954

### Replacing the emergency housing sites

Built in a hurry to meet the urgent need for housing, the first emergency housing sites did not age well. In late 1961, Emmaus was forced to contemplate renovating the Aulnay and Le Plessis sites, followed by those at Saint-Ouen, Pontoise and Conflans. These plans were quickly brought forward when the public began to turn against the emergency housing sites, while at the same time the communes began to rail against the concentration of poverty, social misfits and ex-offenders within one place and the detrimental effects this had on local life. In the face of such criticism, there were two solutions on the table: either keep these people where they were and offer them real opportunities to live as part of a community, or spread them across France to allow them to integrate into normal life once more. Emmaus HLM opted for the first of the two. However, the emergency housing sites were swallowing vast sums of money, due to the expense of maintaining the damp, unsanitary homes. The cheap, basic accommodation, or LEPN, was gradually demolished and replaced by PSR (social rehousing programmes for families living in substandard accommodation) and new social housing.

### Waging war on unpaid rent

Since 1955 the main problem faced in Argenteuil and Bezons had been the amount of rent left unpaid. As we have seen, in 1960 these two emergency housing sites alone accounted for 82% of Emmaus' bad debts. Initially, the company was determined to use hard-line tactics, such as evictions or taking people to court. However, such tactics had to be quickly reconsidered after the Noisy camp was served with an eviction order forbidding the company from rehousing those who had not paid their rent. At Abbé Pierre's request, a member of staff was hired to "liaise with the residents of the camp on a human level". It was clear, however, that the Abbé and the board of directors were diametrically opposed in their stance on the issue. On an ideological level, Abbé Pierre bemoaned "the problem faced by the poorest members of society", "the failings of the authorities" and "the cruel dilemma confronting the social housing company". The board of directors, more pragmatic and preoccupied with robust management, directed his attention to the fact that "the social housing company's current situation and the responsibility it has towards the supervision authorities mean it cannot afford the luxury of continuing to house tenants who make no effort to pay their rent." Such an attitude would be fiercely criticised by the families who honoured their financial commitments, often going without the basics to do so. Paying rent was viewed as "an educational necessity".[2] A compromise was found between coercive and educational methods, and a policy of indifference, and the company gradually clawed back the money it was owed from Argenteuil and Bezons.

However, although the level of unpaid rent dropped to 2.4% in 1962 and reached its lowest of 1.1% in 1965, overall, unpaid rent would continue to steadily increase after this point, until it reached levels which were considerably lower than those of the early years, but significant nevertheless (6.3% in 1980). This new increase, which this time affected social housing organisations across the board, was the result of "the growing discrepancy between rent prices and tenants' financial means":[3] between 1963 and 1966, salaries increased by 16.5% and rent in the Paris region by 49%. Social housing congresses and appeals made to the authorities often raised the issue of house prices and the creditworthiness of tenants, but it was only in 1977 that the solution arrived, with the reform of housing benefit and the government's decision to withdraw funding from social housing in favour of providing those in need with direct financial support.

## ATD: the life of the organisation and its study of Noisy

Emmaus HLM remained deeply concerned about the "running sore" of Noisy, another burdensome legacy from the early years. The camp was becoming a permanent fixture and beginning to operate in an organised fashion: in 1960 the launderette was opened, along with the men's hostel and the children's club, while plans to open a site designed to promote family life received the green light from the Ministry of Construction. In 1961, ATD, an association independent of Emmaus, was set up. The scientific research and international relations sector of this new association began to expand, with the launch of its *Igloos* magazine and the first international symposium on abject poverty, held at UNESCO in 1961. This was followed by a second conference in 1964. Inspired by his meeting with Father Wresinski, on 8 July 1963 the author François Mauriac launched a mass appeal for volunteers in *Le Figaro*. The arrival of Geneviève Anthonioz-de Gaulle, niece of the general and soon-to-be president of the movement, allowed ATD to make new opportunities available. Volunteer training was developed and given to all volunteers as a matter of course. Finally, in 1963, ATD was officially recognised by the UNESCO coordinating committee for international voluntary services.[4]

The work to restore dignity to the poorest members of society also continued. For women, the arrival of a volunteer beautician allowed ATD to open a beauty salon. The salon established itself as the site's central meeting point and a place where women could flourish. It included a launderette, kitchen, library and relaxation room, complete with sewing and knitting machines, a weaving loom and records.[5] Its aim was to help women acquire or rediscover a taste for all things beautiful, and the desire to care for their body and mind. The home set up a mother-and-child clinic and hired a part-time nursery nurse in order to replace the Red Cross clinic which had left the site following vandalism on the premises. The number of teenagers on the site increased as the children grew up.[6] The difficulties parents experienced in exerting their authority and the large number of thefts in the neighbourhood led ATD to set new activities in motion, including a mechanics' workshop and a theatre.[7] In 1964, ATD was given official status as a "club and team working to prevent crime". Collections were organised to provide study grants, and the library and the "cultural hub" expanded.

Original in its qualitative approach to abject poverty, the camp was also unique in the research it carried out. A medical survey conducted in 1963 revealed that out of the 165 families interviewed, forty-eight had already buried a child and forty had (and sometimes hid) a sick or disabled child; out of one hundred children aged between one and five, forty suffered from rickets, eighteen from nervous disorders, eight had motor difficulties, thirteen suffered from untreated ear infections, fifteen had learning difficulties, and thirty had blood clots on their lungs.[8] This tragic health situation was accompanied by an acutely challenging social one. Between 1962 and 1963, the latter was the subject of a rigorous analysis by Jean Labbens, a sociologist who came to ATD following the 1961 symposium. Labbens demonstrated that the camp was no longer a temporary solution, but a long-term one: in 1963, 31% of the people at the camp had arrived since 1954, and 13% since 1955, while only 15% had arrived since 1960. Prior to arriving at the camp, many of the families had stayed for a time in a hotel, which had become too small and unstable a solution once children were born.[9]

Made up almost entirely of French families, the camp also allowed ATD to better understand and deal with the circumstances that led to French nationals being excluded from their own society. The majority of the camp (85%) came from urban regions of metropolitan France, and most of these (45%) from the Paris region. The socio-professional standing of the men was particularly low (80% had no professional qualifications whatsoever) and, at a time when France was witnessing a return to full employment, 23% were out of work. Female unemployment was almost non-existent. As a result, 16% of families could be classed as "destitute" and 55% as "poor". The study revealed that these groups had not descended the social ladder but rather that they had "inherited" poverty: 21% of the parents had been in receipt of state benefits and 57% had lived their childhood in poverty. This poverty was the reason behind the high cohabitation rate (37%); marriage being viewed as too costly and divorcing a former spouse as an overly complex procedure. For all that, many couples were in very long-term relationships. It also emerged that unlike married couples, where the man was older than the woman, the opposite was true for cohabiting couples: the woman almost always had children from a previous relationship and ended up finding herself a younger man, but one with only basic professional qualifications, in an attempt to"combine two sets of difficulties in order to survive".[10]

The situation did not appear to be any better for the next generations: the teenagers in the camp were even less qualified than their parents and, furthermore, were in no great hurry to get a job. Tests hinted at the extent of their psychological difficulties: their experience of poverty had coloured their perceptions of the world; they were on a desperate quest for material, psychological and social security; they felt powerless to change their fate; they were "incapable of coping with reality"; and they experienced an "acute sense of inferiority and powerlessness". In short, they suffered "a weak sense of self".[11]

This new scientific approach to abject poverty can in some respects be likened to the social research conducted in the 1830s, and was a major step forward in fostering an understanding of the phenomenon. It also left its mark on sociology. ATD were pioneers in their will to view poverty not simply as a lack of material wealth, but as a multifaceted phenomenon, which forced victims to leave their cultural, psychological, social and spiritual needs unfulfilled. Lastly, contrary to popular belief, ATD showed that far from playing a pathogenic role, the camp protected its residents from poverty: it gave a roof to families unable to afford their own home, and was also "a unique group which did everything in its power to ensure the survival and security of its members, as part of its small contribution to global society [...] It prevented more serious social problems [and] performed a positive function."[12] Despite frosty relations between Association Emmaus, Emmaus HLM and ATD, several issues of *Faim et Soif* relayed the findings of this research.

## The camp is reabsorbed

Despite the ATD research, in 1959 the camp was officially declared unhygienic and told it would be shut down. Two opposing plans for the camp's future emerged. One was the plan to keep the residents on site but house them in a renovated camp. In 1960–1, an architect drew up plans for a future housing village, social housing loans were granted, the benefits agency for the Paris region agreed to finance communal facilities, and the proposal received the support of the

Ministry for Construction. The second plan was to scatter these residents, seen as pathogens, across France. This proposal was endorsed by the Ministries of the Interior and Public Health, and by the council. With the two sides unable to reach consensus, discussions dragged on until 1965. Still the owner of the land, Association Emmaus ceased to finance the maintenance of the site and, from 1964 onwards, paid only the water bill, fire insurance and taxes.

However, from 1965 onwards, the problem was tackled head-on, both as part of the new government policy to combat slums, which became official when the Debré Law entered into force (1964), and as part of the plans to build new towns. It was then that Emmaus HLM, to whom Association Emmaus agreed to resell the land at cost price, entered into talks with the ministry, and the reabsorption of what had become the Noisy slum began in June 1966. The process was far from problem-free. In an interview, Henri Camus recalled how "the problem was with Father Joseph. He was all for us building new homes, but every time we evacuated an igloo, he'd put someone else back in there! [...] The man just wasn't playing the game. He was over the moon that we were rehousing families, but then he'd go and do that... He was just the same as Abbé Pierre, one of those guys with charisma, there'd be a family in need and before you knew it, in they went! [... So] we'd arrive early in the morning, in lorries from the Community at la Réserve, put them [the residents] in the lorries with all their furniture, take them to their housing and get straight out of there! We had it down to such a fine art that by eight or nine in the morning, everything had been cleaned out and we'd left. That's how we managed to get things done."

By the end of 1968, half the families had been rehoused, be it in emergency housing sites (Plessis, Aulnay), Emmaus social housing (Aulnay, Argenteuil), or in other government-funded accommodation. In May 1969, there were still around one hundred families living on the site and, by late 1970, this number had dropped to sixteen. In the end, out of 223 families living on site in June 1966, 23% were rehoused in social housing, 25% in LEPN housing (the majority in Le Plessis), 20% stayed on site in the temporary accommodation provided, 13% were placed in the Paris region, 12% outside the capital, and 7% in caravans. All the families were consulted before being rehoused: moving costs were covered along with the first three months' rent and, if necessary, the Companions provided the poorest families with furniture. On 10 July 1971, the operation was finally complete: it had cost Emmaus HLM a total of 500,000 francs.[13]

The reconstruction phase was then set in motion, comprising two key elements: the Ministry footed the bill for 1,012 social houses, and the seventy-eight PSR which were in the pipeline were eventually turned into sites providing temporary accommodation, in order to ensure the organisation was eligible for grants. Relations with ATD remained difficult. In 1971, ATD signed a contract with Emmaus, which saw them gain the right to manage the temporary accommodation site free of charge and commit to guaranteeing rent payments for the next eight years. However, one year later, the financial commitments agreed upon proved impossible to uphold and ATD terminated the contract. On 18 May 1972, it was noted: "Negotiations are under way. These are proving arduous, like all negotiations with ATD."[14] After lengthy discussion, it was ultimately decided that the Emmaus social housing company would once again manage operations. The ATD would continue to oversee social welfare initiatives and would, henceforth, guarantee the rent of only twenty-four houses. Consequently, from that point on, it was Emmaus HLM which was forced to shoulder the financial losses: Emmaus-Habitat noted that Noisy-le-Grand was "a site providing temporary accommodation reserved for French families", and that "many of them [were] unable to afford the rent requested."[15] Faced with the prefecture's refusal to finance the deficit, a compromise was finally reached whereby the ordinary temporary accommodation site opened its doors to migrants, who tended to be a creditworthy group. A Not-for-Profit organisation was also created to make the organisation eligible for funding under the government's family benefits system. Furthermore, with the foundations of the first house laid in 1974, Emmaus HLM built 874 new houses, as part of Marne-la-Vallée's "Operation New Town". It is clear that dealing with Noisy was a long and painful process, beset with problems. It exposed the difficult relationship between Emmaus and ATD (renamed ATD

Fourth-World in 1968), which was a conflict of both people and viewpoints. Abbé Wresinski was almost a prodigal son to Abbé Pierre. The two men had a great deal of admiration for each other and, in substance, their viewpoints were very similar indeed. However, Wresinski leaned more towards research and activities on the ground, and dealt with the poverty affecting families, while Abbé Pierre, more at ease in the media spotlight, focused mainly on supporting single men, and had already moved outside Emmaus to bring the issue into the political arena. The conflict was also undoubtedly a clash of two fiery personalities.

However, the illness and isolation of Abbé Pierre meant that, very quickly, the conflict was no longer so much a conflict between the two Abbés, as a conflict between Wresinski and Emmaus. While the primary concern of both Emmaus HLM and Association Emmaus was to get things back on track and ensure robust management was in place, Wresinski's main focus was housing families. In this respect, the conflict shared many similarities with that which had set Abbé Pierre against Association Emmaus between 1954 and 1958.

Lastly, the Noisy camp was symbolic of the difficulty France experienced in dealing with its slums.[16] This is made clear by the fact that those in power took an ambiguous stance on the matter, with various authorities each adopting entirely different points of view. Despite the fact that Emmaus, soon joined by ATD, had been debating the extent and complexity of the Noisy problem since 1954, it was not until 1964 that the French government, with the help of Michel Debré, began to wage its "war on slums", and it was not until 1966 that an "interministerial standing committee" was created and tasked with looking into the matter. There are several reasons behind the government's delayed response. First, slums were considered to be places housing large groups of single men, until surveys conducted in the 1960s revealed that they were also home to large numbers of women and children. This revelation saw slums shoot straight to the top of the political agenda. Furthermore, there was a dramatic increase in the value of such plots of land and, in the 1960s, the state declared its desire to be "the body which remedie[d] all social ills."[17] Finally, demolishing a slum was an extremely complex and lengthy procedure

– numerous plots of land had to be requisitioned and expropriated and, if there was a shortage of permanent accommodation, temporary solutions had to be found.

Belatedly reabsorbed, the "running sore" of Noisy spawned the creation of ATD Fourth-World: a new movement, separate from Emmaus, which was highly original and quickly independent. As the sign placed outside in 1954 read, the camp was also "a credit to those whose work or donations allowed it to be built, and a place which should make a society unable to provide its workers with a decent home hang its head in shame."

## An Organisation Ahead of its Time in the Construction Sector

### The 1960s: the difficult problem of being small and building small

After struggling for years, 1955 marked the start of an extraordinary boom for the French construction industry. Between 1954 and 1975, housing stock was increased by 50% as 9 million new homes were built.[18] Quantity rather than quality was the main concern and the houses were built at breakneck speed. Industrial production methods slowly replaced traditional building techniques, thanks to the use of prefabrications, the streamlining and merging of companies, the reuse of identical building plans, and the standardisation of the end products. Large housing estates, defined as groups of more than 500 homes, were the key to the quickening pace of construction and were built by public, semi-public and private developers. Often built with little thought for quality and designed to last no more than one generation, these estates were nevertheless a considerable improvement on the urban slums they replaced: the houses were larger, brighter, and offered all the comforts of a modern home, including running water, electricity, a toilet and a shower or bathtub. Until 1975, the working classes were, to their great delight, finally able to enjoy a comfortable, hygienic existence. The social housing stock in particular grew considerably in size, both in relative terms (as a proportion of all rental housing stock) and in absolute terms: in

1954, it comprised 380,000 homes. By the end of the 1970s, this number had increased to 2.5 million.[19]

Broadly speaking, the Emmaus social housing company followed this trend. It experienced rapid growth between 1954 and 1963, reaching the 4,500 homes mark by the end of this period. Growth slowed slightly after this point (5,200 homes in 1970) and then began to increase once more (7,900 houses in 1975). However, unlike the large housing estates, Emmaus wished to build on a more human scale. It also sought to build quality housing, by increasing the surface area of its properties, improving facilities, creating green spaces, parking spaces, shops, and social and cultural centres. Emmaus declared it "necessary to ensure these housing sites are increasingly integrated into the area where they are built, rather than being cut off, as they once were."[20] However, it quickly became difficult for Emmaus to get this policy included in new construction policies developed by the government, for several reasons.

First, social housing companies were not given priority when plans were being made to build on available land. Emmaus attempted to take possession of land in the ZUPs, empty plots of land which the government wished to develop into new, residential areas. These were established in 1958 and were to be the main testing ground for the government's new policy on large housing estates. But this land was not the longed-for eldorado. According to Emmaus-Habitat archives, "the company encountered difficulties stemming from the fact that offices for both major companies and the council were given priority when it came to building on empty land. They were ahead of us in the queue when it came to new building programmes."[21] Furthermore, the very principle of a ZUP was not entirely compatible with Emmaus' end goal. The ZUPs aimed "to build medium-sized groups of houses, with a total of one hundred homes built on a one-hectare site. Exceptions [could] be made for larger housing estates."[22]

The increasing scarcity of land suitable for construction in the Paris region also impacted severely upon the company's activities. From 1962 onwards, plans to regenerate the Paris region, and soaring land prices, notably due to the sudden quickening of the rural exodus and the return of the pieds noirs who had been driven out of North Africa, meant that opportunities to purchase land were limited. In 1962–3, Emmaus targeted members of the clergy and town mayors in the Paris region as part of a campaign to find appropriate building land. Their efforts turned up nothing, despite the fact that the campaign had been endorsed by a letter from Abbé Pierre and a new brochure had been specially produced. By 1964, all of the company's land reserves had been used up. Available plots were further and further away from Paris. This meant that residents were forced to travel excessive distances to and from the centre, on journeys which were proscribed under government plans. Land that was classed as belonging to a ZAD, where public organisations had first refusal on land being sold, was too expensive, the owners of the plots were reluctant to sell or the authorities themselves blocked the sale, unsure of the intended use of the land. This increasing scarcity of land available for development explains why the pace of Emmaus' construction slowed between 1963 and 1970.

In addition, the industrialisation of the construction industry, and the mergers which created large construction companies, appeared to have a detrimental impact on smaller building firms. After the ZUPs failed to provide the necessary land, hopes once again focused on the new towns being built. The pet project of the prefect Paul Delouvrier, these new towns aimed to redress the population balance within the Paris region and bring inhabitants closer to the jobs, leisure facilities, and culture on offer. Five sites for new towns were selected in the mid-1960s, which meant an enormous market had to be created out of nothing. In 1968, Emmaus HLM entered the running for the sites at Evry and Cergy-Pointoise and was assured by its supervision ministry that success was all but guaranteed. Those working at the ministry provided Emmaus with "kind and unwavering support".[23] Nevertheless, the company was brought back down to earth with a bump. In order to maximise production capacity, the large construction firms merged their business operations to form Groups of Economic Interest, or GIEs, which far exceeded Emmaus' capabilities, while working their way into the social housing market. In a bid to ensure its survival, Emmaus HLM attempted to create its own group of builders, but "[the] project came up against serious difficulties. These were a result of the stances adopted by the powerful groups who were far from enamoured by the idea that a rival group was to be created."[24]

Lastly, the 1970 social housing finance reforms "did little to benefit small and medium-sized developers."[25] "The reforms were borne out of the government's wish to reduce ceiling prices by encouraging mass construction." Cost-reduction policies were adopted and priority for credit was granted to buildings with low construction costs. There were two possible solutions to Emmaus' predicament. The first was to reduce the funds allocated to new building projects in order to meet the cost criteria. However, Emmaus-Habitat believed that the Movement "continue[d] to suffer too greatly as a result of the low-cost, low-quality projects of the 1950s for us not to have serious misgivings about overly restrictive price policies."[26] The second was to join forces with bigger organisations. Emmaus HLM decided to turn to OCIL,[27] a major organisation in the social housing field of which several Emmaus directors were a member. But their efforts bore little fruit.

And so, after little more than ten years in existence, Emmaus HLM was faced with wholesale changes and a construction industry which differed greatly from that which it had entered at birth. The social housing projects it was able to undertake were increasingly entrusted to SEMs, companies that combined public and private capital, or to major construction groups. Small and medium-sized companies could only obtain contracts for smaller projects. Furthermore, Emmaus was "automatically excluded" from the SEMs of which its main rivals were members, including the housing company *Logement Français*, *Banque de Paris* and its subsidiary companies,[28] and from the ZACs, or integrated development zones, which were placed in the hands of OCIL. OCIL had its own social housing companies.

## The 1970s: Emmaus social housing under threat?

The government then did a U-turn in its housing policy. While "in the reconstruction period, public opinion, acutely aware of the problem and affected by the housing shortage, graciously agreed [...] to live in uniform, high-rise tower blocks,"[29] surveys conducted in the mid-1960s revealed that all social classes aspired to live in their own, individual house. The housing shortage began to ease and savings increased. The construction industry was increasingly less inclined to focus on quantity and the building of large housing estates. These housing estates had come under fire for their poor workmanship, structural defects, and the fact that they were cut off from the surrounding area. The lack of streets, meeting places and communal facilities was also criticised, along with the substandard quality of the building materials, and the poor insulation and soundproofing. At the end of 1967, the ZUPs were replaced with the ZACs. The ZACs attached greater importance to diversity in urban areas, the living environment, and creating facilities for the residents.[30] In 1969, the Minister for Housing, Albin Chalandon, launched a competition for architects to design cheap, individual houses, which quickly became known as "*Chalandonettes*". The 1971 Building Plan which followed aimed to pioneer new ways of housing urban populations as alternatives to large inner-city housing estates, and advocated the controlled expansion of housing estates on the outskirts of towns. The Plan marked the beginning of a period where houses were built over longer periods of time and to better-thought-out plans. The election of President Valéry Giscard d'Estaing consolidated the victory of this policy, which aimed to spread urban populations over larger areas. Social housing was to play its part in this move to create more humane living conditions in urban areas, in particular as part of urban renewal projects.

However, despite these developments, things did not get any easier for Emmaus HLM. As far as the urban renewal programmes were concerned, the 1973 decree, which made it easier for council départements and social housing companies to acquire former rental buildings, proved restrictive. Given that the total cost of works and the purchase price could not exceed 10% of the ceiling price of a comparative new-build project, the decree was not easy to enforce in the Paris region (the only area under the control of Emmaus HLM) except as part of projects conducted under the aegis of the PACTs, or Federations for Propaganda and Action Against Slums. Consequently, Emmaus decided to contact these Federations through their President, Yves Salaün, who also sat on the board of directors of Emmaus HLM. In 1974, the company became a member of the Association for the restoration of social housing in the Paris region. As far as construction was concerned, Emmaus HLM found itself increasingly excluded from the market, now in the hands of major town-planning organisations. These were multi-purpose organisations that both sold and rented accommodation in the public and private sphere. Furthermore, projects to build new social housing were gradually being shelved, and the new houses built by Emmaus, which did little to satisfy the prevailing desire for individual properties, were casualties of the stagnating market, and were therefore increasingly difficult to lease. No longer able to strike the right balance on the new programmes, in late 1975 Emmaus took the decision to focus solely on ventures that were more specifically concerned with protecting social welfare – the PSR and PLR social housing schemes, retirement homes, or urban regeneration programmes.

Lastly, so far as its rental activities were concerned, the rent freeze and excessively low ceiling prices, lower than the cost-balanced rents, had a detrimental impact on social housing companies. At the same time, meagre housing benefit payments, soaring loan rates, and the increasing difficulties faced as a result of the economic situation on both a national and international level, led to a "significant increase in rent prices, which became impossible for many families to afford."[31] The French system, which at the time was based on government subsidies designed to encourage investment in property, also worked against those who built and leased social housing. In the 1970s, this housing was not, in reality, all that "social", and instead tended to house the upper echelons of the working classes and the middle-class members of society. The Emmaus social housing company was vehemently critical of this social housing, "built and allocated in such a way as to make it no longer social",[32] and was even rumoured to have considered filing for bankruptcy in order to protest against the changes.[33]

As we have seen, the *Trente Glorieuses* were not glorious for everybody. Nevertheless, this period was used to embark upon a programme of major repairs: between 1970 and 1975 an average of 3 million francs a year were ploughed into this project, which was later scaled down, as such unbridled spending threatened to plunge government finances into a state of ruin. Emmaus HLM also managed to build several thousand new houses and, as a precautionary measure, launch a policy of buying up land, vital if it was to see building projects through to completion, even if the plots were not suitable for development upon purchase. Nevertheless, growth was very sluggish indeed and it was painfully obvious that a small company would struggle to survive, despite the fact that the circumstances of and around 1954 – the housing shortage, public support and the availability of land – seemed to render anything possible.

## A Business Begins to Develop

### The growth of the business

While it is impossible to deny that there were many bumps in the road, it is equally impossible to deny the growth of the business side of things. Between 1960 and 1975, the number of houses in the business' possession went from 2,515 to 7,920, and the number of employees increased from 140 to 164. The wage bill rose throughout the 1970s; the number of shareholders went from 149 to 440; and the firm's capital increased from 812,000 francs to 7 million. However, the structure of the group of shareholders underwent radical changes. The Emmaus organisations were the majority shareholder only up until 1963, thanks to the Association's 5,000 shares. While in 1964, the Association remained the largest shareholder, four businesses held between 1,990 and 2,700 shares;[34] and by the early 1970s, several organisations working in the housing field held more than 5,000 shares.[35] The business' net assets and liabilities experienced the most spectacular growth, going from 73.5 million to 377 million francs.

The growth of Emmaus' services meant that the organisation quickly outgrew the premises available at 32 Rue des Bourdonnais. From 1962 onwards, Emmaus HLM, which had up until that point occupied part of the second floor, spread to the *Faim et Soif* offices, together with the CGL. The move of Les Halles to Rungis in 1970 freed up the neighbouring building; it was divided between Emmaus HLM (upstairs) and the Association (basement, ground floor and mezzanine). Finally, in 1974, the organisation spread to a second building, on Boulevard Sébastopol.

## A first-rate board

The profile of the members of the board of directors consolidated, as much as it mirrored, the development of the company. Between 1954 and 1956, the board was made up of Emmaus activists who agreed to invest a great deal of time and effort into making it a success. It included some people from Emmaus' core (Abbé Pierre, Lucie Coutaz, Jean Bouchy, Suzanne Bourboulon-Renard) and others who worked closely with the Movement. There was a member of the clergy, two secretaries, two engineers, a private-school head teacher, and a CEO. The turnover was high – with the exception of Abbé Pierre, who was in the post for thirty-nine years, and Jean Bouchy, who died four years after taking up the position – none of the board members made it to the two-year mark.

From 1956 onwards, the board began to find its feet, dividing itself into three groups. The first, made up of Emmaus representatives, grew in size and strength: Abbé Pierre continued to be a member, and Lucie Coutaz became a member once more after rejoining the Movement, having resigned in 1955. In 1958, a representative of Association Emmaus joined this group, along with a representative of CGL. The board's second group brought together housing specialists and included an architect, a builder, two OCIL directors, a former tax official, and the CEO of the SEM for town planning and facilities in the French département Seine-et-Oise (SEMEASO). Finally, there were the representatives from the top ranks of the civil service, who significantly elevated the average socio-professional standing of members: the assistant director of a major bank, a CEO and graduate of the prestigious engineering school *École Polytechnique*, a company administrator, a former tax official who had gone on to become a trustee of mutual insurance companies, an Inspector General for the Ministry of Finance, and a member of the Council of State.

With this new team in place, the board developed into an incredibly stable body. The members who joined between 1956 and 1976 held their seats for an average of eighteen years,[36] and Abbé Pierre, who took up his place in 1954, remained on the board for thirty-nine years. The consequence of members staying in their posts for sustained periods of time was an ageing board: all were below forty-five in 1957; in the 1960s, the average age on the board stood at fifty-four; and by 1977 it had risen to sixty-two, with three members of the board over the age of seventy. New members were recruited through co-option.

## The Social Policy of Emmaus Housing Sites

The difficulty in striking a balance between activism and professionalism, between social welfare and robust management, was reflected in the policies of Emmaus HLM. Nevertheless, in spite of the difficulties faced, the company remained open about its genuine desire to protect social welfare, and it fought tirelessly to do just that.

### Social welfare through social housing

The company's social policy was reflected in four tangible ways. First, in the nature of the houses built: by building some social housing which catered to more exclusive tastes,[37] the company could finance accommodation designed to house the poorest members of society. The company focused in particular on extending its reduced rent programmes (PLRs) which replaced its social rehousing programmes (PSRs) in 1968. Other social housing companies generally refused to undertake PLRs, as they were difficult to complete below the allowed ceiling prices. In the early 1970s, 8% of the company's housing stock was LEPN, 5% was PLR/PSR, and 10% was LEF (cheap, family housing).

Furthermore, Emmaus HLM was the only one to build temporary accommodation sites for French families living in abject poverty (Noisy and Le Plessis). Unlike the temporary accommodation sites designed for migrants who worked (and were therefore solvent), these sites operated at a significant loss owing the fact that their tenants were not creditworthy.

Standard rents were a third integral part of the company's social policy. Under PLRs, these were systematically lower than the rents for profit – the losses incurred were offset by the rent payments from HLM social housing. A low rent policy was also applied to elderly tenants whose sole source of income was the housing benefit and government payments made to pensioners.

Finally, the company conducted a number of experiments whereby it rehoused so-called "difficult" families in individual houses outside its housing sites, either in the suburbs outside Paris or in the countryside further afield. This "original policy" gave families with a farming background, who were likely to be able to easily reintegrate into a rural environment, the chance to better themselves. The experiments also benefited families of scrap-metal dealers who were better placed to do their job in an individual house, with an adjoining plot of land, rather than in communal accommodation.[38] The families received a payment to help cover relocation costs, the company ensured that both social services and a school were available, and the Emmaus Communities helped them to move into and furnish their new home.

## The development of the socio-cultural support framework

Another, less obvious, manifestation of the company's social policy was the socio-cultural framework which was gradually developed. 1959's summer of the "teddy boys" cemented the place of a supposedly "directionless" youth in newspaper headlines. Legislation adopted in 1961 aimed to provide the legal framework necessary to improve the situation and deal with the coming of age of the baby-boomers by advocating the further development of leisure, sport, social and educational facilities. Consequently, in the 1960s, the number of square metres given over to such facilities became an all-important benchmark, and activity leaders and educators were granted additional responsibilities and began to work in a more professional capacity. Emmaus HLM expressed similar concerns about the younger generation, after it observed on numerous occasions throughout the 1960s, the presence of gangs of youths, vandalism and insecurity on the streets.

We have seen that in the 1950s, money was in painfully short supply and that the fact that it was financially impossible to develop facilities and support structures was one major regret. With Emmaus' financial situation growing steadily more stable and with the 1961 legislative framework in place, the Movement's old readiness to use its own initiative returned once again to the fore. At the end of 1963, joint management committees were set up on the largest Emmaus housing sites. The impetus for this new venture came in part from Association Emmaus, the majority shareholder, and from its president, Henri Camus. In 1964, anxious to breathe life back into the Association, Camus suggested that it should "take the problem of socially isolated or ill-adapted families in hand." It was a problem on the agenda of the authorities and a growing number of associations.[39]

The site at Le Plessis, the first but also the most slapdash of the emergency accommodation sites, became the main testing ground for this joint involvement. A "guidance centre" was set up in 1964 to rehouse and support the Noisy families: according to Emmaus-Habitat archives, "this initiative would take the social housing company back to its roots, by ensuring it focused on efforts to reduce the numbers of poor, vulnerable families."[40] However, Le Plessis was merely one link in the chain. Upstream, small hamlets were reserved for the "difficult" families, and downstream, families ready to leave the site were provided with social housing. The social centre, subsidised by the local DDASS (authority for health and social affairs), was managed by the Association, while Emmaus HLM used its own funds to open a youth centre and a PMI (mother-and-child protection unit). This was followed by a total renovation of the living environment.

This experiment went on to become the model which other sites followed, including Bobigny, Blanc-Mesnil, Verrières-le-Buisson and Aulnay-sous-Bois. These sites did so without the Association's involvement and, it would seem, with a lesser degree of success. They did, however, continue to receive financial support from local and departmental authorities.

Housing proved to be emblematic of the way Emmaus worked: the Movement would vehemently criticise the state of society but this criticism would always be accompanied by experiments with new ideas and practical solutions. Between 1960 and 1970, despite the numerous economic and structural problems of the time, Emmaus HLM's sole focus was ensuring the commercial viability of a social housing company whose policy was truly social, both in terms of its rental housing stock and the support it provided to residents. The company's efforts to achieve this goal would, on more than one occasion, cause tension on the board. The CGL, the Association and Abbé Pierre often championed the cause of society's most disadvantaged members, while others would hammer home the need for projects to make a profit.

While social housing companies specialised in rental accommodation, another company in the Emmaus family, about which very little information is available, began to develop in parallel. This was the company in charge of property-buying cooperatives, whose headquarters were also at 32 Rue des Bourdonnais. As the younger siblings of the building sites on which work first began in 1952, they became Emmaus accommodation sites in 1956, and Henri Camus remained at the helm. In legal terms, until 1968, the company was an agglomeration of cooperatives, which were then united to form a limited property whose aim was to help people get a foot on the property ladder, called *La Madeleinière*. By 1973, the property-buying cooperatives owned 9,000 houses and housed 6,000 people. Think small, but be innovative and make it viable: this could easily be an Emmaus maxim, and could equally be applied to its Communities.

# *Chapter 5* / THE COMMUNITIES COHESION AND DISSENSION

We have seen, within the world of the Emmaus Communities, the development of conflicts between those who espoused "the ethic of conviction" and those who defended "the ethic of responsibility". Over the course of this new era, the divide between the two camps became a permanent one and crystallised in the form of two Federations. One, the Central Union of Emmaus (UCC), was created early on, and the other, the Union of Friends and Companions of Emmaus (UACE), came later. In the 1970s, UACE split into two further Federations. They did not have acronyms, but went by curiously republican names: "Liberty" and "Fraternity".

The extent of these internal divisions may come as a surprise, but the reasons behind them are in fact twofold. On the one hand, the Community model was incredibly flexible and could be adapted to suit a multitude of needs, as it was underpinned by only a handful of principles (providing refuge, collecting waste, and dividing up any profit made in such a way as to benefit those most in need). The model therefore lent itself to extensive diversification. There was a vast range of Communities and leaders: Community types (open or closed, apolitical or politically active, etc.), sites (urban or rural etc.), and Companion profiles (female, male, or a mixed group, with or without children). On the other hand, Abbé Pierre, who now focused primarily on Emmaus' activities across the globe, tended to encourage those who wished to set up new types of Community to seek independence from the Movement and strike out on their own.

Acting as a catalyst to this process, which saw a whole host of different models take seed, the years 1968–75 (or the events of May '68) marked an important "before and after" in the Movement's history. Indeed, with the revival of the concept of Community and fervent support for it within the socio-political sphere, Emmaus witnessed the emergence of new approaches and new figures as the younger generation came to the fore.

## The UCC: "The Ethic of Responsibility" and Development from Within

From May 1956 onwards, existing Communities were, in theory, brought together under a large umbrella Federation, which was the brainchild of Abbé Pierre. However, in reality, this Federation appears to have been very quickly shelved following the conflicts that erupted with Paul's departure in November. Consequently, during the Abbé's long period of ill health, a new Federation was created and was a more direct expression of the Bourdonnais team's wish to take things back in hand. Named "The Central Union of Emmaus Community Associations" (UCACE, quickly shortened to UCC), its constituent assembly was held on 21 June 1958 and the organisation was officially registered as a Not-for-Profit organisation at the prefecture on 7 August. Its headquarters were at 32 Rue des Bourdonnais.[1] Jean Bouchy, the acting president of Association Emmaus, was the first president of UCC, appointed to ensure "there was a concentration of power during this difficult time, in order to guarantee that Emmaus could present a united front to the various authorities."[2] However, in October, the Association judged the "difficult period" to be over, and UCC became independent, both organisationally and financially. It appointed a new president, Jean Deroubaix. He went by the name of "Captain Jean", and had been the operations director at the *Gare d'Orsay* in winter 1954 and then the founder of a Community in the Nord département. Born in the lap of the Association and out of the wish to depersonalise the Movement and disassociate it from its founder, this new Federation derived legitimacy from its solid structure and competence. In order to guard against a hesitant beginning, the Federation opted for training and social work and decided to ensure it operated as a thoroughly professional outfit.

### The introduction of paid employment

Despite the fact that in principle Communities were run solely by volunteers, the Federation made the decision, viewed by some as heretical, to take on paid members of staff. The first paid employee, Bernard Weiss, was hired in May 1959. A former accountant, he had served Emmaus as a volunteer for two years. Then, wanting to start a family and earn a wage, he announced his return to the accountancy profession. The problem being purely financial, he was offered the chance to stay on as a paid employee. At the time, the organisation was in dire need of administrative support, to avoid "careless managerial mistakes, administrative irregularities and various oversights, which occurred even in the best of faith." This support was also required to "continue with the thankless but necessary task of regulating our work to ensure that we were operating as an association and not as a private business, and to deal with property, furniture, insurance, taxes, social security matters and the like." Finally, the support "would also allow us to ensure that a qualified secretary provided a service to all of the Communities by carrying out this work, avoiding a situation whereby each Community in turn restarted each task from scratch, with the inevitable trial and error, and time-wasting this would cause."[3] It would seem that the organisation's decision to take the plunge and hire paid staff was more the result of a desire to remain pragmatic rather than being a premeditated decision to break with the ideologies of the past. The principle quickly developed: in November 1959, the organisation hired a social worker and a secretary. These staff members were joined in January 1960 by a teacher, a teaching assistant and a second social worker.

In 1960, the practice of hiring paid employees was extended to Community leaders. As a result, Community leaders were no longer, as they had been in the revealing terminology of the Movement's early years "Community members", but the "first among equals", promoted to a position of greater responsibility than the others, with just as many rights and just as little money, but more duties.[4] They moved up the Emmaus hierarchy, the higher status justified by their responsibilities and sealed by their pay packet. This system provided greater stability. Furthermore, leaders were no longer obliged to remain celibate as they had been until then, and could now have a family. In 1976, out of the thirty-eight permanent leaders, thirty-one were married.[5] In the early 1960s, another important change took place: gradually, leaders no longer received their wage in the form of a payment made by the Community. Instead, Communities each made a payment to the Federation, who then gave the leaders their salary. The change reshaped the hierarchical pyramid: previously possessing nothing more than a moral authority, the Federation now became an employer. Lastly, the wage bill quickly swelled – by May 1963 there were already twenty members of staff on the payroll.

However, Emmaus' decision to hire paid employees did not mark the demise of selflessness. The first wages paid were such that employees were still forced to make sacrifices. The money was just enough to meet a family's basic needs: in 1963, a Community leader in the Paris region with two years' seniority earned 550 francs a month – the same wage as a court reporter who did not type his notes. Given the working hours, the need to be available evenings and weekends, the responsibility of overseeing and motivating a group of around thirty men, and the managing and coordinating all of the Community's economic and social affairs, this salary was strikingly low, and permitted a life of militant selflessness, rather than a comfortable existence. However from 1964 onwards, the salary was indexed to seniority and number of dependents, becoming "a needs-based salary".

Nevertheless, this policy was still not enough to attract reliable leaders for any length of time. As a result, Michel Lefebvre, who had been appointed the new president of UCC in 1971, decided to increase wages. However, as Christiane Lefebvre has remarked, "he did so with great difficulty, as there were certain members who did not wish to be paid – the issue nearly split the organisation in two. It was a whole way of thinking that had to change. It's all very well, and indeed, very kind, to spend every moment looking after others, but Michel [Lefebvre] worked on the principle that caring for those in difficulty was an incredibly tough job. If, on top of that, you had to constantly scrimp and save to raise your own children, you wouldn't be able to do the job properly; you couldn't endure all these difficulties on a daily basis. You needed to have at least a minimum level of financial security to then be able to give to others."[6] However, it was clear that in return for increased wages, employees now had to give something more. As UCC archives note, "[Emmaus now had the right] to demand that the efficiency of each employee's work matched the salary they earned. They were also required to possess knowledge of the job, an ability to perform the role of educator, management skills, and a desire to achieve perfection in all areas of their work [...] It also needed to be possible for leaders themselves, their local committees and the national support office, to measure this efficiency."[7] The principle of paying a wage in return for valuable skills began to clearly supersede the original ideal of a selfless individual who was the first among equals, working for free.

However, the sole aim of hiring paid leaders was to better support Companions deemed too weak for the job and to ensure that the system as a whole was robust. Developing the organisation's socio-medical support structures was also part of the same aim. In 1959, a female social worker was hired to serve all the Communities in the Paris region. Then, following the example set by the Community in Bougival, the 1963 general assembly declared that every Community needed a team comprising a doctor and a female social worker – often the only female presence among a Community of men. This team was to have a consultation room and an infirmary at its disposal. A year later, every one of the twelve Communities had brought a doctor on board, three had a nurse, and six had a clinic. The following year, there was a doctor and a female social worker working in almost all the Communities.

## Supporting the leader: friends, coordinators and assistants

In the early days, the substandard quality of leaders forced Emmaus to search for ways to alleviate the difficulties. The 1962 review stated that the leader of the Nantes Community "had not received adequate training", was "too weak psychologically", had left the Community's books untouched for more than eight months, and allowed unpaid rent to mount up. The review declared that the leader of the Nice Community was weak and "stubborn". The criticism continued.

The "Friends" and the "coordinator" were the first source of support. The Friend was a volunteer who brought his time and skills to the Community and provided a link to the rest of the Emmaus system. He spent his time both working in administrative bodies and alongside Companions, helping them with specific tasks. He was able to act as the Companions' confidant but was there first and foremost to provide the leader with valuable support, and was a stable presence within the Community, which counterbalanced the high turnover of the support teams. Initially, the leader appeared so incapable that the Friends and the socio-medical team even had to "take charge of him, organising his holidays, sorting out his wardrobe..."[8] He relied almost entirely on others. This was the consequence of an overly hectic schedule, but also of the celibate existence, which took its toll, and of a certain weakness of character, a worrying trait in those who had been appointed precisely to provide support and strength to between thirty and fifty "hard nuts" who had been discarded by society.

The "coordinator", a secular term for the "brother" or *fraternitaire* that Abbé Pierre wished to see working in each Community, was a priest "appointed with the Bishop's agreement, because his personal vocation and the other activities, which form[ed] part of his ministry, meant he was in close contact with, and accustomed to, serving the most vulnerable and neglected members of society."[9] The Franciscans appeared to best fit the bill. Living within the Community, or at least paying regular visits, the coordinator was a "straightforward man", the Community member responsible for recalling and enforcing the moral and spiritual content of the Emmaus message.

Very quickly, the leader also began to receive support from one, if not several, "assistants". Indeed, it was noted during the 1962 general assembly that Community leaders were often obliged to carry out time-consuming tasks that could easily be delegated, such as shopping at the market. The assembly concluded that "the leader [did] not choose his tasks, they [were] forced upon him." The shortage of leaders also made it extremely difficult to go on holiday or take Sundays off. Consequently, many would work themselves into a state of exhaustion. And, if a leader fell ill, the Community's very survival was suddenly under threat. As a result, in 1963, it was declared that each Community had to have at least one assistant on the payroll. In 1964, this was extended to several. These assistants were generally recruited from amongst the most stable Companions and those who were best suited to the job (although it was permitted to recruit from outside the Community if no suitable candidates were found). Companions who were promoted kept their Companion status, but received a more generous wage: in 1964, a Community leader earned 850 francs a month, an assistant received fifty francs a week (200 francs a month) and a simple Companion, ten francs a week.

## Emmaus adopts a policy of recruitment and training

It is clear then that the substandard quality of leaders was a major problem for UCC. In 1961, awareness-raising and recruitment campaigns were launched in organisations "of Catholic inspiration" and in organisations "concerned with social welfare" (movements in aid of families or trade unions). In the early 1970s, recruitment went from being "a process undertaken when the need arose" to a "permanent process", which Emmaus undertook to pre-empt needs and survive long-term. In 1974, the general assembly even declared that recruitment had become a veritable "obsession".[10] Posts were advertised in the local, regional and national press, but also in the press specialising in work in the social sector. However, recruitment remained difficult: from August 1972 to November 1974, out of the 248 applications received, only nine were seriously considered; the majority of the candidates were "lacking motivation" and were put off by the difficulty of the work, the prospect of a pay cut and need to sacrifice their family life (they would, for example, be posted to a different region and forced to work long hours in the evenings and at weekends). In 1972, the organisation hired Hervé le Ru, who was put in charge of recruitment and training. He first worked at Emmaus in the Brest Community as a priest coordinator. From 1974 onwards, interviews were also conducted with the help of a psychologist who was a Friend of the Community.

The job of Community leader was unique, and as such required both initial and ongoing training. From 1959, leaders simply learned on the job, attending meetings on the organisation's problems and practices. These were led by seasoned leaders and by Father Jacques Vreck, who was the "head coordinator" at UCC until 1973. The years 1963–4 saw the introduction of a two-and-a-half-day quarterly training session for Community leaders. Paul Lavaud and Michel Tavernier, both sociologists and professional trainers who worked as teachers at the Paris Chamber of Commerce, gave "lessons in psychology based on real-life experience". The sessions covered general topics (alcoholism, communal living, accountancy, etc.), how to draw up common rules, and how to divide up responsibilities. Providing successful training initially required a great deal of trial and error. The sessions were either too heavy on theory, which disappointed the participants who criticised the "artificial nature" of the talks given, or would involve the trainers engaging in the overzealous dissection of specific cases. This would turn the course into a detailed review of all problems encountered, problems that were often practical in nature, and gave participants the impression that they were being forced to "spill the beans" about the difficulties that they themselves had experienced. Nevertheless, even in the early days, the sessions were a valuable source of support to these leaders in the making. In an interview, Henri Camus remarked, "they really helped us to think. About man, about who man is, why he's there, our attitude towards him... Abbé Pierre's jargon wasn't enough; it was a starting point, but it didn't teach us anything we could put to practical use."

The July 1971 law on professional training as part of lifelong learning, which made it compulsory for bosses to pay 0.8% of their wage bill to the state or a training establishment, coincided with the appointment of Michel Lefebvre as president of UCC. As a result, UCC decided to make training a priority. On the advice of the National Federation for Housing and Social Reintegration Centres (FNCHRS),[11] of which UCC had been a member since the 1960s, the organisation founded INFAC, its new training institute. Community leaders were henceforth able to acquire the Dapasse, a diploma providing them with an official qualification to work as "a coordinator of adult groups". Leaders were strongly encouraged to obtain the qualification as "it was viewed as a seal of quality by the government and official organisations." It also opened up new possibilities outside the social sector for the Community leaders. Specific measures were adopted to benefit trainees. In addition to a one-year practical placement spent in four Communities, trainees also completed a three-year theory course. Lastly, internal training sessions became mandatory. These sessions dealt primarily with topics such as sales techniques, market situation, and the trading of goods between Communities. Political topics such as "What is politics?", "What form does politics take in France?" and "Emmaus and Politics" were cautiously introduced in 1970. These topics were further developed in 1972 to include questions such as "How do we view society?" and "Where do we stand in the social-work sector?" By 1973 racism, immigration and "Emmaus and immigrants" were also covered, before all political topics later disappeared from the programme once more.

## A centripetal way of thinking

The direct result of this very inward way of thinking was that there was a negligible increase in the number of Communities. UCC had a significant head start, due to the fact that until the mid-1960s it was the only legally recognised Federation. In spite of its status, it was slow to expand: there were ten Communities in 1959 and thirteen in 1971. Again, these were endogenous creations: Marseilles created Cabriès, Brest opened Rédéné and Saint-Prix was the offspring of the Bougival Community.[12]

It was not until the 1970s that things really began to take off with a sudden realisation: "For years, new Communities at various different sites had been in the pipeline. Not one had been opened. Why?"[13] An investigation into the issue pinpointed a whole host of causes, both external ("the animosity of the administrative authorities" who were reluctant to give the go-ahead to a refuge centre for adults in difficulty; and the shortage of affordable land and premises), and internal (the "fear of risk", "gentrification", the difficulty of finding leaders and Friends who were capable of managing Communities, and the "unfortunate experiences" which fuelled misgivings). The investigation galvanised UCC into action: in May, the opening of the Plessis-Trévise and Strasbourg Communities was officially ratified (the latter was the joint creation of the Communities at Cernay and Metz), and it was announced that in October, Nantes would begin work on another Community at Limoges. The following year, Marseille created Aubagne, Brest created Rennes, and Neuilly-sur-Marne opened Quincy-Voisins. In the space of two years, the number of affiliated Communities increased by half, going from thirteen to nineteen. This dramatic expansion of UCC then ended as quickly as it had begun.

In 1973, with a few, significant phrases, UCC's white paper clearly revealed the extent of the changes that had been made in little over ten years: the role of the leader was now deemed to be "very complex", involving "responsibility for staff, finances and economic affairs", "management" and "marketing". Leaders had to be able to "ensure the survival of a business in a market", estimate needs, calculate and manage. The role was now utterly unrecognisable from what it had been in the 1950s – it was a paid position designed to require a great deal more technical expertise and increasingly inspired by the world of business. Nevertheless, it was vital that the spirit of self-sacrifice continued to underpin leaders' work. An article in *Faim et Soif* declared: "There [was] no timetable. The leader [could be called] upon twenty-four hours a day,' and he had "to be at everybody's service", even if it was acknowledged that he had the right to "a personal life."[14]

To a certain extent, the organisation's decision to throw itself fully into social work bypassed the leaders who had encouraged the move. In April 1968, leaders asked for a thirteenth month. The Federation was increasingly viewed as a service provider, "a sort of mutual insurance company that came to the aid of Communities in difficulty,"[15] and less and less as a militant organisation. Contact with Emmaus became more administrative; the board was seen as a distant, irrelevant body. The policy of centralisation sparked misgivings, which occasionally developed into open conflicts. Furthermore, Abbé Pierre, for whom UCC was far from the favourite offspring, did nothing to hide his disapproval of an organisation perceived to be a bureaucratic body engaged in mundane activities. A letter from November 1975 addressed to the Federation on the eve of its general assembly – which was itself significant in its attempt to remind members of the importance of order and continued interference in the running of Communities – was moderate in form but scathing in substance. It called upon members to ensure that "order [did not] take priority over a meaningful existence and real justice [...] Before continuing to rigidly codify new organisations, a process that tends to follow the wishes of the majority or those best able to organise, might it not be a good idea to stop for a moment and take a year out, in order to work together with other branches of the Emmaus tree?"

## The UACE: "The Ethic of Conviction" and Centrifugal Development

While UCC opted to derive legitimacy from a solid structure and competence, the UACE was based on absolute loyalty to the founder – who, incidentally, made no attempt to conceal his own predilections. Attachment to either group was as much emotional as it was ideological; as much to individuals as it was to attitudes and values. At a meeting of the UACE in January 1978, Abbé Pierre declared, "When the organisation split in two, one camp [UCC] was in favour of *planning out everything down to the last minute detail*, wanting to rule everything with an iron rod, and the other [UACE] was anxious to preserve the *values of spontaneity* as far as possible."[16]

### The belated and gradual structuring of the organisation

We have seen how November 1956 marked the coming into being of Normandy's travelling Communities. They were created out of supposed loyalty to Abbé Pierre and as an attempt to reject top-heavy forms of organisation. The Communities were nevertheless brought together under an umbrella association: "The Association of Friends and Companions of Emmaus". The Association's headquarters were in Alençon and it fell within the boundaries of the Normandy–Picardy section of Emmaus. The adventure, which drew to an end in 1964, later recommenced. Paul remained at the helm and the group still functioned as a travelling Community, this time working their way down to the Loire region. Meanwhile, in 1962, UACE (Union of Friends and Companions of Emmaus) was officially declared a Not-for-Profit organisation. Over the course of the 1960s, two other organisations joined the family of Communities, youth camps and committees of Friends with no Community attached, and in 1966, UACE became a Federation in order to incorporate these new organisations.

These committees of Friends that had no Community attached were created after a travelling Community had visited the area (this was the case with Blois in 1973, Saint-Omer the following year, and Orsay). A visit from a youth camp would also spark the creation of such Communities, including Decazeville and Rodez in 1973, and Brive in

1978. In these Communities, a group of volunteers performed the same tasks as Companions (collecting, sorting and selling waste), but did so in their free time and without a Community of Companions behind them. With the exception of Fougères (1959) and Beauvais (1954), which were created in the wake of a visit from one of Normandy's travelling Communities, almost all of the long-lasting Communities were created in the 1970s. With no Community costs to be borne, the lion's share of the profits was used to fund initiatives in aid of those outside Emmaus. In France, homes for the mentally handicapped were opened (Beauvais), and homes for the elderly received financial support (Carmaux), as did local branches of *Secours catholique* and *Secours populaire*. Profits were also used to provide emergency assistance to those in distress and to promote development, through donations to Sister Emmanuelle in Cairo (Decazeville). Money was given to leper hospitals (Carmaux), clinics in remote areas (Chalon-sur-Saône), and sent to support civilians in conflict zones.

Faced with the increase in the number of Communities, committees and camp staff, in 1970 UACE, which had up until that point been a very informal organisation, decided to impose a minimum of structure. The headquarters were moved from Alençon to Ormes, near to Orléans, and three friends of Abbé Pierre – Roland Jeanniot, Roger Lacaze and Henri Pallière – brought the organisation back under control.[17] Pallière was appointed "key coordinator". Following his death in late 1972, he was replaced by Hervé Teule, treasurer (1972–3), secretary-general (1973–5), then president, while Paul became key coordinator.

This new structure satisfied the organisation's desire to function as a coherent whole. However, imposing this structure was far from easy, as Abbé Pierre and UACE behind him were deeply opposed to the changes on principle. Abbé Pierre was said to have often jokingly referred to what he called "the risk of vaticanisation", which he viewed as diametrically opposed to the spirit of the "catacombs". In spite of his misgivings, it was the Abbé himself who, in 1963, began to realise the need to properly organise the international,[18] and then the national, Movement. As an article published in a 1972 issue of *Faim et Soif* stated: "The organisation [sought] to preserve the spirit of dynamism, which imbued the organisation's beginnings, and to implement the minimum level of structure necessary to ensure our work could continue in the long term."[19] Structure was kept to a minimum in order to avoid risking the "gentrification" for which UCC was so heavily criticised, but the bare bones of structure were put in place to produce an organisation that functioned as a coherent whole and was "both solid and flexible". General Assemblies were held from 1973 onwards and a property association was set up to take charge of purchases and management.

However, Paul's departure from UACE as its founder and guiding light also caused the process of imposing structure on the organisation to gather pace. His far from conventional double life and his embezzling of funds,[20] which had been kept hidden for twenty years, finally emerged in a blaze of scandal in 1974 with the discovery of a mistress, a house and a sizeable jewellery collection. In 1975, Paul was finally forced to leave Emmaus. He was exiled abroad by Abbé Pierre for a brief period of time, and then returned, this time to fleece the Chartres branch of *Secours populaire*, before he was hunted down by Interpol... There is no doubt that Abbé Pierre had been aware of Paul's embezzlement and his double life for a long time, but Paul was an organisational genius and a charismatic leader, who kept alive the prophetic message and spirit of adventure of the early days, who brought more money to the organisation than he cost it, and who, last but not least, had carefully compiled a detailed file of information on the private life of the founder...

The second half of the 1970s was, it seems, the apogee of the process that gave the organisation its structure and returned the house to order. In 1978, a secretary was taken on and the organisation's headquarters moved to Charenton in Val-de-Marne, just southeast of Paris. Abbé Barral was also appointed as the new key coordinator. It was also in 1978 that UACE decided to properly organise the committees of Friends once and for all. These committees had hitherto been left entirely to their own devices and had no ties with the Movement. The issue had been raised repeatedly since 1975, in particular by Abbé Pierre. In a UACE meeting held on 5 September 1973, Abbé Pierre declared: "In continuing to use the Emmaus name, these committees risk throwing all our efforts off course."[21] He went on to state: "It is unbelievably foolish to leave in place under the Emmaus name, committees who are working on initiatives and handling big money without anyone keeping them in check."[22]

Furthermore, no one knew exactly how many of these committees there were. Some put the number "in the tens", others at "over one hundred". An inquiry eventually revealed that around thirty were properly up and running. However, it was impossible to incorporate them into UACE's framework – the organisation's statutes stipulated that votes had to be divided equally between leaders and Friends at the general assembly. Unable to join the UACE, they were granted independence, and on 8 June 1980, the CNAE (National Committee of Friends of Emmaus) held its constituent assembly as an independent body.

## A niggling concern: the poor quality of leaders

In terms of its structure, UACE's model differed greatly from that of UCC's. First, until the early 1970s, the notion of hierarchical management was rejected outright and leadership at national level was non-existent. The organisation was represented nationally by Paul alone – a moral authority who "[himself] received his powers from Abbé Pierre", like the king or the Pope from God. Secondly, each Community had only one leader – this structure made it far from easy to keep them in line. Finally, the leader could not be recruited from outside, but had to be a Companion who had ascended the ranks – this was the natural culmination of the Emmaus principle of "getting men back on their feet".

From then on, the poor quality of the leaders was a constant source of concern. The personal background of the promoted Companions and the fact that they had never had a partner or a family meant they were often unstable and "unbalanced".[23] In addition to the difficulties they experienced in trying to manage men who were themselves in difficulty, the organisation lost count of the number of leaders or assistants who made off with the takings or the wage money. However, opposed to the training programmes in place at UCC, UACE offered nothing more than informal, sporadic, "on-the-job" training sessions[24] and, as a way of putting would-be leaders through their paces, the men were offered gradual promotions. They went from Companion to assistant, to leader of a small travelling Community, before finally being appointed leader of an established Community.

In 1972, the chronic instability and weakness of the UACE system prompted the organisation to declare that no new Community would be given permission to open until the management was satisfied that a reliable leader was ready and able to take the reins. As a result, UACE was forced to follow in UCC's footsteps and recruit leaders from outside. However, while the lack of other viable solutions made this course of action necessary, it went against the original vision of the organisation and saw UACE reflect the UCC model that they so bitterly despised. In 1975, Abbé Pierre was still, in typically euphemistic fashion, accusing the practice of hiring paid employees as "not always being compatible with the desire to give of oneself freely and come to the aid of those suffering most." Recruiting leaders from outside also caused difficulties when it came to paying wages – the Companions who had been promoted only received a very small salary. In 1975, ten years after it had first been introduced, UACE finally adopted UCC's model and began work on centralising payments. In 1979, the first pay scale was put to the test.

By contrast, UCC's deputies' system was much more developed than that of UACE. A distinction was made between the "local deputy", who was a person rising up through the ranks, appointed by his leader and paid by the Community, and the "official deputy", who was experienced and moved between Communities, appointed by the national bodies and paid by the Federation.

## The travelling Communities or centrifugal development

While UACE could boast a wealth of diverse organisations, it had, as a result of its ideological choices, very few "fixed" Communities until 1970 (only Ormes, Bordeaux and Longjumeau). "Travelling Communities" were the lynchpin of the organisation's development.

Sending a travelling Community to an area involved a core group, set up in advance, who would scout out and prime an isolated location where no (Emmaus-type) organisations already existed. The local population would then be informed of the travelling Community's plans, waste-collection operations were organised, and then, if possible, a permanent UACE organisation would be established. These visits by travelling Communities also allowed the organisation to put men to the test by placing them in positions of responsibility, or to temporarily isolate problem Companions. Above all, they roused Companions' enthusiasm. As Laurent Desmard, who would go on to lead a UCC Community before being appointed Abbé Pierre's private secretary, remarked in an interview, "Paul le Roch in Brest had taken travelling Communities to Morlaix and Quimperlé [UCC]; people loved watching Communities being set up: a whole army of heroes descended on the area and performed magic. The same thing happened at UACE. The Companions liked to ensure that their time away was structured, but they did like to leave the Community, experience a change in routine and get away from the daily grind; to have the opportunity to surpass themselves. But they quickly needed to be back working in a structured environment – if not, they'd get out of their depth."

While at UCC, travelling Communities remained an atypical method of expanding the area covered by the organisation, for UACE they were a veritable way of life: the settled or "fixed" Community was viewed as gentrified, and only the nomadic way of life allowed the organisation to revive the adventure time and time again. In very pragmatic terms, another advantage of the travelling Communities was their low cost price: there were no permanent premises to maintain, the group could be flexible, and only a small number of Companions had to be provided for. Thus, at a time when the settled Communities were required to hand over 10%, then later 15%, of their monthly turnover to UACE, the travelling Communities were able to give as much as 75%.

At UACE, Paul and Jules were the heroes and heralds of the travelling Community. Having travelled the length and breadth of Normandy and created Communities in Amiens (1960), Caen (1961), Alençon (1964), Esteville (1965), Notre-Dame de Bondeville (1966) and Elbeuf (1967), Paul's next focus was youth camps. Every year these produced new Communities, including Orléans (1968), Bordeaux

(1969), Lyon (1970), Tours (1971), Cherbourg (1972) and Dijon (1973). Jules focused to a greater extent on creating organisations outside youth camps, and helping Communities in trouble to get back on their feet. He once said: "I don't like settled Communities, I'm a bohemian [...] When we were going around as a travelling Community, we stayed for six weeks, two or three months, tops. The Friends wanted a Community, so we stayed to set up a Community. Me, I'd go off again then to set up other ones. I've founded them in... I don't know where. I've been here, there and everywhere, I've spent a little bit of time in pretty much all of France [...] I'll tell you why I didn't like the settled Communities; because you'd get stuck in a rut. I've not got a problem with sticking to what you know and letting life just chug along nicely. Noticing something and having a problem with it are two different things. But I did notice that we were getting stuck in a rut; that we were becoming boring, comfortable, set in our ways. A travelling Community was a bit like a Community of missionaries, we stirred consciences, shook up the world..."[25]

And so, while UCC increasingly favoured settled Communities, UACE still had three or four travelling Communities in action until the mid-1970s: Dunkirk, Moulins et Châlons-sur-Marne until late 1971, Châlons-sur-Marne, Épernay, Moulins, Dunkirk and Dijon until early 1972, and Berck, Reims, Clamecy and La Palisse until late 1972, etc. The latter, Jules' pet project, finally closed its doors in 1978 in Puy-Guillaume, marking the end of an era. The 1970s was the decade in which UACE's travelling Communities gradually settled. It would appear that this triggered a sharp increase in the number of settled Communities – from three in 1970 to seventeen in 1979, which brought the total almost level with that of UCC, who had nineteen at the time.

## Youth camps: a breeding ground for activists

The other symbol of UACE's nomadic way of life was the youth camp, which was born in the summer of 1963 in Normandy within Paul's travelling Communities. This camp came into being by happy accident. After having worked as the coordinator of the Pontault-Combault Community (La Pépinière), following the 1954 appeal, Abbé Barral returned to work as a secondary-school teacher at Sainte-Croix in Neuilly. However, deeply affected by his work at Emmaus, he quickly requested that he be posted to work as the head of a technical high school in Yaoundé, Cameroon. Having remained in contact with former pupils who wished to help Africa, he recommended them to Paul in Normandy, as youngsters who could spend their holidays working in Yaoundé and in doing so, collect material to support Cameroon.[26]

After 1963, it was decided that camps would be held every two years, for two months during the summer, and they grew exponentially: there were around twenty participants in the camp at Le Havre in 1963, fifty in Rouen in 1964, 350 in La Manche in 1965, 750 in Le Val-de-Loire in 1966, 1,500 in the Sud-Ouest in 1968, and 3,800 in the Vallée du Rhône in 1970. In addition to spreading across the whole of France, a development which acted as a catalyst to the territorial expansion of UACE, these summer camps went international, with 4,000 participants in Italy in 1967 and 5,500 in Denmark in 1969. However, right at the beginning of the 1970s, UACE's youth-camp movement began to lose its momentum in France. This was a direct consequence of the parallel development of international camps and of Paul's departure in 1970. Generational changes were also undoubtedly responsible: the number of participants dropped to 2,700 in Languedoc in1973, to 2,100 in Gard in 1974, to 750 around Montluçon in 1975 and to less than 300 in Corrèze in 1978.

These camps were coordinated by experienced youngsters, who had volunteered with Emmaus for at least six months. Between Easter and the start of summer, they had to find a site, raise awareness of the camp among the local population, and come up with the broad brushstrokes of an action plan. Any young person over the age of eighteen who committed to working at the camp for at least twenty days could take part. The work was voluntary and participants had to meet their own transport costs, but they were provided with board and lodging at UACE's expense. Like the Companions, young volunteers had to abstain from alcohol while at the camp. Tasks were divided up amongst committees: the "sites and accommodation" committee was in charge of hunting down premises and available plots of land, while the "finance and management" committee was responsible for food, maintenance and the running of bric-à-brac operations. The "awareness-raising" committee liaised with the press, put up posters, handed out brochures and organised conferences, and the "waste-collection" committee sought out vans and divided up the site. Participants had an early start (7am or 7.30am, depending on the year) and, after a quick wash and breakfast, the day's tasks were shared out. The working day tended to run from 8.30am to midday and from 1.30pm to 6.30pm. Workers then enjoyed a shower, which was as deserved as it was necessary, an evening meal and the evening off. Lights out was at 10.30pm during the week and 11.30pm at weekends. They did the same work as the original Ragpickers: collecting old papers, rags, scrap metal and household goods; sorting and cleaning objects for bric-à-brac stalls; maintenance work; and domestic tasks. These camps generated a significant profit – as much as 2.4 million francs in one summer. The profits were divided equally between local social initiatives, the development of Communities in France and across the world, and aid for developing countries. By the time these camps packed up and left, they had often sown the seeds of new Communities or Committees of Friends.

Attending a youth camp provided a comprehensive crash course in activism at Emmaus. In the 1960s and 70s it was seen as *the* way to train the young in Emmaus ways. Lasting only one or two months, the camp was limited in what could be taught. It allowed the organisation to recruit and mould a whole generation of leaders: for UACE, these camps were a genuine breeding ground for activists – the place where tomorrow's leaders were born. Like Scout camps, these youth camps bound young people together as they took concrete action in aid of those in need. In the early 1970s, this generation of young hippies was, it would seem, a shock to the system for the considerably more bourgeois "Friends". In a supplement published in *Faim et Soif* it was noted:

> "[A] number of Friends were instinctively wary of the physical appearance of the first volunteers. They had beards, long hair, hippy-ish clothes, a dubious sense of personal hygiene, and a life on the open road had stripped them of any sense of urgency. They weren't what

> the majority had in mind as the ideal young volunteers for the international holiday camps that Abbé Pierre had founded. The more of that type of volunteer that arrived, the more that followed [...] There were a few short haircuts here and there, but these more often belonged to girls than to boys. But it was this meeting of two ways of life, two generations, two civilisations almost, that marked the start of an unforgettable experience for those who lived it and accepted it. Adults, whose lives tended to be settled, who had a secure job and were established members of the society in which they lived, agreed to work for young boys and girls who appeared to have no qualms whatsoever about rejecting any form of conformism, and not only where their wardrobe was concerned."[27]

In terms of the message they wished to convey, the camps did not perceive themselves as "a mere act of charity or a place where occasional generosity was displayed in response to a particular set of difficulties, but on the contrary, as an affirmation of justice and a place where goods were rightfully restored to those who had been stripped of their possessions."[28] The camps made it clear that their desire to remedy political, social and economic ills was at the heart of their work – a message that the often more conservative Friends were loath to accept. In an interview, Yves Godard said of the camps:

> "(They) only came into being because the town's residents, what we call the Committees of Friends, rallied together to take care of the logistics – because all the young people did was pass through. These were mostly middle-class people who were coming together to help Abbé Pierre more than anything else. When the two groups came together was when sparks really began to fly. There were the young people with a whole political discourse similar to that of Cohn-Bendit at the time, with grand statements, slogans and provocative remarks. They'd say 'poverty is political – we come here to work for the summer but we know we'll only ever solve the poverty problem through political action'; and then there was the local press and those middle-class people who'd build infrastructure and set up Committees of Friends, and they'd talk about that wonderful generation of young people who were organising holidays for the poor... As you can imagine, the two sides clashed bitterly – there were the most almighty arguments. We

(the young, long-term volunteers), we got the Friends on board so we'd have infrastructure, and at the same time we knew very well that the young ones would put a spanner in the works, and we were on the young ones' side..."

Finally, the archives appear to point to a development within the Movement that is difficult to interpret. In 1967, while the camps continued to grow and move beyond France's borders, becoming an international initiative, the organisation enthusiastically insisted how "far from the truth it is to state that the youth of today no longer understands and has lost the taste for sacrifice." However, by 1976, things had turned sour and in a meeting on 30 September of that year, one participant noted that the organisation was beginning to witness "a complete change in motivation among the young volunteers compared to ten years ago. They come searching for something, but they don't know what they want. They are lost, lacking direction. They are really, I think, the reflection of today's society." They no longer accept the term "leader" and agree to "coordinator" at a push; they no longer wish to receive "orders", but rather "explanations".[29] Was this remark justified within the context of a younger generation undergoing profound changes in the aftermath of May '68 and the questioning of all forms of authority? Was it a cynical remark made in reaction to the decline in the number of camps? Or was it a comment from the mouth of a young volunteer from the glory days, hankering after a bygone past whose view was inevitably subjective?

Whatever the answer may be, these camps, running from 1965 to 1975, marked a turning point in the history of UACE and in that of Emmaus more generally. They were the veritable building blocks and symbols of activism amongst teenagers and young adults and a way of breathing new life into an entire generation, just as conscientious objection had been some years before. The camps were also emblematic of the organisation's nomadic way of life, which was arduous but convivial and allowed them to travel the length and breadth of France to put up the Emmaus flag – a flag in which a whole generation continues to recognise itself today.

## Liberty, Fraternity and the Independents: the Internal Exit Strategy

According to the American economist Albert O. Hirschmann, there are three ways of resolving conflicts: exit, voice and loyalty. In other words, by either side leaving, taking the floor and speaking out or remaining loyal to those in power.[30] At Emmaus, activists had traditionally opted for an internal exit, either by distancing themselves physically from the Movement or by breaking away ideologically and creating an independent group. The attitude displayed by Paul, who left to revive the Emmaus adventure in 1956, was symptomatic of this way of dealing with conflicts. It was an attitude encouraged by Abbé Pierre himself who, rejecting monolithic forms of organisation and excessive structure, empathised with the more adventurous members who attempted to bring back the spirit of the early days in a way that suited them. Over the course of the 1970s, this exit strategy was put into practice once more when two new organisations splintered off from UACE: Liberty and Fraternity. At the same time, the Communities which rejected all forms of affiliation remained "independent".

### The Communities of the Nord département, Northern France

The majority of the independent Communities were located in the Nord-Pas-de-Calais region in Northern France. The first of these, Lille-Wambrechies, was founded in September 1954 by Jean Deroubaix, in a large, disused fort. Eugène Dubois, or "Gégène", as he was known, was the Community's first leader. He had been with Emmaus since the very beginning. The Community initially became a member of UCC, of which Jean Deroubaix was president (1959–61), then left in 1967 to become a totally non-affiliated Community. The second independent Community was founded in Quincy in 1957 – and then transferred to Raimbeaucourt. Then came Nieppe-Armentières, which opened as a Committee of Friends in 1964 and, at Abbé Pierre's suggestion, became a Community in 1972; Saint-Omer (1967) and Denain (1973), which transferred to Paillencourt a year later, also followed suit. Others were soon added to the list. A number of independent

Communities were also founded following a visit to the area by a travelling Community. One such example is Caen, which was founded in 1962 and later opted to become affiliated to the UCC in the 1980s. Some independent Communities also sprang up in eastern France. But the Nord département remained entirely unique within Emmaus, with a group of Communities that had stubbornly resisted any attempt made to give them structure, despite the fact they had a multitude of informal connections to the mother ship and felt a real sense of loyalty to the region.

Nevertheless, some attempts were made to unite these Communities and bring them into the fold. In November 1965, the Association of Companions of Hope was born, and brought together the various groups in the area surrounding the town of Douai in Northern France. Nevertheless, the name became increasingly inappropriate as all "hope" within the Association began to fade: in the early 1970s, members reported that "nothing is working any more", "everything is falling apart", the Association "[is] morally bankrupt", and the "Emmaus spirit is completely absent from daily tasks".[31] The two leaders were tearing strips out of each other, as much on account of personal differences as their opposing visions of the Association. Abbé Pierre was called in to rescue the situation and at the end of his visit emphasised "the urgent need to improve Communities' financial situation".[32] April 1973 then marked the birth of the International Union of Emmaus Communities. This was a cross-border union designed to bring together the isolated Communities in Germany, Belgium, and the Nord département and city of Grenoble in France. However, once again, the attempt proved unsuccessful.

For a long time, the groups in the Nord département were characterised by their tendency to choose quantity over quality – to the detriment of the latter – and by their perception of Communities as a quick fix rather than as a lasting solution to the problems faced by man and society. In the Communities led by Father Léon, the guiding principle was a simple one: "We needed to fill up all the rooms we could find, and then push back the walls of these rooms... We needed to keep taking people in. For as long as there were people needing help and places to put them, we'd keep taking them in."[33] These

Communities were rough and ready, and investment was rare. In the aftermath of a fire in 1974, the Nieppe-Armentières Community began to rebuild the premises, installed showers and bedrooms with central heating, and re-laid the roof. In a series of articles published in *Faim et Soif*, one member wrote: "On that level, we are proud of what we have achieved for these men. However, during last week's meeting of the board of directors, we all began to experience a deep-seated sense of unease... all that building work... all that money... of course there was the welfare of these men to consider, which was undoubtedly vital if we were to give them their lives back, but was improving their surroundings really our end goal?"[34] The following year, the Douai shelter threatened to close its doors, noting that "[t]he authorities find it difficult to accept the way in which we take people in. Given that we have always been short of money, we have never been able to comply with regulations; failing to comply with regulations has meant we have never been entitled to funding..."

Religion heavily influenced the organisation's work, and the anti-clericalism of certain leaders did not stop it from regularly calling upon local parishes for financial support. The Raimbeaucourt Community embarked upon group pilgrimages to Lourdes and published brochures closely resembling prayer books. Most significantly, the key figure of the Communities in the Nord département was Father Léon himself. Born in 1938 to a farming family in the Nord, he received his calling late in life. He was ordained in 1968 and became a curate in Cambrai. When in 1970 the Cambrai-Paillencourt Community was in need of someone to provide cover, he was snapped up and became its leader, despite the fact that he dreamed only of going to Africa. Then, in the early 1980s he created and managed the Béthune-Bruay Community. He would later become one of the key architects of the movement that saw the Nord département groups united behind the common goal of injecting a real sense of life into the region.

## Emmaus-Liberty or the four forms of liberation

Like a number of Emmaus organisations, Liberty was first and foremost the creation of one man. Born to a poor family on a small farm in Morbihan in 1920, Henri Bouriscaud entered the seminary at the age of eleven. He then went on to become a Redemptorist missionary, in order to seek out and assist society's most impoverished individuals. Throughout the 1950s he conducted regional missions. In 1954, Abbé Pierre's "example" inspired him to act and the Vatican II council opened up new avenues for him to explore. In 1965, he decided to become a worker-priest[35] and embarked upon an accelerated training programme for scaffolders. He went on to complete his qualification in Portugal, gaining practical experience on the construction sites manned by immigrant workforces. Upon his return to France, he refused to re-enter his old convent and, in late 1956, having been posted to work at the nearest chapel, he settled close to the Champigny slum (Val-de-Marne) with its large Portuguese population. He took his first steps into the world of trade unions and worked as an activist in the associations providing support to foreigners in the area. Evicted in 1969, he set up home at the Villiers fort, again in Val-de-Marne, where the majority of the population this time hailed from the Maghreb. Evicted once again in 1971, he found a house in Pontault-Combault and began working in a parks and gardens firm.

It was in February 1971, while working on the garden at the Plessis Community, that le Bouriscaud first met Abbé Pierre. He agreed to one week's work experience in the Beauvais travelling Community and then, having been completely won over by the Movement, he was called upon by the Abbé to become a fully-fledged member of the Emmaus team. With his superior's blessing, he entered Emmaus as a Companion in the Ormes Community [UACE], of which Jules was the leader. He was then asked by the Abbé to manage the operation that sent bottles of milk to Bangladesh. The operation's nerve centre was a disused chapel at 2 bis, Avenue de la Liberté, Charenton, which the Movement had bought up for next to nothing and used to store the goods.

And so, in mid-February 1972, Henri le Bouriscaud arrived in Charenton, anxious to get a Community off the ground as soon as possible. Premises were gradually made fit for purpose and then completed with the purchase of a building in Champigny. With no room to expand, the Charenton Community was forced to remain a very small one, with only four or five Companions. As a result, it functioned primarily as a place providing short-term accommodation, support and guidance. In spring 1973, the Community was named Emmaus-Liberty after the street in which it was located, but in the words of le Bouriscaud himself, "there was something more that made us give it this name, we were sure of it."[36] However, it was not until the late 1970s that this "something" they felt instinctively would take tangible form.

His desire to develop Emmaus' activities in the region prompted him to search for a site on which he could build a new Community. He signed the lease on an old run-down hunting lodge in Dreux, the home of a Redemptorist seminary. The three Companions who entered the Community in March 1976 soon became twelve – that biblical number making yet another appearance – and in 1977 a third Community opened its doors. It was located in Monéteau, near Auxerre, and run by a retired couple. 25 April 1977 is hailed as the date on which the Liberty organisation came into being as an official, constituted "family".[37] In 1978, the Alençon Community, which was created following a visit to the area by the travelling Communities of Normandy, came back into the fold. Lastly, in April 1981, Liberty founded its fifth Community in Berry-au-Bac, between Laon and Reims, in the Champagne-Ardennes region.

The creation of Emmaus-Liberty satisfied the desire of a maverick, politicised priest to form his own school of thought within the Emmaus Movement, but it was also an organisation with its own, unique approach. Unlike UCC and UACE, Liberty sought only to create small Communities (of ten to twenty Companions) and to reduce "the Family" to a small number of Communities (a maximum of six).[38] It differed again from UCC, but also from UACE, which was undergoing a gradual process of "gentrification", in the way it kept internal expenditure to a minimum in order to leave as much money as possible for initiatives in aid of those outside the organisation. These included housing migrant families and making financial contributions to development aid in Africa. The lack of legal structure was in line with the organisation's desire to maintain very flexible ties with Emmaus. Finally, in September 1979, this "something" that earned the organisation its federal name was given tangible form in the Manifesto, which enshrined the organisation's desire to help men free themselves from four different shackles: “alcohol, money, authoritarianism, and the paternalism of Friends”.

First was the need to free the men from money and its “corruptive powers”. Le Bouriscaud was “convinced that money [was] the root cause of all decadence.” He therefore underlined the need “to make being as frugal as possible a point of honour” along with not wasting a thing, given that any surplus resources were to be given to the poorest members of society. This detachment from money went hand in hand with a utopian vision of total equality within Communities, where there was no reward scale or even salaries, and where the leader had to work like any other Companion.

Secondly, the organisation wished to free members from the clutches of alcohol: out of solidarity with the addicts, the Liberty Communities followed the example set by UCC and to a lesser extent by UACE, and chose to operate a no-alcohol policy. They also decided, “out of friendship”, to come down hard on those who fell off the wagon. It should be noted that since the late 1950s, Henri le Bouriscaud had also been a member of *Vie libre*, a working-class movement which also placed the notion of freedom/liberation in its title. Furthermore, both the concept itself and the methods used to free people from alcohol appear to have been directly transposed, at least in part, from *Vie libre* onto Emmaus-Liberty.[39] Thirdly, the desire to provide freedom from “authoritarianism” stemmed from a problem that was as characteristic of “the 1968 years” as it was recurrent when new Communities were tried and tested. The organisation declared that there were to be no “leaders”, only “coordinators”.[40] Le Bouriscaud remarked, “indeed, if you’re not careful, it is only too easy to go from being in charge of things to being in charge of people” and “we are radically opposed to one man wielding power over the group”. Communities had to operate instead on the basis of co-management and mutual understanding. Lastly, liberation from the “paternalism” of Friends was seen by the volunteers as going hand in hand with liberation from authoritarianism. Here, the organisation’s target group was those quick to take unfair advantage of the bargains on offer at the bric-à-brac sales, or those who were seen as too picky and perpetually dissatisfied.

## Emmaus-Fraternity or the post-68 communitarian utopia

While the Fraternity "family" only officially came into existence in 1982, its slow gestation was profoundly rooted in the post-1968 context. For that reason, I will discuss the organisation in this part of the book. In the same way that Emmaus was the creation of Abbé Pierre, UACE of Paul, and Liberty of Henri le Bouriscaud, Fraternity was the brainchild of Yves Godard. Born in 1951 in les Deux-Sèvres, in the Poitou-Charentes region of western France, to a family of deeply Catholic farmers and a father who was a left-wing Christian activist, Godard was called to the priesthood very early on and entered boarding school at the age of seventeen. He would derive little pleasure from his studies and leave before having completed the final exams. Traumatised by the Biafra tragedy which played out in the media's glare he grew depressed, left school and discovered Emmaus in 1969 at the age of seventeen and a half during an Easter camp where Paul was in charge. In an interview, Godard declared: "What saved me was that they set me to work the day after I arrived. The day after I arrived I was standing in front of my pile of cardboard. And that, that's something I'd continue to defend a long time after the event, because what they did there was crucially important. They didn't give me any speeches, they didn't tell me 'you're too young'. Instead they said,'if you're here, you've got your reasons'."[41] Taken on as a young volunteer, he followed for a while the usual pattern of summer at camp and winter with the travelling Communities. In 1971 he met his wife at a summer camp and, in 1973, welcomed his first child into the world. The couple then decided to set up a permanent home and left for Poitiers to found "a long-term travelling Community" (three years). In 1977, the Community was declared as a settled Community.

Life as a volunteer in the Poitiers Community was marked by a style of communal living, which was both very intense and obligatory, and by deep religious fervour. Godard remarked that "in the Poitiers Community there was a sort of coming together of Companions who wished to get involved and the young people who had come in search of something to which they could commit for life. The religious side of things was fairly important in that group – there was a chapel and a service every morning and evening – but no one was under any obligation to get involved." It was also the only Community run by a couple, a couple with children at that, and the only Community that allowed couples to enter together as volunteers. Parents were in charge of their own children's upbringing, but were asked to hand over all of their family allowance to the Community who would then pay for anything the children needed. Fraternity also set great store by the principle of keeping Companions who were elderly and/or disabled within the Community, and of giving them an important place within it. Lastly, it was a Community that, wishing to foster equality, quickly refused to take on paid employees: "[I]n the early years, we were the paid employees of UACE because there was no other solution to the problems we faced. But we'd quickly ask to be taken off the payroll and become Companions with Companion status once more." UACE refused to make such an exception; Abbé Pierre initially attempted to stall proceedings but would later give the Communities' decision to break away "his blessing" and, in June 1982, Poitiers, La Roche-sur-Yon and Naintré came together and created Emmaus-Fraternity.

The group expanded at breakneck speed. Godard once said: "There were more and more of us all the time because I started to behave in a way that I'd come to understand some time later. I found that even if things were going well, even if everything was wonderful, for me that wasn't enough, and the young man who'd been taken in in 1969, he was still suffering. And so I'd find myself no longer able to turn away anyone who appeared on our doorstep. Things got to a point a few years later where there were 117 of us in the Poitiers Community. My wife had made it clear: when number one hundred arrived, she was off. But when the 117th Companion arrived, she still hadn't left. I started to lose it a bit, but I also began to realise that I was the one who agreed to take on new Companions every time."

New branches of the Poitiers Community began to spring up one after another, and allowed this growth to be absorbed: "The Poitiers Community first exploded in Poitiers. We'd gone from being one Community in one place to being one Community in several locations. After that, the Community began to explode in different towns and after that, things got really crazy. We really had to grit our teeth then – things got really tough: it was the same every time – the most capable, the strongest and most balanced members of our Community, or at least a number of them, left the mother ship to open a Community nearby, taking a few of the strongest Companions with them. It was like what happens with immigrants, it's always those who are, in one way or another, the strongest who leave, because you have to leave and start again from scratch, and nothing is easy. So for the ones that left, it was a new adventure while we were left with a gaping hole in our workforce. We'd start again, take on new members and three months later, another new team would leave. It was an extraordinarily fertile period, but one where the Community didn't have a penny and was constantly opening up new Communities." These Communities were indeed surviving on next to nothing. They experimented with new ways of bringing in money, namely growing crops and rearing livestock.

## 1968 and the Community Utopia

All the Federations and "families"[42] were also affected by 1968 fever and the renewed enthusiasm for Community utopias. However, each managed these new phenomena in their own, unique way.

### Liberty and Fraternity – the Community as a post-68 Christian and political utopia

Liberty and Fraternity are the two groups that best fit within the post-1968 context of forms of action whose aim was to uphold utopian ideals, defy authority, and break the mould.[43] Espousing traditional Emmaus principles and spreading the period's renewed enthusiasm for Community life as a way of experiencing the joy of being together and satisfying the desire to campaign differently,[44] these organisations were political, religious and social, and these three dimensions of their work were inextricably linked.

First, the social dimension: unlike the first generation of Emmaus Communities, this new wave, that sought to foster total equality, developed rules, which declared that living together in harmony was to replace any form of authoritarian regime. Fully in line with the spirit of the time, this model emerged as markedly different from that of the first Christian Communities, and from the traditional Emmaus model. It also differed from the famous Community of Le Dauphiné, which was founded by Marcel Barbu in 1940 to make watch-cases and served as inspiration for Father Lebret.[45] All of these models closely mirrored those which structure families – they were strictly hierarchical.

Religion also ran deep in the veins of these organisations, which openly affirmed their Christian identity. This Christian identity was in no way concealed at either UCC or UACE, but it was brandished as a badge of honour at Fraternity, where a quick read of the internal press throws up an abundance of terms with religious connotations ("hope", "witness", "love", etc.) and where daily Mass was part and parcel of Community life. Religion was also present at Liberty, although to a lesser extent: founded by a priest, the notion of "liberation" was captured within the very title of the organisation, and was also a reference to the South American theologies of the same name.[46]

Lastly, the political dimension: despite the fact that politics and to an even greater extent partisanship were taboo within both UCC and UACE, both Liberty and Fraternity actively sought to be both political and partisan. This was a stance adopted against the backdrop of two social phenomena which were emerging in parallel: the excessive growth of politics during and in the aftermath of May '68 on the one hand,[47] and the Christian Community's gradual reacceptance of all things political on the other. This change came about following a letter from Paul VI to Cardinal Roy, which led to bishops officially acknowledging in 1972 that Christians came from across the political spectrum and that socialism and the Christian faith fit hand in glove.[48] Politics at Liberty were shaped by the personal convictions of the founder and focused on "liberating mankind from the increasing number of tyrannical forces to which it is subjected [... and] the many forms of servitude which it is forced to endure." The organisation looked to "change lives" and embark upon a "non-violent revolution" to combat all forms of servitude.[49] At Fraternity, "the way in which people were taken in and helped each other, the way people lived and worked together, the way they stood shoulder to shoulder with those in need, became *a political alternative and fuelled people's desire to rise up and create another world.*"[50]

## UCC and the fall-out from May '68

However, "May '68 fever" and the new spirit of community did not bypass the "old" Federations. They too were affected by the arrival of a new generation of leaders who saw in Emmaus a place to perfect or adapt the utopian ideals of the day. Laurent Desmardre stated in an interview that "there was a prevailing trend of returning to the land, returning to a simpler life, to Community life and a desire to return to the experiments of 1968–70, hippies and all that. At that time, I had a boyfriend who was older than me – he was about thirty and I was twenty. He'd studied this concept of returning to the land and bought a farm in the Ardèche. I'd been blown away by what he was studying – all that stuff about returning to the land, Community life – all that really interested me. I went with him. But I hadn't realised that I was a city-dweller at heart – the countryside bored me and after six months, I couldn't take any more. But he had a copy of the book about the Emmaus Ragpickers, and I read it. I'd heard my father talk about Abbé Pierre one day when we had to move house [...] I came across all that again in the book, it all seemed really interesting and I said to myself 'that's what I want to do'."[51]

And so, from 1972–3 onwards, UCC was rocked to the core by a series of crises, which were the result of the clash between two models. The new generation of leaders, for whom the value of work was not such a fundamental belief, who had an acute political conscience, and who were deeply concerned with issues relating to how people lived their lives, found themselves coming into conflict with the visions and beliefs of the organisation's stalwarts. At the same time, their desire to see groups splinter off and go it alone went against the wish of the organisation's new president who aspired, on the contrary, to make UCC "a proper movement" with "working methods worthy of a political party or union".[52]

Two significant conflicts pitted UCC against the Strasbourg Community on the one hand (1973–4), and against the Limoges Community (1974–5) on the other. In the case of Strasbourg, the conflict centred on ways of life within Communities and involved a local leader whom Hervé le Ru described as "more an eco-warrior of the day, into the 'alternative' lifestyle and very much influenced by May '68 [...] This leader imposed his own choices on the rest of the Community, deciding what they should eat and how they should live. As we saw it, that went against our belief that Companions and their own personal choices should be respected."[53] The Federation argued that there was a risk that this "would see the movement evolve into a series of sectarian groups."[54] The leader in question was dismissed but rehired almost immediately by his local committee, which was then cut off from UCC and became an independent Community once more. As far as Limoges was concerned, the issue at the heart of the conflict appeared to be more the place given to work. Indeed, the new generation who arrived at the organisation during 1972–3 displayed a different relationship to politics and economics. They looked to the Communities more for a way of life that would constitute an alternative to that offered by the capitalist, consumer society. The more established members of the organisation viewed this attitude as "[a way of claiming] the right to do nothing. At that time, you could feel it in the air [...] The new lot were saying 'why collect five lots of rubbish if three are enough?...' They were questioning the very economy of these Communities, which was based on the work of Companions; and that sparked huge tension with all the organisation's old pioneers."[55] Those attached to "the right to do nothing" were ultimately ejected *manu militari*.

The issue of the relationship to politics, which was a key area of concern for Liberty and Fraternity, only slowly began to capture the interest of those at UCC. It was first tackled at regional level, when the question was asked: "can a Friend of Emmaus be socially or politically neutral? There were a number of things which suggested that such neutrality was not possible. The very existence of the Community, which was in itself a disavowal of all that kept man down, and our membership of this Community involved both thinking and acting in line with those who were fighting for the liberation of mankind and developing a better understanding of the causes of servitude (profit, exploitation, discrimination, housing conditions, alcoholism).

Ignoring these factors or remaining indifferent (and therefore neutral) towards them would mean our action would only ever be limited and paternalistic, and would see the Community trapped in a ghetto. If we remained neutral, we could even be accused of being complicit in this servitude. The organisation's Friends occupy a privileged place in this fight against its causes."[56] Nevertheless, political neutrality remained a dogma that had to be reconciled with the militant activism of a growing number of Friends. A compromise was found with the "choice of a movement of a militant nature",[57] which spoke out against the causes of servitude and took a definitive stance on the problems in question without coming across as quasi-partisan. In reality, the activists and volunteers of UCC seemed to be of two very different persuasions: some were very close to the "second left" and the Unified Socialist Party (PSU), while others appeared conversely to identify with the traditional right, attracted to the Movement more by the charitable aspect of its work.

## An All-Consuming Commitment

The poor enforcement of rules and regulations, the process of trial and error used to turn the organisation into a professional outfit, and the constant reinvention of the Emmaus model made it possible to call in individuals who were motivated but ill-qualified and who then learnt the ropes and built up the organisation on the job. "For those of us who'd been there from the early days, our time was up. But we'd experienced something extraordinary, which allowed us to both set up our own Communities and to move on to the next level, because there was nothing there. We'd built everything and now we needed to build again."[58]

Generally speaking, being a Community leader at Emmaus until the early 1980s, at a time when Abbé Pierre's Movement had once again faded into obscurity, meant coming up with alternative, militant forms of action. Working as a Community leader was, for some, nothing more than a hiatus, a temporary change of direction, but nevertheless it was an all-consuming experience. Laurent Desmard has remarked: "When it was me and Raymond [Étienne] working in a Community, we worked all the time and we were always together. There was the Community of Mont-sur-Meurthe, the Metz Community and there was only the two of us, so we had to go. And on top of all that we had to do Emmaus France, sort out this or that... it never stopped. We gave every ounce of our energy to the job."[59] The small number of leaders also meant that interpersonal relationships and friendship occupied a central place within the organisation. For both of these reasons, it is entirely justified to conclude that working within the team at that time was an incredibly intense experience.

UCC archives available reveal another factor that made working with Emmaus an increasingly all-consuming commitment: a more rigid structure was gradually imposed upon the Federations' managerial bodies. Indeed, the increase in the number of Communities led to increased numbers of counsellors, while developments at Federation level (the recruitment of leaders and the decision to make them paid employees, an internal press, the regionalisation of the organisation, training, etc.) caused the workload to increase significantly. As a result, a system of internal "commissions" was introduced in late 1972. Meetings were spread over the weekend, with Saturday afternoons set aside for commission work and Sundays given over to plenary sessions. In 1973 alone, thirteen *ad hoc* committees held meetings including the "national meeting", "provisional budgets", "press" and "presidents-employees" commissions. From 1974–5 onwards, this system became the rule. The committees' opinions tended to have the value of official decisions and they developed an increasing number of their own, independent initiatives (surveys or more informal attempts to gather information, analysis of working practices, and the diagnosis of problems). If we add to this the development of specific training programmes for leaders, presidents and treasurers, it quickly becomes clear just how marked the increase in time spent in meetings was, particularly at weekends.

At UACE, no such system of commissions existed, but the organisation did experience the same process of expansion. This expansion was even more apparent given that the Federation grew out of nothing – the first general assembly was held only in 1970. In 1972, the organisation's boards and bureaus were joined by Community leader meetings. Meetings which brought together both leaders and Friends later followed. At the same time, minutes became more comprehensive documents. This was a sign of the growth in activity, but also of an increasing desire to circulate information about their work and to ensure records were kept.

This growth in activity at Federation level played a crucial role in making involvement with the Movement an increasingly intense commitment – both in terms of working relationships and the time devoted to Emmaus. Commitment to the Movement was even more all-consuming given that the prevailing uniformity of Emmaus' work at the time served, if not to produce cohesion, then at least relative consistency. Indeed at UCC, the average age remained relatively stable, fluctuating between forty-two and just over forty-six; the youngest members were around thirty years of age and the oldest no more than sixty-seven. There was almost nobody in retirement. At the same time, the organisation witnessed a decrease in the socio-professional standing of its members. In the 1950s and 60s, UCC Friends were industrialists or engineers. In the 1970s, they were manual workers even though there were still a handful of executives among them. The last defining feature of the social profile of the Federation's bodies was its feminisation: reading the available lists of names, it would appear that until the 1970s, there was not a single woman on the board of directors. However, in1976 five of the board's eighteen members were women, and in 1978 there were three. While this feminisation remained moderate, the process was nevertheless well under way; the women who arrived on the board were, for the most part, social workers (paid members of staff) or manual workers (volunteers).

If the previous era was the one which sealed the first major divisions within the organisation, this was the era that formalised and multiplied them. The world of Emmaus Communities grew bitterly divided, but the animosity was sometimes so strong that rather than trading insults, groups would remain entirely unaware of each other's activities: it was quite simply inconceivable that UCC and UACE would sit down and talk. These internal divisions were even encouraged by Abbé Pierre who, after having given Paul's plan to create the travelling Communities of Normandy his blessing, did the same again to

Henri le Bouriscaud with Liberty and Yves Godard with Fraternity. At the same time, he continued to pay regular visits to the groups in the Nord département, when he was asked to do so. As a result, the organisational model was never set in stone. It continued to perpetuate while constantly reinventing itself, adapting to the location, times and leadership in place.

At the same time, the "tripod" caused the centre of gravity to change. While in the beginning Friends were obliged to compensate for the poor quality of leaders with their own reliability and strength, these leaders, with an increasing number of qualifications to their names, gradually became the anchor of the organisation, whether they were social worker professionals recruited from outside (UCC), leaders who had been subject to stricter surveillance as they rose up through the ranks (UACE), or leaders chosen from among the most solid and reliable activists (Fraternity).

In conclusion, one of the major characteristics of the period was the birth of a new generation within Emmaus. Politics cemented its place within the Movement, the religious element began to reinvent itself and the Federations adapted to the changes, each in their own, individual way. From this point on, two generations of organisation coexisted – the Federations of the 1950s and 60s, and the Families of the 70s. However, within the organisations themselves, two generations of leaders also lived side by side. This coexistence sparked considerable tension and saw the Movement's early model called into question.

# *Chapter 6* / EMMAUS COMPANIONS OF THE "TRENTE GLORIEUSES" (1945–1975)

*"Some of them had lost everything. At Emmaus, they got it all back: work, the safety of a roof over their heads, a bed, a place at the table, the warmth that comes with being known and recognised, friendship and in helping others, they regained their self-respect. Sometimes, they found love."*[1]

Almost all of the Companions were broken men; some were more seriously and permanently fractured than others. For many, war had left its mark – the Second World War, the wars in Indochina and Algeria – and former legionnaires were found in every Community. Others, or the same ones, had been devastated by the death or illness of a loved one, the breakdown of a relationship, or homelessness. Many had already spent time behind bars. However, one of the fundamental rules of Emmaus meant that no one could be forced to reveal their past: "No one of our number shall be judged using any yardstick other than his value as a man in the here and now, whatever his background, his past and his opinions."[2] In the words of Abbé Pierre, Emmaus sought to become "an extraordinary mental health clinic where the staff were recruited from among the sick,"[3] where the broken man, through his work and Community life, became the saviour of others and, consequently, of himself.

Despite all this, a Community at that time was first and foremost a place Companions came to by default, a place of shame. In an interview, Laurent Desmard recalled: "I arrived at UCC and said: 'I want to volunteer in a Community.' [The woman at reception] stared at me, her eyes wide open – that just didn't happen: she only ever met Companions who were ashamed of coming to Emmaus. Because although Abbé Pierre had for a while, throughout the catacomb period, galvanised the masses into action, from 1965 right through to about the 1990s, coming to Emmaus was regarded as something to be ashamed of. We were in the middle of the *Trente Glorieuses*, so there was plenty of work, and the people who came to our Communities didn't have a job, they'd been cut off from society. And if they didn't have a job, it wasn't because there was a lack of available work – it was because they were incapable of working. For those reasons alone, a large number of the lorries owned by Communities didn't feature the Emmaus name [...] One day, I went to the local café with two Companions, just down the road from the Brest Community, and the guy who worked there said to me, 'Where've you come from?' So I said, 'I'm from the Emmaus Community.' My two colleagues just sat there and didn't say a word. Once we were outside the bistro, one of them said to me, 'Next time you say we're from Emmaus, I'll punch your lights out.'"

Having considered the Communities from an ideological perspective and from the top down, it would be useful to change focus and examine them from the bottom up, in order to appreciate them as places where people lived, worked and supported each other, as well as to understand in sociological terms one aspect of the exclusion suffered during the *Trente Glorieuses*. Indeed, despite their varied individual profiles, the Companions represented only one part of the poverty and insecurity of these years of prosperity, given that by definition the Communities attracted only a certain type of profile. The vast majority of Companions were men, already marginalised, but who agreed, either permanently or temporarily, to live as part of a group, work and remain celibate. Anyone knocking at Emmaus' door was making a specific choice – they were not choosing a homeless hostel, the street, a B&B or a slum, but something else. For all that, appreciating the extent to which Emmaus Communities have, over time, been able to come up with responses adapted to Companions' problems is an integral part of understanding the history of poverty and the fight against exclusion.

## The Profile of Community Members

Communities were frequently forced to ask themselves questions of a historical nature in order to appropriately refocus their efforts: How is the profile of an average Community member changing? Are there more or fewer young people in Communities than before? What about elderly Companions? Or people living a very precarious existence, with no professional qualifications? Aside from common perceptions, which are often entirely inaccurate or at least only partly true, a number of official sources of information can be used. The main one is the major survey carried out by two Parisian sociologists, Sorbonne Professor Gilbert Murry and his assistant Nicole Carlier. The study was based on UCC's central records (now missing) for the period running from 1 January 1964 to 1 April 1965, containing information on each of the 1,460 people who were Community members at the time.[4] This chapter will also be based on the fairly comprehensive figures from UACE Communities in the mid-1970s. It will no doubt be said that given that these two sets of figures do not come from the same Federation, they cannot be reliably compared. However, studies conducted since the 1980s show that Companions travelled across France and that, while they could be sent by one Community to another "sister" Community, in reality they moved fairly freely between them and were naturally disposed to care little about the ideological differences between Federations. Each local organisation remained first and foremost an Emmaus Community characterised to a much greater extent by its location, size or the personality of its leader than by the particular Federation to which it belonged.

## Arriving and leaving

In the years 1964–5, the average age of a UCC Companion was 41–42. The age curve is bell-shaped, with the majority of Companions falling into the 35–39 and 40–44 age brackets (each group accounted for 16.5% of all Community residents); the line rises as adult age increases (5.7% below 25 years of age, 9.5% aged 25–29, 14% aged 30–34); and falls with old age (23.7% aged 45–54, 12.3% aged 55–64, 1.8% 65 years of age and over). This drop can be explained by the fact that often in poor health and the grip of alcoholism, Companions did not survive into old age. The rare few who reached retirement could go into the Esteville home (UACE) but would choose, more often than not, to remain in a Community. Murry and Carlier believe that judging by the frequency of their stays in hospital, Community members could be said to reach "old age" at around 45. Figures from the

Cernay Community (1955–60), which are broken down into different age brackets, reveal a slightly higher average, but the age curve is again bell-shaped: 2% aged 15–20, 17% aged 21–30, 24% aged 31–40, 23% aged 51–60 and 7% aged 61–70.[5]

A graph of the age at which Companions first entered a Community produces the same curved line, but the two are not entirely in sync: 9.4% arrived before the age of 25, 12.4% aged 25–29, 33.6% aged 30–39, 36% aged 40–54 and 8% aged 55–64. 0.7% of Companions entered a Community for the first time after the age of 65. The disparity between these figures and those relating to the age of Community members points to a high departure rate among the youngest members. These figures also clearly demonstrate that only a small minority looked to solve their problems by entering a Community late in life.

The average Companion was a person forever on the move. Even among those who returned to a Community several times, stays were often short-lived: Association Emmaus has described Communities as "a permanent place of transit for a certain number of men who become regulars."[6] There was also a tendency to switch between different Communities: 40% of those who stayed for a second time tried out a second Community, 20% of those who enjoyed a third stay tested out a third Community, 10% of those who decided to stay for a fourth time experimented with a fourth, and so on. In total, 13% of the Companions who had enjoyed eight or more stays in a Community had stayed in the same one, 9% had divided their time between two different Communities, 11% between three, 28% between four or five, and 38% had been to six or more Communities. These Companions either actively looked to pursue a nomadic existence or were forced to do so having broken Community rules and therefore unable to return. Some simply believed that the grass was always greener on the other side and so constantly looked elsewhere. Whatever the case, this nomadic way of life was as much a demand as an offer at Emmaus, being as it was an organisation with many different Communities scattered across the length and breadth of France.

These figures also convey a wide range of different attitudes to Communities among Companions: some were looking for a place to settle, others a place of transit. Association Emmaus once noted, "If we look at the men in a Community on a given day in the year, we see that a significant proportion of them are Companions who have been in a Community for a long time. However, if we look at all the men together who stayed in a Community during a given period of the year, the proportion of those who stayed for a long time is significantly smaller."[7]

The more stays a person undertook within a Community, and/or the older he was, and/or the longer the first stay had been, the longer the subsequent stays became. Those under the age of 30 stayed for only short periods of time (61% stayed for less than four months, compared to 29% of those over the age of 55) and vice versa (14% of those under 30 stayed for more than a year, compared to 43% of those over the age of 55). Furthermore, the longer the first stay was, the more often it was followed by further, frequent attempts at life in a Community. To a certain extent, adaptation to Community life had to take place from the very beginning if the experience was to last and improve. "If, instead, a man felt his first attempt at Community living had been so unsuccessful that he left again after only a short time, the chances of him later returning and staying put were very slim."[8]

## The social profile and psychological state of an Emmaus Companion

Data relating to the social profile of Emmaus Companions in the mid-1960s are also available. On entry into a Community the Companion declared a profession (which could just as easily be the job last held, or the profession for which he had originally been trained, as it could one of the trades mastered during a professional life on the move, or the job he dreamed of getting. Figures show that 30% were manual labourers (39% in Cernay from 1955–60) and 30% skilled labourers. 50% of this group worked in construction (but only 10% of skilled workers in Cernay were in construction). 6.3% of entrants declared themselves to be craftsmen or tradesmen (13% in Cernay), 6.4% had worked as chefs or in hospitality (7% in Cernay), 8.5% had worked as a heavy-goods vehicle driver (10% in Cernay), 3% had been office workers, and 5% had held non-manual posts, sometimes of a high socio-professional standing (legal clerks, translators, etc.). In the rural Community of Cernay, a further 10% were agricultural labourers. Many Companions had no official profession, declaring jobs which were either very unstable (lorry driver, waiter, etc.), or on the contrary, jobs which forced people to live and work in a very structured environment (former soldiers or legionnaires).

Looking at the names given by Companions when asked who was to be contacted in the event of an accident reveals that more than a third had no close relationships: 38% did not put a name forward. Of the others, 36% gave their father or mother, 23% a brother or sister, 14% another relative, 14% a friend, 4% an organisation (welfare authority, hospice, etc.), 5% their wife, and 4% their child. According to data on the marital status of Companions in Cernay, between 1955 and 1960, 74% were single, 19% divorced,[9] 5% widowed, 1% married and 1% separated.

Lastly, the statistics reveal that 28% of Companions came from western France, 20% from the north, 20% from the Paris region, and 15% from the east of the country. However, these statistics are only indicative, and largely specific to UCC, as they reflect the geographical distribution of UCC Communities (the organisation had strongholds in the Paris region, Alsace and Brittany). Nevertheless, while in these regions Communities attracted a large number of locals, conversely there were cases where the existence of local Communities had only a negligible impact on the number of Companions attracted from the surrounding area (Bouches-du-Rhône, Gard, Alpes-Maritimes and Sarthe): the majority of those who entered the southern Communities hailed from all over France, while Companions in the Sarthe Communities were mainly native to the region.

It also becomes apparent when analysing the statistics that the larger the town, the lower the turnover and so the more stable the workforce was. And yet the Communities located in major towns and cities tended to have a larger workforce, which contradicted the theory often put forward by the organisation; that a small Community in a quiet area encouraged stability. Indeed, Association Emmaus once declared: “It can be argued that the large Communities, when located in the largest cities, act more as places providing temporary refuge from the more hostile outside world. They become places where men either stay for longer or places they leave never to return. The fact that Community members are less inclined to come and go encourages newcomers to stay for longer periods of time. This is especially true given that new members come to the Community from all over France, that they've already spent their life on the road, and that they no longer feel at home in their native region. By contrast, Communities in the smaller towns, and generally speaking when they are small themselves, tend to function more as places which men simply pass through and to which they often return."[10] It should also be added that a Community in a larger city enjoyed a greater degree of anonymity that one located in a small town. This served to lift the shame associated with being a Companion and further promoted stability.

The majority of Community members suffered serious mental health problems. This was clearly highlighted by a study by psychiatrist Dr Geier conducted in 1963 at UCC's request. The study examined 500 Community members and had the additional advantage of presenting a different classification, based on the age of Companions.

The young Companions interviewed (aged 22–30) were often suffering from progressive neurosis and had arrived at Emmaus for that very reason. It was particularly difficult to treat these individuals within the Emmaus organisation ("all we can do is to limit the damage") and their chances of being reintegrated into society were minimal. They often returned to Communities on several occasions and stayed only briefly. They were incapable of recovering independently and had never had personal relationships, a family, or professional ties. It appears that, as a result, the road to adulthood was very rocky indeed. The study reveals an abnormally high frequency of hospital stays, but the reasons behind them are unknown. Fully-fledged adults (30–45 years old) were often suffering from alcohol addiction on arrival at Emmaus. They did not adapt to Community life straight away and stayed a number of times, switching between Communities. For these people, this was a difficult period – one where they accepted failure and a new form of dependency in exchange for financial security. Finally, the older Companions (over 45 years of age) were "weak characters [...] who, having been dealt a series of tough blows, were finally ground down by the terrifying machine that is today's society [*sic*]". The Community proved to be well adapted to these individuals' needs, providing them once more with a social and protective environment – a refuge that became a permanent way of life.

Besides mental fragility, afflictions common to all those interviewed were panic and anxiety. Community members sought to overcome these difficulties through intense work, which stopped them from thinking and looking back, and/or through Community life, alcoholism or regression to childhood (accepting the authority of the Community leader). The Community was a particularly suitable environment when the fragile individual was seeking security and agreed to accept authority.

## The Community, a Place of Work

No two Communities were alike. Besides the fact that each Community operated differently depending on the Federation to which it belonged, the form which Community life took depended on many factors: the personality of the leader and friends, whether or not it was close to the town, the number of Companions and their profile... Nevertheless, each Community was built on a certain number of basic principles. The Community was a place where people both lived and worked, and therefore a place that Companions would leave only occasionally. Initially, the places where Companions lived and worked within a Community merged into one. However, from 1964 onwards UCC committed to systematically separating the two, first by dividing up the time in the day. The place where goods were sold was closed in the morning to allow Companions time to collect, sort and deliver items. UCC then sought to physically separate "work" from "home" by recommending that a specific plot of land be set aside for the sale of objects. This would ensure that Companions enjoyed a certain degree of privacy when in their living quarters.

### Work at the heart of the Communities

The Community was first and foremost a place of work. This was true from an economic perspective in that collecting unwanted items and sifting through rubbish dumps for goods to sell constituted the main source of income. It was also true from an ideological point of view because it was believed that work "[got] men back on their feet". The majority of Communities thus displayed a placard with one of two phrases written across it. These phrases enacted the second rule of Emmaus: "You are not in a refuge here. We stand on our own two feet. We work. We earn our crust by helping others less fortunate than ourselves."/"Never will we accept that our survival depends on anything other than our work."

The central importance of work was explained to the Companion upon his arrival, and allowed Communities to declare themselves the antithesis of charity. Abbé Pierre explained how "from the moment he arrives on our doorstep, the newcomer must feel welcomed as a friend. The leader must show him around the Community, explain the role of the Community to him and make it clear what is expected of him. Indeed, it is vital that from the very beginning he appreciates that he is not entering a homeless shelter but that here, we need him, with his strengths, his skills and, above all, his good will and his friendship, so that together all members of the Community can do more to help those living in deprivation."[11]

Work began with tours around the local area to collect unwanted goods (these were carried out by the drivers and the porters, i.e. the removal men) and items collected were supplemented by donations that homeowners brought into the Community. Bernard Eidenschenk recalled: "At the beginning, we rarely received telephone calls asking us to go and take items away. For a time, the priest of the parish would announce at Mass on a Sunday morning that the Emmaus lorry was coming round, which made it easier for us to collect unwanted goods. We didn't set days or times for collecting these items, because there'd always be someone at the house." For a long time, one of the main difficulties Emmaus experienced was "finding people who could drive heavy-goods vehicles. There were very few of them. There were even fewer who were teetotal."[12]

The goods collected were then sent to a number of different sorting workshops (clothes, books, knick-knacks) and, if necessary, to workshops where they were repaired (electronic goods, domestic appliances, wooden furniture, chairs that needed the straw seat replacing). Sorting was an operation where careful attention to detail and a delicate touch paid dividends. Describing the work in 1971, Roubaix wrote: "Companions needed to know how to separate what was immediately useful from what could be sold or given away. They also needed to be able to distinguish between six different qualities of paper and two of cardboard. It was delicate, but dusty work. Items that were useless to some were turned into items others could use [...] Non-ferrous metals and scrap metals were treated in a similar way. The work required equal attention to detail, because as with paper items, the price offered by the wholesalers depended on how thoroughly the goods had been sorted."[13] "Any newcomer was systematically assigned to paper-sorting: it was a simple, easy job that involved working in a team."[14] Finally, in the last stage of the process, the goods were sold in the Community shop.

Upon arrival, each Companion was assigned to a particular task, which could also be a job within the Community itself (cooking, cleaning or laundry). However, no job was ever assigned on a permanent basis. Instead, tasks were constantly reassigned as some Companions left and others began to settle. Certain tasks were particularly coveted. These included jobs that involved touring the local area on the lookout for unwanted goods (driver and porter), as it allowed Companions to escape the Community and enjoy contact with the outside world. These jobs also provided Companions with the opportunity to earn the occasional tip, which did not always find its way to the Community pot, and to drop into the local bar, away from prying eyes... Jobs were also divided up according to the skills of each individual Companion, some absolutely invaluable to the smooth running of the Community.

In return for their work, Companions received a weekly allowance. This comprised a lump sum which was paid into his bank account to cover any big purchases or for use after he left the Community, and a small amount of pocket money. This was handed out on Sundays, first after Mass, then at breakfast or lunch. Each Community was free to decide how much of the allowance was to be handed out as pocket money and how much was to be set aside. In addition to this, Companions were provided with free board and lodging and had long received a generous supply of cigarettes (a minimum of two or three packets a week, sometimes four or five). As a result, the amount of "pocket money" (as it was somewhat childishly known) given to the Companions was small and for a long time, the Federations paid little attention to the matter. For Abbé Pierre, the sum had to remain symbolic in order to ensure that as much money as possible was available for initiatives outside the Community and not to encourage people to stay at Emmaus because it was a financially attractive option. It was also often believed that increasing pocket money served only to increase Companions' expenditure on alcohol. At UCC, the sum remained unchanged between 1960 and 1968 (ten francs a week),[15] and increased only slightly between 1968 and 1973. However, from 1973 onwards, the amount of pocket money given to Companions increased dramatically (seventy francs a week in 1980),[16] the raise counterbalanced at least in part by the increased cost of living. The same thing happened at UACE where the allowance, which was still ten francs in 1972, rose to sixty francs by 1979. In addition, both Federations provided an allowance to be used specifically for holidays.

## An economy based on collecting waste

Since 1952, Companions had worked by recovering unwanted items. In a market where there was little competition, Communities earned a comfortable living, especially since they were not taxed, benefited from reduced fiscal charges, had minimal management costs and no salaries to pay. Emmaus operated outside the rules of the market, with no concern for either profit or performance and was guided instead by a powerful social ethos. The concept of service replaced that of profit in full measure.

Despite the fact that Communities in the Paris region conducted a huge number of waste-collection operations outside the capital, Companions were sometimes forced to "go that extra mile",[17] comb vast areas of land and constantly raise local residents' awareness of their activities. As a result, claiming a "waste-collection zone", which offered attractive spoils, was crucial to each Community's success. As Jacques Loch noted in an interview:

> "More than half of the conflicts in the history of Emmaus were linked to the waste-collection zones. In their heyday, one Community would not tolerate another turning up and taking away its crust or the crust it was scared of losing. Today, that's not the way we think at all because for the most part we've got more work than we can handle. But the history of Emmaus is peppered with stories of Communities encroaching on another's territory if there were valuable items to be had, or sending colleagues to a place where they knew there was nothing worth collecting. That was fairly common. If it was too far away or the item in question was an old straw mattress on the fifth floor of a building with no lift, Companions would sometimes pass it on to another Companion, or put the collection date back three weeks... But of course, getting your hands on the good stuff meant collecting as quickly as possible, and moving outside your zone! Of course, what shouldn't be hidden either is that throughout Emmaus' history, all Communities had an unmarked lorry. Tradition dictated that we were all meant to have lorries with 'Emmaus' on the side, but often Communities had an unmarked lorry quite simply so they could enter another's zone to look for one or two juicy pick-ups, because people didn't ring us to ask us to go and collect things as much as they do today."

Getting to grips with the job was a gradual process. In an interview, Henri Camus described: "At the beginning, we didn't sort the items properly and we burned the wrong things, what we were doing was neither use nor ornament. But we quickly learned how to properly sort metals, card and paper. We kept a careful eye out for bottles. What was really important was to collect small items that at first glance didn't appear very valuable. We were careful not to miss bits of furniture; in the early days there was a lot of furniture that we had to leave outside in the rain or even burn... Slowly, we learned to appreciate the value of furniture, either through Community members themselves or through leaders like Paul le Roch, but at the beginning we didn't understand its worth." The types of items collected changed over time. "Initially, we brought home mainly newspapers, comics, rags, scrap iron and sheet metal. Later, people increasingly began to get rid of old pieces of furniture, beds and stoves."[18] While there is no exhaustive list of items collected in the 1960s, more is known about the 1970s: in 1973, the forty-seven Communities in France processed 30,000 tonnes of raw materials – a tenth of the total amount of waste that was recorded as having been collected in France at the time.

In terms of tonnage, 35% of the material collected by the Metz Community in the mid-1970s was cardboard, 23% paper, 21% scrap metal, 1.5% non-ferrous metals, 7% cast iron, 5% glass, 3% textiles and 1% plastic.[19] In 1979 and 1980, 20% of takings in UCC Communities came from cardboard, 23% from paper, 17% from scrap metal, 17% from non-ferrous metals, 5% from cast iron, 1% from glass and 16% from textiles. Everything that could be resold was resold. The label "Emmaus quality" was sometimes attached to the items by those who had collected them as a sign that they had been sorted with meticulous attention to detail. A defining characteristic of this period was the significant proportion of takings that came from selling on raw materials to those who collected and restored them, despite the fact that bric-à-brac sales remained the main source of profit. At UACE in 1979, the sale of raw materials accounted for 42% of takings and bric-à-brac sales for 58%. Anything that could not be resold was burned, without a second thought for the environment. Goods were burned in the open air and the fumes were so strong that burning had to take place at night. Bedsteads, mattresses, wood, tyres and plastics were all piled up and set alight. Drums of acid that could not be used were emptied out on to the ground.

Finally, levels of prosperity varied greatly from one Community to the next, and depended on both the Community's size and location. At UACE in 1976, total sales ranged from 215,900 francs at Le Blanc, a small women's Community, to 925,750 francs at Ormes.[20]

## The campaign to see the job of Companion receive official recognition

At that time, Emmaus was an association unlike any other and Communities operated in a legal vacuum with no official status. As far as social protection was concerned, systems varied from region to region and there was no national standard. The ministerial decree of 28 November 1960 theoretically made the payment of social security contributions mandatory. The decree came into effect very quickly within Emmaus, albeit in only a handful of Communities, including Caen. However, in 1969 UCC – the Federation which had initially been most attached to the principle of providing Companions with medical and social care – had yet to decide whether it would in fact pay the mandatory contribution for each Companion. UCC was reminded that such a decree had been issued on several occasions – a clear indication that the Federation was failing to comply. When Communities did pay these social security contributions, the sum paid stood at a tenth of the benefit which senior citizens on a low income received from the state. These contributions did not entitle Companions to health insurance until they had been made for a quarter. This meant that Communities receiving requests for medical care from Companions before the end of this first quarter were forced to shoulder further costs. Companions were therefore placed under a different social security system – the system covering hostels. However, this solution was nothing more than the best of a bad lot. Furthermore, the system covering hostels appeared "inconsistent" and somewhat arbitrary, meaning it was interpreted differently depending on which Community required assistance and on which civil servants were in charge at a given point in time.

UACE Companions, however, were able to present a letter from the head of social security in 1962, which stated that any man who had lived in a Community for six weeks or more was entitled to cover under the standard social security system. However, some directors of URSSAF, the French social security and benefits agency, refused to comply with the letter, arguing that a letter did not have the value of a decree and that the Companions, who received cash payments, should be forced to pay the same social contributions as manual workers.[21] The Nord Communities refused to join this system on principle, believing that the state had a duty to protect the poorest members of society.

Lastly, contributions to ASSEDIC, the association in charge of issuing unemployment benefit, were made by only a handful of Communities. All this meant that the level of confusion surrounding the legal status and obligations of Communities was matched only by the disparity between the situations of Communities in different regions. In 1974–5 this series of problems prompted the Emmaus Communities to contact the Ministry of Social Affairs and to embark on an internal process to standardise contribution practices. With Abbé Pierre expressing the wish to see Emmaus recognised as "a Community providing shelter and services",[22] the Movement set about compiling a case to see the job of Companion officially recognised. However, negotiations were unsuccessful, and were in no way encouraged by the war between the Federations – the wounds of which were still raw.

## The Community, a Place to Call Home

The Community was also a place people called home, a closed world and a world of men. Like any total institution, it covered all living costs (board and lodging, clothing, care) and both abstinence and the strict observance of different forms of discipline were defining features of day-to-day life.[23] Nevertheless, as Bernard Lacroix has pointed out, there were a number of significant differences between Communities and total institutions, because members chose to enter and serve Communities of their own free will and agreeing to do so could be seen as making a bid for freedom.[24] Choosing to live within a Community had inherent consequences: members were isolated from the outside world, forced to leave behind old circles of friends, saw their opportunities to meet others become limited, and the world in which they moved become smaller. Furthermore, in a Community everything tended to become a public act (eating, working, having fun, etc.) and "as in the porcupine fable, close to Schopenhauer's heart, in coming together to give each other a sense of warmth and intimacy, Community members create more opportunities for tension and increase the risk of friction. Therefore, the concept of bringing people together to share the same space can, by its own logic, cause them to feel alienated from the environment in which they exist."[25]

### Community infrastructure

Beyond the rationale behind the work of UCC and UACE, and the ways in which both chose to operate, there are important distinctions to be made between the two Federations during this period. At UCC, the Community was viewed as a protective cocoon, where the broken man could get back on his feet. This belief in the need to provide support and protection was reflected in the careful attention paid to Community structures, with the pioneer Community in Brest created and led by Paul le Roch. In 1962, refurbishing premises to make them suitable for Companions' needs became a priority at UCC: showers were built, along with toilets and three- or four-person bedrooms to replace the large dormitories. Other initiatives included the construction of more functional kitchens and various workshops, each one appropriately equipped for a specific part of the Companions' work. Opened in 1957, the Nice Community acquired showers and toilets in 1966; Lille-Wambrechies, set up in 1954, got its first bedrooms in 1963 and toilet blocks and showers in 1964. Nevertheless, in many Communities living conditions remained second-rate. In an interview on his time spent in Communities, Raymond Etienne recalled: "When I arrived at Metz, I had [to fight to get the kitchen redone], because I was fed up of cockroaches falling into the coffee. We had to use a blowtorch in the kitchen in order to kill the cockroaches." Etienne continues, highlighting that the attention paid to infrastructure was inextricably linked to the Federation's desire to restore Companions' dignity: "In Brest, we'd watch them arrive, sometimes as tramps, drunk out of their minds, often without teeth, without glasses. For Paul le Roch [the Community leader] the most important thing was to get them back on their feet. If you'd lost all your teeth, we'd go to the dentist; if you didn't have any glasses... There was a doctor, a social worker, a psychiatrist. After that, they could choose whether to stay or go. It was Brest that convinced me to stay. There was work to do with people, people who weren't tramps through and through, and when they said to me, 'that bloke there, he arrived five years ago, he arrived in the same state as that one, and now look at him'..."

At UACE, where the focus was on providing support to those outside the organisation, progress was a lot slower, more moderate, and hampered by the fact that there were a large number of travelling Communities without their own premises: by the late 1970s, there were still Communities without heating or proper toilet facilities. A review of various Communities in June 1974 revealed that in Ormes, a Community which opened its doors in 1966, work had only just begun on building bedrooms; that in Lyons, set up in 1970, leaders were considering possibly installing central heating and bedrooms would not be built before 1977; and that in Tours, which opened in 1971, work on the living quarters was almost complete. In Dijon, set up in 1973, lavatory blocks were only completed three years later.

In contrast, at the end of this period, at UACE everything was gathering pace: in 1980 alone the Toulouse Community built a laundry room, a doctor's consultation room, two television rooms and a bar. These developments caused many to rail against what they saw as sudden "gentrification", which went against the Federation's traditional ethos. In 1981, the president spoke of his "embarrassment at the ease, flippancy even, with which some have announced their investment plans: in the space of a few minutes, more than 3 million were spent... The only place where money urgently needs to be spent is on rehousing the Bourg-en-Bresse Community; but even here the amount of money set aside could still be significantly reduced. At a time when no one can claim not to know what's going on elsewhere, we need to be absolutely sure that, as our slogan goes, those 'who suffer most' are not amongst ourselves."[26] This commitment to living a life of austerity harked back to the ideal of the catacombs, total self-sacrifice and immersion in work and efforts to help those in need. Inherent to this lifestyle was the difficulty in reconciling the service of others, which had to come first, with the need to look after your own life, an activity seen as selfish and as an unnecessary luxury.

## Elements of everyday life

Work dictated the structure and pace of everyday life. Companions awoke (for some early risers the day began as early as five o'clock), ate breakfast and worked from eight o'clock to midday. The morning would be broken by a brief coffee break that would often turn into a generous, mid-morning snack. Lunch was at half-past twelve and was followed either by a card game, a nap or a television break, depending on each Companion's individual taste. Work began again at half-past two, finished at six o'clock, dinner was served at around seven o'clock and Companions were then free to spend the evening as they wished. In Cernay in the 1960s and 70s, "the menus were simple. In the morning: coffee and sardines, coffee and dried sausage,[27] coffee and sausage meat, coffee and pig's head, coffee and soft cheese, or coffee and black pudding. Lunch was soup, potatoes and salad; soup, tripe and potato purée; soup and soft noodles; lentils with streaky bacon and potatoes; pilchards and potatoes; or soup, kidneys and potatoes. In the evening, there were potatoes and salad, potatoes and tripe salad, potatoes and lettuce, carrots and eggs, noodles and tomato sauce, potatoes and Munster cheese, or potato and lettuce omelette. Fruit (and greens) were rare and there was little call for them to be served."[28] As far as personal hygiene was concerned, "after four o'clock on a Saturday, Companions were able to take a shower or bath (in the municipal baths at Cernay hospital) and go to the barber's, armed with a voucher but with no money in their pocket."[29]

Sunday was a dark day. Already, by around 1953–5, "Sunday had become Emmaus' number one enemy. On Sunday morning, everyone attended to their own business: doing their washing, getting their hair cut, having a shower and, for some, going to church. However, after lunch, with nothing to do, no purpose and no commitments or expectations, many sought refuge in local bars where they would slowly drown the ghosts that haunted them."[30] In 1977 still, "Sunday was often a slow day, if not deadly boring. It was a serious problem within Communities."[31]

Mass was not hugely popular. In Cernay, "every Sunday morning, the coordinator would hold Mass in an old hut that served as a chapel. Newcomers would turn up the first time (thinking that Mass was compulsory). The following Sunday, apart from a few, rare exceptions, the coordinator would be alone in the hut... For the blokes in the Community, religion was the preserve of the healthy, the privileged and the priests – it wasn't for poor guys like them."[32] Religion appeared to occupy a more central place in UACE Communities, many of which had their own chapel and continued to perform two rituals that had been first introduced by Abbé Pierre. In memory of the "spirit of the beginnings", the first ritual involved placing a statue of the Virgin Mary in the common room. This statue stood "as a sign to all the men who no longer had any family left of a maternal presence within the Community that was not simply religious."[33] The second ritual was that of saying grace before meals, despite the fact that the wording from the early days had been replaced by the more flexible and open verse that was introduced by Paul (of Normandy) during the youth camps:

> "Friends and Companions,
> In sharing this meal which we have earned
> Let us renew our desire to work together
> To give bread to those who are hungry
> And hunger to those who have bread."

For older Companions, UACE had a retirement home in Esteville, Normandy. The home also welcomed Companions worn down by illness or convalescing, and was occasionally used to host international gatherings. This Esteville home was a small, early eighteenth-century castle, surrounded by two acres of woods and meadows. Its owner, Georges Lanfry, had been a close friend of Marc Sangnier in his youth, whom he first met through Sangnier's religious and political movement, *Le Sillon*, and then again through the academic association *Jeune République*. Organiser of the *Congrès de la paix* in 1926, a member of the Resistance during the Occupation and co-founder of the group *Résistance*, he was also the director of a public works company. Between 1938 and 1959 he was the head of the trade union for employers in the construction industry and was the brains behind the creation of many apprentice training centres. At the time when the travelling Communities were touring Normandy, Lanfry was informed by Paul that a retirement home for Companions was needed and donated his property to the Federation in 1964. He passed away in January 1969, at the age of eighty-four.[34] In addition to the bedrooms, the house had a library, lounges, some craft workshops and a chapel. In 1972, the property was officially accredited by the social services of Seine-Maritime in Normandy and, at that point, a price for a day's care was introduced (eighteen francs per person in 1973). Nevertheless, the majority of older Companions at UACE and almost all of those at UCC remained in a Community. However, very few actually reached retirement age and, when they did, they were not expected to live for more than another five years.

## Alcohol – a problem that would not go away

The main problem faced by all Communities was alcohol. From the very beginning, some Communities were "dry", either on principle (Brest) or due to the fact the leader was a recovering alcoholic (Wambrechies). In 1959, the team at Le Coutumier were still allowed to drink freely, but were reminded that "the majority [of Communities were] dry,[35] and that a decision had been taken to either limit or prohibit the consumption of alcohol within the Communities."[36] In 1961, UCC decided to impose an alcohol ban, which did not prove easy to enforce in the south. By the following year, Nîmes and Nice were still drinking beer and those in the Marseilles Community were still able to drink wine. What's more, the ban on alcohol did not stop bottles from being passed around, particularly in the evening, nor did it stop Companions from spending the evening or Sundays in the local bar.

UACE took a more flexible approach. At a UACE bureau meeting in 1972, Abbé Pierre reminded members "just how sensitive an issue temperance [was]". He declared: "Drink should not be considered a shameful vice. The drinker trying to give up is making a huge effort; he must feel supported and never be punished if he falls off the wagon. All failures can be excused, except the failure to be honest."[37] Furthermore, it proved impossible to wean some Companions off alcohol completely. As a result, Abbé Pierre reminded his audience that "however much [he wished] that Communities were, in principle, alcohol-free, it would perhaps be a good idea if some were not, in order that they might take in certain Companions."[38] In fact, within UACE in the 1960s and 70s, there were still some Communities that allowed alcohol and others that did not. This allowed Companions to be moved from one type of Community to another and to keep those who were simply unable to kick the habit within a Community. As we have seen, Liberty banned alcohol in the Community as a matter of principle.

The Federations tackled the problem of alcohol head-on, each in their own, unique way. Until the 1980s, the majority of Communities remained "closed", i.e. going out in the evening or at weekends was banned. In all Communities, if Companions had clearly committed a misdemeanour under the influence, they were either asked to leave immediately (such misdemeanours accounted for between a fifth and a third of all exclusions) or, at the very least, were driven some kilometres away to walk it off. However, the fight against alcohol involved more than imposing a ban: the Community at Le Coutumier declared that it would "primarily recommend providing Companions with counselling aimed at eradicating the causes of alcoholism."[39] Indeed, providing this kind of support was where the leader, doctor and social worker focused almost all of their efforts. Almost all Communities also endeavoured to offer ways of decreasing alcohol dependence (medical care, courses of treatment) and used simple, everyday tricks such as serving sweet drinks at mealtimes that were more pleasant than water (non-alcoholic beers, fizzy drinks, fruit juices), as well as sometimes using more radical means – such as forcing Companions to swallow sachets of *Hespéral*, which caused them to vomit as soon as alcohol passed their lips.

## The Community, a Place of Solidarity

*"Emmaus is the one who is suffering helping the one who is suffering more."*[40]

Just as it was a place where men worked and lived, the Community was equally a place of solidarity. This solidarity was first internally focused – the older Companions would support the new, and experienced Community members would assist the inexperienced. Richer Communities would also help those in greater financial difficulty, by awarding grants or informal subsidies. However, the Community was, above all, a place where members displayed solidarity towards those outside, in accordance with the third rule of Emmaus, that of serving the most disadvantaged members of society. This was enshrined in two statements: "The aim of our common endeavour is to rescue anyone in distress and in so doing, to further the cause of real, lasting peace."/"Serve others in greater need before yourself."

Until 1962, UCC focused heavily on supporting those outside the Movement. At that point, the concept of developing the Communities themselves caused the Federation to focus inwards instead and investment in the well-being of Companions was considered a priority. Despite this, initiatives continued in support of local residents in difficulty. Such initiatives were more targeted and tangible, and hence more gratifying – it appeared "easier to get Companions to give to a local family than to India."[41] 1967 marked the start of an era which focused more on international work and development aid. However, UCC seldom went through Emmaus International, an organisation it viewed at the time as "Abbé Pierre's plaything". Ultimately, it primarily continued to provide assistance at a local level: supporting local families in difficulty (providing money to cover emergencies, refurbishing apartments, donating furniture, sponsoring children); donating money to local branches of *Secours catholique*, to associations for the handicapped and the elderly, to centres for social reintegration and to centres providing social and cultural activities; and helping those just out of prison, immigrant workers, etc. Links were also established, notably in the form of individual networks, with *Vie libre* (an association combating alcoholism) and *Le Nid* (an association providing support to prostitutes and a pioneer of the Social Catholicism movement).

By contrast, UACE clearly favoured initiatives in aid of those outside Communities. Since the heyday of Normandy's travelling Communities, local initiatives had included providing emergency funds to local families in difficulty and donations to *Secours catholique* or *Les Petits Frères des Pauvres,* just as they did at UCC. However, they also focused, to a much greater extent, on opening or supporting homes for the physically and mentally handicapped, children, young workers and the elderly, as well as hostels providing medical treatment and detox centres. From the very beginning, UACE displayed a marked interest in initiatives in aid of those abroad and in the work of Emmaus International, to which the Federation was connected through Abbé Pierre and through its own president, Hervé Teule.

In addition, it appears that the choices Communities made regarding which specific sectors of society they would support were linked to the causes that French society chose to champion at a similar point in time. These decisions followed a sequence partly similar to that followed by other organisations such as *Secours populaire*.[42] In the 1960s, and even more so following the publication of François Bloch-Lainé's 1968 report, the maladjusted and the handicapped were viewed as being among the groups most "excluded" from society. In the 1970s, international initiatives became increasingly important. Lastly, from the mid-1970s onwards, two new causes came to the fore. One was an internal cause within Emmaus, *SOS-Familles* (an organisation fighting household debt),[43] and the other was external, the creation of night shelters for the homeless. These shelters were almost always created in cooperation with other associations (*Secours catholique*, the Red Cross), and even on occasion with the authorities (the town or département council).

## The Prost Home: the Debate on the (Re)integration of Companions Begins

The extreme vulnerability of many Companions and UCC's perception of the Community as a protective cocoon in no way hindered the development of initiatives that sought to reintegrate Companions into society and to adapt them once more to a fluid labour market offering work in abundant supply.

### The difficulty in (re)integrating Companions

In October 1955, Association Emmaus acquired a building at 11 Cité Prost, near to Place de la Nation in Paris. It quickly came to be used as a house where Companions could escape the daily grind of Community life and rest for a time in Paris, albeit in a huge dormitory with few creature comforts. From 1958 onwards, while the Association was offloading the last of its responsibilities to other organisations, management of the Prost home was transferred to UCC.

Records show that the home was primarily occupied by men anxious to return to the world of work. It thus began to act as a potential halfway house between the Community and the outside world. In the years 1960–1, extensive renovation work was carried out in order to make it more comfortable: the dormitories were converted into eight three-bed rooms, the kitchen was refurbished, and a dining hall, common room and television room were installed. The Federation also hired a leader-tutor to work at the home. The Companions worked outside the home during the day and slept there at night. They were only asked to pay for their rent and food. The process to select residents was conducted within UCC Communities and decisions were taken jointly by the Community leader, doctor and social worker. As far as was possible, these Companions were required to be abstinent and needed to be established Community residents.

The Prost home was the stage for a ground-breaking debate within Emmaus on how to (re)integrate Companions into society. The home was created following an increased awareness of the difficulties faced by the Companion leaving a Community. These included difficulties of a material nature, such as finding a hotel room or eating properly; and psychological difficulties, such as coping with solitude in the evening. It sought to become "a type of family boarding house where communal living would provide workers with the material and, above all, the emotional support needed to thrivewithin society and better themselves."[44] The home would "free the Companion leaving the Community from a number of material worries, but would also, on a psychological level, extend the role the Community had formerly played."

In February 1963, the home broke away from UCC and became an independent Not-for-Profit association: the Association of Friends and of the Prost Workers' home. In order not to be subject to restrictions on the length of time Companions could stay, the home did not claim any state funding. As a result, the home's only sources of income were the money boarders paid for their rent and meals; and subsidies from UCC Communities in the Paris region. In theory, it was to be nothing more than a temporary home, where residents would stay for a maximum of six months. However, in practice, many set up home and were unable to leave. The leaders, chiefly Henri Camus (president of the home 1963 to 1965, as well as, at the same time, president of UCC and Association Emmaus), Thérèse Frontier (social worker), René

Cesbron (leader of the home and former Community leader) and Michel Lefebvre (vice-secretary-general of the CGL and Henri Camus' successor as president of the home), consequently decided to "Carry out an in-depth analysis of what the home is now and what we would like it to become. Indeed, if we're not careful, there's a risk that Prost will fairly quickly become more of a hotel than a home. Generally speaking, the men arrive all fired up, with the hope of reintegrating into normal society. And yet, sooner or later, almost all of them come up against 'something', which causes them to cease to flourish and even go backwards."[45]

Sociologists Gilbert Murry and Nicole Carlier were charged with conducting this "in-depth analysis", which as we have seen turned, more than anything else, into a vast study on the profile of Community members. This study was supposed to be an introduction to a subsequent analysis of the boarders' profiles, but the two ultimately merged into one. Nevertheless, one conclusion emerged from the study: the home's boarders were generally selected on account of the fact that they had settled comfortably into Community life, and yet the longer their stay had been, the less likely they were to reintegrate into society. Successful reintegration was gradually jeopardised as they acquired new reference points in many key areas of life: work, their relationships to others (the absence of women and children, etc.), and domination (of an often "semi-charismatic" boss forcing members to remain loyal). And yet, "it is no exaggeration to state that the Community member is someone who finds it very difficult to leave behind one way of life and adapt to another; someone who cannot reuse past experience in a setting that is overly different. Consequently, entering the Prost home puts someone who is well integrated into Community life at significant risk – still fragile, he is forced to come face to face with a threatening society."

## From a "follow-up home" to a shelter

In the light of this conclusion, the report recommended that the home should instead focus its attention on the long-term unemployed and those ill-adapted to the world of work. In doing so, it would simultaneously be able to fill the places Community members had not taken, and thus become more financially viable. By 1965, non-Companions already accounted for eight out of twenty-two boarders; in 1971, they accounted for twenty out of twenty-five residents. From the early 1970s onwards, the home no longer claimed to act as an extension of Community life. Instead, it primarily housed isolated men who had been referred by hospital social services, businesses, town councils or homeless shelters – many had spent time in psychiatric hospitals and/or prison. In 1972, Association Emmaus opened a new shelter; a workers' home in the Rue des Bourdonnais. The Bourdonnais shelter received state funding and was thus subject to restrictions on the length of residents' stays. As a result, Prost took in those leaving the shelter.

Like the Communities, the purpose of the Prost home was ultimately twofold: it provided short-term support, in particular to young people, and also a home in the longer term. The figures clearly show that after having stayed at Prost for more than a year, Companions began to settle on a permanent basis. Over time, laying down roots at the home became the norm and Prost went from having a majority of men in the 30–40 age bracket (in the 1960s), with no resident over 50 (an age group viewed as "too difficult to reintegrate"), to having a majority of residents aged 40–60 (in the 1970s). For those who stayed at Prost long-term, settling into a stable job remained problematic: out of the forty-six boarders who passed through the home in 1969, twenty stayed with the same employer, but five were temporary workers, six changed job once or twice, six switched posts three or four times, and nine changed five times or more. It was concluded that residents suffered from "a pathological need for change", which meant they could only survive if work was in abundant supply. Furthermore, outside the professional sphere they had few ties. Finally, just as it was within Communities, alcoholism was a real problem and often led to residents being evicted from the home. In addition, the home received no state funding and, as a result, was permanently in the red. In 1979, the dire state of the home's finances prompted them to reduce the number of beds from twenty-five to twelve, and the maximum length of stay to one year.

With the labour market thriving, the Companions of the *Trente Glorieuses* often made only fleeting visits to Communities and moved on from one to another. Mentally very fragile, with no ties and often profoundly affected by traumatising experiences such as war, these were broken men who rarely laid down roots. They often held few professional qualifications but were nevertheless skilled with their hands and no strangers to hard work – qualities that proved invaluable when collecting and restoring unwanted items.

At a time when regulation was weak, even non-existent, the Community was also an enclave where rules and obligations were waived. Exempt from professional taxes and operating in a sector where there was no competition, Communities were free to collect and burn items as they wished, using practices that today would turn the faces of any work inspector or environmentalist white with horror. Living conditions were the same in every Community: there was a lack of standardised social protection, or indeed of social protection in any shape or form, and premises were little more than habitable. This lack of both competition and regulation allowed Communities to build on the impetus of 1954 and become a permanent feature of France's social and economic landscape. Built on the three rules of shelter, work and service, Communities introduced a revolutionary system, which saw the poorest members of society work to give to those who were poorer still, and in so doing reclaim some of their lost dignity.

# *Chapter 7* / THE INTERNATIONALISATION OF A CATHOLIC MOVEMENT

Abbé Pierre's increasing distance from the French movement, his penchant for international initiatives, and the impact of the 1954 appeal abroad combined to open a new door for Emmaus: from 1955 onwards, the Movement's founder received a constant stream of calls for help from across the globe. He both created and uncovered replicas of the Emmaus model abroad; nurturing and supporting them in every way he could. The internationalisation of Emmaus took effect in two clear stages: in the 1950s and 60s, a whole host of isolated initiatives began to appear; in the 1970s efforts focused on consolidating and strengthening initiatives already in place.

In addition to looking at the organisational issue that is the birth of Emmaus International, this chapter aims to conduct a deeper analysis of the transformation of Catholic development ideologies, and of the place which religion and politics occupied in the humanitarian sphere. Indeed, the influence of religion was of crucial importance during this period: development aid was one of the many areas which repeatedly received pontifical support. Many of the Emmaus leaders abroad were priests, the vast majority of activists were Catholic, and it was firmly believed that development initiatives were the tangible expression of a modern, active form of charity on a global scale. Conversely, just as religion appeared to unite the troops, politics was the source of deep-rooted divisions within the Movement and restricted its ability to make its political voice heard. Divisions existed between the western branches of Emmaus who kept politics at arm's length and groups in Latin America who, seduced by liberation Christianity, placed politics at the heart of their work. There were divisions within both the North and South; between youth groups and their older counterparts; and between those who advocated helping the poor to become independent and those who believed that charity was the way forward. As a result, one of the main issues debated within

Emmaus throughout this period was whether or not (and how) religion should act as a basis upon which causes could be analysed and political action taken.

## Individual Initiatives Blossom

### The West: relaying the message of Abbé Pierre

In many western countries, the extensive media coverage of the mass mobilisation of the French people in 1954 inspired the creation of new Emmaus organisations. The appeal immediately struck a chord in Switzerland. Abbé Pierre was initially invited to give conferences in Zurich by Abbé Jolliat, and in Geneva by Caritas. Clothing collections were organised in aid of the French poor and "Committees of Friends of Emmaus" were promptly created. Switzerland also rallied behind the cause in the bitterly harsh winter of 1956. Invited to speak once again, Abbé Pierre's words inspired Marcel Farine to take action. Defender of social Catholicism and champion of many a cause, Farine granted Emmaus his unwavering and continued support. Born in the Swiss Jura in 1924, to poor and deeply religious parents, he first campaigned within the conservative Christian trade-union movement, before joining the fight in the 1950s, along with his wife, to protect the underprivileged. Meeting Abbé Pierre encouraged him to properly organise his own charitable initiatives and to found Emmaus Switzerland, of which he remained president until 1989. In 1959, he met Raoul Follereau and consequently brought Emmaus Switzerland on board with the fight against leprosy. As well as having eight children and a job as a postal worker, Follereau simultaneously held the presidency of fifteen associations,[1] including Emmaus International. He was the Association's first president and remained in the post for a decade (1969–79).

Northern Europe quickly became an Emmaus stronghold. In 1954, Abbé Pierre was invited to give a talk in Denmark. An Emmaus organisation began to develop in the country, slowly at first, but in 1965 the process began to gather pace when around sixty young Danes took part in the camps organised by Paul. In 1969, Denmark played host to the international camps. Conference tours and the mobilisation of young people were also behind the birth of Emmaus Sweden. Approached by Father Dureau, a Dominican priest,[2] Abbé Pierre was invited to revitalise a morose generation of young people who were visibly short of "reasons to live".[3] He spoke in favour of altruism and support for disadvantaged nations. Following this rallying cry, a small group launched *Les Hirondelles* – the name "Emmaus" had already been adopted by a sect – to dispatch volunteers to countries in need. The organisation established close links with Peru and India before spreading to both Norway and Finland. Communities also began to take root across Northern Europe. In Finland, the first Community was opened in 1964 (Helsinki) with the help of Father Guy Barbier, a former worker-priest in France; Sweden in 1965 (Björkå) and Denmark in 1970 (Aalborg and Aarhus). Local social initiatives were also developed in these countries. The Helsinki Community supported students from very deprived backgrounds: it paid the salaries of, amongst others, two teachers for those in prison; a leader for a camp for young drug addicts; and a social worker for alcoholics. In Holland, Lisbeth and Jean Wilken, two former volunteers who had come to Paris in 1954, decided upon their return home to create a Foundation of Friends of Emmaus. Jean would later become the second president of Emmaus International. As well as other Committees of Friends, Communities began to open from the mid-1960s onwards in Holland (Har Zuilens in 1966, Langeweg in 1969), and 1958 saw the publication of the first Dutch version of *Faim et Soif.*

Thanks to the efforts of the younger generation, Emmaus also began to take root in Italy in the early 1960s. The first Community of Ragpickers opened its doors in Verona in 1962. An information letter from Emmaus International described the Community as "the creation of a few young Catholics who no longer accepted traditional forms of charity and decided to set up home alongside the poor who lived off their work collecting and restoring unwanted household items."[4] However, in 1968 the Community became worker self-managed, as well as becoming involved in various social struggles and later in violent conflict; it ceased all activity before starting up again in 1982. Similarly, in 1966 a new Community was created in Bologna, at the instigation of young people who had attended the summer camps. It struggled to find its feet and in 1970 merged with the Community in Rimini (originally established in 1967) in order to form an economically viable organisation. Young people also set up the Laterina-Arezzo Community (1972), which then spread to Prato (near Florence) and Padua (1978).

Small organisations also sprang up in Germany, Belgium and, from 1970 onwards, in Spain. Outside Europe during this period of growth in the western world, Emmaus took root in Canada from very early on, following Abbé Pierre's tour of the country in April 1955. The first Community was created on the initiative of Father Grégoire, and Father Vaugel offered his property as a place for it to set up home.[5] The support of Cardinal Léger also enabled the team to commandeer Father Robert Laporte in order to further develop Emmaus Canada, and groups were created in Granby, Hull and Quebec. In the USA, a Community was created in Harlem in the 1960s.

It is clear that the spread of Emmaus throughout the western world was far from insignificant, even if the countries. In question only ever spawned a handful of groups, rather than the dozens which appeared in France. These groups shared three salient characteristics: they were generally created following conferences given by Abbé Pierre, the support of priests was often crucial in their success, and many of them were set up and managed by members of the younger generation.

## Emmaus in Asia: a Christian initiative

Asia was a continent with few Christians and even fewer Catholics. In 1960 Emmaus operated in Japan, where just 0.3% of the population were Catholic; in South Korea (2.1% Catholic); in Indonesia (1.3% Catholic); and in India (0.9% Catholic).[6] Emmaus was only able to gain a foothold in Japan and Indonesia thanks to the role played by the traditional figure of the missionary priest in the two countries. In South Korea, the success of Emmaus depended upon local priests, and in India, Emmaus watched as the new humanitarian-development model emerged.[7]

In Asia, Emmaus was born in the Land of the Rising Sun.[8] At the end of the war, Japanese businessman Mr Ozawa found himself stripped of all his possessions. In 1949, he joined forces with a group of poor citizens to set up a Ragpicking operation on the outskirts of Tokyo and to found the housing site La Cité des Fourmis (literally, Ants-ville). As was the case in France, bourgeois "Friends" were pivotal to the initiatives' success, with two key figures on board. Satoko Kitahara was the daughter of a university professor, who was born into the Shinto faith but who converted to Catholicism. Kitahara would later write a book on La Cité des Fourmis, which reached a nationwide audience. The second key figure was Mr Matsui, writer and representative, who in 1959 would succeed in forcing the town council to officially recognise the site.

Meanwhile in 1950, Father Robert Vallade, a Paris priest of Foreign Missions, arrived in Japan. Struck by the extent of the country's poverty, he decided to set up home in a shantytown and, having learned of Emmaus' existence in Japan, wrote to Abbé Pierre to ask his advice. Abbé Pierre suggested living and working alongside a group of Ragpickers and in 1955 Father Vallade consequently spent a period of time living in La Cité des Fourmis, before going on to launch a sister initiative in Kobe: the Gyokokaï Association, or Association of the Morning Light. An article published in a 1970 issue of *Faim et Soif* declared: "For the poor of Japan, there was nothing poetic about the name. It evokes the moment when a man, after sleep has crushed all thoughts of his destitution, awakens to find it staring him in the face once more. But here, in this new Community [...] light once again came to symbolise hope and creation."[9] In other words, the Community was a model of the "enthusiastic disillusion" so dear to Abbé Pierre. With Father Vallade still at the helm, the Movement then spread to Osaka, Mino and Nagano. With the financial support of the French, Italian and Danish Communities, the Japanese organisations gradually began to provide an array of both medical and social services, including clinics, shelters, children's gardens and hospitals for the elderly and those who were paralysed.

As was the case in Japan, the development of Emmaus in Indonesia pre-dated Abbé Pierre's appeal and rested on the shoulders of a missionary priest: Father Antoine Van Dam, a Dutch Capuchin monk who helped the poorest urban populations living in the north of Sumatra. In 1961 he approached Emmaus and asked them to buy a mobile clinic for the islanders. Paul's travelling Communities footed the bill. Ten years later, following a meeting with Abbé Pierre, Van Dam opened a social welfare centre with a maternity ward, healthcare services, a day nursery, an orphanage and a home for the elderly. Emmaus covered part of the cost, but money also came from local efforts to collect and recycle old bottles and paper, as well as from the sale of calendars. In 1972, his association became a member of Emmaus International.

In 1966, Emmaus finally gained a foothold in South Korea when Park Su Kil, a former international leader of the JOC and a refugee from North Korea, read about Emmaus in a Japanese newspaper.[10] He illegally took possession of a plot of land in Seoul and the first Community began to grow, providing a home for children and teenagers who had lost their parents to war. A second Community was opened in 1967 in Taegu, with the support of the groups in Japan. During the day, the youngsters living there collected and recycled waste as well as shining shoes, and at night they continued their studies. By 1977 the Community was home to 200 teenagers. In 1972, a Community for families was founded on land belonging to the town. Lastly, alongside these Communities was the Community for young offenders who had been orphaned by war. This Community had been in operation since 1964 and was also built on land which the town lent to the Association. In 1973, it was placed in the hands of the Vicar General of the diocese, Father Kim, who made it part of the Emmaus family on the advice of Father Vallade.

The case of India was markedly different. It was the only Asian country where Emmaus was the fruit Abbé Pierre's visits, and not a result of the work of Catholic networks. It was also the only country where the Association relied on the support of young, non-religious volunteers and was built on the humanitarian-development model. Abbé Pierre first visited the association in 1956 to meet Prime Minister Nehru. He returned in January 1959 at the invitation of a group of Christian students. During this second visit, he made the acquaintance of Indira Gandhi (who later became India's first female Prime Minister), and spent a number of days shadowing Vinoba Bhave. Bhave was the "apostle of modern India" and spiritual successor of Mahatma Gandhi, and was just as efficient in "the cleansing of religious values" as he was in redistributing land for the benefit of the poorest members of society.[11] Emmaus began by supporting the work of the international civil service, which since 1958 had been building houses on land made available by the Indian government.[12] In 1963, the Swedish association *Les Hirondelles*, whose efforts had until that point been in aid of Peru, made India its second area of focus, and the Danish and Finnish branches of the association soon followed suit. Initiatives in support of the Untouchables gradually began to develop in the Madras region. There was a crèche, nursery school, night school, medical centre, clinic for undernourished infants, family-planning clinic, dressmaking school, joinery workshop, fishing cooperative, an agricultural development programme, and so on. These initiatives constituted veritable integrated development programmes characteristic of the new humanitarian-development model that was emerging across the globe.

## Latin America: between awareness-raising, Ragpicking and social action

Just as it had been some years earlier for Father Lebret, it was Latin America which became a veritable testing ground for Emmaus. The region developed into the largest Emmaus stronghold outside Europe and brought groups from the North face-to-face with new ideological perspectives.

In Argentina and Peru, the associations which later became Emmaus pre-dated the appeal made by Abbé Pierre. They were created and managed by priests, and Ragpicking and social action formed the lion's share of their work.

In 1958 while recuperating in a clinic in Switzerland, Abbé Pierre received a visit from Father José Balista, a teacher at the Jesuit college of Buenos Aires, who offered him a ticket to Argentina. He made the trip with Lucie Coutaz in 1959 and observed the initiatives already in place. He was told: "We got the ball rolling in 1952. There were three of us: an architect, a law student and myself. We were twenty-five, eighteen and thirty-five, respectively. After spending just one day experiencing the reality of life in the slums first-hand we were shocked to the core and thus felt obliged to take action. We shared our concerns with various groups of young people, in particular with university students. In two months, fifty people were doing what they could in five shantytowns."[13] Formed into an association in October 1955, the group had already taken the name of Emmaus by the time Abbé Pierre paid a visit, "more [out of] a desire to follow the philosophy which had guided Abbé Pierre in his work than [out of] a wish to adopt his working methods. We'd always believed that these should be adapted to our working environment and to the forms of action which we were capable of taking."[14] Two years later, the association had 2,000 volunteers working in seventy shantytowns. Initiatives included awareness-raising activities; social-policy lessons, which were open to all; the publication of a magazine; the trialling of micro-projects to aid the development of poor areas (installing drinking water and electricity, building roads, schools, clinics, etc.); and establishing cooperatives to organise the local population. In 1967, Emmaus was approached by the government to draw up a plan to eradicate the shantytowns. In addition to its work in Buenos Aires, a "Community development plan for impoverished rural regions" was created, underpinned by the same principles as the plan for urban regions, but paying particular attention to herd yield, small industries and crafts. One area where the fledgling association in Argentina broke new ground was in its focus on refurbishing sport and leisure facilities which the poorest members of society could use. Finally, the main source of income was from the *trapería* (a Community of Ragpickers) based on the traditional Emmaus Community model.

In Peru, the group was founded by a French priest, Father Gérard Protain, who in 1959 set up a Ragpicking operation with a team of young Peruvians on a Lima rubbish dump.[15] Abbé Pierre's visit spurred the troops on and an Emmaus association was formed. From 1960 onwards, the organisation began to grow with the arrival of the first volunteers from abroad; Canadians first, followed by teams from Sweden and France. This growth continued when in 1961, the Ministry of War donated a vast area of land in the heart of the desert in Atocongo in the outer reaches of Lima. Despite its extremely remote location, a group of around ten shantytowns rapidly grew up around the land and Emmaus set to work improving the living conditions of residents. Crèches were opened to care for abandoned children and to allow women to work (1964). These were funded by a joint sponsorship scheme with Sweden and France. Carpentry courses were introduced (1965), followed by a mechanics' training centre for young boys, a family clinic and a primary school (1966); electricity was installed in 1967 and the centre was officially endorsed by the Ministry of Public Education. 1968 saw the opening of a social and cultural centre offering activities including theatre performances, film screenings and debates. Open-air activities and summer camps were developed. In addition to the funds and volunteers which Emmaus provided, this vast project was also supported by the local committees of CCFD, the French Catholic Development NGO. Other initiatives followed later in Cristiana (a domestic-science school and a technical training centre and workshop, both for women and both funded chiefly by Emmaus Norway), and in Santa Maria (lessons for orphans in agriculture and pig-rearing, funded by Emmaus Sweden).

Though rooted in partially similar soil, Emmaus' growth in Brazil followed a markedly different course. The Movement first took root in the country thanks to the efforts of a major national figure, Dom Helder Câmara. Câmara was the national secretary of Catholic Action, secretary-general of the National Conference of Bishops (1952–64) and auxiliary Bishop of Rio (1952–64). He would go on to become the Archbishop of Olinda-Recife (1964), the man who instigated a significant debate on the Church and the poor, champion of the grass-roots ecclesiastical Communities and in 1970, the first countryman who dared to speak out abroad against the torture carried out by his government.[16] In 1955, to combat the poverty in the Rio shanty-towns, Câmara created a "Welfare Bank", built on gifts of money and voluntary work, which made loans to the poorest members of society and enabled the infrastructure for healthcare, education and training to be created. He then called upon Abbé Pierre for help. Abbé Pierre responded by sending Câmara one of his protégés, Jean-Yves Olichon. Olichon was a former leader of *La Réserve* and the Pontault-Combault construction workers, and had been frozen out of the Movement by the Bourdonnais team for his authoritarian methods and malpractice. In March 1956 he arrived in Rio and found "a piece of waste ground, one large shack, a huge pile of rubble, snakes and the rubbish dump next door."[17] With the government's support, the team built a warehouse, buildings for bedrooms, toilet blocks, a games room, a large dining hall, and a dentist and doctor's surgery. They set up carpentry and shoe-repair workshops, installed radio and electricity and built furniture and houses. The Rio site took on colossal proportions: in 1963 it occupied 4,200 $m^2$, fifteen years later it stretched over 33,000 $m^2$; in 1963 it had only a handful of residents, by 1978 there were 820. They were a hotchpotch of prison inmates referred to the Community by the prison administration, men recently released from jail, young offenders sent by juvenile court judges, and the unemployed. Accounts suggest the site was run more like a prison or army barracks than an Emmaus Community and was managed with an iron rod.

Finally, Emmaus was present in Chile thanks to the work of Father Hurtado (whose achievements included clinics, a bottle cooperative, a workers' hostel, an "institute for social advancement", Communities in Santiago, Temuco and Concepción); in Uruguay thanks to Father Sierra (who set up initiatives in aid of the homeless, general clinics and a teaching farm); and in Paraguay (where Emmaus sought to acquaint Indians with their rights). Work in Chile was severely disrupted by the coup d'état of September 1973. The coup prompted Emmaus to launch initiatives in aid of the political prisoners, and schemes to send milk and food to children's canteens and clothes to support the Communities.

## Two isolated pockets: Lebanon and Rwanda

Two locations conclude this overview of Emmaus initiatives around the world: the isolated pockets of Lebanon and Rwanda. En route to India in 1959 and again on his way home, Abbé Pierre visited Beirut, triggering an influx of volunteers and prompting the Greek Catholic Bishop of Beirut to donate a plot of land. A Community, christened The Oasis of Hope, quickly began to take shape, surviving on income made from recycling waste and producing fuel using traditional methods. However, the premises which had been made available free of charge were gradually reclaimed, and were too small to allow the

Community to really develop. In the 1970s, competition from cardboard-collection firms led to a decline in activity. Most significantly, Community life was severely disrupted by the Israeli–Palestinian conflicts of 1967 and 1973, and their attendant batch of refugees.

In Rwanda, Emmaus was slow to come into being. In 1954, Father Joseph Fraipont was among the Belgian volunteers who came to Paris to work as Emmaus Ragpickers. In 1957, he read the encyclical appeal encouraging dioceses to send priests to build African churches as part of the decolonisation process. He decided to respond to the call and left for Rwanda as a *Fidei donum* priest. Initially, he taught Latin and Greek to a few privileged members of society, before discovering the extent of the poverty affecting physically handicapped young people.[18] He was given permission to use a bare hill and an old, run-down house in Gatagara, and formed an association in April 1960. The first residents arrived in 1961 and it wasn't long before operations picked up pace: the first crafts school for boys opened its doors and a female doctor and nurse arrived from Europe. In 1963, a crafts school for girls was also set up and a unit for very young children followed in 1964. New blocks and workshops were added to the site in 1965. By that time, 250 disabled children had made the site their home and the hill had become a fully-fledged village including schools, houses, a medical centre and a church. Emmaus Rwanda was a truly local development initiative. Its aim was to reintegrate physically handicapped youths into society, by first bringing in Europeans to operate on them and to provide rehabilitation before handing the task to local staff. All residents received training in professional skills. Boys were taught welding, car mechanics and farming, while the girls attended lessons in, amongst other things, cooking, sewing, ironing, cleaning, childcare, embroidery, winnowing and beading. A clothes-making workshop was opened in 1970, enabling the Community to export the items made to other parts of the region, while the workshop which assembled transistor radios became an independent cooperative. A "pilot village" was also created to familiarise the youngsters with independent living. In 1975, Father Fraipont gradually began to withdraw from the project and Rwandans became solely responsible for the centre.

## Emmaus International: Uniting Diversity

It is clear that the Emmaus organisations across the globe were hugely diverse. Some pre-dated the 1954 appeal and later aligned their work with Abbé Pierre's vision, some were created from scratch, and some were offshoots of the Emmaus model. With the exception of Europe, where there was a slight predominance of organisations set up by non-religious individuals, almost all associations were set up and managed by religious figures. Some focused heavily on charity, while others advocated the empowerment of society's most disadvantaged members and sought to make them aware of their rights. The challenge for Emmaus International was to assemble this disparate and fragmented group to ensure that every one of them could survive within a Federation.

### The genesis of Emmaus International

In Lausanne, Switzerland, in November 1957, three phenomena formed the backdrop to a first but fleeting attempt to create an Emmaus International: the development of small movements which declared their commitment, be it renewed or continued, to Emmaus in Europe; the internationalisation of issues that preoccupied Abbé Pierre – apparent both in the increase in the number of conferences held abroad and in the creation of ASCOFAM; and, last but not least, the founder's personal difficulties. Abbé Pierre was the president and the small handful of members included Georges Lillaz, managing director of the department store BHV and a loyal friend and key member of the Bourdonnais team; and Raymond Saillet, founder of the first Emmaus Community in Switzerland.[19] The group's aim was "to coordinate the various activities which [had] grown across the world spawned by the efforts and initiatives of Abbé Pierre, and to ensure they [could] offer each other mutual support." However, Abbé Pierre's lengthy stay in hospital and the many conflicts which erupted appeared to get the better of the venture, which was shelved as quickly as it had come into being.

In late 1958, Abbé Pierre began to regain his strength and respond to requests for help from across the globe. In 1959 he went to

Argentina, then to Mumbai with a stop-off in Lebanon. In 1962, he travelled to the Sahara. However on 11 July 1963, on another visit to Latin America, the boat on which he was travelling sank in the River Plate and, for a time, he was believed to be dead. It was then that the team realised that he was the only person, besides Lucie Coutaz, who knew every single one of the Emmaus groups emerging across the world and that he was the Movement's only figure of moral authority. The years which followed were devoted to laying the foundations for a new Emmaus International and the organisation was officially launched six years later. The first leaders were a group of five members chosen for their seniority within Emmaus and on account of the fact that they represented a variety of continents: Marcel Farine from Switzerland, Dutchman Jean Wilken, the Canadian Robert Laporte, the Chilean José Aravena and Robert Vallade from Japan.

And so, on 24–25 May 1969 Emmaus International was reborn, again in Switzerland, but this time in the Federal Palace in Berne. At that time, Emmaus had sixty-one groups working in twenty-five countries. During the ceremony, the Association adopted the *Universal Manifesto*, a fundamental text, comprehensive yet brief, which ensured that organisations would be bound by the same basic principles but would have the freedom to enforce these in a way that best suited their working environment."[20] It was decided that a directory of Emmaus organisations would be created, that work would begin to coordinate the training of volunteers and leaders, and that a communications bulletin would be produced. Father José Balista from Argentina was made permanent secretary and Marcel Farine appointed president. It was decided that the headquarters would be in Geneva.

The second general assembly took place in Montreal in July 1971, and focused on the adoption of statutes. Following the offer made by Father Laporte, a leader in Canada for fifteen years, to volunteer as the Movement's part-time secretary, the headquarters were moved to Montreal. Marcel Farine remained president and Father José Balista was made vice-president. The third general assembly was held in Paris in September 1974. Here, members "looked for the optimum conditions which would enable [them] to put the Emmaus house in order, a process made necessary by the considerable growth of the Movement, and in order to protect the legitimate diversity within it."[21] It was decided that each group would submit annual reports to the organisation and pay a contribution, even if this was only symbolic. This issue was raised again in 1978, with Abbé Pierre insisting on equilibrium between prophecy and institution: "It is my belief that the institution is crucial, particularly for those who are very far away, very isolated and in need of this support [... But if] the institution is necessary, we must try to improve it so as not to lose the prophetic aspect of our work."[22] Meanwhile, in late 1976 the general secretariat was placed in the hands of Hervé Teule, already president of UACE, and in 1977 it was transferred to Charenton (Val-de-Marne).

## Religion affirmed in the fight for development

As we have seen, a significant number of Emmaus groups were founded by members of the Catholic Church. In that sense, the order of the "monks of poverty", which Abbé Pierre had dreamed of establishing in the 1950s, came much closer to fruition abroad than it did in France, based both on a missionary ideal which, despite being in crisis, remained present, and on the major social encyclicals of Jean XXIII and then Paul VI.

World hunger, an issue close to the Catholics' heart from the mid-1950s onwards, continued to occupy a central place in Emmaus' work until the mid-1960s. As the FAO launched the World Campaign Against Hunger in 1959, so too did the papacy began to take a more affirmative stance on the issue. In 1961, it charged French Catholics with creating a federative body akin to the German *Misereor*.[23] They accepted the mission, creating the Catholic Committee Against Hunger, or the CCCF. In 1966, the committee was officially registered as the Catholic Committee Against Hunger and for Development, and became a permanent body. Most importantly, a series of encyclicals was issued affirming the importance of the Church's social teachings. While Emmaus did not reprint *Mater et Magistra* (1961), it did commend the statement made by Jean XXIII in March 1963 for the World Week Against Hunger. The Movement was even more generous in its praise of the encyclical *Pacem in Terris* (April 1963). The text was published in *Faim et Soif* in the July–August issue of that year and inspired by the text, Emmaus also published in the same issue a beautiful "tribute to the Pope of reconciliation",[24] following his death. His successor continued with the work already under way and Emmaus enthusiastically reprinted both the speech on local development which Paul VI made to the UN in October 1965 as well as the encyclical *Populorum Progressio* (March 1967), which was devoted entirely to the development of the Third World and advocated an integrated human development strategy combining the fight for peace with that against hunger, education and culture. From that point on, the Church officially defended positions which Emmaus had been advocating for the previous ten years, following the lead of Father Lebret.

Emmaus was particularly keen to relay socially progressive, even political, doctrines. An extract from the encyclical *Populorum Progressio* was reprinted in a 1967 issue of *Faim et Soif*: "While in some regions of the world an oligarchy lives a life of luxury, the rest of the population, poor and scattered, is deprived of any opportunity to pursue personal goals and occupy positions of responsibility and is even forced to endure living and working conditions unfit for human beings [...] There is no one for whom private property is an unconditional and absolute right. Nobody is justified in keeping for his own exclusive use anything more than what is necessary when others do not even have what they need to survive [...] The desire to own property should never be pursued to such an extent that resources are no longer available to meet the needs of one and all."[25]

In the 1960s, Emmaus' religious sensibilities came to the fore, displayed clearly through the integration networks they set up, their enthusiastic approval of Vatican policy, and the personal convictions of many of the Movement's leaders and activists. The 1974 general assembly made no effort to hide the religious aspect of Emmaus, despite the fact it took care to ensure that religious affiliation remained personal to each member. As Roubaix stated in 1974: "As far as religion is concerned, it is entirely logical that the stances on global problems adopted by members of Emmaus stem, to a greater or lesser extent, from their religious beliefs. However, the

Movement as such must refrain from declaring itself a denominational movement."[26]

## The controversial place of politics within Emmaus: liberation Christianity comes up for debate

Religion's prominence within the Movement soon began to fade and debates on the place of politics within Emmaus took centre stage. But while there was broad agreement on religious issues, the place of politics was controversial to say the least. This was due to the fact that one, deliberately ambiguous principle was at the very core of the Emmaus system. Since the very beginning, the Movement had made plain its desire "to fight against the causes of poverty, in all its forms, until they are completely destroyed" (*Universal Manifesto*, article 6). But it did so without ever explicitly stating how far it would go to achieve this goal.

In the 1960s, politics began to come to the fore through a series of articles on Latin America and specifically on the political situation in Brazil, a country which in 1964 had been the victim of a military coup and subsequently, of an increasingly bloody, authoritarian regime. However, the Emmaus newspaper only ever relayed the official positions of the Church. In spring 1963, a lengthy article drew readers' attention to the major "revolutionary strike" in São Paulo and to the workers' demands. At the same time, the driving force behind the strike, the National Labour Front, wholeheartedly endorsed the principles of the encyclical *Mater et Magistra* and the Archbishop of São Paulo, followed by several priests and bishops, gave the cause their full support.[27] In 1966, the newspaper backed Brazil's democratic opposition, comprising the Left and a Church led by Dom Helder Câmara, with the discreet support of the apostolic nuncio and the more open support of Pope Paul VI.[28]

However, it was not until mid-1968 that the place of politics began to emerge as a key issue, with the students' and workers' movements in the West and, in Latin America, the General Episcopal Conference in Medellín.[29] Members of the conference were increasingly insistent upon the need to reject "the charitable deeds of old". Their aim was to "cause the famous and the eldest among their privileged children to feel ashamed of their often profound neglect of the poor, and to compel them to devote themselves to the battles waged as an integral part of serving those who suffered most."[30] The debate made waves at the first general assembly (1969), and continued throughout the 1970s. Broadly speaking, two camps went head-to-head. On the one hand, there were those who advocated helping the poor to become self-sufficient, who were staunch defenders of liberation Christianity[31] and/or Marxism. On the other hand, there were those who believed in a more charity-based approach, who were more conservative in their outlook.

The first camp was a very political one, comprising the main groups in Latin America outside Brazil[32] and *Les Hirondelles* from the Nordic countries. The political conscience of the South American subcontinent was becoming increasingly acute, and Argentina became the vehicle through which it was expressed. The country condemned the binary opposition between the developed and developing world, declaring that "the aim of Emmaus must be to fight to abolish the organisations which underpin this order of things."[33] It was supported by Sweden's Marxist-inclined thinkers who "attacked those who did not cut off ties with people who continued to live within existing organisations and adapt to them."[34] Four years later, liberation theology[35] offered a new historical framework. Chile became the herald of the fight to establish a new world order: "In aspiring as we do to stand shoulder to shoulder with the oppressed in their suffering and their struggles, we note that in the countries which make up South America, the clash of interests between the ruling class and the class of the oppressed is becoming increasingly apparent. We aspire to remain faithful to the spirit of Emmaus and to play the role that is incumbent upon us to play in the fight for liberation. Furthermore, we seek to demand that Emmaus groups in developed countries provide effective support in the fight against the imperialist forces which exploit our countries and are primarily responsible for the poverty our people endure, with the complicity of our ruling classes. The oppressed, those who have nothing, will never experience true joy until we have eradicated the root causes of poverty, and until we have made sure that it is no longer possible for one class to be exploited by the other [...] The duty of the poor is to take power."[36]

During its assembly in early 1974, Sweden followed suit. Roubaix declared: "Emmaus-Björkå is a workers' collective based on the concept of proletarian internationalism. This concept holds that there are fundamental common interests uniting the proletariat of imperialist nations and the people of oppressed countries in the fight against imperialism. Our task is to deepen our knowledge of the fight against imperialism through close study of Marxist-Leninist works, and to provide national liberation movements with as much material support as possible, because these movements are the most powerful weapon in the fight against imperialism; we must also support the fight for liberation in oppressed countries through political action..."[37]

By now it will be clear that two opposing currents of thought were beginning to converge: one in the South and primarily religious, liberation theology; the other in the North and primarily political, Marxism – the Swedish group *Björkå* supported several African liberation movements supported by the Soviet camp, including the MPLA in Angola, the PAIGC in Guinea-Conakry and the SWAPO in South Africa. It continued to do so throughout the 1970s and 1980s.

However, there were other groups who maintained a more cautious stance. Towing the official line of Catholic Action, Italy "ruled out any possibility of taking direct political action."[38] An article published in a 1970 issue of *Faim et Soif* stated, "There is no way that the fight against the causes of poverty can be separated from the political struggle. As a Movement, we must refrain from making two mistakes: either disregarding political action [...] or allowing the Movement to form ties, as a Movement, with any of the bodies or parties, or groups of parties, through which political action is carried out. Such ties would make it impossible for the Movement to act as a political agitator. In order to accomplish its specific mission, a Movement like Emmaus must, as a group, [...] restrict itself to what are known as the preliminaries of politics."[39] Lastly, other groups advocated a more charity-based, even conservative approach, starting with the most powerful groups (France) and those who most clearly emerged as leaders (Switzerland and the Netherlands). Undoubtedly out of a desire to remain realistic, but also perhaps as a result of the fact that he had, for a long time, been a staunch anti-communist, Abbé Pierre settled the debate with the following decision: "We must fight against the causes of poverty together, as a matter of urgency, but how exactly this is to be done remains a matter of personal choice. We must respect the differences within the Movement and avoid creating a political party under the Emmaus flag."

And so, while some Catholic supporters of the Third World became involved in political struggles,[40] Emmaus International, as a result of the divisions between groups and internal power struggles, resolutely defended more cautious positions but wished in no way to remain neutral in the political and religious debates of the time. This line of action was recalled, and explicitly enshrined, in a text adopted in October 1978 entitled "The Scope and Limits of Emmaus' Social Action'. The text encapsulated both the Movement's desire to encourage social action for social justice and to avoid partisan behaviour:

> "1) In addition to being both the starting point for, and complement of, any struggle for social justice, Emmaus as a Movement fights alongside the most vulnerable members of society. Its mission involves not only coming to their aid in their hour of need, but also enabling them to demand their own rights and make their own voice heard.
>
> "2) It is implicitly understood that such action means that Emmaus is, and remains, in conflict with all those who, consciously and unconsciously, cause poverty, particularly through various forms of domination at a national or international level [...]
>
> "3) It is fully in line with the *Universal Manifesto of Emmaus* to arouse, inspire support and assist social or popular movements seeking rights which are not respected.
>
> "4) However, for Emmaus groups, campaigning as part of, or working with, political parties or movements whose objective is to achieve power, exceeds the scope of the *Universal Manifesto.*
>
> "5) Membership of any political party, or programme, whether or not these are based on a specific ideology, is a matter of individual concern for each member of Emmaus, and not for the Movement as a whole."[41]

Following publication, the text was constantly referenced and today continues to serve as a doctrinal basis for the Movement's relationship to politics.

## The Many Forms of Emmaus' International Activity

As was the case of the early days, the polymorphous fight against the causes of poverty led Abbé Pierre to invent new means of action, or to import and transform those already in place.

### SOS-Milk Cartons

The first instance of Emmaus sending cartons of milk abroad dates back to late 1960. The Movement declared: "While we wait to be able to destroy or contribute to destroying the causes of poverty, it is vital and urgent to save the newborn babies who are actually dying from a lack of milk."[42] Emmaus groups in Belgium, Germany and the Netherlands then launched an operation to collect cartons of concentrated, sweetened milk, calling on children to make donations to help their young comrades in poor countries. The operation was centrally coordinated by a Belgian couple, Mr and Mrs Laroche. In order to ensure the operation could continue in the longer term, the couple then decided to manage requests from missionaries received by Abbé Pierre.

In 1963, the famine in Bangladesh prompted Abbé Pierre to launch a new appeal for cartons of milk. In response to the appeal, the organisation SOS-Milk Cartons was set up in France, with headquarters at Rue du Faubourg-Poissonnière in Paris. It would appear that none of the association's activities continued over a sustained period of time. Instead, it would spring into action periodically, organising operations as and when the need arose. In fact, its initiatives during this period were significantly out of sync with those launched by Emmaus, which sought to eradicate poverty rather than relieve its symptoms. In 1971, Hervé Teule took up the presidency of the association, followed by Paul Chamont. These appointments kept SOS-Milk Cartons in the Emmaus family.

## Emmaus and Bangladesh: from twinning committees to Craftsmen of the World

While SOS-Milk Cartons remained tied to Emmaus' apron strings, two other associations were to gain independence: UCOJUCO (today known as *Peuples solidaires* or People United) and *Artisans du monde* or Craftsmen of the World. While *Faim et Soif* did discuss the Biafra tragedy (1967–9) on several occasions, Emmaus was not an emergency aid organisation and did nothing specific to help those affected. By contrast, two years later, the Movement as a whole made an all-out effort to support Bangladesh.[43] Indeed, Abbé Pierre received a personal request from Narayan Desai, a militant Indian pacifist and disciple of Gandhi, to raise awareness of the tragedy among French people and to galvanise the country into sending food, supplies, clothes and medicines to the refugees. On several occasions, *Faim et Soif*, "echoed the cry of the Bengali people" with strong political conviction – Narayan Desai declared the tragedy "genocide", while *Faim et Soif* called it "the most heinous of crimes against human values and their greatest challenge since Nazism."[44] Cartons of concentrated sweetened milk, clothes and blankets were sent to Oxfam, the main organisation working within the camps. By late 1971, Emmaus had already collected and sent eighty-one tonnes of milk, 340kg of medicines, a tonne of plastic for roofs and more than 1 million francs, divided equally between the camps and efforts to get the villages of Bangladesh back on their feet.

Upon his return from India, on 1 November 1971, Abbé Pierre sent a letter to every mayor in France suggesting that French towns be twinned with refugee camps. The idea was not entirely new: since the late 1950s, Emmaus had displayed a keen interest in twinning committees, regularly relaying the annual congresses of the Federation of Twinned Towns, a body created after the Second World War in an attempt to further Franco-German reconciliation. However, the concept was hijacked and took on a new, unprecedented form. This time, it was not two towns which were twinned, but a town and a camp. More than 700 French town councils took part in the initiative.

The principle of sponsoring Indian camps was later shelved as the refugees returned home. Nevertheless, the population's needs remained great and to ensure the initiative would continue long-term, Abbé Pierre suggested that it instead become an initiative which twinned French towns with Bengali villages, in order to support reconstruction and development. As a result, on 1 July 1972 around sixty committees, created in response to this appeal, came together to form the Union of Twinning-Cooperation Committees (UCOJUCO). UCOJUCO became a member of the World Federation of Twinned Towns; its headquarters were in Charenton, Hervé Teule was the treasurer and Paul Chamont, also responsible for Emmaus Volunteer Support, was the secretary-general. In the space of a few months, the committees spread to the majority of western countries where Emmaus had taken root.

While the committees focused their efforts on fostering development in Bangladesh (training midwives, opening clinics, hospitals, primary schools, orphanages, secondary schools, vocational training centres, support for livestock rearing and agriculture), the country was deliberately not mentioned in the statutes, in order to allow for the possibility of providing similar assistance to other parts of the world in the future. In 1973, committees also appeared in Burkina Faso (for reforestation, the construction of small dams and wells, support for food-producing crops and cooperatives, and the promotion of the craft industry) and in Tanzania, Mali and Senegal in 1978. In late 1977, the UCOJUCO general assembly decided to officially rename itself the Union of Committees for the Development of Peoples (UCODEP).

The concept of twinning-cooperation was deeply rooted in development-aid thinking, but also harked back to Abbé Pierre's previous involvement in the Universal Movement for a Global Confederation: the aim was, in the words of Roubaix, to "bring about a desire, a way of being and of living, which might accurately be described as *global civicism.*" He went on to state that "in order to do this we must go *beyond pity and charity*, we must dare to tackle *the political dimension* [...] With charity, we simply pass the hat round; it is as individuals that we dig into our pockets and give what we see fit. Faced with problems of this kind, I am convinced that we need to go further, beyond individuals and their goodwill, and call upon human communities that work."[45] In 1983, UCODEP merged with the movement, "1% to the Third World for Solidarity in Development", created in 1974, and which would later form Peoples Together or *Peuples solidaires*.

It was also as part of the twinning initiatives and at the instigation of Abbé Pierre that the first *Artisans du monde* (Craftsmen of the World) shops would open their doors. UCOJUCO, which sought in particular to develop local craft industries, opted for this original solution. It allowed Third World products fair access to the market (with "maximum satisfaction of the worker – the guarantee that he would receive the actual price paid and that no intermediary would cream off a significant share"), as well as allowing information and awareness-raising points to be set up in western countries ("to open people's eyes to the international mechanisms which perpetuate these exploitative organisations through imperialism, multinationals and the arms trade").[46] This idea was not entirely new; similar shops were already up and running in the Netherlands, England (Oxfam shops) and in Switzerland (*Magasins du monde*). The first Craftsmen of the World shop opened in France in the Les Halles district of Paris in early 1974, and the concept quickly spread, in particular, it would seem, to places where there was an Emmaus Committee of Friends nearby. The same formula was also used to support Chile. It enabled goods handcrafted by Chilean political prisoners to be traded across France and meant that awareness of the country's situation continued to grow from 1974 onwards. For all that, *Artisans du monde* remained the brainchild of Abbé Pierre and it became independent from Emmaus almost immediately.

To conclude, it would seem that to an even greater degree than in France, Emmaus abroad was a patchwork of various, fragmented organisations which had nothing more in common than their attachment to the figure of Abbé Pierre. Some were drawn to him on account of his political discourse, others for his charitable deeds, and the majority for his charisma and prophet-like aura. As a result, organisations were united more by the crucially important religious aspect of the Movement than by its relationship with politics, which was inherently ambiguous and a major bone of contention. Finally, the vast range of Emmaus initiatives and its central aim of "getting men back on their feet" put the Emmaus International of the *Trente Glorieuses* at the crossing point between traditional missions, the new humanitarian-development model and more radical ways of supporting the Third World.

# III – 1980–2000: EMMAUS RETURNS TO THE MEDIA AND THE POLITICAL ARENA

The *Trente Glorieuses* came to a slow and gradual end as a series of devastating blows brought France to its knees. For the associations, the first signs of a social crisis caused by the deterioration of the economic situation appeared on the ground in 1975. From then on, slowly but surely, the authorities became aware of the unemployment problem facing French society, with 1 million unemployed in 1977 and 1.5 million by 1980.

The Left's arrival to power initially triggered a change in policy, with the government moving away from liberal economic strategies and towards a new form of Keynesianism:[1] there was an increase in the minimum wage, in payments for the elderly on a low income, in family allowance and in housing benefit. Measures were adopted to support young people and encourage the building of new homes, industries were nationalised, and laws were passed which reduced working time, increased paid leave, etc. However, these measures, which defied Reaganism and Thatcherism, did not produce the desired effects. In 1982, France plunged back into recession. In May, the number of unemployed passed the 2 million mark and all economic indicators turned red, while the municipal elections of 1983 saw the opposition stage a dramatic recovery. Consequently, 1983 sealed the beginning of a new phase of austerity and of the process that would gradually convert the socialists to economic liberalism.

Nevertheless, unemployment continued to rise, with 2.4 million unemployed at the end of 1984. After a slight improvement in 1985, the figures soon returned to their former dismal state: the unemployment rate went from 2.8% in 1974 to 5.9% in 1979, then 8.3% in 1983. In 1985 it passed the 10% mark and reached 10.6% in 1987. In particular, the crisis caused long-term unemployment to become significantly more widespread, and triggered an increase in casual labour. The decline, even disappearance, of traditional family and rural support networks; the crisis of workers' organisations – chiefly communist – which had previously structured the social fabric; and the gradual breakdown of the traditional family unit (a decrease in marriage and an increase in divorce, single-parent families and single-person households) caused the barriers, which at one time would have prevented people from sinking into poverty, to disappear.

It was at that point that the so-called "poverty-insecurity" issue began to feature in national political agendas. It first appeared in the form of reports: Henri Péquignot's 1979 report to the Economic and Social Council entitled "The Fight Against Poverty', and Gabriel Oheix's report two years later, "The Fight Against Poverty and Insecurity: Sixty Proposals', which was commissioned under Giscard d'Estaing and eventually delivered under Mitterrand. The issue then appeared in the form of symbolic gestures: in 1981 the Ministry of Social Affairs became the Ministry of Solidarity. Finally, the issue came to the fore as a series of action plans: January 1983 saw the launch of an initial phase of action focusing on improving the provision of emergency support and social welfare payments, and emphasising the need to combat the causes of poverty (debt and illiteracy). October 1984 then marked the start of a second phase, which saw an "unprecedented level of mobilisation" on the part of the government, as it focused its attention on emergency accommodation, social housing, the use of agricultural surpluses, and improving the situation of the older unemployed.[2] Meanwhile, at the end of March 1983, Prime Minister Pierre Bérégovoy received the major associations working to support the poor, including Emmaus, for an initial review of the situation on the ground. In light of this review, the second action plan set aside the vast sum of 200 million francs a year to be divided between twenty major associations, which once again included Emmaus. However, for the government, the first plan was nothing more than "a bare minimum" and the second a "stopgap measure"[3] brought in before the introduction of a guaranteed minimum wage. This was a policy that the associations had long hoped to see adopted, a policy that was championed by all presidential candidates of 1988 and a policy that the French had approved by an overwhelming majority.[4] Following the Wresinski report[5] and a lengthy consultation with associations, the minimum wage (RMI) finally saw the light of day in December 1988. The wage aimed to provide social protection to the increasingly large sector of the population who were not eligible for such support. It strengthened the basic social rights of the French people by reviving a more administrative form of state intervention.[6] Two centuries after the French Revolution and a few months away from the bicentenary celebrations, the nation fully acknowledged, once again, its duty to assist the poorest members of society.

To conclude, this third and last part of the Emmaus story played out against the backdrop of an economic and social crisis which put both authorities and associations to the test as they faced new audiences and problems. It emerged gradually with the issue of unemployment slowly gaining prominence over a ten-year period before being suddenly catapulted into the spotlight in 1984, with media interest in the issue of the "new poor", the major government plan to tackle poverty and insecurity and, for Emmaus, the thirtieth anniversary of the 1954 appeal, all accelerating the process. Abbé Pierre returned to centre stage: the brown beard had turned grey and the prophet appeared to have become an old sage, but his sparkling oratory and ability to charm the media had remained entirely untouched.

Beyond the problems specific to each association within the Movement, the challenge facing Emmaus as a whole was twofold. On one hand, it had to transform from an entity based on a charismatic but ageing founder to an organisational and institutional authority. This authority, known as Emmaus France, was a late addition to the Emmaus family, created in 1985 and its foundations were only gradually consolidated. On the other hand, it was forced to manage a rapid and dramatic shift in the Movement's centre of gravity: while the Communities had, since the 1960s, been the only type of Emmaus organisation known to the public, and almost the only one with social housing, from the mid-1980s onwards, the organisation chart became strikingly different. Association Emmaus resurfaced, now focused on meeting the most pressing social needs. *SOS-Familles* developed at breakneck speed, in order to fight against household debt. The Movement also created two new key players, the Abbé Pierre Foundation for the housing of the underprivileged, and a vast array of organisations which aimed to reintegrate those whom society had cast aside. However, the rise of these organisations, concurrent with that of a nascent Emmaus International, was not without a number of problems of power and balance.

# *Chapter 8* / EMMAUS BEGINS TO SPECIALISE IN MEETING URGENT SOCIAL NEEDS

In 1983, Association Emmaus was little more than the relic of a bygone age, with only three disparate activities under its control: a shelter at the Rue des Bourdonnais, the Prost home in crisis, and a social centre that was tied to the Emmaus social housing company of the Plessis-Trévise Community. In the space of a few years, the arrival of the economic and social crisis radically altered the state of play: the Association threw itself into meeting the urgent social needs on the ground. No other Emmaus organisation was working in this sphere and it became the Association's new pet cause. Association Emmaus then began to expand considerably, its growth based largely on state subsidies. It was spread over more than fifty sites, almost all of them in the Paris region. In 2007, it notched up 297,000 day visits and 436,000 overnight stays in accommodation centres. In 2008, it had more than 430 employees on its books – that was more than the total number working for *Secours populaire* across the whole of France. The team managed a budget that soon exceeded the €32 million mark.

This spectacular renaissance, that was above all a process that restructured the Association, resulted from a combination of factors. 1979 brought with it the arrival of Michel Lefebvre, former secretary-general of the General Confederation of Housing[1] and former president of the Prost home and UCC. Lefebvre was the architect behind major changes within the Association. However, also responsible for the renaissance were the new government action plans launched in 1983–4, as well as the media campaign of winter 1984–5. From that point on, every fibre of the Association's being worked to establish a coherent chain of responses that – in the words of the slogan adopted by the team – would allow the socially excluded to move "from the street back to society". This development, the result of the increased number of organisations and initiatives, went hand in hand with a process that saw the Association become a thoroughly professional outfit. It was a process that the Association itself found more than a little difficult to reconcile with its militant identity.

## Emergency Aid

Abbé Pierre's 1954 appeal in aid of the "street sleepers" had, first and foremost, been an attempt to raise the alarm about France's housing crisis. Housing supply later began to catch up with housing demand and this, combined with the prosperity of the *Trente Glorieuses*, meant the issue was no longer discussed. In the early 1980s, the issue reappeared in a different form: the homeless now victims not of a housing shortage, but of unemployment. Nevertheless, it was the images of 1954 that re-emerged from the archives in the winter of 1982 as those freezing to death became front-page news. Every winter since then, the issue has continued to haunt both the press and the national conscience in a bizarre seasonal pattern that has seen the homeless become people to be housed in the winter and evicted again in the summer.[2] After the authorities' and associations' first clumsy attempt to take the issue in hand between 1983 and 1993, a visible change in funding and organisational methods saw Association Emmaus cement its place as a highly professional outfit in the sector working to meet the population's widespread and urgent social needs.

### Winter initiatives begin to develop

In the winter of 1982–3, the press once again began to draw the nation's attention to the homeless freezing to death. The following winter was the harshest of the decade. After the January 1983 plan and the March circular recommending that every major French town set up emergency social services that remained open 24/7, in 1984 the government adopted a plan for the winter fight against poverty and insecurity. One notable feature of this plan was the grant of 10 million francs awarded to twenty associations, including Emmaus, to fund emergency aid initiatives (shelters, food parcels and emergency funds).

These measures and this new focus on social exclusion, in particular during the winter, coincided with the thirtieth anniversary of the 1954 winter appeal. The Emmaus Movement chose to commemorate the event with a new appeal from Abbé Pierre. At the same time, the urgency of the situation prompted the Association to organise night soup runs in major French towns, using the funds newly provided by the government – an operation that, with the support of the Communities, was repeated every winter until 1989. These soup runs were typical of the palliative approach to social problems that prevailed at the time, and were created almost concomitantly with *Les Restos du cœur*, an initiative masterminded by Coluche in late 1985.

Funding from the DDASS, the local health and social care authority, also allowed the Association to open several emergency centres from winter 1985–6 onwards. These were set up in old railway wagons at Quai de la Gare station, in hospital annexes (according to the year: Claude-Bernard, Sainte-Anne, La Salpétrière or Esquirol), and sometimes in metro stations. Associations also joined forces to organise the shelters: the collective *Solidarité-Paris*[3] was created in winter 1986–7 as a manifestation of the associations' desire to coordinate their efforts and allowed them to keep track of the number and location of places available at any given moment. In the year 1984–5, 10% of those taken in by the Claude-Bernard centre were single women, 2% were children and 20% were over the age of 45. The proportion of women later seemed to decrease (they accounted for only 7.5% in 1993) before increasing again in the late 1990s and then decreasing once more, which it has continued to do ever since (3% in 2003). It was not until the 1990s and the law on the minimum wage that any specific provisions were made for the under-twenty-fives; this group accounted for 13% of those taken in by the shelters in 2003. Finally, the phenomenon of the "poor workers" became more visible: in 1985, 20% of the people who visited the emergency centres were in work, compared with 50% in 1993. However, by 2003, this proportion had plummeted to 10%, a figure far below the average for the Île-de-France region (24%).

In the 1990s, the formula was working well, and there were several major developments. Following the introduction of the minimum wage in 1988 and the 1990 Besson Law that aimed to guarantee housing for the poorest members of society, the government's poverty-insecurity funding – initially for the benefit of *all* of society's poor – was increasingly directed specifically towards those living on the streets. Thus, while the total amount of funding available decreased as a result of the proliferation of initiatives, the sum allocated to the homeless increased, particularly from 1993 onwards.[4]

Elsewhere, the network of shelters run by Association Emmaus continued to expand. Between 1984 and 1992, only two centres a year were opened; three were opened in winter 1993–4; then five during the following winters. In 1993 the Association lost its railway wagons when it was forced to return them for use during the Left Bank regeneration scheme. However, new centres, old factories and unused business premises allowed them to increase the number of places on offer.

Finally, 1993 saw the creation of the Paris *Samu social*, a travelling health and social care unit providing emergency support to those living on the street, and its creation radically altered the state of play in the social sector. A joint initiative from the state financial institution *La Caisse des dépôts*, the multinational French water company *Compagnie des eaux*, Paris City Council and FNARS,[5] the *Samu social* formed part of a new approach to begging and vagrancy. Indeed, until 1993, beggars and vagrants were considered criminals and were dealt with by a special police squad at the police headquarters. "The Vagabond Pick-Up Team" was created in 1955, and renamed "The Homeless Support Squad" in 1968. The homeless could be forcibly taken to Nanterre, where a former workhouse had been transformed into a centre providing shelter and medical care. Until 1989, the centre was managed by the Paris police headquarters before being handed to Paris City Council.[6] However, in 1994, the forcible removal of beggars was made illegal, and it became mandatory to establish a dialogue with the people concerned.

The *Samu social* operated using a network of minibuses with a team of social and healthcare workers on board. Between the hours of nine o'clock in the evening and four o'clock in the morning, the team came to the aid of those who had phoned for help as well as searching the streets for those in need. Those living on the street were offered the chance to come to one of the network's centres. Receiving a great deal of support and funding from the authorities, and devoted solely to this task, the *Samu social* managed an increasing number of emergency beds. As the service became a key player in the Paris emergency accommodation sector, Association Emmaus' own importance within the field decreased. While in the 1980s, the Association was one of the sector's "heavyweights", from 1993–4, it began to lose ground, chiefly to the *Samu social* (which managed 45% of beds in 2000), but also to the Centre for Protestant Social Action (CASP). CASP also experienced a meteoric rise to fame in the 1980s and managed 12% of all beds in the sector in 2000. Nevertheless, Association Emmaus remained the second largest organisation in the sector with 14% of beds under its control.[7]

The last important part in the fight against winter poverty was the "big freeze" protocol, which entered into force in 1999. In 2002, it became the "big freeze" plan, featuring three different levels, each for different night temperatures. The Association took part in the plan every year.

## Taking in people from the street

Created in the 1980s and 90s, these new initiatives were symptomatic of a shift within the authorities and in public opinion. Indeed, the issue of people living on the street was a matter of increasing concern, despite the fact that it appeared difficult to demonstrate the numbers had actually increased. In contrast, it was very clear that the homeless were becoming more visible, for several reasons.[8] First, because they were the exposed tip of the poverty-insecurity iceberg, out in the open for all to see. Secondly, the decriminalisation of vagrancy and begging, enshrined in the new penal code of 1994, led the police to refocus their policies on the fight against crime. The opening up of numerous public places since the 1970s (railway and metro stations), along with the move of the Les Halles district towards Rungis, in the southern suburbs of Paris, and the fight against insanitary housing, served to spread out the homeless shelters, which had previously been grouped together. This meant that the number of places where the public were brought face to face with the homeless increased. In addition, street newspapers began to appear in 1993. Increasingly on display in public places and holding the attention of the media, the homeless also found that public opinion was hugely sympathetic towards them. This sympathy stemmed in part from the fact that many of those surveyed feared that they too would one day find themselves alone on the edge of society, struggling to survive.

Association Emmaus devoted its attentions to these groups of people from the outset. The Rue des Bourdonnais, the shelter that had provided social support since 1955, served as the foundations of initiatives in aid of the homeless and witnessed exponential growth: 3,000 people were given a bed in 1984, and 1,200 were given shelter in February 1988 alone. To cope with this growth, in 1986 the Association purchased the neighbouring premises. Soon receiving funds from Paris City Council, the shelter provided a listening ear, help with administrative procedures, allowed the homeless to use the premises as their registered postal address and/or directed them towards organisations best adapted to their individual needs. This shelter also housed the largest free locker room in Paris, later moved to the railway station Quai de la Gare.

### The minimum wage

Adopted on 3 December 1988, the bill introducing a national minimum wage (RMI) created another government post. The law stemmed from Father Wresinski's report submitted to the Economic and Social Council.[9] According to Wresinski, who founded ATD Fourth-World following his decision to break away from Emmaus, poverty was not simply material, but something that took many forms. To him, poverty was a social, cultural *and* civic state, each form of insecurity following on from and reinforcing the other. This view prompted him to recommend a greater degree of coordination between work on education, housing, healthcare, employment and vocational or other forms of training, through initiatives more tailored to individual needs. From the very beginning, Association Emmaus was at the forefront of the campaign for the minimum wage and recruited members of staff responsible for running this new service at the Rue des Bourdonnais. The Association's sat on the various Departmental Integration Councils[10] and through its general secretary it chaired one of three Local Integration Committees located in Paris.[11]

However, the Association opted to deal exclusively with the homeless; people with a fixed abode were referred to the social services. And yet the initiative, designed as a temporary measure to provide support on a long journey that would see them ultimately reintegrated into society, clearly did not serve the same purpose for this group: the longer the time spent on the street, the more difficult reintegration became, particularly if the period of time spent on the streets exceeded the two-month mark.[12] This meant that broadly speaking, the aim of the initiative was not to get the homeless back into the world of work, but first and foremost, to get them back into society: to get them to agree to detox, a health check and psychotechnical tests, and to encourage better personal hygiene. This process was made all the more difficult by the shortage of accommodation centres and by the fact that many of those receiving support were unable to work.

### The development of day centres

1993–4 marked the start of a new phase in the care of society's poorest members, with the development of day centres. These had of course existed at the Association since the mid-1980s, set up in prefabricated buildings on three small plots of land on loan from Paris City Council. However, at that time, they occupied a secondary place among the Association's initiatives in aid of the homeless.

However, in the mid-1990s, the day centres enjoyed a new boom. At the instigation of and thanks to funding from the newly created Abbé Pierre Foundation, one of whose aims was to try out new, innovative ways of combating social exclusion,[13] the Association opened its "Solidarity Boutique" in 1994 on Rue Bichat, in Paris' 11th arrondissement. With daytime opening hours complementing those of the night shelters, the idea behind the boutique was to group together under one roof a whole host of services beneficial to those living on the street. These included hygiene and healthcare services (washing machines, showers, footbaths, medical and dental care, facial treatments, a hairdresser, help with alcohol addiction, etc.); and workshops providing support in finding a job and paid internships and in getting paperwork in order, help with finding accommodation, and a service that allowed those of no fixed abode to register the boutique as their official address. Visitors were also able to cook their own food and partake in outings and cultural activities on offer at the weekend. With sixty to seventy people arriving through the doors daily, and an initial workforce of only two paid employees plus the 110 volunteers who quickly followed, the boutique soon reached saturation point. As a result, the concept was reproduced, under different names, in the Paris suburb of Créteil and at the Pitié-Salpétrière hospital.

Another centre that opened its doors in late 1988 was, from the outset, every bit as successful as it was geographically central: l'Agora in the Rue des Bourdonnais. A large subsidy from the Paris transport company, RATP,[14] and funding from the DDASS and the DASES,[15] enabled the association to transform an old shelter whose activities had ground to a halt into a "Solidarity-Integration Centre". The principle here was the same, but was applied on a very large scale. In 2000, the centre provided support to 91,000 people; by 2005 it helped 200,000. In 2000, L'Agora also began to offer breakfast to the homeless, and began to open at the weekend, meaning it henceforth provided support seven days a week, 365 days a year. In late 2003, a partnership with Microsoft France enabled the centre to set up a "cyberspace", an initiative that received extensive media coverage. The centre was now able to offer free and unlimited internet access to those living in abject poverty. The resources available included a registered virtual (email) address, the opportunity to create data-storage sites (to store family photos, copies of administrative documents, etc.), a webcam to keep in contact with friends and family, and the opportunity to browse adverts for jobs and accommodation, and so on.

Broadly speaking, the 1990s were characterised by the significant development of these shelters where the homeless could receive help free of charge and without giving their name. In addition to the traditional changing rooms, these shelters offered a wide variety of practical services. The aim was to create places adapted to the problems of homelessness where the person living on the streets could find as many solutions as possible to their needs. These needs could range from the most urgent to the need "to reintegrate into society, reclaim a sense of citizenship and once more enjoy fundamental human rights." Furthermore, "taking in the homeless and meeting their basic needs provided the Association with an opportunity to ensure they did not slip through the net and to direct them towards the services best adapted to their particular situation."[16]

### Summertime social exclusion

Association Emmaus also considered how best to care for the homeless during the summer. While the problem was as old as the homeless themselves, it took an exceptionally long time to enter the public's radar, and they were ambivalent in their response. From the mid-1980s onwards, the associations constantly emphasised the lack of organisations open in the summer. This shortage meant they were flooded with requests for help, and in particular for food. However, despite the demand, the holidays taken by both volunteers and paid employees caused almost all of the centres to close over the summer.

In 1987, Association Emmaus began to call loudly for winter shelters to open all year round. In 1994, Paris City Council declared that centres could remain open throughout the year. The Association immediately seized this opportunity and opened one of its centres all year round. At the request of and with funding from the DDASS, the Association then opened a *restaurant social* in the Rue des Bourdonnais. The restaurant provided free meals to the poor during the summer and an increasing number of diners came through the doors: 713 meals were served in July 1997; 3,000 in July 1999. At that time, 97% of diners were men. Also in 1999, Paris City Council launched its own *Camions du cœur*, vans offering meal hampers and coffee to those in need. However, as late as 2001, of the forty-six associations providing food to Paris' homeless, only nine remained open during the summer.[17] In this season, the emergency hotline for the homeless was flooded with calls from the moment it opened in the morning.

In addition to these quantitative goals, the Association aimed to better respond to the unique characteristics of summer poverty: solitude as the environment begins to wither in the heat, the gruelling ordeal of walking in soaring temperatures, the risk of serious burns as a result of falling asleep in the sun, dehydration, the explosive cocktail of heat, antipsychotic drugs and alcohol, and so on. The 2003 heatwave brought the issue to the fore once again, despite the fact that proportionately, the homeless were not greatly affected. It was then that the Association called in vain for a "heatwave" plan to be established. In 2004, it launched a campaign to raise awareness of the issue.

### The development of the "maraudes"

In view of the fact that those most excluded from society rarely come to the associations and institutions for help, the trend in recent years has been to go to them. The *maraudes*, or homeless support teams who travel on foot or by minibus, are an age-old phenomenon in the history of solidarity in France. St Vincent de Paul had already pounded the streets searching for prostitutes in need of his help and, in winter 1954, Abbé Pierre similarly toured Paris, this time providing the "street sleepers" with emergency support. However, these initiatives failed to spread and remained very sporadic. In 1993, the creation of the *Samu social* gave new impetus to this system which involved travelling around offering coffee, soup and blankets to the homeless or a place at a shelter where they could receive support. The law of 29 July 1998 on the fight against social exclusion broadened the scope of initiatives in aid of the homeless by providing for the creation of services that would operate at street level. Today, like many other associations in the solidarity sector, Association Emmaus has a walking *maraude*, that has been up and running since 1999.

Finally, the Association has been involved since 2002 with the collective *Aux captifs, La Libération* and, more recently, with the association, *Les Morts de la rue*. Literally meaning "The Dead on the Street", the association was set up in 2003 and aims to raise awareness among the authorities and the general public of the extent and causes of these deaths, to give decent funerals to those who die in the street, to track down the families of those who have passed away and, if necessary, to organise a religious funeral service.

## Accommodation Centres: "From the Street Back to Society"

Asylums and hospices were the successors of the eighteenth-century workhouses, created to provide shelter to a hotchpotch of the sick, vagabonds, the elderly and the mentally ill, in large, dilapidated communal halls.[18] Until the 1970s, these institutions had a pitiful reputation. However, in November 1953 and December 1954, the first regulations for accommodation centres entered into force. These regulations notably stipulated that those newly released from prison and those at risk of prostitution were to receive state subsidies. Organisations specially designed to meet their needs would be created, along with hospitals and treatment centres. However, until July 1959 these regulations did not cover vagabonds who were now fit to practise another profession, and as a result they were regularly imprisoned. A new decree issued in May 1960 laid down the standards that had to be met for a centre to receive official ministerial approval, and made it mandatory for those attending the centres to receive both physical and psychological follow-up care. In the 1960s and 70s, two types of centres were in operation: shelters for the homeless, which replaced the workhouses in major towns, and accommodation centres in the stricter sense of the term that began to increase in number following Abbé Pierre's 1954 appeal. These were often religious associations that in 1957 came together to form the Federation of Accommodation Centres.[19]

The centres were restructured again in the mid-1970s. The law that entered into force on 19 November 1974 officially sanctioned housing benefit, extended it to other beneficiaries (chiefly families) and formalised the Accommodation and Social Readaptation[20] Centres (CHRS). The law of 30 June 1975 officially acknowledged the role the centres played in the government's mission to reintegrate the homeless into society. Finally, the September 1979 circular broadened the scope of this mission to include both social and professional reintegration.[21] At the same time, having been financed solely by the private sector, these centres began to draw on both public and state funds, even if today [2008], the private sector continues to fund these organisations to the tune of 90%.[22]

## Emergency accommodation centres

Emmaus' emergency accommodation centres (CHU) initially opened as winter shelters and were thus classed as temporary organisations or "level 1" centres. These centres could be CHRS organisations to which specific places were added, chiefly in winter, funded by other parts of the budget, but also buildings made available by local authorities or public bodies (hospitals, barracks, metro stations, etc.) and managed by the associations.

Since their creation in the mid-1980s, the CHUs have undergone significant changes, starting with their exponential growth: Association Emmaus, which did not manage a single CHU in the early 1980s, today [2008] has twenty under its control. The system has also grown more complex over time. The CHU themselves allow visitors to stay for between one and five nights, depending on the centre. The Association, however, refuses to renew a person's stay on a night-by-night basis. It views the practice as running contrary to its principles, as it means it is unable to take any steps to help a visitor reintegrate into society. Following the creation of the CHU themselves, "Vagrancy Stabilisation Centres" (otherwise known as "level 2" or "2 bis" centres) were also set up, designed for people who expressed a desire to come off the streets. Stays in these centres were longer (between a fortnight and a month). In addition to showers, launderettes and paramedical care, visitors had access to a social worker and could attend workshops where they received help with their search for a job or accommodation. Staff were also on hand to help set the wheels of visitors' personal projects in motion. It would be both pointless and tedious here to comb through this jungle of initiatives that were in a permanent state of flux and in which the social workers themselves could lose their way. Suffice it to say, each centre had its own characteristics that varied according to the association by which it was managed and the funding on which it depended. These included the maximum length of stay, and the centre's particular target group (paying residents or those who stayed free of charge, single women, single men or couples, etc.).

Until the mid-1990s, the management of the CHU was the subject of extensive debate within the Association: they were wholeheartedly endorsed by some as the essential apex of the system, while others rejected them, viewing them as incompatible with Emmaus' desire to eradicate the root causes of homelessness. The first point of view prevailed and has been the Association's official line ever since.

## Accommodation and social reintegration centres

There was, however, much broader support for the Accommodation and Social Reintegration Centres (CHRS). These centres had begun to take root with the opening of the Prost home, followed by the registration of the Bourdonnais hostel.

In 1979, the Prost home's large deficit prompted management to drastically reduce the number of beds and limit the length of stay. However, the home's approach also became more qualitative, with residents receiving a greater degree of support in their journey towards independence and social (re-)integration. The home then began to become a more official organisation. Registered in 1984 and later subject to an official purchase order as part of the regeneration of the area, the home was finally moved, after countless twists and turns, to Pré-Saint-Gervais in Paris' 19th arrondissement. Reopened in 1994, it divided into a CHRS and a follow-up service of apartments for those living in extreme poverty. In addition, the main body of another building housed a cloakroom and a space for cultural activities. The traditional hostel in the Rue des Bourdonnais also closed in 1995–6 to make way for administrative buildings (the Association's headquarters and the offices of UCC) and a better homeless support service; half of the residents were transferred to Quai de la Marne (a new CHRS for single men) and those best able to stand on their own two feet were sent to shared accommodation in various locations. The Association's first generation of CHRS, the Prost and Bourdonnais homes, that each complemented and later mirrored the work of the other, acted as testing grounds as the Association attempted to design a process that would ultimately see single men reintegrated into society.

In 1987, the Association also began to discuss accommodation for couples and children, which at that time in France was very thin on the ground. Not only did keeping the family unit together increase the chances of reintegration, but the almost total lack of accommodation available to women and children was at odds with the prevailing increase in the number of single-parent families. In 1990, the Association purchased a building in Passage de Flandre, in Paris' 19th arrondissement. Following a plan developed by Jacques Lazard, who had been a member of the Association's board of directors since 1954, the building was converted into a "social hotel". The hotel had fifty beds, meaning that in addition to those leaving the CHRS and those on the minimum wage, it was able to take in women with children and single-parent families. The facility was a "social hotel" and not a CHRS – it provided only "basic support"[23] on a temporary basis while residents waited to be rehoused. Paris City Council funded the project as part of its Departmental Integration Plan. Each room had a sink and a hotplate and the maximum length of stay permitted was three months, but was renewable – in 1994, the average length of stay was fourteen months, as the lack of social housing meant there was nowhere else for the residents to go.

In early 1992, the Association then reclaimed the CHRS at the Quai de Valmy,[24] where the national management of Emmaus France set up home on the ground floor. Each family had a kitchenette and a bathroom. The renovations carried out at the beginning of the 1990s prompted the Association to conduct a wholesale review of the ways in which they provided social support and to go from being "an organisation that placed a strong emphasis on living as part of a group, to being an organisation that accorded greater importance to a private life and a family's right to live as an independent unit."[25]

## The creation of stabilisation and integration organisations

The last stage of the journey towards reintegration was a visit to a stabilisation organisation. At Association Emmaus, the stabilisation process took place at SARAH (the Short-Term Support Service for Adults in a Hotel), in apartments across various locations or in a hotel.

SARAH was opened in October 1985 and was the first organisation of this kind to be created by the Association. Financed by the DDASS and with a small contribution from the residents themselves, it enabled the Association to offer single people and those temporarily excluded from society a room and social support. Since its start, the maximum length of stay at SARAH has remained at fifty days, with the possibility of an extension.

From the mid-1990s onwards, the stabilisation-integration system began to develop considerably. It was able to mirror the Transitional/Temporary Accommodation (ALT) system already in place and an agreement was signed between the Association and a social hotel. The Association incurred no extra costs as these were covered in part by CAF, the family benefits agency, and in part by the residents themselves. Only those in work or with a job in the offing were eligible to receive support from the ALT system; the agreement provided for three-month stays, which could also be renewed. Today [2008], this period has been extended to six months, again renewable. In 1998, the Association signed an agreement with the DDASS, agreeing to increase its capacity from eighty to 120 ALT beds. Today [2008], 140 such beds are available.

Other types of accommodation designed to facilitate social integration began to appear: supported apartments[26] and homes with variable leases[27] (1990s); social residences[28] and family hotels (2000). The Abbé Pierre Foundation in particular was keen to encourage the development of these new forms of accommodation.

Cross-cutting initiatives were developed for the residents of these various centres (CHU, CHRS, Stabilisation and Reintegration Centres). The battle against illiteracy was the first to be waged, beginning at the very start of the 1990s and following the recommendations of the Wresinski report. Workshops for both illiterate French people and foreigners wishing to learn French were set up, led by volunteers who had been trained by the Association. A whole host of new initiatives were also developed, including those providing access to healthcare help with claiming the minimum wage, and help with the searches for housing and employment.

## The system is called into question

The evolution of this support-accommodation-integration system was spectacular. Starting almost from scratch in the early 1980s and contending with continuing economic and social crises, within two decades it became an extremely complex and highly technical system.

In theory, its wheels seemed well oiled and, in the words of the Association, allowed the homeless to go "from the street back to society". In practice, however, the system ground to a halt, with every part of the machine choked up. It first entered a state of gridlock when the CHUs opened their doors. The centres were only ever reluctantly attended due to their rigid opening times (they were closed during the day), the lack of privacy, insanitary accommodation and the prevailing violence.[29] However, despite this they were constantly full to capacity, and the emergency services for the homeless were inundated with calls, sometimes from the minute they opened in the morning. Furthermore, the Association's archives reveal an increased bottleneck in the system from the end of the 1990s, caused by the arrival of large numbers of illegal immigrants and asylum seekers, who hailed from eastern countries, and black or North Africa. Arriving in France without a penny to their name, but often with professional qualifications and an ardent desire to integrate into both society and the labour market, they were unsuited to the traditional mechanisms that provided social support on the journey towards reintegration. The length of OFPRA[30] procedures, the shortage of places available in CADA (the national network of shelters for asylum seekers) and the 1991 law that banned them from working or applying for social housing all served to block the process. As a result, "the associations lacked ways of meeting the needs of these people, who often required little more than a gentle push in the right direction to find their feet, settle down and integrate."[31] Meanwhile, the number of asylum cases rejected by the courts gradually reduced many to vagrancy. At the other end of the chain, the blockage was caused by the lack of options available to those who wished to leave the system. From 1988 onwards, the relative improvement in the economic situation enabled some of those housed in the centres to return to work, but access to housing remained problematic: there was a shortage of housing for large families, council flats, family hotels, etc. In 2002, Association Emmaus declared: "This housing shortage is stifling the development of the CHRS and means that they are unable to keep people moving through the system. It is forcing residents to remain in the centres, and to live a life foisted upon them rather than one they have chosen, when all they require is a small amount of support. It is preventing centres from taking in new people who would benefit from the support on offer, and creating a sense of lassitude and exasperation."[32]

Social workers were ultimately rendered helpless in the face of the growing number of people who were mentally very fragile or suffering from psychiatric disorders and who had been refused treatment by specialist hospitals. Indeed, the June 1990 law on the hospitalisation of people with mental health disorders, and the November 1992 circular on reducing hospitalisation in favour of treatment within alternative organisations, changed the social treatment of mental illness. Support organisations found themselves attending to "a large number of people with schizophrenia, psychotic disorders and manic depression, the majority of whom were incapable of taking sole responsibility for continuing the treatment of which they were so desperately in need,"[33] and were people whom the social workers were often powerless to assist.

The "tent phenomenon", spearheaded by organisations from *Médecins du monde* to *Enfants de Don Quichotte*, ought to be viewed as an expression of the exasperation felt by associations and their users faced with a system in a state of gridlock. The groups' first demand was that centres should be open all year round and not only in winter. Since 1995, it is true that the authorities have in fact allowed associations to leave some centres open throughout the year – the CHU at Choisy, run by Association Emmaus, is one such example – but the practice remains limited. The second demand was that no restrictions should be placed on centres' opening hours and the 2006–7 campaign to achieve this goal bore fruit: following the "Reinforced Action Plan for People Experiencing Homelessness" (PARSA) of 2007 and the DALO Law that was passed two months later, emergency accommodation centres are now open twenty-four hours a day, seven days a week, with no restriction on the length of stay.[34] However, the associations observed that these laws and action plans in fact had a pernicious effect: the shortage of places in accommodation centres and, further downstream, in social housing, meant that while the new system saw associations no longer forced to send people back out on to the streets every night, and thus enabled them to provide those sleeping rough with stability and help them draw up a long-term plan, a new bottleneck in the system was created. This came about at the expense of the homeless who remained on the streets, unable to find even decent emergency accommodation. In addition, the lack of both financial and human resources made it difficult to provide social support.[35]

## For the young: the holiday for those on the outskirts of society

As part of the reintegration and stabilisation process, a unique initiative was developed in 1999 in Esteville. It was designed for young people who were living on the outskirts of society. Having functioned for some time as a retirement home for Abbé Pierre and Companions who wished to make use of it, La Halte d'Esteville had a structural deficit as a result of its low productivity. This deficit, together with the increase in the number of Companions who preferred to spend their retirement elsewhere (in a Community or other organisation) and the new legislation on communal support facilities for the elderly, which would have necessitated extensive renovation work on the site, prompted UACE to relinquish the house and, with the agreement of Emmaus France and Emmaus International, to donate it to Association Emmaus.

The new project resulted from the realisation that young people accounted for a significant proportion of those within the support facilities of the Association (in 1998, more than a fifth were under the age of twenty-five) and from a report newly published by the Ministry for Employment and Solidarity that recommended the creation of "living spaces away from everyday life where [young people] could design and carry out their own projects."[36] The Association wished to specifically target young people living in extreme poverty or as vagrants, and provide them with a place where they could receive support, a listening ear and relief from the pressures weighing heavy on their shoulders. They were also offered guidance and a whole host of activities designed to inspire them and restore motivation which had long faded away, such as an introduction to the crafts industry and open-air activities organised in cooperation with local associations and professionals, such as horticulturists and nurserymen. In 2006, one hundred young people participated in the scheme.

## Professionalisation and Militancy

The extraordinary growth of Association Emmaus, which had picked up from almost nothing in the early 1980s, forced the Association to question whether or not it was able to deal with the frenzied pace of this development. In addition, the relationship between the quantity and the quality of services was an issue frequently raised. In 1988, the Association expressed its intention to henceforth "limit the number of people who benefit from our support but ensure the quality of the service provided."[37] In 1995, former president Henri Camus reaffirmed his desire to see a more moderate pace of growth, but one that would in turn produce "high-quality social support". This statement "followed a discussion from which it emerged that in the view of the directors, this philosophy ought to underpin all of the Association's activities: it should aim to create small services that were dynamic and run with infectious enthusiasm. In turn, this ought to inspire others to do the same. Indeed, since the very beginning, it is this role as the driving force behind new initiatives that the Association has endeavoured to play."[38] The 1997 general assembly decided to pause the development of the Association. In 2001, it reaffirmed its desire to adopt a holistic approach when attending to those who sought help, to treat them with dignity and respect, in a way that would allow them to benefit from real support in their journey towards reintegration. The Association was delighted to have "resisted calls for it to develop its activities in other areas, for example, facilitating reintegration through the provision of financial support. Instead it preferred to develop the solutions already in place [...] It wish[ed] to remain a militant and innovative association."[39] However, behind the speeches, any pauses in development were not as clearly apparent as the spectacular rise in activity.

### Professionals in the field of social action

The first salient feature of this increase in activity was the exponential growth of the wage bill, affordable due to the predominance of public funding – whether from the state, the DDASS, DASES or CAF. This public funding allowed new staff to be hired across the various centres: in 1973, a total of 49 paid employees worked for the Association; there were 53 in 1983, 154 in 1993, 260 in 2000 and more than 430 in 2008. This increase in the wage bill meant the headquarters had to be extended to make room for the work of the secretariat and coordination and accounting services. In 1984, there was only one paid employee at the headquarters, Michel Lefebvre. In 1987 he was joined by a full-time accountant and his wife, who worked part-time at the secretariat. In 1989, the Association was still a family business. Christiane Lefebvre became a managerial assistant and a full-time typist was appointed. In 1993, there were still only nine people on the team. By 2008, however, it occupied the entirety of the Bourdonnais premises... From then on, it had all the defining characteristics of the major associations and businesses: a works council was set up, the workload of the board of directors increased, staff were divided into committees, the power balance shifted away from elected members in favour of paid employees, audits were conducted, the Association was restructured, and the staff even went on strike...

## The development of a communication policy

This growth was due first and foremost to the work conducted in a sector where needs were overwhelming and which received generous subsidies. It has also been due, for some years now, to better communication. It was not until 1995, following the development of its activities, its increasing weight within the sector and its expression of a desire to make its presence known, both within Emmaus and outside it, that the Association implemented a real communication policy. The policy was initially internal and was to "train, educate and organise meetings for donors [and] volunteers [...]" It affirmed the need to "promote the Movement, encourage militancy and bring the Association to life."[40] A brochure was created as well as a new logo, inspired by that of Emmaus France. However, until 2000, the sector depended entirely on volunteers and interns.

The policy quickly came to include a section on external communication. The Association launched a recruitment and membership campaign for Easter 1988, with the creation of their first poster. In launching the campaign, it followed in the footsteps of the CCFD,

*Secours catholique* and *Secours populaire*, who had long been active during this period when people were willing to dig deep into their pockets. The Association employed the services of CIME, an agency specialised in fundraising. Following the realisation that the public knew next to nothing about the various organisations within Emmaus, a Movement viewed as an homogeneous mass that focused on collecting and restoring waste items, the Association's aim was to forge its own identity and ensure it had a visible presence in the field. This would allow it to hold more sway with donors and volunteers, but also with the authorities and financiers, which would in turn allow it to reach the world of business. New communication tools were created (posters and leaflets, and a website in 2002), and a study was carried out to better target donor profiles and adapt the content of messages. In 2002, with the help of the agency Proximity, the Association developed campaigns to find new donors and retain those already on the list. The policy was a success; the number of donors went from 6,000 in 1997 to 19,500 in 1999, to 27,800 in 2006. In 2004, the gross profit of these campaigns stood at €960,000. Challenges currently facing the Association are the need to mitigate the damage caused by excessive demands on donors and to respond to the arrival of the baby-boomers and their "child of '68" mentality,[41] vastly different to the previous generation, along with the need to appropriate the new means of communication available (internet, text messages, etc.) – in short, to survive in a world where the competition for donations is increasingly tough.

This new visibility also allowed the Association to establish partnerships with businesses, in the framework of the July 1987 law on corporate patronage and the August 2003 law on economic initiative. The first partnership was formed with the AXA insurance group in 1995. AXA notably offered the Association its premises in Choisy-le-Roi for a very attractive price. The buildings were unused and the mortgage had already been paid off. The venture was in the interest of both parties. The Association noted in its archives that, "as with last winter's emergency shelter experiment at Pigalle, AXA wishes to mobilise its staff around this project,"[42] and be able to claim involvement in social initiatives. Cooperation with businesses has accelerated sharply since 2003, with the material and financial support of partnerships as varied as *BNP Paribas*, *Bayard Presse*, *Carrefour*, Paris Airports, the *France-Télécom* foundation, the *Société générale*, Microsoft and *Pinault-Printemps-Redoute* (now known as PPR). In 2004, corporate patronage accounted for €230,000 in funds and represented €256,000 in exchange value of goods in kind.

## Campaigning at Emmaus

As was the case with the majority of associations, campaigning at Association Emmaus was characterised by a significant gap between the bottom and the top. Top management was typified by the strong influence of people with a taste for militancy. As was the case in the social housing companies, these people were, first and foremost, activists who campaigned on several fronts and historic figures. Such was the case with Henri Camus, born in 1925. Camus was the president of UCC (1960–8) and the president of the Prost home until 1965. He worked his whole life as the paid director of Emmaus' property-buying companies. Alongside these commitments, he was a member of the board of directors at Association Emmaus (1958–60), then president of the Association (1960–93). Jacques Lazard, born in 1919, bank director and member of the Association's board of directors from 1957, moved to the bureau in 1960 and stayed there for four years. On his death in 1988, he bequeathed two apartments to the Association. Yves Goussault, member of the bureau (1955–7), sat on the board of directors in the 1960s and once again from 1992 to 1994. At the same time, he founded and managed IRAMM.[43] Born in 1927, Bernard Weiss, the first paid member of staff at UCC and a Community leader, sat on the Association's board of directors between 1976 and 1994 and on that of the Prost home from its opening in the 1970s.

This strong tradition of fighting on multiple fronts lives on today [2008]. Marie-Françoise Legrand, who was president of the Association from 1998 to 2001 and who has since remained a member of the board of directors, was the director of the National Federation of Social Housing Companies and member of the board of directors of the Emmaus social housing company from 1990 to 1996. Claude Michaud, president from 2002 to 2008, was a voluntary member of the board of directors from the 1980s, then president of the Emmaus Community at Neuilly-Plaisance.

Some key paid employees followed the same trajectory. Born in 1929, Michel Lefebvre was secretary-general of the Association from 1985 to 1993. Arriving at Emmaus in 1954, he was soon given a permanent position as assistant secretary-general at the CGL, a post he held from the 1950s to the 1980s. At the same time, he agreed to become the president of the Prost home in 1965 and of UCC from 1971 to 1977. On his retirement in 1993, he stayed on as president of the Association until 1998, when he fell seriously ill. Like Henri Camus, both a volunteer and paid employee, Lefebvre devoted his whole life to Emmaus; his wife also campaigned with the Movement. When he finally did go into retirement, the Association searched for a successor who was "an activist who champions the social cause and who has experience of working within associations" and of staff management. A leader of the Rural Christian Youth Movement (MRJC) was appointed to the post. In 1997, the position was passed on to Alain Raillard. Born in 1946, Raillard was a primary-school teacher turned housing specialist (director of publications at the CGL, head of the Île-de-France agency of the Interprofessional Housing Committee, technical consultant in charge of housing policy in the cabinet of the Ministry of Housing, and secretary-general of the High Committee for the Housing of the poor). Recruited for a short time by the Abbé Pierre Foundation, he ended his career as secretary-general of the Association before retiring in 2006. At the same time, he had been the president of the CGL and the National Observatory for Rental Prices, a member of the National Housing Council, vice-president of the social council of the UNFO-HLM, a municipal councillor in Aubervilliers (for the left-wing party Union des Forces de Gauche), and president of a French youth and cultural centre (an MJC). Lastly, the current secretary-general is a former regional leader of the CFDT-Métallurgie, a trade union for those in the metalworking industry. It is clear, then, that the top of the hierarchy were unequivocal in their support for militancy.

The issue was not quite so clear-cut at the bottom, namely due to the fact that the Association, which had enjoyed a recent revival, had lost its militant culture. Having long been out of the media spotlight and operating solely in the Paris region, it also had few volunteers: 290 in 1970, 415 in 2007. By way of comparison, *Secours catholique* boasted 66,000 in 2007 and *Secours populaire* 86,000 in the same year, albeit across the whole of France. To mitigate the absence of a militant culture and the deal with the increasing demand on resources created by a population living in extreme hardship, the Association began to organise training sessions, the first of which took place in 1991. A survey conducted in 1997 on the profile of volunteers revealed that 80% were women, half were over the age of fifty-five, half lived alone, and three-quarters had joined the Association in 1993. The greater proportion had volunteered in order to be useful to others (39%), or to use their skills or do something constructive (30%); very few had come out of religious belief (4%) or political affiliation (3%); and just 1% named Abbé Pierre as the reason they entered the Movement. For two-thirds of those surveyed, the Association was the only place they worked as a volunteer.[44] Since the survey's publication, it would appear that the average age of volunteers has decreased and the proportion of male volunteers has increased – in 2003 40% of applications to become a volunteer were from those between 18–30 and 41% came from men.[45]

In the early 1980s, the Association sprang to life once more in order to tackle serious social exclusion. This phenomenon received extensive media coverage but was broached by very few associations at the time. Consequently, in combating this scourge, the Association was able to ensure that Emmaus championed Abbé Pierre's new emblematic cause while still continuing to work on the streets. The Association's growth was remarkable, and it is today one of the most important branches of the Movement. However, two major issues continue to spark debate. The first of these is whether it is entirely appropriate to have within Emmaus an organisation that is two-thirds dependent on subsidies, when until the 1980s the Movement fervently defended the concept of independence through work. However, despite the misgivings expressed by some, in order to meet the urgent social needs of the poor the Association had no other choice but to look elsewhere for funding and members were consequently quick to accept that it would not be financially independent. The second issue is growth. Bubbling away beneath the service is the tension between the desire to provide high-quality support and the temptation, given the extent of poverty, to simply help as many people as possible. The solution adopted since the 1990s has been a circular one, whether vicious or virtuous, a matter of individual judgement: faced with an increase in the number of people in desperate need of social support, the Association must expand its workforce in order to maintain a high-quality service. And expanding its workforce in turn allows it to increase the number of people who benefit from the services available.

## *Chapter 9* / EMMAUS RETURNS TO THE FIGHT FOR HOUSING

As the *Trente Glorieuses* came to a close, the Emmaus social housing company (Emmaus HLM), like the majority of its counterparts, came to the depressing conclusion that it was impossible to both effectively manage property holdings and implement a genuine social policy in a system based on subsidies aimed at encouraging building. But in 1997, this system was called into question by the Barre law, which saw welfare payments for people begin to prevail over subsidies for the construction industry. It also marked the start of a new era for the housing industry, all the more so given that the economic and social crisis made the position of tenants highly insecure and given that the image of social housing continued to deteriorate. 1977 marked a clear before and after both in the history of social housing in general, and in that of the Emmaus HLM in particular. However, the challenge facing Emmaus remained the same: to defend social welfare in a sector which was increasingly concentrated, regulated and dependent on outside funding. Moreover, the changing profile of those renting accommodation prompted Emmaus to develop new methods of management.

At the same time, Abbé Pierre, who had turned his attentions to international initiatives in the 1960s and 70s, was called back to France in 1983 to take centre stage in the campaign to defend the "new poor". He returned to the issue which had originally made him famous – one he continued to hold dear –that of housing. In 1987, he laid the foundations for an organisation specifically devoted to housing the poorest members of society. Its aim was to analyse the problems these people faced and to test out innovative solutions. Five years later, the association was officially recognised as a *Fondation d'utilité publique*, a Not-for-Profit organisation serving the general interest. Unlike the other organisations within Emmaus, it opted to take on the name of the founder and became the Abbé Pierre Foundation for the Housing of the Underprivileged – to the great consternation of many within Emmaus. Like the Association, it too developed at lightning speed. In less than a decade, it acquired expertise which made it a force to be reckoned with, developing a truly professional mastery of communication, fundraising and the art of rousing the public to action.

## From Emmaus HLM to Emmaus-Habitat

After a difficult phase, 1976 marked the start of major restructuring process within Emmaus HLM. Following the discovery that some staff members had embezzled funds, the company opted to completely reorganise the management. Claude Néry, a former national member of the JEC who joined the New Left before becoming a member of the PSU, the CFDT and the construction company Adels, was a construction industry professional and was appointed as general director (1977–92). His assistant, Georges Dunand, also a member of the CFDT, took over the role in 1992. The presidency also changed with the simultaneous arrival of André Chaudières; a member of the board of directors since 1966, of the CFDT and Adels, a construction industry professional and Claude Néry's former manager. The new management were united in their social and political values and bound by friendship. The company's general services were overhauled and the tasks involved in the day-to-day running of the company were decentralised. The system was gradually computerised, a personnel department and salary scheme introduced, and a business mission agreed upon. Having outgrown the premises at the Rue des Bourdonnais, they also relocated. If the 1977 landmark reform of French housing policy is added to the mix, the extent of the transformation which took place in just a few years can be readily appreciated.

### The 1980s: reforms and experiments in social welfare

The system based on welfare payments for those in need notably began to materialise through Personalised Housing Benefit (APL). Designed to make low-income households financially solvent, the benefit involved lessors signing an agreement with the state, which would then award the lessor monthly payments. Originally intended as a temporary measure to stimulate economic recovery, the APL was introduced on a permanent basis to alleviate the increasing poverty of French households.[1] For Emmaus HLM, this reform would allow it to "return to a more normal level of housing construction".[2]

While in numerical terms there was only a negligible increase in the number of houses the company built (7,920 in 1975, 8,090 in 1984), behind the figures, the company had in fact embarked upon a large-scale policy of renovating the housing stock it already ran, as well as demolishing properties and replacing them with new-builds. The policy was rolled out as the government decided to improve the state of its run-down social housing by introducing PALUOS, subsidies for the improvement of rental accommodation and buildings occupied by those on benefits.[3] The fact that there was little change in the overall figures was also due to the company's decision to focus on carrying out extensive repairs on existing stock, on bringing this stock in line with current standards and on improving its quality. In 1984 alone, 19 million francs were spent on "essential" work, 17 million on "necessary" work and 12.5 million on work deemed to be "desirable..."[4] However, the company was forced to slow the pace of this work in view of the cost and the significant difficulty it faced in obtaining funding – large construction groups and more sensitive areas were given priority when it came to allocating grants. Meanwhile, other sectors were gripped by construction fever, and shops, community facilities and homes for the sick and elderly all began to appear.

After a brief recovery (8,875 houses were built in 1987), construction at Emmaus HLM once again ground to a halt, as a result of two problems. First, the lack of land available in the suburbs close to Paris led the company to build accommodation sites further and further away from the city itself. However, from 1987 onwards the company refocused its attentions on building in the inner suburbs, after a number of operations were declared bankrupt. Secondly, the operations funded by PLA[5] were based on repayments at a progressive interest rate and the costs became increasingly difficult to shoulder. Coupled with the rent freeze, which remained in force for a number of years, the second half of the 1980s saw these repayments plunge many social housing companies into a serious operating deficit.

By the late 1970s Emmaus HLM was aware of just how difficult it was to break even by building traditional social housing. It thus began to experiment with new initiatives aimed at making significant improvements in social welfare. The economic crisis, the growing desire to see social housing make a profit, and the de facto exclusion of the poorest families from social housing proved that this was the right course of action to pursue. A notable change was the company's decision to build detached houses, some of which were designed for people who wished to get on the property ladder and for families unsuited to traditional social housing (rural families, large families or families on the very fringes of society). This development of cheap, versatile wooden houses opened up new perspectives. However, very few local authorities responded favourably to the experiment. The company also planned to build housing for immigrants, vital if they were to eventually settle and integrate into society.[6] These plans became reality with a substantial number eventually built in Paris and Les Hauts-de-Seine, through cooperation with the social housing company Sonacotra homes.

Finally, in the early 1980s, the company extended the area it covered, until then limited to the Paris region, by agreeing in 1980 to build a "follow-up home" in La Vielle-Aure, in the southwestern French département of Hautes-Pyrénées. This home was built to house young people with problems and to help them reintegrate into society.

## The 1990s: the social policies of housing estates

From the mid-1980s onwards, social housing companies were faced with the increasing poverty of their tenants. During the *Trente Glorieuses*, a significant number of places in social housing were given to members of the middle classes mounting the social ladder and looking to buy their own property. A minimum income was required to sign a lease. Combined with the obligation placed on tenants to produce deposits and guarantees, this prevented the most disadvantaged members of society from accessing accommodation. Consequently, the aim of the social housing companies was to "offer rental accommodation, at below market price, to people who came from across the social spectrum but who had a stable, albeit modest, income."[7] The economic and social crisis stifled this social mobility, as it prevented an increasingly large number of French people from leaving social housing and buying their own property, and created new groups within society who faced Herculean difficulties in finding alternative accommodation (large families, foreign families, single-parent families, etc.). At the same time, the gradual disappearance of cheap B&Bs, sub-letting systems and cheap rental accommodation, which had until then provided an alternative to social housing and acted as buffer solutions, increased this new trend towards the concentration in social housing of those living in poverty.

As was the case with the national minimum wage, state policy changed according to the amount of housing available. To curb state spending while at the same time meeting the needs of society's disadvantaged sectors, the largest benefit payments were henceforth reserved for those on the lowest income, and the social mission of social housing was reinforced. The Besson Law of 31 May 1990, which declared that "guaranteeing the universal right to accommodation constitutes a duty of solidarity for each and every member of the French nation", made it mandatory for each French département to draw up a Departmental Action Plan for the Housing of the Disadvantaged and created the Housing Solidarity Fund (FSL), centralising benefit payments and the social support measures in the housing sphere. The Guidance Law on Towns (July 1991) attempted to reverse the prevailing trend, which saw those responsible for planning urban spaces plump for either private or social accommodation and obliged large towns to construct a mixture of the two. Given the fact that welfare payments were insufficient to meet the needs of a growing proportion of the population, the state also introduced the PLA-TS, a heavily subsidised government loan intended to enable those whose income was 40% below the PLA limit to access rental accommodation.

These two major pieces of legislation were finally rounded off with the following initiatives: *Contrats de ville* – contracts for new building projects signed between the state, local authorities and their partners; *Zones urbaines sensibles* – sensitive urban areas which received special state subsidies; *Zones de redynamisation urbaine* – areas with high unemployment selected for regeneration; *Zones franches urbaines* –

larger *Zones de redynamisation urbaine* in need of greater assistance from the state; the National Programme for Urban Regeneration (1999); and *Les Grands Projets de ville* – designed to improve the living conditions for residents. In 2000, the Solidarity and Urban Regeneration Law (SRU) entrenched this proactive spirit by adopting a holistic approach to the issues it tackled and the obligation it placed on local authorities to meet a 20% social housing quota.[8] Authorities failing to meet this quota were fined. Meanwhile, new legal instruments were created for constructors and those renting out social accommodation. The two most important of these were the PLUS, created in 1999 (loans granted to constructors if at least 30% of the houses built went to tenants on a limited income), and the PLA-1, created in 2001 (loans with an interest rate far below those offered on the market). In 1988, the government also introduced a reduced VAT rate of 5.5% for social housing construction projects and declared such projects exempt from property tax. This veritable myriad of mechanisms, which remain in place today, clearly conveys the extent to which this new social issue had entered the political sphere. It was an issue which had (re)emerged in the 1990s: the housing of the poor and disadvantaged members of society; people trapped in areas where a whole host of social problems converged, lacking the means to escape.

Supported by these new measures, construction once again got under way in the early 1990s at Emmaus HLM; the pace picking up in the first decade of the new millennium. In 1989, the company had 8,090 houses to its name. By 2007, this number had increased to 13,011. With the price of land making it almost impossible to build in Paris' inner suburbs, the new homes once again spread towards the outer suburbs of the capital. At that point, the number of requests for new building projects from outside the capital also began to increase, and in 1992 the Ministry of Housing officially extended the area within which the company was able to build.

Efforts to renovate the existing housing stock also continued and the last of Abbé Pierre's emergency housing sites – Chaville – was demolished in 1996. However, this period was marked above all by the rising cost of major repairs and everyday maintenance work; partly a result of the changes made to housing standards (new standards were introduced in areas including heating, rubbish chutes, insulation, lifts, heat and smoke vents, play areas, asbestos use, and the sorting of household waste). However, costs also rose due to the fact that from 1977 onwards, the homes suffered increasing damage, with new cases constantly being brought to light. As life on certain housing estates became more difficult, the company was forced to increase security in the homes, which often caused structural damage in the process: shutters were fitted on the ground floor, burglar-proof doors fitted in communal areas, intercoms and fire doors installed, cellars closed off, and enclosing walls and speed bumps built. Lastly, the homes suffered increasing wear and tear as a result of the company's attempts to repair wilful damage, an issue regularly brought to the leaders' attention from 1994 onwards. Such damage included: fires in the rubbish chutes and management offices, graffiti on the walls, damaged entrance-hall doors and letter boxes, vandalised underground car parks, and broken windows and street lights. In 2000, the prevailing sense of insecurity and the damage caused to homes prompted the development of more aggressive action plans. These included continued liaison with the police, procedures for filing complaints and the training for staff working on the ground. The company strengthened its dialogue with the children and teenagers living in the homes, introducing cleaning operations, with the youngsters sometimes being paid for their efforts. It created sports and leisure areas; and launched *"prévention été chaud"* operations, designed to protect vulnerable groups of the population from the effects of a heatwave. It also paid greater attention to the needs and views of tenants, adopting cleanliness charters, advisory councils, councils of building representatives, and undertaking work to smarten up and modernise the accommodation. These initiatives were launched following the company's realisation that "[it could] no longer adopt a purely 'administrative' approach to 'the entitled', however meticulous that approach might be; [it needed] to actively seek to attract a 'clientele' which often has other competitive options to choose from. We need to adapt our offer to their needs or their constraints."[9] The company worked to repair torn social fabric and revive Community spirit through meals served in the streets, outdoor furniture sales, fêtes, "stairwell meetings" for those living in its blocks of flats, parties with enormous pans of couscous cooked outside, and new local newspapers. In order to combat the problem of unpaid rent, support services were set up, offering help with applying for government benefits, committees to look into difficult cases, and personalised support plans were drawn up by the buildings' caretakers to help residents in financial difficulty get back on their feet. Since 2000, initiatives have also been in place to help families with the maintenance of their accommodation. In general terms, since the mid-1980s the decentralisation of activities and working closely with the residents themselves have been the very lynchpins of Emmaus HLM's social policy. It no longer acts simply as a builder and lessor but as an accommodation manager providing both a service and social support.

Finally, the launch of new government policies prompted the company to pursue the same line of action it had done in previous years, but this time with greater fervour, and it continued to develop housing for those whose social needs were the most acute. Despite the fact that this form of social housing was truly unique, it continued to represent only a minute proportion of all social housing stock: in 2001, it accounted for no more than 4.5% of individual houses, 0.1% of homes and 1.7% of adapted accommodation. The birth of the Abbé Pierre Foundation allowed new partnerships to be established. One such example of these is the 1992 partnership for the construction of housing designed for families evicted after their home had been declared a dangerous structure. This focus on those in acute social need was again given tangible form in May 1990 with the creation of an association working solely in this area: France Euro Habitat (FREHA). FREHA was created within the framework of the Besson Law and specialised particularly in rehousing immigrant families and buying up and converting dingy B&Bs used to house the homeless. Ten years later, FREHA had bought, leased or made available almost 700 homes spread across Paris and its inner suburbs.

## Housing stock with a truly social agenda?

Beyond the small sector of social housing designed for those in acute social need – a sector symbolically important but somewhat insignificant in terms of the total number of houses it encompassed

– it is important to examine whether or not there was anything unique about the profile of Emmaus tenants. This question merits consideration, because while the Emmaus social housing company was viewed by its social housing counterparts as one whose primary aim was the protection of social welfare, it was regularly accused, within the Emmaus Movement, of having evolved into nothing more than a simple, profit-driven social housing body.

There is no doubt that the company took on tenants whose income was lower than that of the average social housing resident. Proof of this was the type of housing that the company built (the significant quantity of LEPN and PSR housing in the 1960s and of PLA-TS housing in the 1990s), and the reports produced within the social housing sector which showered praise on Emmaus for their social welfare-oriented approach. The Movement itself also made comments such as, "care must be taken to ensure that Emmaus does not earn itself a reputation as an organisation which takes on only the more difficult tenants refused elsewhere".[10] The clearest proof has come in the form of statistics, in particular since the 1990s, where precise figures are available: in 2000, the number of unemployed or insecurely employed tenants living in Emmaus social housing was twice as high as the regional average for the social housing sector. A larger number of its occupants were of foreign nationality (31% in 1995, compared to a social housing average of 20%), and more of them lived in large families. With regard to regional averages in the social housing sector, a significant proportion of Emmaus property holdings were in areas classed as *Zones urbaines sensibles* and on the very fringes of the capital. In the early 2000s, more than half the tenants were on an income below 60% of the social housing income ceiling and in 2006, three-quarters of tenants were in a similar situation. This social welfare-oriented approach was very much deliberate. In an interview, Claude Néry declared: "As far as allocating housing is concerned, as soon as a person needs a home and we sense that he'll be able to pay for it, if there is someone else who also needs the home but who is financially more comfortable, we take the person on the lower income. In all the other big companies, it's the other way round. They take the person who can pay and who'll give them peace of mind; they even ask on a fairly regular basis for a list of several candidates to choose from."[11]

For all that, this margin of freedom quickly began to shrink. In the same interview, Néry explained: "At the beginning, we had guaranteed funding from the city council and, in providing us with that funding, the council was entitled to 20% of the housing. As soon as the law was passed which forced those running businesses above a certain size to contribute 1% of their wage bill to social housing, these heads of business also had the right to allocate a certain percentage of social housing, depending on the size of their contributions. Consequently this meant that we'd launch social housing operations where, of the one hundred homes built, twenty were for the city council, thirty for the council of the département who also requested some, and twenty–thirty for the heads of businesses who'd made contributions under the "1% law". We were left with around thirty to allocate, however, with the state increasingly withdrawing its support, the proportion of funding provided by heads of business (and therefore the houses reserved for them) increased; all the more so given that when accommodation was renovated, employers who had already contributed to construction were asked to contribute further. They agreed to do so on the condition that they were given even more properties to allocate. This process meant that social housing companies were increasingly stripped of the right to allocate their accommodation and that was the case for Emmaus too, because funding largely dictates what we do."

## Protecting social welfare and running a business: a complex identity for Emmaus as a social housing company

The very statutes of Emmaus' social housing company meant it was constantly torn between two ways of operating: as a business and as a social endeavour. The former ensured its survival and the latter was its raison d'être, neither one could be renounced without threatening either the company's identity (by overdeveloping the business side of things) or its survival (by focusing excessively on social welfare). As a result, the company was constantly forced to strike a balance between contradictory trends: maintaining the buildings without having to excessively increase the rent; keeping a firm hold of the purse strings without restricting tenants' benefits; repairing and renovating the housing stock without being forced to withhold staff pay, etc.

So far as the business side of things was concerned, the company emerged as an increasingly formal, professional outfit. After significantly increasing in size during the 1970s, the number of paid employees levelled out (208 in 1978, 217 in 1994), before increasing again to 245 in 2005. The business-oriented approach appeared to prevail with the introduction of pay scales, staff elections and, from 2000, profit-sharing bonuses. Specialists continued to fill the post of managing director: after Claude Néry, who worked in the housing sector, came Jacques Oudot, who had studied banking and graduated from *Sciences Po* and *L'Institut de sciences sociales du travail*, the higher-education establishment specialising in social sciences. Oudot was also a specialist in local authority management and administration, and was succeeded by Nelly Lordemus, who has been in the post of managing director since 2002. Lordemus previously worked as regional director at the French National Housing Authority, where she was responsible for the management of 10,000 homes in areas where housing was a particularly sensitive issue. This affirmation of the business-oriented approach, linked to the company cementing its place in the world of professional social housing firms, was also reflected to a certain extent in the profiles of the board of directors, the average age of which remained stable and relatively high until the mid-1990s: 63.2 (1977), 63.7 (1987) and 62.9 (1997). Among the directors were: Yves Salaün (1956–86), president of the National Federation of the PACT (Propaganda and Action Against the Slums), government commissioner to the French Property Investment and Management Company, and CEO of *Crédit logement*, the French bank guaranteeing property loans. There was also Maurice Combes (1976–93), retired from the Ministry for Public Works. Marie-Françoise Legrand (1990–6) was the director of the National Federation of Regional Associations of Social Housing Bodies, before being appointed representative to the managing director of the National Union of Federations of Social Housing Bodies, the UNFO-HLM. A second group on the board comprised individuals who were just as highly specialised but in areas not directly related to social housing:

the departmental director of the French property loans provider, *Crédit foncier*; the director of the CAF; referendum counsellors at the Court of Auditors; representatives from the Ministry for Social Affairs; CEOs, etc. Typical of this group was Bernard Brunhes (board member from 1996 and chairman from 1998), a graduate of the prestigious *École Polytechnique* and chairperson of an international consultancy firm. He had worked at *Insee*, the National Statistics Institute, the United Nations Statistics Office, and the Plan Commission, was responsible for drawing up five-year plans for the French economy, had been a member of the Prime Minister's cabinet for Social Affairs, and worked for the managing director of the state-owned railway company, SNCF.

For all that, the company continually reaffirmed its commitment to protecting social welfare, and to campaigning actively on behalf of those in need. From the mid-1990s onwards, Emmaus organisations were an increasingly significant presence on the board of directors: Abbé Pierre sat on the board until 1992, when he left his seat to Emmaus France; Association Emmaus held a seat throughout the period; the CGL was a member of the board until 2005; and UCC held a seat between 1978 and 2004. Emmaus International has been a member of the board since 1996 and the Abbé Pierre Foundation has held a seat since 2000. Emmaus is also represented by individuals who campaign as part of several organisations: Maxence Faivre d'Arcier (1957–80) simultaneously held a seat on the boards of the social housing company and Association Emmaus, while André Chaudières was also the first president of the Abbé Pierre Foundation. There were also cases where individuals progressed through various bodies within the Movement: Marie-Françoise Legrand (Emmaus HLM, then Association Emmaus), Claude Néry (Emmaus HLM, then the Abbé Pierre Foundation) and Jacques Oudot (Emmaus HLM, then UCC). Lastly, following the 2003 Borloo Law, which made it mandatory for limited social housing companies to have a main shareholder, the company entrusted this role to the Abbé Pierre Foundation, which had both the necessary funds and sectorial interest. In his interview, Claude Néry remarked: "Those collecting the 1% contributions had begun to realise that the shares to which they had subscribed often represented a significant percentage of all capital raised for the protection of social welfare. They realised that by owning shares in civil companies and buying up other shares they did not own, they could take power at the OCIL and in other social housing companies. As a union member and someone who represented the union on several CIL,[12] I'd seen the way people were operating and I could sense that the time had come to take action; I said to myself: we can't dilly-dally any longer [...] I'd prefer us to stay in the Emmaus Movement and not get swallowed up by the CIL [...] With that in mind, I requested that the Abbé Pierre Foundation henceforth made its contribution to the running of Communities by subscribing to shares. Which they did. Having got several representatives of the Emmaus Movement on to the board, we already controlled a small amount of capital; getting the Abbé Pierre Foundation on to the board in exchange for its contributions meant that with the two combined, we represented around 33–35% of the company's capital, which was more than that controlled by the two CIL. But we only just managed to get there; had we started the process three or four years later, we would have risked seeing our company kick the bucket."[13]

Conversely, Emmaus HLM contributed in another fashion when it decided in the 1980s to build facilities for Emmaus, whether these were buildings for the Communities or accommodation centres for the Association. Finally, it is not without significance that the name chosen for the company in June 2003 further highlighted the fact it belonged to Emmaus – Emmaus HLM Ltd was renamed Emmaus-Habitat, Social Housing Ltd. This decision to strengthen ties with the Movement followed the 1960s and 70s, a period during which Emmaus HLM had kept greater distance from its mother ship. In strengthening ties with Emmaus, the company both aimed to ensure that those working to protect social welfare had a voice within the social housing movement and to raise the Emmaus Movement's awareness of housing issues.

## The Abbé Pierre Foundation: A New Giant in the Emmaus World

### A slow genesis (1987–94)

In the 1980s, Emmaus continued to wage the fight for better housing through its social housing company, but it made very few public statements on the issue and its social initiatives were hindered in part by the triumph of the business-oriented approach. Yet the need to raise public awareness of the issue of homelessness, the increasingly overcrowded state of the accommodation centres, the reluctance of many elected representatives to continue building social housing, the annual media coverage of the summer closure of shelters, and the end of a period of respite for the homeless meant there was still ample opportunity to issue a rallying call and take action, which Abbé Pierre decided to seize.

1987 was declared "The International Year of the Homeless". From 9 to 11 October, the Abbé oversaw the organisation of "international humanitarian meetings" on the issue in Pont-Saint-Esprit in the southern French département of the Gard. André Chaudières and Claude Néry, president and managing director of Emmaus HLM, respectively, were the two men chiefly responsible for coordinating the meetings, which were held before a panel of government representatives, members of parliament, local councillors and heads of humanitarian associations. At the time, the number of families living on the streets or in poor accommodation was estimated to stand at 200,000. The meetings, relayed by some of the media's key players, concluded with the statement that "decent housing for every individual, every family, is a fundamental right [...] key to social advancement and integration", and announced their decision to create an Abbé Pierre Foundation for the housing of society's most disadvantaged members, the aim of which was to inspire the launch of and encourage initiatives that "would quickly see each and every homeless person guaranteed accommodation and ensure they were provided with social support".[14]

The organisation first saw the light of day as an association in December 1987. In February 1992, it was granted the official status of an organisation serving the public interest, after having squirreled away the 5,000 francs required for the statutory reserve. During this four-year period, a communications plan was launched, a prestigious committee of political support was created (bringing together members of the Senate, government ministers, MPs and secretaries of state of all political colours, although the majority were socialist), and a file of donors was drawn up. In 1991, with Abbé Pierre president of the Foundation, a regional delegation was established in Marseilles, the home of vice-president André Chaudières.

In the view of Emmaus France, "Abbé Pierre made no attempt to hide the fact that he had been presented with a *fait accompli.*"[15] However, for Emmaus HLM, "what André Chaudières said was true; Abbé Pierre let his hand be forced, but he let it be forced gently. And he had no regrets later on."[16] Abbé Pierre did in fact subsequently always remain very close to his Foundation. Whatever the reality of the situation, the creation of the Foundation did spark both controversy and criticism within Emmaus. It was criticised first of all on account of the fact that the Foundation was born long after the other Emmaus bodies but monopolised the name of the founder, defying the usual custom of making only tacit use of Abbé Pierre's name. It was also criticised, as in the eyes of Communities "it went against the values we had always held dear to ask others for funds while Companions worked to earn money by the sweat of their brow. It was bad enough that Emmaus HLM worked with state money, but then to have a Foundation that beyond money from the state, went looking for donations from the public, well that was absolutely unthinkable. So right from the start, relations between Emmaus and the Foundation weren't exactly great."[17]

Lastly, the space initially cleared for Emmaus France on the Foundation's board of directors was limited to say the least, and it was only after lengthy negotiations that the number of seats they were given was increased to three (out of eleven), including the vice-presidency, then to five (out of thirteen), including the seat of the vice-president who had since been appointed president. Lengthy negotiations were required because the boards of foundations were forced to adhere to very precise rules: at the Abbé Pierre Foundation, there were four founding members who were given a seat for life, four *de jure* members appointed by the French and European authorities[18] and, finally, four co-opted members, chosen for their skills and approved by Emmaus France.

## Trying, testing and encouraging innovative initiatives

One of the Foundation's main missions was to try out and encourage innovative initiatives aimed at overcoming the housing problems faced by the poorest members of society.

### Solidarity boutiques

For the Foundation, helping people access housing began with helping the homeless, from the very beginning of the 1990s, when the "solidarity boutiques" opened their doors as "veritable service stations for people and families of no fixed abode."[19] Introduced at the initiative of Housing for All, an association created by André Chaudières and devoted to the protection of social welfare, they were taken up by the Foundation from its very inception as an original and appropriate way of meeting the needs of the homeless. The Foundation opened the boutiques following the realisation that "Searching for a roof, a bed, food and a job on a daily basis requires a superhuman effort on the part of those people and families who find themselves in a situation where it is impossible to manage any kind of personal project. The lack of a fixed abode – therefore of an address – immediately excludes these people from basic civil and social rights. In order to break the spiral – no house, no address, no job, no health – the Abbé Pierre Foundation opened these 'solidarity boutiques' and made them available to families and individuals who were excluded from such rights."

The vast range of services offered allowed the Foundation both to meet the urgent needs of the homeless and to achieve their goal of reintegrating them back into society: those who came to the boutique were provided with a registered address (a letter box, a place to store their luggage and the services of a letter writer to help them with paperwork), personalised support and guidance, somewhere to rest, and information (on employment, housing, health, social rights, etc.), but they also had access to services and facilities which allowed them to clean themselves up and tend to their personal appearance: they could get a wash, change their clothes, do their laundry and ironing, repair their clothes, have their hair cut, get medical treatment, participate in leisure activities, writing workshops and even in sporting activities or trips to the theatre. Hardly surprisingly, archives in fact reveal that the users of the boutiques admitted to suffering as a result of their lack of accommodation (95%) and from a lack of money (86%), but many also confessed to suffering seriously from solitude (94%), cold (90%), fatigue (74%), the judgemental attitudes of others (65%), malnutrition (42%), violence (41%), and a lack of personal hygiene (28%). Furthermore, 99% had pathological conditions, be they dermatological, pulmonary, of the ear, nose and throat and/or hepato-gastroenterological.[20]

Open for business during the day, the opening hours of these boutiques complemented those of the accommodation centres. They quickly began to spread throughout metropolitan France and La Réunion: two boutiques in 1991, fourteen in 1993, and twenty-six since 1999. Subsidised by the CAF, the Ministry for Social Affairs, local authorities and regional and departmental councils, they were managed by one or several permanent members of staff and a team of volunteers. The system was flexible: while some of the boutiques were managed directly by the Foundation, the majority simply opened under its name, as a guarantee that it would run smoothly. This also meant that in the absence of subsidies, the Foundation could accept money from elsewhere to cover the boutique's costs. In addition, the Foundation was responsible for organising staff training, for centralised purchasing and for the provision of technical and financial advice for the whole network.

From 1994 onwards, the solidarity boutiques were considered by the authorities to be an integral part of the fight against acute social exclusion and were enshrined in the law on exclusion (29 July 1998) as organisations essential for the protection of social welfare. However, over the next few years, the boutiques became more widespread, causing a division between the small boutiques of which Emmaus was a fervent advocate, and larger organisations created at the instigation of the authorities, which were sometimes designed more to keep vagrancy under control than to help the vagrants themselves. This was particularly the case in towns thathad issued by-laws forbidding begging (1993–7).

While the boutiques were designed first and foremost for the homeless, after ten years had passed, reports noted significant developments necessitating certain changes. First, the boutiques were providing support to a growing number of young people under the age of twenty-five with no income, no training, no job and no plans. These people had no family and no access to the education system: they accounted for 20% of users in 1995 and 29% in 2003. Some of them lived on the streets or in squats, trapped in a haze of alcohol and psychotropic drugs; for others it was early separation from their families that had left the deepest mark. Despite these developments, there were a number of significant flaws in the systems put in place: the Route to Work programme (TRACE) did not reach the most marginalised, while the local missions and the Support, Information and Guidance Centres (PAIO) worked largely with those who were potentially employable. As a result, the Foundation sought to launch initiatives that were better adapted to the needs of the homeless, in particular where health and housing were concerned. Secondly, while in small towns the vast majority of service users were French, in the major cities, a growing number of asylum seekers (representing up to 90% of those receiving support) came to the Foundation in search of a registered address and administrative assistance. In 2001, reports also noted the arrival of entire families at the Foundation, often from Algeria or the East. However, those whose asylum application had been rejected rarely came to the Foundation, aware that they were living illegally. And yet the problem for the social workers was not so much the presence of asylum seekers, despite the fact that their arrival in large numbers could often bring the system to a standstill, as the lack of solutions they were able to provide. Thirdly, an increasing number of women came to the Foundation for support, sometimes with children (12% in 1995, 23% in 2003) and indeed, this group of women represented an increasingly large share of the homeless population. In the early 2000s, several solidarity boutiques introduced women-only days. Finally, the sharp increase in the prevalence of psychological disorders among service users sometimes sparked outbursts of violence in the face of which social workers and medical teams were utterly powerless. The Foundation's 2004 activity report declared that "The policy currently in place in the mental health sector, which seeks to keep the mentally ill within normal society while providing them with hit-and-miss medical care rather than with systematic support, is of great concern to the associations."

These developments should undoubtedly be considered with caution. While they were duly noted on the ground and records of exact numbers kept, they were nevertheless flagged up with some hindsight (around ten years), which suggests that we should not be too quick to take cyclical and structural factors into account. Whatever the case, these new sectors of the population, who flocked to the Foundation in dire need of support, tended to drive the homeless out of the very solidarity boutiques that had originally been set up with them in mind. Furthermore, the influx of requests for help (an average of eighty to a hundred a day in 2001, double the number for which they had been designed) made it difficult to maintain a truly convivial atmosphere. Lastly, the arduous nature of the daily work prompted the Foundation to set up a counselling service for its staff and volunteers. The Foundation's 2001 activity report stated: "We will never tire of hammering home the message that working in a solidarity boutique is a difficult job. Support workers are brought face to face with painful, heartbreaking and utterly shocking life stories. The vulnerable state of those who turn to the Foundation for help, their physical and moral decline, become impossible for the boutiques' teams to bear when there is nothing in place to provide relief, nothing in place to improve the situation in the short term."

### Integration through housing

Initiatives in favour of housing constituted the lion's share of the Foundation's activities, accounting, on average, for 60% of the annual budget. These initiatives involved building, restoring, improving individual or communal accommodation, and helping people to find somewhere to live. Until 1996, the Foundation focused more on temporary accommodation – emergency shelter for people attempting to reintegrate into society and residential centres and hotels for those in need of social support. However, following the adoption of the Périssol plan in 1996, which favoured emergency accommodation, the Foundation began to turn its attentions to long-term accommodation and helping people to stay in their homes. Finally, since 2000, the focus has been on adapted accommodation (helping improve accommodation, helping tenants to carry out their own renovations, and providing them with support). One of the Foundation's most recent major campaigns (2007) focused on the fight to demolish the slums.

Some initiatives also targeted specific groups of people, with certain sectors of the population receiving special attention: rural families received aid to help them stay in their homes; from 1999 travellers were assisted in the purchasing of caravans and the development of sites on which to keep them; and those suffering from isolation saw the Foundation step in from 2000, with the ground-breaking development of family boarding houses. Additionally, in Paris, 1999, housing support also involved the creation of a Solidarity-Housing-Space (ESL) to attend to families' needs and provide them with social and legal support.

### Cultural initiatives and social development in deprived areas

Cultural initiatives, which formed part of the Foundation's initial plans, only really took off in 1996 before once again being placed on the back burner where they have remained for a number of years. Culture was understood in the broader sense of the term. On 25 September 1996, the Foundation's board meeting stated the need "to pursue a vision of culture whereby each man is seen as capable of producing wealth and in which both the individual and collective are able to express themselves, without upholding that other vision of culture in which the world is filled exclusively with would-be artists."[21] In order to combat the negative image of deprived areas promoted by the media and the boredom which produced antisocial behaviour, culture had to allow people to escape from what imprisoned them, provide them with a focus and break the cycle whereby victims of violence themselves become the perpetrators of violent acts. It had to facilitate the strengthening of communication and Community spirit and to allow the potential of both individuals and groups to be fully exploited so that the images promoted by the media might once again be positive, rather than negative. There was nothing particularly innovative about this approach. Nor did it herald any great change –as far back as the 1950s, Father Wresinski had attached great importance to culture – but what was important was how this vision of culture was put into practice.

The Foundation's aim was to develop cultural initiatives at a local level (access to art and culture, development of the residents' own artistic and cultural projects). These initiatives would unite the generations and open up areas which existed as ghettos, cut off from the outside world. The groups targeted as a matter of priority were women, children and young people, and the Federation's favoured activities were those which brought people together and promoted participative democracy.

## The development of international solidarity

From the very beginning, the Foundation also initiated international action programmes, even if these were originally very limited and primarily took the form of financial support given to humanitarian organisations. However, from 1995 onwards, the multiannual programmes managed directly by the Foundation itself were given priority, while at the same time some resources were kept aside for smaller, occasional projects. In the early days initiatives were directly related to housing, but the concept was quickly broadened to include the living environment and lifestyle (social support services, healthcare and medical facilities, social and cultural initiatives), with housing viewed as a lever. Initiatives remained focused on the development of (very) poor countries and were carried out in cooperation with the local population. The aim was to improve social and economic conditions, and to "focus on providing high-quality, innovative initiatives that would stand as examples to be followed, rather than simply launching as many as possible."[22] The Foundation was the contracting authority and co-financer of the initiatives. The overall budget earmarked for international solidarity was 10% of the Foundation's total budget: 300,000 francs (1991), 1.5 million francs (1994), €895,000 (2001) and €1.3 million (2006).

The first major programme was launched in Bamako, Mali, where a "makeshift" residential area was regenerated and legalised: land was given official status and houses were built along with a Community hall, open-air theatre, etc., and in the Kayes region, where houses were built, and water-conveyance systems and solar panels installed. This programme was conducted in cooperation with Malian associations working in the Paris regions. Getting these associations on board was a way of offering training to young Malians in Paris, who assisted with the work. These programmes were monitored over a ten-year period. India was the Foundation's other main area of focus, where initiatives were launched to support exiled Tibetans, those with leprosy and women of the "untouchable" caste.

From the mid-1990s onwards, the Foundation aimed to foster the active participation of the local people themselves in these initiatives. It did this first through solidarity lending in order to provide them with the means to improve their living environment: such as micro-credit, savings accounts and cooperatives. Such assistance was provided in the belief that "solidarity lending, informal or formal, but effectively adapted to the reality of the situation faced by the world's poorest people, means that today we do not simply have to issue handouts. Charity should be limited to emergency situations and shown only in the aftermath of disasters or wars. Solidarity lending brings people together and allows the various residents of an area to discover or reclaim a sense of dignity."[23] It then sought to bring local residents on board by encouraging them to physically participate in the building of their own homes (self-construction). The practice was first introduced by homeless Malagasy people who were the victims of a cyclone in 1997.

### Post-disaster support

This new type of operation in aid of disaster victims was quickly extended to help victims of conflict and from 1999 onwards, the Foundation laid out significant sums for "post-disaster support". Despite the fact it was not an emergency aid organisation, it collected money to help with the rebuilding of houses. After Kosovo, funds were once again collected primarily in aid of disaster victims: in 2001 €230,000 were collected for the victims of floods in the Somme and €600,000 were collected following the explosion of the AZF factory in Toulouse; in 2002 €640,000 were raised for the victims of floods in southeast France; and in 2003 €400,000 were donated in the aftermath of the

Algerian earthquake. The Foundation released more than €700,000 in aid of the victims of the tsunami in southeast Asia. These sums were just as impressive as those garnered by organisations who were recognised experts in the field, and even exceeded them. The Foundation did not take action itself, but instead pinpointed partner associations working on the ground who would receive and utilise (Red Cross for logistics, *Médecins du monde* for the provision of counselling services, etc.). It also provided caravans to victims, helped with moving costs, paid for furniture to be put in storage, re-equipped accommodation, and set up facilities allowing locals to renovate their own homes.

## Raising public awareness and calling the authorities to action

Following in the footsteps of its eponymous founder, protecting the public and calling them to action were two of the missions of the Foundation.[24] In 1989, at the request of Abbé Pierre, a working group drafted a Bill on housing for the most disadvantaged members of society. A summary note was sent to Ministers for Housing and Social Affairs, to the representative of the President of the Republic, to the main social housing bodies and to the MPs who sat on social committees; a "black book" of all the cases which the Foundation had received was compiled and published. That same year, the release of the film *Winter of '54: Father Pierre* allowed the Foundation to continue its work raising public awareness and rousing people to action.

After the 1980s, a decade which saw campaigns focus primarily on the "new poor" and prioritise the provision of emergency aid and relief from the effects of homelessness, the 1990s saw the launch of campaigns which were more specific in their target audience, more aggressive and more political in their approach. Efforts were concentrated in particular on campaigns in favour of those "without", including illegal immigrants without papers and those without a roof over their heads.[25] With these campaigns, the issue of housing for the disadvantaged returned to the fore and was tackled with new fervour. In 1990, the Besson Law was passed, welcomed by the Foundation as it included some of its own proposals and strengthened the

Foundation's campaigns. 1990–1 also saw the birth of the association Right to Housing (DAL) and rallies at the Place de la Réunion and later at Quai de la Gare, which played out in the glare of the media. Abbé Pierre played a key role at the rallies, while the Foundation acted as a go-between.[26] Following the speeches made by Abbé Pierre calling for a ban on winter evictions, which received enthusiastic support (autumn 1990), the Foundation also spoke out in March 1991 in favour of maintaining state loans for social housing, creating "one-stop shops" at departmental level for housing advice and support, allocating 10% of unused state land to social housing in urban centres, and making it mandatory to provide alternative accommodation before evicting a tenant from his home.[27]

Between 1993 and 1995, the Foundation's main focus was calling those in power to action during the elections. A letter was sent to all candidates of the legislative elections of 1993, signed by both Abbé Pierre and Emmaus France, demanding that housing be guaranteed to all, that a national enquiry be conducted into the situation of the homeless and those in substandard accommodation, that a law be passed on the renovation and construction of social housing and that a ban be placed on the eviction of tenants before decent alternative accommodation had been found.[28] Printed by all the major newspapers, the letter was sent to 3,500 candidates and signed by 750, resulting in 136 of the 577 candidates elected having signed the letter. The signatures came from across the political spectrum and included seven ministers. For the presidential elections of 1995 a text calling for the adoption of a framework law was addressed to the candidates and during the local elections a communiqué was published in the form of a poster.

In addition, the Foundation joined the mysterious world of associations, institutions and para-institutions, working with UNIOPSS,[29] FNARS[30] and the High Committee for the Housing of the Disadvantaged. The Foundation enjoyed a close relationship with Louis Besson who, after having worked as Minister for Housing, became a member of the National Council for the Fight Against Exclusion (1993) and president of the High Committee. From 1992 until 1997, when he was appointed Secretary of State for Housing, he was also a member of the board, then of the bureau of the Foundation. By bringing before the Secretary of State for Housing several spokespeople close to the Foundation, such as Louis Besson and but also Frédérique Rastoll (CGL and a member of the Foundation's board since 1992), the unexpected change in majority in 1997 allowed the Foundation to wield greater influence in the redrafting of the law against exclusion (1998). Conversely, Patrick Doutreligne, member of the High Committee in 1996, technical advisor to Louis Besson's Secretary of State (1997–9), then secretary-general of the High Committee (1999–2002), was later appointed secretary-general of the Foundation. During these years, links with the left-wing members of government who specialised in housing issues were vital to the Foundation's efforts to raise awareness and take action on the matter.

However, in broader terms, from 1995 onwards the Foundation's attempts to publicly express its concerns also involved the annual publication of a report on substandard accommodation in France, which since 1998 has been supplemented with one version for the press and another for general consumption.

With an initially modest readership, the annual report, whose publication coincided with the end of the winter ban on evictions, became, from the early 2000s onwards, a veritable barometer of the housing situation in France and was widely circulated in the media. With its long version comprising around 200 pages, it sought to stand as a clinical study into the housing situation of the disadvantaged, containing extensive descriptions, comparisons and analysis. It delivered critical opinions on government measures, recommendations and proposals. The 2002 report was the first time that the number of French people housed in substandard accommodation was recorded as 3 million[31] – a figure which people and publications everywhere have since cited time and time again. Since 1990, several attempts had already been made to place figures on the situation, Indeed, it was calculated that in 1990 2.5 million were living in substandard accommodation and 400,000 were homeless in 1990, but these figures never reached such a large public audience.

The credibility of the report was largely due to the importance accorded to research within the Foundation. In the early years, research was primarily compiled in the journal *Fondations*, which was published biannually through a prestigious editorial committee (Serge Paugam, Julien Damon, etc.) and a sponsorship committee (Geneviève Anthonioz-de Gaulle, Martine Aubry or Louis Besson). However, the amount of research conducted internally remained limited. Things changed in 2003 when an agreement was signed with a specialist research office, FORS, and a full-time sociologist was recruited to manage the research sector.

Today, the Foundation's power to galvanise both the public and politicians into action is impressive. In addition to the report's success as a tool used by the media, almost all political parties, except those on the far Right, now consult the Foundation before drawing up their housing programmes. In 2002, the Foundation was crucial in maintaining the 20% quota for social housing per town in force, a quota established under the Law on Solidarity and Urban Renewal. The Foundation was also largely responsible for the passing of the DALO law upon the Abbé Pierre's death, a law it had helped to promote.

## Communication professionals

It is clear that the fact the Foundation came to occupy a central place within the housing sphere was due to the reputation of Abbé Pierre and the quality of the research it produced. However, it was also due to the importance consistently accorded to communication, a field in which the Foundation quickly became a veritable professional. Such a professional, in fact, that it almost relegated organisations who made extensive use of the media, such as *Secours populaire Français*, to the rank of humble amateur.

## The development and professionalisation of campaigns

The very status of the Foundation meant it survived first and foremost on donations. Abbé Pierre was a major asset as it got off the ground: during its very first press campaign, in spring 1989, the Foundation was given a free page in *Le Point*, a page at negligible cost in *Le Figaro*, *Le Monde* and *La Croix*, a free half-page in *Le Progrès*, *Le Dauphiné*, *Lyon-Matin*, *Paris Match*, and a free quarter-page in *Le*

*Provençal, Ouest-France, La Dépêche du Midi, France-Soir, Le Pèlerin, Le Républicain lorrain* and *Témoignage chrétien*.[32] A new campaign followed in December for the release of the film *Winter of '54: Father Pierre*, with the creation of a patronage committee and a poster campaign. In 1993, the Foundation earned the title "major national cause", which gave it the right to broadcast messages on state radio and television at preferential rates and also opened doors in the world of private media.[33] The campaign was deliberately focused on fundraising and brought in more than 50 million francs in donations for an initial outlay of only 2 million francs. At the same time, from the start, the organisation also used mailshots, although these were rapidly divided into those seeking to attract new donors and those aiming to elicit further donations from donors already on the books.

Symptomatic of the way the Association operated in the early days, the communication sector was initially "a family business". Carlo Fortunato, an Italian friend of Abbé Pierre, secured for his agency the job of managing campaigns, but the contract was vague, issued without a call for tender, awarded for a number of years, and stated that the agency was to receive performance-related pay – all principles that went against the Charter of Ethics to which the Foundation acceded in 1991. The situation was regularised when the contract was renewed in 1994 and communication was placed in the hands of a large agency, *Publicis*, which resolved to make the Foundation "a point of reference in the housing field, in order that it might be recognised as a pressure group and a group capable of rousing the public and the authorities to action."[34] It was *Publicis* that suggested the publication of an annual report on substandard accommodation.

In 1994, the Foundation adopted a strategy which would see it roll out a far-reaching media campaign based on rousing the masses to action: press releases, a forum for debate, the circulation of the research journal and newspaper (220,000 copies) and the production of videos. It was quick to make full use of sponsorship and corporate patronage, activities encouraged by the 1993 law (distributing 1 million fundraising envelopes at the exits of large Carrefour supermarkets and BP and Total petrol stations, and eliciting sponsorship from fashion designer Agnès B and cosmetics company Lancôme). Finally, on 21 December 1994, it organised a national awareness-raising day, appearing free of charge on the television channels TF1, France 2, France 3 and M6, while continuing to issue mailshots at a breakneck pace. In one year, 60 million francs were collected and the Foundation's profile was significantly raised.

1995–6 marked the start of a phase which would see the Foundation beset by a series of economic difficulties. The ARC scandal, the Périssol plan on housing for the most disadvantaged members of society, and the major strikes of late 1995 caused donations to plummet. Then, in the throes of the Garaudy affair, the Foundation was forced to realise the disadvantages of being the only body within Emmaus to bear the name of the founder. While donations did not suffer hugely as a result, *Publicis* terminated its contract, many partners in both the institutional and the private sector distanced themselves from the Foundation, and the media steered clear of the press releases it produced. This "loss of a real audience" prompted the Foundation to take a long, hard look at its strategy and change tack, "in order that the Foundation might henceforth be identified not in relation to one figure, but as an institution act[ing] as the voice of the socially excluded and those deprived of their rights, and rely on Abbé Pierre not as a passing celebrity but as an historical figure".[35]

The new agency hired, *Stratis*, specialised in business communication. The challenge now was to remedy the general public's ignorance of the Foundation[36] and to give it a unique identity within Emmaus, but progress was slow.[37] In fact, between 1998 and 2002 attempts to meet these challenges remained discreet, with communication based first and foremost on the mailshots and the report on substandard housing. Fundraising became a slick operation, with the introduction of a cycle: after launching appeals for new donors and appeals to retain those who donated for the first time, the Foundation would either begin attempts to keep second-time donors on the books or chase up those who had donated in the past. The final stage of the cycle aimed to get inactive or "dormant" donors to dig deep once again. Every year, several campaigns were conducted corresponding to each stage of the various cycles. The exchange of donor files between associations and the use of "mega" databases,[38] which collated donor information from a number of organisations, enabled campaigns to attract donors to yield the best results possible. The use of corporate patronage continued to develop with business partnerships directly supporting the boutiques (luncheon voucher company *Chèque déjeuner*, and home store BUT) or those which helped the Foundation to equip accommodation (IKEA).

Lastly, since 2002, the Foundation has once again begun to make extensive use of the media. The fiftieth anniversary of the 1954 appeal notably sparked a far-reaching publicity campaign and the annual report, recast specially for the occasion as a document tracing the Foundation's development. It was also presented in the main lecture theatre at the Sorbonne, in the presence of Abbé Pierre. In 2006, the Foundation launched a "committee of ambassadors" as a symbol of the media spotlight's move away from Abbé Pierre and towards a group of public figures. The move mirrored that made by *Les Restos du cœur*, when media attention was deflected from founder Coluche and instead placed on *Les Enfoirés* ("The Tossers"), the group of performers who took to the stage for the organisation's annual charity concert. However, in addition to bringing the artistic world on board (Jean Réno, Lambert Wilson, Mathieu Kassovitz, Jean Dujardin, Nolwenn Leroy, etc.), the committee sought to include key figures from the world of journalism (Elise Lucet), sport (Éric Cantona, Abdelatif Benazzi), science (Thomas Piketty, Boris Cyrulnik), literature (Marek Halter) and of course, housing (Louis Besson). This eclectic committee of ambassadors was created in order to allow the Foundation to target a more mainstream audience via media campaigns which would run throughout the year, and to help it move from a database largely comprising elderly donors on a modest income to one where the majority of donors were younger and better-off.[39]

### Communication in fundraising: striking the balance between tugging at the heartstrings and lifting the lid on injustice

In the same way that in its public communication, the Foundation combined showbiz with a fervently critical, political attitude towards injustice, in its fundraising communication the Foundation constantly sought to strike the balance between *"tugging at the heartstrings and lifting the lid on injustice.*"[40] The black-and-white poster for the "major national cause" campaign (1993), depicting a woman and her children sitting on a suitcase in the street tagged with the line "Mummy, where are we sleeping tonight?", sparked fierce debate. As the Foundation noted during its board meeting on 4 November 1993, "This type of campaign, designed to stir emotions, in particular by choosing to focus on the issue of eviction, places the Foundation to a greater extent than before in the category of charitable organisations, by leaving its role as an agitator to one side. At the same time, we should recall that the aim of the campaign is to raise funds to increase the financial resources which the Foundation has at its disposal."[41] Six years later, they faced the same problem: the mailshots issued by *Stratis* used sad, depressing and sordidly realistic images. Moreover, the issue of housing itself was largely absent. The images did, however, bear relation to and reflect the reality of the people who came to the boutiques for support.

Caught between these two opposing campaign styles, the Foundation came up with a compromise. Determined as it was not to "sell its soul", while accepting the rules of a fundraising game now played in an increasingly competitive market, the Foundation's 2001 activity report concluded, "We cannot seek to raise funds by describing life as a picture seen through rose-tinted spectacles; because if life is that rosy, what reason is there to donate to the Foundation? Neither can we bombard the donor with images which are excessively brutal. All of us know deep down that we give money because we are moved by a picture of someone who is suffering, by a poignant photo, by the stories of people who have experienced real hardship and whom we wish to help. This is the dilemma with which we are constantly faced. But not wanting to show images of misfortune out of a sense of propriety, not wanting to recount people's difficult, painful journeys, as if they didn't exist, will have a detrimental impact on our fundraising efforts and, ultimately, therefore on the people who benefit from these funds [...] Showing positive images is not the role of the material accompanying a fundraising appeal. We don't give money when everything's fine. We give money to ease suffering."

This dilemma was notably resolved by using posters and mailshots in tandem. While the posters showed a great deal of respect for the image of the people in them, the mailshots were keener to make use of life's darker side. People's journeys through life were presented as stills from dramatic films, black-and-white photography was used, and a small piece of cardboard placed in donation envelopes as a symbol of the cardboard on which the homeless slept. This two-pronged approach was also born of the Foundation's need to target different groups of donors in different ways: while the most loyal donors reacted favourably to messages focused on housing, "attracting new donors, in a very competitive market, requires us to adopt so-called 'dramatic' tactics".[42]

Launched late 2007 by the Foundation's new director, the campaign against the slums was undoubtedly the most successful in asserting the Foundation's identity. Innovative[43] in the tone it chose to adopt, it neither *tugged at the heartstrings* (it used hard-hitting words and images) or *"lifted the lid on injustice"* (no one was presented as responsible). Indeed, the posters no longer depicted the lack of housing (through images of street sleepers) or the suffering of individuals (through images of their faces) but instead portrayed the abomination that was the slums with empty outlines of men accompanied by phrases designed to shock. Examples include the image of a child's bed by a mouldy wall tagged with the line: "When we're ill, we stay at home. But what if it's your home that makes you ill?" And the photo of an apartment block in flames, recalling the Paris fires that hit international headlines in 2005–6, tagged with: "Slums: the problem is not only that people live there, it's that they die there."

The campaigns were made all the more effective by the fact that more was now known about the donors themselves. The donors targeted were primarily those who gave to several organisations and who were ill-informed about the Foundation's work: in 1999, only 18% spontaneously mentioned the issue of housing(!), and 66% made no distinction between the Foundation and Emmaus. The newspaper, even if it was skimmed rather than read, was used to remedy such ignorance. Studies revealed that the average age of donors was 65 but that there were two generations within this group:

those born before the Liberation (51% in 2002) and those of the *Trente Glorieuses* (49% in 2002). For the first generation, Abbé Pierre was a key reference point. Donating money was just as much part of an *ethos* as a *praxis* heavily influenced by a Christian and family-oriented background. However, members of this generation were also driven to donate by their own personal experience of war and illness. In contrast, for the second generation, Abbé Pierre was less significant; the experience that had defined their lives was not so much war as May '68, and the ideology to which they adhered was not so much charity as humanism. While the first-generation responded to messages calling for charity, the second was more receptive to messages that were political in nature. As a result, the Foundation's aim was to subtly alter the behaviour of these two generations of donors, gradually targeting first-generation donors with material on donations and bequests, while modernising the mailshots to consolidate the second generation of donors. Communication also became more selective and "third-age" donors were targeted in appropriate places (the *Notre Temps* exhibition fair for the elderly), through appropriate television channels (TF1 rather than M6), and during appropriate slots in the television schedule (lunchtime and afternoon rather than evening).

Finally, as the only Emmaus organisation to depend primarily on fundraising, and the only organisation together with UACE to be officially recognised as a body serving the public interest, the Foundation at last experienced spectacular financial growth. Climbing rapidly up till 1995, when donations totalled 64 million francs, the annual total raised decreased temporarily in 1996–7 before increasing once more: 93 million francs in 2000; 122 million francs in 2005 (€18.6 million) and €23 million in 2007. Donations and bequests also increased sharply: 255,000 francs in 1993; 7.5 million francs in 1999; €2 million in 2004 and €4.5 million in 2007. The number of active donors[44] followed the same trend: 1,000 at the end of 1988, 147,000 in early 1994 and 410,000 in 2001.

Marginalised within Emmaus during the *Trente Glorieuses*, the housing sector made a strong comeback even before the issue returned to the media and the political arena in the early 1990s. This comeback was first due to Abbé Pierre's desire, from 1987 onwards, to re-address the sector. It was also the result of the desire of social housing companies to play an active role within the Movement. Finally and above all, this comeback was the fruit of the spectacular growth of the Abbé Pierre Foundation, which in the space of only a few years became a force to be reckoned with in both politics and the media. The Foundation and the social housing companies complement each other and since the early 1990s, the two have worked to shift the Emmaus centre of gravity back towards its roots in the housing sector.

# *Chapter 10* / THE WORLD OF WASTE COLLECTION AND RECYCLING IN THE FACE OF CRISIS AND COMPETITION

The economic and social crisis that ravaged France from the mid-1970s onwards dealt a sharp blow to the world of waste-collection and recycling, the Communities and Committees of Friends, and led to the gradual development of two types of responses. These were initially quantitative and inward-focused: while poverty was on the rise and the Movement was forced to turn people away on a daily basis, the number of places available had to be increased. This growth was particularly characteristic of the 1980s: Emmaus had thirty-three Communities in 1978, sixty-five in 1983 and ninety-one in 1989 – the total number had almost tripled in a decade. Growth then began to slow, with 112 Communities up and running in by 2007. However, the Movement also devised responses which were qualitative and outward-looking: with the rising problem of social integration, an increasing number of young people and women falling victim to social exclusion and Emmaus' awareness that it was not a place suited to these people's needs – in 1989, only 2% of those who came to UCC-were successfully reintegrated into society – the Communities and Committees decided to create and develop organisations whose aim was to facilitate the reintegration process. These organisations later became independent bodies. Finally, the Movement began to reshape the way it supported the most vulnerable members of society, with profits increasingly allocated to the creation of accommodation organisations, the provision of emergency support and the fight against household debt.

In addition, Committees, Communities and organisations designed to facilitate social reintegration were faced with the profound changes affecting the waste-collection and recycling economy. The Movement's decision to go back to basics and focus on bric-à-brac sales was accompanied by a slow and clumsy strategy of adaptation to a sector that was now highly competitive and wrapped in red tape, despite the fact it had previously been, above all else, an unregulated sector developed by those on the fringes of society.

Finally, with the onset of the crisis, the profile of those seeking help from Emmaus changed. The concept of Community saw itself radically redefined, called into question by the individualisation of society, but strengthened by the fact that belonging to Emmaus was now a source of pride – or at least not quite the source of disgrace it had once been. This change resulted both from the fact that unemployment had become socially acceptable and from the fact that the media had developed a new-found respect for the organisation.

## Facing the Social Crisis

In 1980, the Communities began to broach the issue of the crisis and its repercussions in explicit terms. At UACE, the activity report for the summer – traditionally the low season – saw usual trends turned on their head. For the first time in the organisation's history, the number of people entering Communities barely decreased, people even had to be turned away, and all the Community members who had gone on holiday returned to the fold. In a meeting on 26 September 1980, UACE declared that "everywhere, people [were] being turned away daily".[1] The Federation decided to create new Communities in response to this problem, which it continued to view as one of capacity.

Furthermore, from the following year onwards, the Federation began to sense that it was dealing with increasing numbers of young people and was acutely aware that the Communities were not suited to their needs. This was a concern which Abbé Pierre in particular hammered home during several UACE meetings. The Federation considered it crucial "to encourage these people to return to everyday life as quickly as possible".[2] However, between March 1981 and February 1982, 92% of the under-thirties entering the Communities had no professional qualifications and 94% had no affective or family ties – two major obstacles to reintegration. The situation of these young people encouraged the Federation to look at new forms of action. Another new development, which the Communities were even less equipped to handle, was the increasing number of applications from couples and women with children.

## A quantitative response

The desire to remedy the shortage of places available in the 1980s initially led to an unprecedented wave of new Communities being created and saw an equally unprecedented number of unaffiliated Communities join the Movement. UCC had seventeen Communities in 1981, thirty-five in 2000 and thirty-seven in 2007; UACE had sixteen in 1981, twenty-eight in 2000 and twenty-six in 2007. This proliferation of new Communities and affiliated bodies has meant that as far as the 112 Communities currently in operation are concerned, the two major Federations no longer hold almost total power as they once did, and that the *outsiders* have become dynamic members of the Emmaus Movement; whether these be groups that have broken away from UACE (Liberty, Fraternity) or the independent Communities that, since 1994–5, had been organised into families.

The response provided by the smallest Emmaus organisations was also quantitative, with more people packed into the same number of Communities. Looking back on the period in an interview, Jacques Loch stated, "Back then, we were still in the days where quantity was important. We often talked about the quantity of accommodation, the quantity of people catered for and the quantity of Companions we took on, because we could see just how serious the poverty was. Several people slept in each room, it was a squeeze and we didn't think about the material conditions we were living in, we got by as best we could and built what was necessary. In the Thouars Community [Fraternity] it was caravans, mobile homes; we had rats, no water in winter for a fortnight at a time, municipal showers... very uncharacteristic experiences that today few Communities and even fewer accommodation centres would tolerate. The authorities would be even quicker to put their foot down, with current building standards and rules on living conditions being what they are."

In 2007, Liberty and Fraternity each had seven Communities. As for the (formerly) independent organisations, *Accueil et Vie* had five, concentrated around the southwest Mediterranean; *Partage* had fifteen, scattered more widely across France; and *le Nord-Pas-de-Calais* had eight. Finally, in 2005, seven Communities remained unaffiliated. This growth in the number of Communities produced an increase in the number of places available, particularly in the 1980s: there were 1,800 places on offer in 1983, 3,730 in 1989 and 3,900 in 2008.

The Committees of Friends did not experience the same growth, with numbers stagnating in the 1980s (forty-one Committees in 1980 and the same number in 1989), then decreasing to thirty-seven in 2007. This lack of growth was due to the fact that Committees, while admittedly less wieldy and more flexible, continued to rely on volunteers to move things forward, and these were difficult to replace. It was also undoubtedly due to the fact that Abbé Pierre constantly reminded the Committees themselves that the Communities, as the "root" of the Emmaus tree,[3] remained irreplaceable and that these should continue to be the Movement's focus and the most important cog in the Emmaus wheel.

## The youth problem

As far as qualitative responses to the situation were concerned, the Movement focused most of its efforts on the growing number of young people seeking support. Time and time again, the increasing number of young people turning to Emmaus for help was presented as a new phenomenon. However, since 1980, it has been suggested that youngsters had been flocking to Emmaus since time immemorial. Consequently, if we are to obtain an accurate picture of the situation, we need to look beyond subjective interpretations and examine the reality on the ground.

The figures available[4] encourage caution. First, in the same year, the situation varied greatly from one Community to the next: every year, several Communities remained unaffected by the phenomenon, taking in no young people at all, while the peak of the decade was reached in Elbeuf in 1993 (39%). Secondly, the situation could change significantly from one year to the next: the average number of young people in UACE Communities reached 16% in 1990 before dropping to 11.5% in 1992, increasing to 16% in 1993, dropping again to 9.5%

in 1994, etc. Furthermore, these changes occurred seemingly without any convincing explanation.[5]

If we put to one side the need to take these significant variations in the detailed figures into account, an analysis of the averages appears to reveal that over the very long term, the number of young people living in Communities remained relatively stable: in 1964–5, 15.2% of those at UCC Communities were under the age of thirty, and this figure was almost identical (15%) across all Communities in France between 2000 and 2003.

Nevertheless, there were developments, and significant ones at that. However, in order to appreciate these, it is not enough to remodel sections of graphs relating to specific points in time – entire charts need to be redrawn. From 1980 to 2000, the graphs displayed peaks and troughs: from the mid-to late 1980s, there were high averages (around 12% of those in Communities were under the age of 30), then a sharp drop in the early 1990s. This was followed by an increase between 1994 and the early 2000s when the figures plateaued. In view of the fact that the drop in the number of young people between 1990 and 1994 coincided with the creation of the minimum wage, it is possible to conclude that this new mechanism, which constituted a complete overhaul of state policy in favour of the most disadvantaged members of society but which was rejected by the majority of Communities, suddenly made them a less attractive option.

Validating this hypothesis means refining the age groups under consideration, as the introduction of the minimum wage did not affect those under twenty-five. In fact, the twenty-fives to thirties were the very group which, eligible for the minimum wage, left the Communities in the greatest number. Conversely, the number of under-twenty-fives in Communities decreased between 1965 (5.7%) and the late 1980s (less than 4%), before increasing again between 1990 and 2000 (8.1% in 2001): after having tried the accommodation centres, young people tended to fall back on Communities, which at the time were rethinking their entire approach to this sector of the population. Lastly, the proportion of very young people in Communities remained negligible. Between 1955 and 1960, 2% of those in the Cernay Community were below the age of twenty and 0.26% of those in UACE

Communities in 1998 were under eighteen, as were an average of 0.8% of the residents in all the French Communities between 2000 and 2003. The second observation made time and time again was that the level of qualification which these young people were thought to possess was ever decreasing. This was particularly true of those working in waste-collection and recycling. The Movement also frequently remarked upon their extremely fragile mental state. In fact, a study carried out by UCC in 1986 on the under-twenty-fives revealed unstable family situations and even a complete lack of family ties: 52% had not been brought up in their own family and had been placed in the care of others (DDASS, homes, childminders), 8.5% did not know one of their parents and 16% had never known either. They often came from large families: only 4% were only children, while 23.5% had between four and six siblings and 24.5% had more than six. The educational level of those willing to respond (many declined) was classed as "low", as was the level of professional qualifications they claimed to have (a third had no qualifications whatsoever; a third had a level of qualification again classed as "low"); the majority stated that their areas of expertise were construction and factory work. Hence, described here is a sector of the population which was socially and affectively disadvantaged, with very few qualifications and only limited experience of working life. However, this profile was in no way new. As we have seen, the Companion of the 1960s was at best a qualified manual labourer and at worst, had no qualifications at all, and it is unlikely that the most highly qualified among them at the time were also the youngest. The psychological study would also reveal their extremely fragile mental state, with many participants showing signs of progressive anxiety disorder and many whose chance of reintegration into society was considered to be "remote".

However, the real change during this period appears to be due to the decline of the labour market. In the 1960s, young people rarely stayed within Communities because, even without qualifications, they were easily able to return to work. In contrast, in the 1980s and 90s, they could find themselves out of work for years, floating between Communities and accommodation centres. Consequently, during this period, young people presented Emmaus with three problems. First, their lack of skills made it difficult to integrate them into Communities, the very lynchpin of which was work. Secondly, accommodation centres and the national minimum wage were new sources of competition which made the idea of work and sticking to a schedule seem altogether less enticing. Finally, the Communities themselves, aware that they were better suited to middle-aged, broken adults than to the young, for whom Community life could be difficult to endure psychologically and constitute a barrier to integration, were sometimes even less keen to hold on to them, given that getting several generations to peacefully coexist was far from straight forward.

## Women and children

The Communities' record was equally unimpressive when it came to supporting women. There were two possible ways of doing so, both problematic: the Movement could either introduce mixed Communities or open Communities specifically for women.

The Community at Le Plessis has already demonstrated just how difficult it was to manage women-only Communities – women were physically weaker than men and so less able to adapt to the demands of waste-collection and recycling work, there were outbursts of violence and jealousy to contend with, and children lived among them. When they arrived in Communities, women, who had often battled life's difficulties for longer than their male counterparts,[6] were also more broken. Only two women's Communities ever existed: Le Plessis opened its doors in 1954 and Le Blanc was set up in 1979, in Indre, Central France. However, both experienced significant difficulties. Failing to make a profit, Le Plessis opted to become a mixed Community in 1980. Le Blanc encountered major problems on several occasions and even closed for periods of time.

By contrast, mixed Communities became increasingly widespread as the number of female victims of acute social exclusion grew. In 1983 there were around fifty women in Communities, in the late 1980s there were 120, and double this by 2007. The consequence of this trend was an increase in the number of children: there were around thirty living in Communities in 1983 and 150 in 2007. But while having both men and women in Communities had its advantages –

tasks could be divided up between the sexes so that each played to their strengths, there was a better balance and atmosphere, and couples could be trained together – it also caused problems. First, many Companions found it impossible to endure, as seeing men and women together reminded them of a past that was too painful to bear – mixed Communities in themselves were effective but the presence of couples was not tolerated. Secondly, mixed Communities raised the issue of what to do about children. Besides the fact that single men were often not at all comfortable with children living among them, accepting children into a Community meant planning to meet their needs and constantly ensuring they were given the opportunities to develop as they should. Finally, it required guarding against and/or laying down rules on sexual relations, contraception, sexually transmitted diseases and so forth. At Fraternity, however, couples who were active within Emmaus were accepted into Communities and very quickly new couples were also welcomed with open arms.

## The 1990s: the development of organisations for social integration

With the arrival of these new groups of young people and women, all seeking help, the Communities devised an original response: organisations for social integration. After innovative pilot experiments with such organisations in the 1980s, they were developed over the course of the following decade.

In 1983, the Strasbourg Community, which was founded in 1971 by UCC and joined the ranks of the independent Communities not long after, started ENVIE (New Business for Economic Integration). In order to help young people reintegrate into society, the organisation created intermediary waste-collection and recycling businesses offering contracts paying the minimum wage for a maximum of two years. Replicating the experiments conducted in Scandinavia since 1979, which had produced encouraging results, the Strasbourg experiment was part of the genesis of so-called "intermediary"[7] businesses officially recognised in France in 1983. In Strasbourg, the business was based on the collection of domestic appliances from Communities, waste-reception centres and distributors, and through agreements signed with the electronics firm *Darty*: 60% of costs were covered by the sale of repaired products, 25% by subsidies and 15% by additional forms of support. Another experiment, this time based on carefully selecting and repairing old clothes and, to a lesser extent, old papers, was developed at the same time by Emmaus-Artois – another independent Community. In 1984, Pierre Duponchel, a volunteer at the Cambrai Community, decided to devote himself to Emmaus as a paid employee to work on creating jobs for young people. He participated in the creation of the Béthune Community in Bruay-la-Bussière, in the Nord-Pas-de-Calais region of France, and drew inspiration from the experiment conducted in the Belgian Community at Namur. In four years, Namur raised enough money to hire 140 employees through collecting and recycling clothes. In order to avoid directly involving Emmaus, the Community created Le Relais as a separate association. As Duponchel remarked in an interview, "You need to imagine we're back in 1982–3: there was something shady about an association that set up in business; people who were meant to protect social welfare and who started a business were seen as people using the social sector to make money." The first operations to collect old clothes took place around Arras in 1985. Le Relais initially operated as an association, hiring people on TUC placements,[8] before becoming a limited company. Since 2000, it has functioned as a workers' cooperative. These initiatives, which were mere experiments in the 1980s, grew in number in the 1990s. Initially, they scattered across France, springing up one after the other: in 1999, ENVIE had twenty-seven associations and 400 integration contracts available, while Le Relais accounted for 730 jobs. Despite the fact that for a long time, relations between Emmaus and Le Relais were tense – several Communities were bitterly critical of these "wild" organisations taking root on the waste-collection patch they had claimed as theirs without any prior consultation – there was a gradual rapprochement, which culminated in each acknowledging the other and full integration in the first decade of the new millennium. Conversely, relations between Emmaus and ENVIE were initially very solid, its Businesses for Economic Integration being held up as examples to follow, but cooled in the 1990s.

The very concept of a Community creating a Business for Economic Integration before then becoming independent began to spread. In the late 1980s, UCC's Chambéry Community embarked upon the creation of *Tri-Alpes*, a business based on collecting and recycling waste from waste-reception centres. By late 1990, approximately ten jobs had been created for a workforce whose members were unqualified, on the verge of social exclusion, and unsuited to Community life. In 1985, a workshop specifically designed for women, where old textiles that could not be made fit for resale were given a new lease of life, opened its doors. Six years later, it was declared a Business for Economic Integration. Located in the heart of a male Community, in 2004 the Business for Economic Integration took on forty members of staff. These were often women of around forty years of age, and the majority were foreigners or people awaiting leave to remain in the country, living alone or with children and with a painful past behind them. The Communities becoming *de facto* mixed establishments sparked the creation of training courses for couples, while both the Businesses for Economic Integration and the Communities offered a relatively stable environment. In 2003 in Poitou-Charentes, around fifteen Emmaus associations, together with two Associations for Economic Integration in the western French commune of Niort, created the Western Textiles Recycling Initiative, or the TRIO platform, which also aimed to increase the number of women reintegrated into society through work in the textile industry. The initiative was a veritable platform where surplus textile products from companies across the region were processed, in order to limit the quantities cast on to the scrapheap or resold to those who collected waste items on behalf of the Businesses for Economic Integration. In Foulain, northeastern France (Partage), the Viaduct Workshop stored, repaired and recycled wooden pallets. In 1997, it already had sixteen members of staff on its books that had been hired on CES contracts.[9] The majority of these were former Companions. One of the features which made the workshop unique was the fact that it had been created jointly by *Partage* and *Secours catholique*, with the local CHRS joining the team in late 1994. Finally, in 1992 the Des Pepins Community (Fraternity) created Hedged Farmland Workshops. In 2003, their joint workforce was

170-strong, and many of its members were former Companions. Located at the centre of Communities, these workshops provided staff with a veritable pathway back to independent living. They began their journey in a Community and then joined an Integration Workshop on either a CES or CEC[10] contract before finally starting work in a Business for Economic Integration. Employees were housed in individual family houses, which together formed almost a village. Alongside professional coaching they benefited from a holistic support package and artistic activities.

The Committees of Friends were far from inactive, themselves sometimes turning into veritable Businesses for Economic Integration. From the very beginning of the 1980s, several Committees took on employees who were initially granted TUC contracts. Then, as government-subsidised mechanisms to help the socially disadvantaged return to work developed, these contracts became CES and then CEC. Presented as a weapon in the fight against social exclusion and unemployment, these posts were given primarily to people living in extreme hardship with little hope of finding a job elsewhere. According to the philosophy behind this initiative, "volunteers steal jobs from people who could do them."[11] The increase in the number of unfilled places across the Communities in the late 1980s was a vindication of the Committees' choice, and prompted them to start paying workers the national minimum wage. As a result of this decision, in 1988, twenty-one out of thirty-eight Committees had paid employees on their books. Thirty-five of these employees were on open-ended contracts, twenty had fixed-term contracts and a further 155 contracts were CES, CEC or CIE.[12] In 2002, some Committees spent 80%, even 90% of their takings on their wage bill and overheads, which itself became a high-risk strategy during periods when sales temporarily decreased...

## Training for Companions: the debate

The Movement also began to consider how best to deal with the Companions who could not be directly (re)integrated into society and to discuss the type of training they should be offered. At UCC, the issue came to the fore in 1982 when the Cabriès Community decided to apply for state funding in order to employ "workshop monitors". At the time, the majority of Communities were so lacking in terms of the training they offered to Companions that it was inconceivable to think that any one of them could be successfully (re)integrated into society in the long term. Similar decisions had been taken previously (in 1954, a joinery workshop was created in Pontault-Combault with a view to providing Companions with vocational training; in 1975, a mechanics workshop was opened in Neuilly-sur-Marne), but the Federation ruled out any possibility of applying for state funding and declared that the project "distorted" the Community. In its view, a Community's purpose was not to reintegrate people into society, but rather to be "a place where people could live, socialise and receive support". Cabriès ultimately capitulated, under the threat of exclusion from the Federation.

Two years later, UCC did nevertheless acknowledge that there was a "real need for literacy tuition and basic training" and encouraged its Communities to meet this need. However, initiatives at local level remained thin on the ground: in 1991, only two UCC Communities in Brittany – Quimperlé and Saint-Brieuc – offered training (for work in the electrical goods industry). Communities continued to be guided by the belief that it was ultimately impossible to (re)integrate members into society, while the Companions themselves, who were interviewed anonymously, believed it was very difficult at Emmaus to enter or return to the world of work. Fixed, inflexible schedules meant they lacked the time to search for a job, received little help with their search, and were of the impression that expressing a wish to leave the Community "did not go down well". The UACE's key initiative was the creation in 1986 of a small training centre whose aim was to provide Companions with professional qualifications, and which initially focused on training them to work in the electrical goods industry. In Communities everywhere, initiatives to combat illiteracy were almost non-existent.

The lack of such initiatives stemmed from the fact that Communities were more eager to foster Companions' personal development, through social activities (holidays, games, leisure pursuits, etc.) and activities which encouraged self-expression. These activities began to develop in the early 1990s. There were writing workshops in

Chambéry and Marseille Pointe-Rouge, and painting and sculpture workshops in Marseille-Saint-Marcel (open to local residents in an attempt to bring together people from different sides of the track), or drama workshops, music workshops, etc.

This shortage of initiatives sparked an original response on the part of Fraternity in 1996: La Maison de l'Aube created by Yves Godard. A place where people could meet, a place where they could search for the ways and means to move forward, and a centre providing training in basic skills and the Emmaus professions. It was located in Poitiers and open to Companions from all federations. However, once again, emphasis was placed on self-expression, communication and personal development. Running at a severe loss and shunned by certain federations, it was finally dissolved in 2004 and converted into the Companions' Training House, which later became part of Emmaus France and turned its attentions to the fight against illiteracy, to basic skills training and to training in the Emmaus professions. Since the very end of the 1990s, local initiatives appear to have followed this lead, with workshops in IT, gardening or cookery, literacy courses and training for budding electricians or electrical goods workers, etc.

However, Communities remained focused on the principle that their role was not so much to reintegrate people into society – a questionable term given that so many Companions had never been integrated into society and seemed beyond hope of reintegration according to the universally accepted criteria – as to get the men who came to them "back on their feet". In that sense, the work of the organisations for integration fundamentally complemented their own.

## The Development of Community Life

Community life underwent considerable change as Communities remained the preferred solution for broken or world-weary men, be it temporary or long-term.

### The Community as shelter and staging-post

The economic crisis radically altered the role the Community played as a staging-post. From the very beginning of the 1980s, members of

Emmaus everywhere bemoaned the increase in applications for Community places, the increase in the number of people being turned away and the decrease in the number of outings offered to Companions (outings to the grape harvests, for example, had been frequent up until that point). Companions lived by the old adage "a bird in the hand is worth two in the bush". With times hard once more, the guarantee of a warm place to stay and a job deterred Companions from trying their luck elsewhere. In contrast, from 1987 onwards, supply once again outstripped demand; many Communities found themselves with spare places and observed a decrease in the number of Companions. This time, however, the problem was not so much one of capacity as one of changing demand, taking place against the backdrop of the development of alternative responses to social exclusion (accommodation centres, the minimum wage). Demand decreased particularly among the middle-aged: 31% of Companions were aged 30–40 in 1988 and 20% came from this age group fifteen years later; 41% were aged 40–50 in 1994, compared to 29% ten years later. It is easy to imagine what such a decline in the number of workers in the prime of life and the consequent loss of skills would have meant for a Community.

As for those who opted to join a Community, there was a sharp drop in the number that stayed for a short time only. In 1988, 35% of stays in all Communities lasted less than three months. In 1998, this figure stood at 25% and by 2003, it had dropped to 17%. The stays became, a fortiori, much longer than they had been in the mid-1960s: while 63% of stays lasted less than two months in 1964–5 and 20% lasted more than five months, these percentages had been more than inverted by 1988–9 (10% and 71%, respectively).[13] These developments chiefly gave way to an increase in the number of six- to twelve-month stays and in the number lasting more than a decade.

However, while Companions tended to stay at Emmaus for longer, they also switched Communities with greater ease. In 1965, 39% of those who were on their second stay were trying out a second Community, and 19% of those who were staying in a Community for the third time were staying in a third Community. In the late 1980s, these figures stood at 83% and 63%, respectively. In the 1960s, 38% of those who had eight or more stays under their belt had tried at least six Communities; at the end of the 1980s, this figure stood at 64%. There is no doubt that this "itchy-feet syndrome" was largely the result of the increase in the number of Communities.

Information is available on the profile of newcomers arriving in the late 1980s;[14] two-fifths came from another Community (more than a third had been moving between Communities for between two and ten years), a fifth were of no fixed abode, a fifth had a roof over their head and a fifth came from an accommodation centre. The new Companions possessed very few qualifications: 59% had not successfully completed primary education, 3% had received a professional skills certificate at the end of secondary education, 22% had not managed to attain the National Diploma awarded at the end of the third year of secondary education and 7% were illiterate. The number of Companions who had broken all family ties was a lot higher than it had been in the 1960s: back then, 38% did not name a next of kin. By the late 1980s, this number had increased to 63%. Finally, just as in the years 1964–5, Companions in Communities in the Nord-Pas-de-Calais region largely hailed from the area immediately surrounding the Community. The vast majority of Companions in the southeastern Communities came from across the whole of France (on account, perhaps, of the south's natural pull, or the increased likelihood of finding seasonal work there) and the other Communities tended to recruit from within their respective regions.

## The Community as a place to live

Life within Communities changed significantly over time, with increasing emphasis seemingly placed on the individual. While in the early years living as a collective was the dominant ideology and practice, Companions were increasingly provided with personal rather than communal spaces and individuals no longer surrendered their own identity to the group. As a result, the concept of Community was radically redefined. However, these changes were nothing more than the natural extension of the policy that had been in place since the early 1960s – dormitories were replaced by small bedrooms, washrooms were installed, Communities kept a watchful eye on the Companions' mental state, etc.

Companions were endowed with growing purchasing power. There was a particularly notable increase in the sum of money given to Companions during the first half of the 1980s (UCC increased the weekly sum received from €24 to €30 per week in real terms) and it continued to rise throughout the 1990s, although not to quite the same extent. However, there was a disparity between the sums given to Companions in each of the two major federations: a Companion earned more in a UCC Community in the 1980s than in a UACE Community in the 1990s. By contrast, in 2000 the two federations standardised the amount of money which Companions received. The decision to do so stemmed from UCC's desire to bring the sum as closely in to line as possible with the changing cost of living, while UACE refused, in the 1980s, to play the game of "the consumer society", and to break with the spirit of poverty that had traditionally imbued its work. At a meeting of friends and leaders in 1984, UACE declared that "to increase the sum of money given to Companions would be to agree to seeing their needs grow in line with the prevailing spirit in our society; despite the fact that at the same time, the economic situation of some people continues to worsen. Not to increase it would be to refuse to simply model ourselves on society in order to express our solidarity with those who are currently experiencing such economic difficulties, and in order, perhaps, to also imply that alternative ways of looking at the world exist, besides that which seeks to increase consumption and the needs of individuals."[15]

Another defining characteristic of the period was that living space within Communities increasingly became individual, rather than communal. Despite the fact that dormitories had already given way to bedrooms for smaller groups, these were now gradually replaced with single rooms. As the economic crisis took hold and the Communities took root, a proportion of Companions tended to make these Communities their long-term home. Keeping a tight grip on their purse strings, they hoarded money away and invested in technology: personal televisions – the arrival of which emptied communal TV rooms – video recorders and hi-fi systems, followed by computers, mobile phones, etc. A Companion who made the Community his long-term home was now able to have all the technology he could wish for at his fingertips. In addition, Companions tended to cherry-pick the parts of Community life in which they wished to participate: they began to sleep and eat outside the Community, particularly if they were in a relationship. The Community actively encouraged them to do so, believing it crucial to their personal development and the process of reintegration. The issue of the Companions' sex lives, previously taboo, was broached in the 1990s and Companions were later encouraged to enjoy sexual relationships.

The federations also widened access to holidays, an issue which was rarely discussed until the 1970s. Initially, the prevailing trend was for each Community to develop its own, unique holiday schemes. However, UCC then adopted a system whereby Companions received a certain amount of holiday, which gradually increased as they spent longer in the Community, and in the early 1990s, UACE followed their example. The holidays offered differed from one Community to the next. For a long time, with its three houses – Primelin (Brittany), la Ferme des Vosges and Lespinassière (Aude) – UCC offered a wider range of activities. For a number of years, the federations also developed "hobby holidays" where Companions could try out new things and get involved in sporting activities. Finally, many Companions went on holiday with their families (more than a third), went camping or stayed in a hotel (both a third each).

The Movement's changing relationship with healthcare was also symptomatic of its new-found desire to focus to a greater extent on Companions as individuals. During the previous period, only UCC had tackled the issue of healthcare in any meaningful way. By contrast, from the 1980s onwards it was dealt with by organisations across the board. UACE even went as far as to hire a federation doctor for two years (1990–2) in order to improve communication with local doctors; develop screening procedures (for tuberculosis, etc.), vaccinations and Community pharmacists; to sort out administrative problems; and to initiate a debate on how best to deal with AIDS. There was, however, one issue which the Movement has grappled with constantly since its very inception: alcohol. However, while UCC began to tackle the problem in the early 1960s, even by the 1980s UACE was still dragging its heels: while the majority of Communities were "dry", some were still serving beer and on several occasions, those attending meetings noted that friends and leaders were not exactly shining examples of abstinence. Since the 1990s, training in the physical, psychological and social consequences of alcohol consumption has been provided as a matter of course and abstinence has become the hard-and-fast rule.

Finally, the Movement's increasing focus on the individual has also been reflected in its very recent decision to ensure that Companions are given the opportunity to express their own opinions on Community life. This issue was raised sporadically from 1992 onwards, when the first "Companions' charter" came into being. The principle was then gradually enforced through trial and error, with Communities sometimes asking Companions for their views more out of a sense of obligation or to keep a clear conscience than because the reality of Community life made it necessary to do so. Now, however, it is standard practice for Companions to decide who exactly will benefit from funds raised to help others in difficulty and to participate in general meetings. Further progress was also made in 2008 with Companions' participation in the decision-making process.

## The elderly man

Upon reaching retirement age, several options were open to a Companion: he could stay in the Community, go into the Emmaus retirement home (Esteville until 1998; la Halte-Saint-Jean for the Communities in the Nord-Pas-de-Calais since the 1990s), or leave Emmaus to set up home in specially adapted accommodation or an apartment. In 1991 at UCC, 50% stayed at Emmaus and 50% went elsewhere. However, the majority stated that had they a genuine choice, they would opt to leave.[16] Conversely, in the Nord-Pas-de-Calais region, the majority of Companions stayed in a Community, a minority moved to the retirement home in Halte-Saint-Jean, but not a single one left Emmaus. Broadly speaking, the decision to stay was often made by default: Companions' lack of qualifications and the periods of unemployment they had experienced left them with pensions too meagre to live comfortably elsewhere.

Demographic changes and the progress in access to healthcare made elderly men an increasingly common feature of Community life:

while in the early days Companions died young, now their life expectancy was increasing. Some also began to carve out veritable "careers"[17] at Emmaus and, as a result, the issue of retirement became an increasingly legitimate concern. Age graphs for 1980–2000 show a slow but marked increase in the number of elderly Companions at Emmaus: on average, 5% of Companions were over the age of sixty in the late 1980s. This average peaked at 8.8% in 1999 and stood at 7% for the period 2000–5. Nevertheless, the average life expectancy of a Companion remained far below the national average: in the period 1990–5, 29% of Companions living in Communities died between the ages of fifty-five and fifty-nine; 54% between sixty and sixty-four. Furthermore, 41% had retired less than a year before they died and 32% had retired one to two years prior to their death. Out of sixty-seven cases examined, eighteen died as a result of an alcohol addiction, sixteen from cancer and fourteen from heart disease.[18]

## The status and protection of Companions: unanswered questions

It has been demonstrated that during the previous period in Emmaus' history, the desire to see Companions receive legal status came to the fore. The issue was tackled repeatedly from the 1980s onwards, but negotiations were never successful. The matter in fact encompassed two distinct sub-issues: social protection and law.

As far as social protection was concerned, all Companions benefited, at least in theory, from Social Security. In August 1982, having been asked to deliver its verdict on the matter by UACE, the Central Agency for Social Security Bodies officially exempted Communities from the obligation to pay social security contributions on Companions' behalf, as any other employer was required to do on behalf of his workers. However, in the late 1980s, Social Security offices across France continued to differ in their attitudes towards the system (demanding differing contributions, awarding different amounts in benefits, etc.), and Companions did not benefit from a uniform registration procedure. The Communities in the Nord-Pas-de-Calais region operated under a specific system: they did not pay contributions to URSAFF, the French organisation responsible for collecting social security and family benefit contributions, but Companions were covered instead by the *bons bleus* financed by the departmental council. This cover allowed Companions to have medical expenses reimbursed. When interviewed on the issue, Pierre Duponchel remarked, "Companions are entitled to social protection; what is at issue is how this protection is to be financed. There is no way that the work of Companions, who have been thrown on society's scrap-heap, will fund the social security system of that same society. For a long time, people said: 'They don't provide Companions in the Nord département with social protection.' That's not true. We provided it; we just refused to finance it. Whereas in Emmaus the usual line is, 'Within the Community, the Companion is a fully-fledged citizen. Therefore, he is entitled to social protection just like everybody else and, therefore, we'll pay into the social security system.'" In 1989, Communities in the Nord département abolished this system, agreeing instead to pay Companions the national minimum wage, which meant they were entitled to social protection. Since 2000, Companions have been covered by the CMU, France's universal health insurance system.

However, the real challenge facing Emmaus was a legal one. As the only relevant legal text in force, the Labour Code only recognised paid employees and volunteers. Companions, who fell somewhere between the two, were tolerated de facto by the authorities. With no specific legal status, they were treated, from 1988 onwards, in the same way as those living in accredited accommodation centres. Companions were placed in this category as they were not "hired" by Emmaus, but "taken in", and did not receive a "salary" rather "pocket money." And yet, spurred on by the vagueness of the legislation, Companions had been calling for the right to be officially recognised as unemployed and to receive unemployment benefit since the late 1970s – some Communities issued "pay slips", which placed the whole system under threat. At the turn of the new millennium, the Miraillès Barons affair put the issue back in the spotlight when UCC was faced with a formal legal battle: a Companion filed a lawsuit against the Federation in order to obtain a pay slip and a certificate of employment, a certificate proving that contributions had been made to ASSEDIC, the unemployment benefit office. The case was brought before an industrial tribunal before being referred to the Court of Appeal who ruled in favour of the Companion. However, the Supreme Court later overruled the judgement. Despite the fact that the case set a legal precedent, Communities are still occasionally hauled up before the courts. These court appearances were the result of the fact that since the late 1980s, calls to see government ministries grant Companions the legal status of "unsalaried worker" and "worker of the solidarity economy" have continued to fall on deaf ears.

## The Changing World of Waste Collection and Recycling Puts Communities and Committees to the Test

Alongside these economic and social changes, the waste-collection and recycling sector was also undergoing a period of radical transformation. In simple terms, the history of waste-collection at Emmaus can be said to comprise three major phases: the golden age, until the 1970s, when broadly speaking waste-collection and recycling was an unregulated sector in which there was no competition; the 1970s–90s, when the raw materials crisis prompted the Movement to focus instead on bric-à-brac sales; and the 1990s onwards, a phase in which Emmaus began to focus once more on sorting and recycling waste, this time in a highly regulated and increasingly competitive environment.

### The raw materials crisis and the development of bric-à-brac sales

From the 1980s onwards, the waste-collection and recycling market, which from the 1950s to the 1970s had barely interested a soul, became increasingly competitive and subject to the laws of supply and demand. This change prompted Emmaus to redirect its attentions towards bric-à-brac sales.

#### The yo-yoing prices of raw materials

In November 1992, waste paper was sold at 300 francs per tonne, but just two months later the price had fallen to fell to fifty francs per tonne. The decrease was due to the fact that in the intervening period, Germany had passed a law banning the dumping and incineration of waste paper and, as a result, the European market was flooded with German waste paper. By contrast, in September 1994, the price increased once more, to 1,100 francs per tonne. This increase was due both to new American laws which saw recycling waste paper suddenly cease to be the cushy number it once was in the USA, and to the economic recovery which sparked huge tension on the global pulp market. This is a prime example of what has been described as "the game of the yo-yoing prices of recyclable materials and the precarious nature of market opportunities."[19] The aim here is not to make an inventory of the fluctuations in raw material prices with which the Communities and Committees of Friends were forced to contend, but rather to simply flag up the mechanisms responsible: the markets were global and the slightest change in the economic situation or legislation of a major country could turn everything on its head. The falling price of raw materials affected scrap metal, paper and cardboard in particular: for example, in 1989, Communities sold corrugated paper for fifty-two francs per tonne, two years later they were forced to pay seven francs per tonne to get rid of it.

Consequently, in the early 1990s the Movement was forced to face the bitter truth: "The golden age of waste-collection and recycling [was] a thing of the past."[20] Raw materials (paper, cardboard, scrap metal, etc.) no longer produced a profit, Communities now had to pay to have skips removed and it was becoming increasingly difficult to move non-recyclable waste (it was forbidden to burn such waste on site, and waste-reception centres and incinerators had reached a state of gridlock). The system had gone from being one in which collecting and recycling raw materials was a lucrative activity to a system based on the provision of services where it cost to have raw materials taken away, with the market increasingly dominated by the large waste-collection, recycling and treatment firms.

Finally, there was a decrease in the actual tonnage collected. Two sets of figures from the Rennes-Hédé Community, produced twenty years apart, speak for themselves: in 1984, the Community collected and recycled 542 tonnes of scrap metal, compared to only 296 tonnes in 2003; 122 tonnes of other metals compared to fourteen; 176 tonnes of paper compared to fifty; thirty-eight tonnes of cardboard compared to none; nineteen tonnes of glass compared to none; and seven tonnes of feathers compared to none. Only the tonnage of textiles collected remained constant (seventy-eight tonnes).

### Attentions turn to bric-à-brac sales

This raw materials crisis caused Emmaus to focus instead on bric-à-brac. In 1979, 58% of UACE's total takings came from bric-à-brac sales and 42% came from the sale of raw materials to those who collected and recycled waste. In 1990, bric-à-brac accounted for 76% of takings. This figure increased to 86% in 1995 (90% at UCC in 1998). As always, of course, the figures differed greatly from one Community to the next: at UACE in 1998, the Community in which bric-à-brac accounted for the highest percentage of the takings was Arles (95.8%) while Cherbourg accounted for the lowest percentage (57.7%).

In the 2000s, on average, 28% of all takings came from furniture, 20% from second-hand clothes, 12% from building materials, 12% from knick-knacks, 8% from electrical appliances and 7.5% from books and postcards. Looking back on the decade as a whole, the main conclusion which Emmaus drew was that the quality of the products sold had declined, as furniture and cheap clothing became more widely circulated and worn-out. Emmaus also faced increasingly stiff competition when trying to acquire bric-à-brac. In the search for furniture, knick-knacks, records and postcards it had to fight off the flea markets, fairs and garage sales which had been springing up across France since the 1980s, while in the hunt for clothes it was forced to compete with the collections conducted by humanitarian organisations. Consequently, while the number of Communities continued to increase, the total tonnage of items collected declined: in 1999, 3.5 million m$^3$ of items were collected following 530,000 collections, compared to only 3.2 million m$^3$ and 484,000 collections in 2003.

## The 2000s: the competitive re-launch of waste-collection and recycling

These developments were inextricably linked to the increase, from the 1990s onwards, in the number of directives on the treatment and recycling of waste. The proliferation of such directives was an attempt to reduce pollution, make living environments healthier and to save energy. The directives' entry into force meant that while in the 1980s the fall in the resale price of recycled materials made it more economical to dispose of waste, waste disposal later became increasingly expensive, which in turn encouraged the selective collection of waste and recycling. The changes transformed the trade of waste-collection and recycling into a highly competitive battleground where the stakes were high,[21] despite the fact that Communities and Committees had, up until that point, survived due to the lack of competition in the sector and despite the fact that they relieved owners of unwanted items for free, unlike waste-collection and recycling firms.

The first major piece of legislation in the field was that of 17 July 1975 on waste disposal and recycling. In addition to banning the large rubbish bonfires, which took place in all Communities, the law made the collection and disposal of household waste the responsibility of each town council, established both the principle of "the collection and recycling of reusable objects and materials, and of energy" and methods of funding (introducing a fee), and created the National Agency for the Collection, Recycling and Disposal of Waste. In 1990, this agency became the Environment and Energy Saving Agency (ADEME), bringing both the French Energy Saving Agency and the Air Quality Agency under its umbrella. The law of 13 July 1992 then provided further impetus for such efforts. It introduced the principle of preventing toxic waste, declared that all so-called "final" waste was to be disposed of by 2002, and made it mandatory for all town councils to draw up a waste-management plan.[22] These two laws radically altered the approach to waste: the "anything-goes" attitude which had prevailed up until that point and which had notably resulted in an increase in the number of rubbish dumps was replaced by a policy that ensured that the treatment of waste was strictly monitored. The policy required local authorities to close municipal rubbish dumps, to set up waste treatment plants and, for final, non-treatable waste, to create highly regulated "technical burial centres". A series of decrees, particularly encouraged by the EU, were adopted (1990–2000) and supplemented these pieces of legislation: they included decrees on polluting activities, the packaging of household goods, classified waste facilities, the classification of waste, batteries and accumulators, and end-of-life vehicles. The "polluter pays" principle became widely applicable, having first been enshrined in the 1964 Water Law: by this principle, the person responsible for producing the waste is responsible for its disposal. These changes had a profound impact on the waste-collection and recycling economy at Emmaus. Two significant cases by way of example: the textile sector and "WEEE" (waste electrical and electronic equipment).

## New challenges for the textile sector

At the symposium entitled "Crunch time in Textile Collection and Recycling: Destroying or Creating Jobs?" organised by Emmaus France in 2006, Serge Sztrakman stated: "[in the textile sector] there are different families. The largest of these is second-hand clothes and it is here where we can make a profit. Then, there are the sub-groups such as industrial wipes. As far as this product is concerned, French industry is not doing well, because metalworking has been relocated to cheaper labour markets, etc. I've been in this trade for thirty-two years and when I started out we made a profit on industrial wipes. Today, we're making a loss. Then there's pure recycling with wool, knitted items, merino, etc. There was a time when we sent these products to Italy to be treated. Italy couldn't withstand the competition from India and China, and so today we send these products to the Subcontinent to be re-treated, and at negligible cost. We also used to deal with felted cardboard, which only one factory in France produced [... It] filed for bankruptcy a year ago."[23]

The extent of the crisis affecting the collection and recycling of textiles is clear. In addition to the economic crisis of the 1980s, the sector was forced to contend with episodes of structural upheaval from the 1990s onwards. First was the crisis of the French clothing banks, which were followed by their European counterparts. The major waste-collection and recycling firms in France, working together under the umbrella of business Recollect, developed a system that was clever but which sounded the death knell for Emmaus' own recycling activities. Working in partnership with charitable associations, the business put clothing banks on public highways, in car parks or near supermarkets. Generally bearing the logo of the French Association for the Paralysed (APF) or of the Red Cross, the principle behind the clothing banks was simple: a major association rented its name to a wholesaler dealing in recyclable waste, which then sold the clothes in countries in the East or in Africa. The presence of such clothing banks, bearing the APF logo, had already been flagged up at a local level by the UCC in 1976, but negotiations with local figures had seen the problem resolved. The system was developed in the USA in the 1980s and spread across France on a large scale in the 1990s. It was then adopted by foreign wholesalers in the late 1990s as a means of penetrating the French market, a veritable gold mine for countries such as Germany or the Netherlands which were much better organised but had exhausted their national stocks of old clothes. In 1996, the largest waste-collection and recycling firm in Germany, SOEX, signed a contract with the French Red Cross to use its logo and place clothing banks across the whole of France, with the ultimate goal of controlling no less than 80% of clothing-collection operations in Europe. Faced with this offensive, Recollect was itself forced to file for bankruptcy in 1990 and was bought up by the firm Vivendi. Associations also began to appear whose name suggested they were every inch authentic charities (Missionaries of the Heart, for example), but whose "charitable credentials were somewhat dubious".[24] They too created networks of clothing banks for the benefit of foreign waste-collection and recycling firms. A small fish in a big pond, Le Relais-Emmaus attempted to fight fire with fire, by setting up its own clothing banks, but ones whose profits were used to create jobs which could help Companions integrate into society.

But the waste-collection and recycling industry was then heavily affected by the decline in the quality of the clothing collected: while it had previously been possible to unravel, darn and re-sew damaged fabric and therefore to sell the items on to second-hand clothes dealers, clothes were now produced at a negligible cost in Asia. They were of abysmal quality and often fit only for the rubbish dump. The "cream" of the clothing (the best of the items collected which could be sold directly to second-hand dealers, the rest of the items known collectively as the "skimmed pile") continued to decrease, and today accounts for only 10–20% of all items collected. At the same time, the very low cost of new clothing meant it could even compete with recycled products. Furthermore, the cost of disposing of waste items, including textile products, continued to increase, which placed an enormous strain on budgets. Lastly, collecting and sorting textile products were very labour-intensive activities (labour costs accounted for 60–70% of the cost price and continued to rise with the introduction of the 35-hour working week, the general tendency to reduce working time, etc.). Large firms responded to these developments by relocating to the Maghreb or eastern Europe, or by further developing their use of machinery to replace a human workforce.

From 1992 onwards, all of these factors combined to jolt Emmaus into action and sparked new debates on the urgent need to adapt to the new lie of the land, or risk disappearing from the textile market. The Movement began by examining what exactly was at stake. In addition to the symbolic importance of the Ragpicker in 1998, Le Relais had created 600 jobs in fourteen years, and textiles produced between 20% and 30% of the turnover within Emmaus Communities; dealing in second-hand clothes was seen as a lucrative activity, a booming trade with a bright future, and the French market continued to display impressive potential for growth. Attempts were also made to pinpoint weaknesses. Emmaus was good at collecting items but performed badly when it came to sorting and selling its spoils. In early 2002, an agreement signed between Emmaus France and ADEME enabled the pair to hire a consultant who diagnosed problems and made recommendations.

Associations also responded to new developments in the market by joining forces. In 2004, collecting, sorting and selling textiles accounted for 3,000 of the posts designed to facilitate social integration, with 2,000 of these at Emmaus. These figures make it clear that while Abbé Pierre's Movement was the major association in the sector, it was not the only one. In early 2002, the first joint meeting between the Emmaus, *Secours catholique* and *Terre des hommes* networks was held and the first joint decision taken. This decision saw the organisations establish common goals (communication with the general public, streamlining the various areas of activity, information exchange, putting joint positions before policy-makers, etc.). In addition to creating jobs for social integration in France, posts often designed for women, these associations also proposed using the textile products to facilitate the independent development of Third World countries, which were in dire need of clothes.[25] Lastly, a series of solutions to these problems were gradually put in place, chiefly through the creation or merging of regional platforms in order to allow the surplus of textile products to be sorted with greater precision and to develop new Businesses for Economic Integration:[26] TRIO opened its doors in 2003 for the Poitou-Charente-Vendée region, followed by Evira in Bourgoin-Jallieu for the southwest, Le Lien in Neuvy-sur-Loire for central France and Retirex in Pontivy for the Brittany region.

The efforts made by Emmaus over several years to push through a bill on a "textile contribution", the implementing decree of which was adopted by the Council of State in 2008, also need to be considered against this backdrop. A contribution to be paid by producers and distributors of clothes and linen for the home, the textile contribution would provide sorting operators with financial support to deal with and recycle waste, and therefore at Emmaus, it would help create jobs to facilitate social integration. Since the early 2000s, around 100,000 tonnes of textile products have been collected each year by either private firms or associations. In 2007, Le Relais alone collected 46,000 tonnes and the other Emmaus groups (Communities and Committees of Friends) collected 17,500 – these figures clearly demonstrate both that Emmaus was a hugely powerful presence within the sector and exactly how much was at stake.

### WEEE

Another more recent example of how Emmaus was forced to adapt to changes in the market comes in the form of WEEE (waste electrical and electronic equipment). In December 2002, a European directive on WEEE[27] regarded this equipment as special waste and stated that as such, the dismantling or disposal thereof was subject to specific rules. Still based on the principle that producers and distributors were responsible for managing the end of life of these products, it also made it compulsory to use approved organisations for the collection, dismantling and disposal of these products, as was the case with packaging. However, while with textiles Emmaus had been caught unawares by a change in the market with which it caught up only by the skin of its teeth, in contrast the Movement adopted a pre-emptive approach to WEEE and carried out extensive preparation work prior to the implementation of the directive in France.

In 2003, on the initiative of several grass-roots groups, a working group was set up to monitor the transposition of the European directive into French law, to pool knowledge and information on the waste-treatment sector, and to raise awareness across the Movement about the nature of the challenge faced (the need to dispose of waste in approved treatment plants, the increase in the cost of waste treatment). In 2004, funding from the state financial institution *La Caisse des Dépôts* allowed the Movement to hire a consultant, who had graduated from the prestigious *École Polytechnique*. Despite the fact that Emmaus held only a 4% market share in this sector, there was still a considerable amount at stake – namely whether or not they would have to pay taxes on the disposal of waste items brought in by individuals. In essence, what was at stake was the very survival of this specific sector of the waste-collection and recycling industry. The Movement finally signed an agreement with *Eco-système*, the largest environmental organisation in France (the equivalent of *Eco-emballages* for the WEEE sector), which provided Emmaus with a free waste-treatment service and even paid them for this waste. In 2007, the year the directive entered into force, the Emmaus groups sent 17,000 tonnes of WEEE to *Eco-Systѐme*.

## Supervision and Commitment: Friends and Leaders

All of these developments had a significant impact on the supervision of waste-collection organisations, both in technical terms and in terms of the new responsibilities to be shouldered.

### The job of Community leader grows increasingly technical

From 1980 onwards, in order to further improve the supervision of the sector and deal with the fact that work therein was becoming increasingly technical, UCC aimed to appoint two to three leaders per Community. Coupled with the increasing number of Communities, this decision forced the recruitment campaign to step up a gear. Job advertisements were most often placed in the Catholic press or in media aimed at converting people to the Catholic faith (*Témoignage chrétien*, *La Croix*, *La Vie*, *Télérama*, etc.) and it was only in 1996 that the Federation began to use publications targeted at a wider audience, as a result of the difficulties experienced in recruiting leaders and due to its desire to cast its net over a larger area (*Ouest-France*, *Actualités sociales hebdomadaires*, *Libération*, *Le Parisien*, *Le Figaro*, etc.). The Federation's ideal candidates would be aged 30–50 and would meet certain criteria relating to their motives for applying, their skills, militancy, and availability.

The constant need to recruit new members of staff and the difficult nature of the job in question prompted the organisation to adapt its training policy. Before being hired on a permanent basis, the trainee underwent a probationary period during which he was first immersed in Community life, before being given a position of responsibility. In 1993, a mentoring system was put in place which saw seasoned Community leaders guide young hopefuls. Once hired, the new Community leader continued his training, which was intense during his first few years in the post and then became more low-key. However, training continued throughout the Community leader's professional career. A Community leader's increasing ability to stand on his own two feet and cope with the demands of the job was reflected in the wage he received: today, a beginner receives a monthly salary of €2,350 gross, and an experienced leader, €3,500.

The grass-roots groups believed that the importance accorded to professionalism would spark the decline of militancy within the Movement. However, this accusation was more a reflection of leaders' desires not to sacrifice their private life than of a lack of conviction: many had worked previously in the humanitarian or social work sectors and those who came from very different backgrounds, of which there were a significant number (the world of cinema, sport, etc.) most often chose to work with Emmaus out of a genuine desire to commit to the cause.

While UCC was always looking to recruit more leaders despite the fact that they were not really in short supply, the shortage of leaders at UACE was drastic for three reasons. First, it was a result of the fact that the Federation remained steadfast in its policy of internal promotion, which continued to be held up as the ideal recruitment method. However, as the job became more complex and the need for leaders with a solid skills base grew, it became an increasingly hypothetical concept. Secondly, there were no guarantees that promoting a Companion to the position of Community leader would prove successful: a man whose mental state was fragile found it difficult to cope with the demands of the job, and as UACE noted in a meeting in 1981, "a deputy leader trained and appointed in the same Community has difficulty in being accepted in his new role for at least six months."[28] The Federation also later remarked that rising through the ranks to become a Community leader "require[d the Companion] to undergo a lengthy process of personal development, make sacrifices and have a certain type of character."[29] Finally, external recruitment itself remained hypothetical owing to the meagre salary on offer – in 1981, a UACE leader with six years' seniority and two children earned the minimum wage. Consequently, the Movement focused primarily on providing internal training, a decent salary and social protection (in 1984, leaders were given cover from a mutual insurance company, pensions were gradually revised from 1988 onwards and supplementary pensions were later awarded). From 1997 onwards, thawing relations between UCC and UACE led to the establishment of common training programmes and then, from 2001, to the development of a common recruitment process and the accelerated standardisation of practices regarding wages, the reduction of working time, paid leave, etc.

In contrast, Liberty remained closer to UACE from the very beginning. In his interview, Jacques Loch remarked, "We are perhaps a little hasty in continuing to believe in and experiment with the internal promotion of Companions. Today, that remains one of the priorities of Liberty. By this I mean that, for example, that we will have no problem with putting people who came to us via the emergency services in positions of responsibility. In fact, my colleague arrived here after four years on the streets, having been sent by the emergency services. We will place trust in these people, a trust which is careful and relative, but we will be driven by the belief that internal promotion is best."

## A crisis of commitment?

In French society as a whole, joining the Emmaus cause remained something of a secondary phenomenon: while *Secours populaire* boasted 86,000 volunteers and *Secours catholique* 66,000, there were only 1,000 volunteers in the Emmaus Committees of Friends in 1985 and 2,500 in 1998. The Communities had the support of 2,800 volunteers in 1990 and 4,400 in 2002. For all that, the difficulties which Emmaus encountered were fairly characteristic of contemporary activism.

While the issue had never been raised before that point, the shortage of Friends (local volunteers) was a problem broached periodically from the 1980s onwards both at UACE and in the Committees of Friends. There was no such shortage at UCC, but from the 1980s onwards, the Federation constantly bemoaned the lack of commitment on a local and national level: the low turnout at meetings, the lack of applications for posts and no real desire to influence the path which the Federation followed. Despite the fact that, in theory, one-third of the members of UCC's national boards were leaders and two-thirds Friends, in the 1980s, the ratio was 50/50 due to the lack of candidates applying for the job.

From 1985 onwards, Friends were portrayed as people increasingly coming to the Movement to perform occasional tasks, looking for an opportunity for personal development rather than to give selflessly to Emmaus. Little by little and conscious of what they were doing to a greater or lesser extent, the majority of Friends left the Movement in the hands of Community leaders, content to provide technical and occasional support. The Friend who performed a technical role within Emmaus (treasurer, cashier, seller, waste-sorter) preferred practical tasks, lending a hand with specific tasks, providing immediate assistance rather than long-term support, making visible changes rather than working to educate others. They were relatively uninterested in taking a holistic approach to the job and turning their hand to the wide variety of jobs it entailed, including evaluating problems and providing guidance, tackling health issues and safeguarding the Movement's future. At best, the majority of Committees limited themselves to playing a managerial role. These associations, which people were initially so keen to form and which essentially acted as protectors of the Movement's principles and spirits, breathing life into Communities, had effectively resigned, choosing to keep their involvement to a minimum."[30]

Without drawing upon controversial macro-sociological theories on the *post-it* era[31] or pointing to hypothetical social crisis, the Friends' gradual abdication of their responsibilities can be attributed to certain internal factors. As we have seen, the Friends were the strong pillar in the Emmaus triangle, making up for leaders who were far from up to the job. And yet since the 1970s, the high quality of the leaders appointed turned the power balance within the Movement on its head. Furthermore, there were the conflicts about the privileges each group enjoyed: the leaders, heavily focused on internal tasks (waste-collection and recycling, providing Companions with social support), now looked for Friends who were able to represent the Movement and defend its values, but the majority of these Friends displayed similar enthusiasm for internal tasks, responsibilities of which they had been partially stripped. There was also the issue of age: in 1983, UACE became aware "that [they were] starting to resemble a third-age club";[32] at the CNAE, 42% were over the age of sixty in 1985 and 59% ten years later, which meant that during this period, the proportion of pensioners within the organisation increased from 48% to 67%; at UCC in 2001, only 9% of the Friends were under the age of forty-five, compared to the 67% who were over the age of fifty-six. It would appear difficult not to link the ageing of the volunteers with their increasing lack of desire to shoulder responsibilities. The hypothesis seems even more likely when we consider the fact that the two phenomena occurred simultaneously. Finally, the increasing complexity of the work required also needs to be taken into account. The CNAE were more than aware that it was "not easy for simple volunteers", particularly older ones, "to keep up to date with new technology, to discuss waste-disposal operations, EU agreements and textile platforms".[33]

However, it is overly simplistic to conclude that the Friends were gradually deserting their duties. There is no doubt that they appeared less inclined to take on responsibilities, both at local and national level. There is also no doubt that when the Federation urged members to take more political action, the Friends often responded with charitable initiatives. For all that, the figures refute the assertion that "they [now] only provided occasional support". In 1993, a survey conducted by UACE revealed that while 5% had been in a Community for less than a year, 30% had been in a Community for one to three years, 30% for four to eight years, and 35% for more than eight years. It is clear, therefore, that at a local level the Friends were deeply loyal to the Association. Furthermore, an exhaustive enquiry carried out at UCC in 2001 revealed that many gave the Federation a great deal of their time: on average, 40% of the volunteers sacrificed one to five hours a week, 28% five to eight hours, 16% eight to sixteen hours, and 5% sixteen hours or more. Moreover, it is clear that it was the pensioners who were and continue to get involved at national level, making up 6% of UCC's board in 1981, 31% in 1990 and 44% in 2008.

Finally, Friends often campaigned on several fronts. This is one last factor which explains their increasing rejection of "total" commitment to the Movement, just as much as it serves to qualify the earlier assertion that contemporary volunteers were abdicating their responsibilities. At UCC in 2001, 43% of friends had their fingers in several pies (compared to 33% in religious associations, 32% in other associations in the solidarity sector, and 28% in sporting, leisure or cultural associations). If this is added to time already spent at Emmaus and time devoted to their loved ones, these pensioners ultimately appear a very active group, and it becomes easy to understand why they would baulk at the thought of more demands being placed on their time.

For many, then, involvement with Emmaus is a retirement activity, following membership of the youth movements and a period spent in politics or the unions as an adult. Often, their motivation for joining is not ideological. Rather, their involvement "is almost accidental, more than it is the result of any real choice. They are driven by the need to feel useful, to occupy their time, to reconnect with society or to in some way continue working life."[34] This does not, however, prevent them from later staying with the Movement out of conviction.

Nevertheless, Emmaus sought to respond to the problems it perceived. UCC attempted to revive the militant spirit of old and rouse people to action through its internal press, brochures and training days. However, the members of local Committees, who often signed up to work on tangible initiatives at local level, showed little enthusiasm for national meetings. In the 1990s, the Federation's decision to refocus its meetings and training sessions on regional matters appeared to produce more effective results.

More than anything else, UACE lamented the difficulty they experienced in attracting young people to the Federation, and attempts were made to transform the camps, former hotbeds of militancy in the 1960s and 1970s, into a new melting pot of political activists from all walks of life. These attempts were not hugely successful: in the 1980s, at a meeting of Friends and leaders, UACE declared: "the clientele of these camps has gradually changed. It is no longer only students, French people or foreigners who participate, but also young people who live their lives on the road, with no work, no home and no family, who come to the camps in search of a place to live for a while. Some of them were even fresh out of prison. The way these people arrived at the camps was in some ways similar to the way in which Companions arrived in Communities."[35] Furthermore, leaders of the camps and of UACE differed in their relationship to Abbé Pierre and in their positions on mixed Communities and abstinence, to the extent that in 1984–5, the Federation was finally forced to create a rival organisation. On their last legs, the camps were slowly relaunched throughout 1991: they welcomed eighty young people in the summer of that year, 180 in 1992, then 250–300 every year after that – a far cry from the thousands of youngsters who had flocked to the camps in the glory days. From that point on, the southwest, chiefly the area around the Pyrenees (Pau, Toulouse), became the epicentre of this renaissance, with the creation in 1995 of GIVE (the International Association of Emmaus Volunteers) in order to train camp coordinators and capitalise on the experience of each volunteer.

Lastly, as far as the Committees of Fiends were concerned, they tended to remedy the shortage of volunteers by hiring workers on government-subsidised contracts whose aim was to facilitate social reintegration.[36]

## The end of the "coordinators"

In the context of the "Catholic crisis"[37] (the decline of religious observance and Sunday worship, the crisis of vocations, etc.), the gradual disappearance of the "coordinators," – Community priests – was initially a source of both concern and distress: not only were an ever smaller number being recruited, but there were"fewer and fewer priests wishing to act as coordinators",[38] preferring instead to remain simple "Friends".

However, coordinators continued to exist at national level until the 1990s. At UCC, while Jacques Vreck, the Franciscan priest who arrived at Emmaus during the 1958 crisis, left the job in 1973, and while the post officially disappeared, the Federation continued to regard the "key function" of these coordinators as vital,[39] and the arrival at the headquarters of Hervé Le Ru, the Breton priest who had left the priesthood and married, ensured that the Catholic spirit continued to imbue the top of the hierarchy. He would occupy the post of secretary-general from 1976–97. At UACE, the role was passed from Abbé Pierre to Paul, and then to Abbé Jean-Yves Barral. A close friend of Abbé Pierre since September 1953, a former volunteer at Neuilly-Plaisance in the summer of 1954 and coordinator at Pontault-Combault for five years, Abbé Barral then left to teach in Africa. Upon his return, he became a leader of diocesan priests abroad – a post in which he remained for seven years. Made available on a part-time basis in September 1979, Abbé Pierre offered him the job of national UACE coordinator and he received permission to take up the post. However, the job became a source of controversy: the boundary between preserving values and surveillance, even discipline, was continually maintained; the remit of the job was unclear; and the presence of a priest at national level appeared increasingly incompatible with the principle of secularity. When he left UACE in late 1994, Abbé Barral was not replaced. Consequently, in the late 1990s, these coordinators disappeared entirely from both national headquarters and Communities, never to return.

## Solidarity Begins to Change

Lastly, the way both Communities and Committees put the concept of solidarity into practice also began to change, as they turned their attentions once more to *SOS-Familles* and the fight against social exclusion.

### A new cause: *SOS-Familles*, the fight against debt

*SOS-Familles* was an organisation born in the bosom of Emmaus during the previous era of the Movement, but until 1975 had only one branch in Rouen. However, the organisation went on to expand considerably. In 1967, Anne-Marie Poinsignon, wife of the sub-prefect, was looking for something to fill her time and visited the Emmaus Community of Notre-Dame de Bondeville, where she was introduced to the work of the Committee of Friends. In an interview with Régis Thimoreau, Poinsignon recalled, "this Committee had inherited a sum of money from the travelling Community when they first started up. For the time, this sum was relatively large. These Friends did a lot with it; many families asked them for cash to pay their rental deposits, to cover an electricity bill, etc. And yet at the end of the day, it was always the same people who returned to ask for more. I began to think that it was quite an odd solution to their problems, one which was costly and did little to teach them better habits [...] That was when I realised that what we needed to do was not to provide stopgap solutions, far from it, but to try to prevent them from getting into difficulty in the first place."[40]

With Abbé Pierre's support, *SOS-Familles* developed assistance for families in debt, together with social workers, guardianship services, family court judges, social housing offices and the CAF. The money needed for the working-capital fund came from the Elbeuf and Notre-Dame de Bondeville Communities, loans from the CAF and local government funding. The principle which underpinned this assistance was that of breaking the spiral of debt, which led families straight to eviction and children straight to care, by issuing families in debt with an initial payment which was limited but which allowed any legal proceedings against them to be called to a halt. However, only families with an income benefited from such assistance, as *SOS-Familles* later had to get back the money it had paid out (by obtaining control over their family and housing benefit and of the payments issued before or after the birth of a child, by agreeing with them that a certain amount would be deducted from their salary, etc.). The scheme was in everybody's interest. It benefited families as they were able to stay in their homes; their creditors, because generally speaking, money which the families made by selling their possessions did not cover all of the bailiffs' costs; the family court judge as they were able to keep families together; and the CAF, because every case dealt with was one less case for their legal service, which was already at breaking point.

However, the scheme was not about issuing handouts. It aimed to educate and support families in managing their money, and it also aimed to help perpetuate the organisation's business activities, with the money paid back by one family then being used to help others do the same. The scheme's long-term goal was always to make families independent and able to manage their money responsibly, a skill which some had never acquired. It also aimed to make them aware of systems whose cogs they knew nothing about: in a document charting the early development of *SOS-Familles*, it was noted that as far as families in difficulty were concerned, "with no prior awareness of what would happen, if they fell behind with their rent, left a bill unpaid, wrote an uncovered cheque, the machine is set in motion: mysterious, incomprehensible warnings quickly followed by court orders then bailiffs. Furniture is seized, summons arrive in the post, the courts deliver their verdict and the families are served with an eviction order."[41] Efforts to educate families in how to manage their money proved effective – the annual rate of non-repayment nearly always remained below 5%. The gradual growth of both the working-capital fund and the local reputation of the Rouen committee led to an ever-increasing number of families receiving help: two in 1967, 129 in 1971 and 250 in 1975.

However, until 1975, this was the only committee in existence. This was in no way the result of a lack of effort on the part of *SOS-Familles* to convince other Communities of the beneficial effects of this social action at local level. The fact remained that *SOS-Familles* was born in the Emmaus bosom, which did little to attract UCC, and at the time UACE was still too lacking in structure to actively encourage the initiative to spread. In the end it was Abbé Pierre himself who urged the organisation to roll out the model elsewhere. In 1973, he published a long article in *Faim et Soif*[42] which brought in a grand total of... two cheques. In 1975 he tried again and suggested to the state broadcasting company (ORTF) that they interview Anne-Marie Poinsignon on the daytime television show *"Aujourd'hui Madame"*,[43] with the Secretary of State René Lenoir also present. The programme prompted many people to make donations over the telephone and finally aroused the interest of those in UACE's circle of influence (Communities, Committees of Friends). By 1983, fifteen branches of *SOS-Familles* were already up and running.

The crisis then acted as a catalyst, plunging more and more people into difficulty. Debt began to plague young couples, bankrupt craftsmen, the unemployed, and divorced couples. It was also increasingly caused by purchases made on credit: in the 1970s, the meteoric rise of chequebooks and later of credit cards meant that for some, spending was pain-free and difficult to control. The work of *SOS-Familles*, which sought to tackle the problem on the ground and which at the time was something quite out of the ordinary in France, also began to interest the authorities. It first interested those on the Right, when in January 1981 Anne-Marie Poinsignon met with the Secretary of State for Health and when *SOS-Familles* were mentioned in the Oheix report. It then turned the heads of those on the left, when in October 1984 Abbé Pierre spoke of the organisation during his meeting with Laurent Fabius, and when in February 1985 the organisation's leaders were invited to visit the Prime Minister's cabinet. In the spring of 1981, the King Baudouin Foundation (Belgium) also requested a meeting.

These signs of respect that *SOS-Familles* was beginning to earn did not go unnoticed and in the 1980s and 90s the authorities began to take decisive action against the debt scourge. They did so first through their political programmes of January 1983 and autumn 1984. They later sought to combat the problem through the Neiertz Law of December 1989,[44] and then through the creation of services which dealt with unpaid housing-related bills within the framework of the FSL (Housing Solidarity Fund). These services were strengthened by the 1998 law on the fight against social exclusion.[45] Finally in 2003, the Borloo Law established the civil bankruptcy and personal responsibility procedure. However, this increase in the number of initiatives was also a reflection of the fact that the problem refused to go away: with the economic crisis, unemployment, jobs becoming increasingly insecure and the increasing availability of credit, the number of people in debt grew –200,000 households were affected by excessive debt in 1989. In 2003, 500,000 households were victims of the same problem.

At *SOS-Familles*, the number of local Committees, which remained attached to a Community or a Committee of Friends, continued to rise (twenty-seven in 1993, forty-nine in 2008) and government funding became more widely available. At the same time, the number of families who received assistance increased dramatically in the first half of the 1980s (the number of requests for help and the number of local associations both increased but the authorities failed to respond), reaching 1,600 families in 1985. Of course, when considered in relation to the scale of the debt problem in France, this figure makes it seem as if the organisation were merely testing out a pilot scheme on a few guinea-pigs rather than doing anything significant. After a drop in the number of families receiving support between 1985 and 1988 (when the first state solutions were put in place), it has slowly, but almost continually increased until the present day (3,600 families supported in 2007).

By contrast, the most marked trend was the constant decline of the families seen/helped ratio (71% in 1986, 54% in 1988, 34% in 2005), which forced *SOS-Familles* to acknowledge the limitations of its work. First, the committees dealt only with solvent individuals, and yet an increasing number of these individuals subsisted solely on minimum welfare payments, which were non-transferrable.[46]

Secondly, they dealt only with families – a rule that became gradually more flexible from 1996 onwards. Cases later became increasingly burdensome and complex and the various branches of *SOS-Familles* found themselves increasingly crippled by the workload and unable to help all those in need.

The fact was that the various branches of *SOS-Familles* remained small organisations. At national level, a liaison committee, "temporary and purely technical",[47] was put together in 1981 and remained the only coordination organisation until 1990. The secretariat decided upon a place to set up home, which would be anywhere where other Emmaus groups were kind enough to make space: the corner of an office in Charenton in the 1980s, in Paris at the headquarters of Emmaus France between 1990 and 1992, then from the Rue des Bourdonnais to the headquarters of Emmaus HLM and on to the headquarters of the Committees of Friends, home from 1994 to 2008. Finally, the organisation settled at new common Emmaus headquarters, where it has been since 2008... At local level, a survey conducted in 2005 revealed that only 16% of all branches of *SOS-Familles* had an email address, the premises of 33% of them comprised a single room and 26% did not even have a computer. One-fifth had an office which was manned for less than three hours a week and only a fifth had an office which was staffed for more than seven hours a week. The recruitment of new volunteers, or even simply replacing those that left the local committees, has been a constant source of concern since 1991: in 1991, there were on average only seven volunteers at each local branch.

It is clear, then, that *SOS-Familles* was a small but significant operation. Its organisations relied entirely on the support of Communities and Committees of Friends: across the whole of this period, around 90% of its income came from these two groups and on average an *SOS-Familles* committee received 65,000 francs a year from the Emmaus organisation, which acted as its sponsor. As far as the Communities were concerned, the majority of support for *SOS-Familles* came from UACE and Liberty, even if the "old" UCC Communities such as Neuilly-sur-Marne, Nantes or Cernay endorsed their work in principle. Committees made contributions proportionate to their size, some were very modest and others far exceeded previous generosity. Such was the case with the Thonon committee which, in 2000, gave the organisation 400,000 francs. Finally, for some years now the Abbé Pierre Foundation has been providing large sums of money to help them take care of the debts of households in grave financial difficulty.

## Support for victims of acute social exclusion

Another facet of the Movement's work to help those in need was its fight against acute social exclusion. In the winter of 1984, Communities took part in "Abbé Pierre's Christmas", in particular by organising night soup runs in major towns and cities, and reclaimed control of the fight against acute social exclusion. They struck up new partnerships with other associations, calling the public to action, creating joint night shelters and day centres, opening grocery stores, etc. Moreover, in doing so, they adopted an all-inclusive approach: while the majority of the Communities' partnerships were formed with associations that were (originally) Catholic (*Mie de pain*, *Secours catholique*, etc.), this was to a much greater extent the result of their overwhelming dominance of the French solidarity sector of the early 1980s than of any desire to keep things within a Catholic clique; records also reveal many local partnerships with *Secours populaire*, a movement of communist parentage, with the socialist *Ligue des droits de l'homme*, with protestant organisations (CIMADE) or with associations of non-religious or apolitical origin (*Les Restos du cœur*). Many Communities also supported local food banks, another initiative that Abbé Pierre launched and of which Emmaus was co-founder.

The Committees of Friends followed the same sequence over the same period of time. Since the early 1990s, their efforts to support those in need have stood out on account of their enthusiasm which they have displayed in (jointly) creating shelters, accommodation centres, Community grocery stores and solidarity boutiques.

The social and economic crisis had radically redefined the challenges facing the Communities and Committees of Friends. The creation of organisations for social reintegration and their becoming independent was undoubtedly one of the great innovations of the time. Encouraged from the outset in view of the fact they were better adapted to the needs of young people and women (women held 50% of the posts for social integration at Emmaus, despite the fact that they made up only 6% of all Companions) and experiencing exponential growth, in 2008 these organisations accounted for 1,850 jobs (for 3,880 Companions) and €61.6 million in funds (compared to €86.6 million for the Communities). Developing at this pace, these organisations soon outperformed the Communities in terms of their balance sheets, even if these balance sheets from the two organisations cannot be reliably compared, given that Communities were fundamentally built on the principles of extending support to those in need rather than making a profit.

In one generation, the waste-collection and recycling economy has also changed considerably. After the golden age, the raw materials crisis led the Movement to return its attention to bric-à-brac, and flea markets continue to be one of the activities for which Emmaus is most widely known. For all that, behind this changing focus there has, for a number of years now, been the desire to fight for survival in the waste-collection and recycling economy, in the face of increasingly complex regulations and the fierce development of competition. Adapting to this new environment has involved using more technical resources and pooling them with those of other organisations, but it has, in a way, also allowed Emmaus to rediscover its trade of old. As Laurent Desmard has recalled:

> "In the old days, we had two types of cast iron and three or four sorts of scrap metal, so it was up to us to deal with them and it wasn't difficult: we just had to break them up and put them in piles. We collected bed bases and springs, and the fabric inside was taken out and carded, so it was really quite simple. On top of that, there were also four or five blokes who dealt with cardboard. So as you can see, there were a lot of people assigned to very basic collecting and recycling jobs, which didn't require any special skills. Today, things are changing again because, oddly enough, that sort of waste-collection and recycling is starting up again. I was at the waste-collection centre in Angers, you had to put the wood with the wood... And yet that disappeared in 1982–3. Construction must have accounted for 7–8% of what we made at one time, because the raw materials were no

> longer sold. Cardboard didn't sell anymore, so we gave up on cardboard: the same thing happened with rags. And nowadays we're going back to all that because people now sort all those things into piles before they put their waste out; because current recycling policies award funds for the collection and recycling of unwanted items, and ask those who produce waste to pay for it to be recycled from the word go. Today, people are increasingly given to collecting and recycling waste items out of a desire to protect the environment. That provides us with an opportunity, it really does, but one that we need to grab with both hands once more, because there was a time when we turned our backs on that trade and focused to a much greater extent on the warehouses where we sold things, which brought in more money. Today, we're going back to the trades we once knew. We're going back to them in a different way, but we are going back nevertheless."[48]

However, the battle is far from being won. While in a magnificent move, Emmaus got out of the WEEE sector while the going was good, that sector remains a small one in comparison to the size of the textile sector or to the challenge that waste-reception centres and recycling plants today represent.[49] The UCC has described these facilities as "structurally dangerous rivals for Emmaus"[50] in that they take material which can be recycled away from the Movement and look to branch out into waste-collection.[51] The future of the trade at Emmaus will also depend on its ability to find new ways to collect and recycle and new sectors from which it can harvest its goods. In this regard, the dynamism of Emmaus organisations such as the Hedged Farmland Workshops and the initiative which saw them collect and treat ink cartridges (1997), and later mobile phones (2004), have reinstilled a certain sense of optimism within the Movement.

# *Chapter 11* / EMMAUS INTERNATIONAL A NEW POLITICAL DYNAMO

In the previous period, Emmaus International had been built on two separate movements. First, the broad consensus that religion ought to enjoy: a movement propelled by the figure of Abbé Pierre, the presence of a large number of priests within Emmaus and the personal beliefs of the majority of activists. Second and later, the bitter controversies over which political stance, if any, Emmaus International ought to adopt. Tentative consensus was finally achieved around a flagship text entitled "The scope and limitations of social activism in Emmaus", which was a summary of both the Movement's desire to combat the causes of poverty and to remain neutral, rejecting all forms of religious or political affiliation.

This text, with its two distinct facets, established the line that Emmaus International would henceforth make its own. The Movement initially used the text in the first half of the 1980s to justify a stance which was neutral and rejected all forms of affiliation but which was also largely apolitical. It was made increasingly so by the fact that at the time, liberation theology was entering a period of crisis. In contrast, from the mid-1980s onwards, the fight against the causes of poverty staged a spectacular recovery, featuring in every speech. The recovery was the fruit of both the process which saw the complete restructuring of international initiatives and, at Emmaus, the arrival of a new president. Meanwhile, it remained to be seen if, and how, this recovery would manifest itself on the ground.

## The Place of Politics is Officially Recognised

The fight against the causes of poverty dates back to the very inception of Emmaus, and Abbé Pierre was its first herald. However, the early presidencies of Emmaus International, Swiss (1969–79), then Dutch (1979–86), proved themselves to be advocates of a more charity-focused approach to action and, above all, anxious not to open the floodgates to Marxism. In contrast, from the mid-1980s onwards, the context changed dramatically. Marxism was no longer in any way an empirical model – we need look no further than the crushing of the Prague Spring in 1968, Solzhenitsyn's revelations about the Gulag in 1973 or the fall of the Khmer Rouge in 1978–9. Western Christianity, Catholicism in particular, was also in crisis. The wealth and prosperity of the *Trente Glorieuses* became a distant memory which neither Anglo-Saxon neoliberalism nor Mitterrand's Left in France were able to bring back to life. As a result, from that point on, the old major ideologies which had long formed the backbone of society entered an historic phase of "movement".[1] With these foundations in place, a transnational cycle gradually emerged where neoliberal globalisation was continually called into question. So far as France was concerned, the cornerstone of this cycle was the coming together of a diverse range of militant traditions – the post-'68 Left, Christian movements expounding international solidarity, farmers' protests and working-class trade unionism.[2]

Another change took place which concerned Emmaus more specifically. In 1986, the Movement's presidency passed to the Italian Franco Bettoli. Inspired by his participation in the first French youth camps held in the mid-1960s, he abandoned accountancy, the career he had agreed to pursue, and devoted himself fully to Emmaus, both founding and leading the Italian branch of the Movement. Having followed the development of Emmaus in Burkina Faso with particular attention, Bettoli was convinced of the need to go beyond the charitable approach that had largely guided the work of the Movement up until that point. Consequently, he devoted his first executive committee to "the fight against the causes of poverty", and called for efforts at all levels to "raise awareness of these causes". In October 1987, the Third World debt (a cause championed by both the new anti-globalisation movement and by the papacy since the Pontifical Commission on Justice and Peace in January 1987), fair trade and the sale of arms, "which fuel[led] wars and allow[ed] anti-democratic governments to thrive", emerged for the first time as issues.[3] In September 1988, the general assembly in Verona officially sanctioned this new line of action.

## From religion to politics: liberation theology comes up for debate (1988)

Where this assembly displayed ingenuity, if indeed it did so consciously, was in the way it brought politics back on to the agenda through the sphere in which there had traditionally been the broadest consensus at Emmaus International: that of religion. Until then, debates within the organisation had almost completely sidestepped liberation theology. In fact, it was a school of thought which appeared connected to a very specific geographical area: designed to meet the specific needs of Latin America, it could not easily be exported to other southern areas in which Emmaus worked, where the context was markedly different. Furthermore, it was deeply evocative of Marxist philosophy. This made the majority of activists in northern groups, charitable or otherwise, uneasy.

And yet, in the 1980s, liberation theology began its decline, the victim of repeated attacks by the new Pope John Paul II and Cardinal Ratzinger; and paradoxically it was when the philosophy began to breathe its last, that Emmaus brought it back to life. The Movement's decision to place liberation theology on the agenda of a world assembly appeared to respond to four concerns. First, the wish to discuss once again the religious dimension of Emmaus, following the "observation that the majority of Emmaus groups in Europe have not, generally speaking, attached a great deal of importance to the spiritual facet of their work, and have even suppressed it, because the Movement is officially non-sectarian, despite the fact that many of those who signed up did so in the name of their faith."[4] Secondly, it responded to the desire to institute a debate on the place of politics within the Movement. Thirdly, it compelled members to reflect on "a school of thought which [was] so crucial to an understanding of the courageous initiatives and work undertaken on a daily basis by so many of [their] groups, particularly in Latin America."[5] Finally, and most importantly, it allowed Emmaus to rethink its relationship with the poor.

The vicious attacks endured by liberation theology, from the papacy in particular, were never mentioned. On the contrary, this school of thought was presented as being fully in line with the social doctrine of the Church: with the post-conciliar situation, with the major encyclicals of Paul VI and with the recently published encyclical from John Paul II, *Sollicitudorei Socialis* (30 December 1987). This text defined the unacceptable laws of international liberalism[6] as "structures of sin". The only misgiving which Emmaus expressed about liberation theology was that "it often reproduced a Marxist vision of things in the most simplistic way possible".[7] It was the chains of this Marxist vision which the assembly intended to cast off, by retaining only its original approach to the poor.

Indeed, Emmaus retained several aspects of liberation theology that were discussed at the meeting. First, the philosophy's relevance to its own work: As Roubaix declared at a meeting of the CAMT executive committee in January 1988, "what is new about liberation theology as a philosophy is that it originated as a *praxis* amongst the poorest members of society. Emmaus also developed from its *praxis* towards the oppressed."[8] Emmaus then took note of the fact that grass-roots ecclesiastical Communities could serve as useful organisational models and as models of how "change could occur slowly, its seeds planted in smaller groups".[9] Furthermore, the Movement also took on board the importance which liberation theology attached to not making decisions for somebody else. In the words of Roubaix, "the problem which we experience in our relationship with European groups is not so much one of money as of ideology. The European groups have their ideology and send their money to places according to their own views and desires."[10] Finally, Emmaus retained the idea that political action was ultimately necessary. Because if it was necessary, as proposed by Leonardo Boff, a Brazilian Franciscan and a disciple of this form of theology, "to look at the reality of the poor with the eyes of the poor", "to take on the life of the poor" and "to champion the cause of the poor", it was also necessary "to identify the mechanisms which cause poverty", namely "the international system of capital and the relationships of dependency and oppression which it institutes between nations at the heart of the system and those on the outskirts."[11]

Liberation theology also included the religious viewpoint, influential within Emmaus, which encouraged people to see the poor as sacred beings. As Boff and Elzondo wrote, "We must never forget that, ultimately, the poor are our eschatological judges. Without the poor, the Church loses its Lord and its theology loses its evangelical content."[12] He went on to declare that "the poor are a theological territory, a place in which we discover the presence of God [...] The poor are a prophetic sign for the world [...] The poor are the eschatological sign of the kingdom."[13]

Encouraged and supported by the Movement's new leaders, this assembly sparked controversy. Certain activists like Robert Vallade, priest of the Foreign Missions and president of Emmaus Asia, believed that discussing liberation theology made Emmaus excessively political and brought it too close to the clergy. Others, however, such as Grégoire Haddad, Archbishop of Lebanon and the leader of Emmaus in this region, were delighted that the topic was on the agenda. For them, "everything [was] political" and Emmaus had for too long lacked strong, political discourse.

## The place of politics is officially recognised and Emmaus becomes an anti-globalisation movement

In reality, liberation theology was, more than anything else, a pretext for discussion and the assembly focused chiefly on political issues. Drawing on a battery of figures to support the idea that the various forms of inequality were both widespread and becoming ever more deeply entrenched in society, the assembly called into question the role played by NGOs who "have developed and develop forms of solidarity and service which benefit poor countries, but which often work against each other. Indeed, many of these NGOs adopt a paternalistic approach to helping the poor and one which is based on issuing handouts. Such an approach perpetuates poverty and exploitation."[14] Jean Ziegler, sociologist, economist and close friend of Abbé Pierre, spoke at the assembly. He presented the debt of poor countries as a "deadly scourge" and concluded with a series of proposals. He argued that Emmaus ought to "become acquainted with and support projects worldwide aiming to provide an alternative to liberal or totalitarian capitalism, to help the poor reclaim the sense that they can actively shape the history of their country." He also believed it should "prioritise practical initiatives which seek to target the structural causes of poverty at a social, political and economic level," that it should look to make those within the Movement aware of "exploitative trade practices and of the deliberate destruction of the environment, in particular by multinational companies", and that when making day-to-day purchases, it should support Third World producers and avoid multinationals, whose aims ran counter to those of Emmaus. Following the assembly, a letter was sent to the IMF and research initiated into "solidarity saving".[15]

For the first time, the assembly adopted a nonpartisan but heavily political discourse as its line of action. It was a discourse which clearly expressed its desire to tackle global organisations and challenge the established order, but to do so with a view to achieving social justice rather than the birth of a Marxist society. Abbé Pierre's outraged conscience was transposed on to an international level. This new approach was in no way unusual but was instead part of the international movement that at the time was in the embryonic stages of development. Indeed, alongside the religious roots of liberation Christianity,[16] the issues of debt and globalisation also returned to the spotlight. Debt was first: faced with the explosion of humanitarian aid, from the 1970s onwards, a field of experts in development began to emerge along with "a discourse which instead of justifying initiatives that simply involved giving handouts to the poor began to challenge the causes of poverty. The discourse of pity became one which condemned the causes of prevailing injustice."[17] Globalisation also began to arouse new interest: in 1984, a network of alternative associations born in Anglo-Saxon countries decided to send delegations representing civil society to each G7 summit, "in order to counterbalance dominant economic thinking".[18]

It was then, against the backdrop of radical changes taking place both internally and internationally, that Emmaus participated both in the development of the anti-globalisation movement and in the founding protest which took place in Paris in July 1989, against the G7 summit, against neo-liberal globalisation and in favour of the cancellation of Third World debt.[19] Launched following an appeal made by the unions (CGT, CFDT, SNSE, SNE-Sup, UNEF, SUD-PTT, etc.), associations (CIMADE, MRAP, *SOS-Racisme*, LDH, the confederation for secular, state education *Ligue de l'enseignement*, the Association for the Unemployed and those with Insecure Employment, the Committee for the Inadequately Housed, etc.) and political parties (LCR, PCF, PSU, etc.), Emmaus International attended the protest with Abbé Pierre, who was a signatory of the open letter to the G7 heads of state and who had been asked to attend the TOES (a counter-summit bringing together the world's seven poorest countries) as an international expert.[20] The summit's final statement echoed the new concerns. Participants committed to postponing debt repayments for Third World countries, banning international loans for arms sales, conducting a wholesale review of the development model which the North foisted upon the South, etc.

The following assembly in Cologne in 1992 saw the Movement consolidate this new line of action, working under the slogan, "Building a united global society, hand in hand with the poor". In the period between the two assemblies, the fall of the Berlin Wall and the collapse of the Soviet empire sealed the victory of capitalism, which was now the only economic model left on the table. However, these two events also saw analysis of the world which had previously pitted East against West now set North against South. In his speech, Pepe Aravena of Chile declared: "It is becoming increasingly clear that the division of the world, which was said to be ideological, is in fact economic." The assembly focused on fair trade, debt, the protection of the environment and the fight for human rights. Latin America continued to be the part of the world which displayed the most combative approach, condemning "the capitalist system as the greatest enemy of humankind" and "the major force responsible for the destruction of the environment". Aravena went on to state, "We continue to be concerned by the fact that there are still people within Emmaus who continue to hope that a solution to the problems of the poor and the oppressed will be found within the capitalist system, and that their attitudes and initiatives are paternalistic in nature."[21] The charitable approach to helping these people appeared to have been well and truly dismissed in favour of a combative and critical discourse which in some groups was close to the Marxist discourse of the 1970s.

But beyond the words, tangible solutions were also put forward: making the groups in the South more self-sufficient, increasing the number of partnerships and twinning initiatives, developing education and (very recently) access to water; taking action to ensure associations acquired greater weight as "a global moral conscience", putting pressure on the GATT, the World Bank and the IMF; developing fair trade – Emmaus had already opened alternative trade shops in Denmark, Finland, Sweden, the Netherlands, Spain and Italy – and forming closer relationships with international bodies already in operation.[22] As far as environmental protection was concerned, in 1992 Emmaus International took part in the preparations for the Earth Summit, at the International Forum of NGOs in Rio and UNCTAD. In the international arena, the Movement wished to act as an "agitator; a force which spoke out against certain models of development and proposed a type of society where the division both of labour and of the income which this labour produced were looked at in a new way."[23]

In 1994, Abbé Pierre, whose political discourse within France was becoming increasingly inflammatory in tone,[24] was once again summoned to the anti-globalisation stage. He was called by the CRID[25] to speak on the fiftieth anniversary of the Bretton Woods agreements;[26] Ricardo Petrella[27] asked him to make a statement at the meeting of "Les Petits de la Terre", which was held in parallel to the G7 summit in Naples. Officially recognised in 1993 as an organisation with advisory status to the United Nations' Economic and Social Council (ECOSOC), Emmaus International also supported the campaign against sexual tourism and child prostitution (1994) in its own right, took part in both the World Summit for Social Development held in Copenhagen (1995) and its preparatory meetings, participated in the G7 counter-meeting in Lyon (1996), in the campaign against the Multilateral Agreement on Investments, and in the *Jubilé* 2000 Appeal for the Cancellation of Third World Debt (1997). The Movement threw its weight behind such initiatives as they were convinced that "work on the ground and lobbying [were] not activities which [could] exist in isolation. Each gave the other greater credibility and coherence."[28]

It is clear, then, that Emmaus International was a fine example of the progression of anti-globalisation principles before they were catapulted into the media arena in 1998 (the creation of ATTAC) and 1999 (the protest in Seattle against the WTO); of how these ideas slowly developed as networks of both political and humanitarian organisations began to work together; but also of the role religion played in redirecting attention towards the political sphere. Furthermore, this approach from a campaign which was not national (the French group played only a very small part in the development of the anti-globalisation movement), but well and truly international, served to temper the notion that "it is in the inner workings of the national political sphere that we must seek to find the dynamism and motivation for campaigns on international issues",[29] along with the idea that "this new cycle of protest [appears to be] less the fruit of economic, political or cultural globalisation than the fruit of changes and restructuring processes which have taken place within the French political arena."[30] Indeed, it was under the combined pressure applied by the Latin American groups, the Movement's Italian president and Abbé Pierre, in an international context experiencing radical change, that a common thread began to bind the groups of Emmaus together, and that ultimately, anti-globalisation initiatives and thought began to emerge. In this campaign, work at an international level was predominant, and demonstrates how Emmaus contributed, along with many others, to the creation of a "global civil society". There is no doubt that this new society was in the embryonic stages of development but was alive, kicking and highly reticular.

In the years since 1998, after a decade of growth and consolidation, anti-globalisation has gained acceptance within the media as a legitimate school of thought, but has also revealed its weaknesses. The discourse it produced and the types of initiative it organised became routine, partly as they had done at Emmaus International: after the major assemblies in Verona and Cologne, the following assemblies appeared less hard-hitting as they were not as innovative in their work. Admittedly, the 1996 assembly did adopt a new text, the charter of "commitments for a united world", in order to "support the tangible steps taken by the poor and the socially excluded to move towards a society built on solidarity and justice [...] [to speak out against] the forms of social injustice and the systems which produce poverty and exclusion both when others are doing so and when we speak as a lone voice and [propose] an alternative social model." Several local groups also joined ATTAC, either providing it with extensive support (*Björkå* in Sweden) or accommodation (*Montevideo* in Uruguay); and Emmaus International continued to participate in meetings of the World Social Forum – Mumbai (2004), Porto Alegre (2005) and Bamako (2006).

However, from that point on more significant progress was made with tackling new issues and, above all, with putting theory into practice on the ground:[31] there were ethical investment schemes (the creation in 2005 of an ethical Emmaus Global Fund which was deposited in La Banca Etica in Padua), the social economy, the solidarity-based economy, the savings and credit experiments conducted at a local level, access to water programmes (with a flagship project at lake Nokoué in Benin) or the fight against human trafficking.

## A new level of political action: Europe

Since the 1980s, the Emmaus message has also taken root at European level. The first networks of associations fighting against poverty began to form in the mid-1980s, a process which in 1989, culminated in the creation of a federation of European associations and networks working against poverty and exclusion. This federation was created in partnership with DG5 to be the body which would represent NGOs.[32] Emmaus International participated in the work of the federation from its very inception and became an official member in 1991. Emmaus also joined several other organisations: in 1992 it became a member of the European Citizen Action Service, an organisation created in 1990 to provide legal and tax aid; in 1991 it joined the Centre of Research and Information for Development (CRID) as an associate; and it joined the French platform for development NGOs, as part of a European co-funding initiative. In addition to organising a whole host of campaigns on the right to asylum or the fight against poverty, these organisations were invaluable sources of information and support on matters regarding EU legislation.

## Emmaus Organisations Change Shape

### Founding members desert the Movement on ideological grounds

In sanctioning Emmaus' movement into the political arena, the 1988 assembly sparked a wave of protest. On 19 June 1990, the executive committee of Emmaus International declared: "It is clear that the new avenues which the Verona assembly adopted are likely to deeply unsettle a significant number of Friends who originally came to the Movement to help the poor, and that there is a considerable distance between this concept and the new initiatives aiming to make people independent and responsible for their own destiny."[33] Four countries were particularly affected by these changes: Japan, South Korea, Canada and Switzerland. All were founding members of Emmaus, all were advocates of a more charity-based approach to the poor and two had a priest as their leader. However, the ideological attacks which they were forced to endure were not the only cause of their desertion: these organisations appeared to have already been weakened by the global economic crisis (sometimes witnessing the drastic reduction in size of their waste-collection and recycling operations), but also by the ageing of their leaders and either their inability to make way for new blood or, on the contrary, by the fact that they left the Movement in order to support other Catholic initiatives. Such was the case of Minoru Murata, who was appointed vicar-general of Kobe in 1995. After latent confrontations and more or less formal boycotts in the 1990s, these groups were ultimately expelled from Emmaus on account of having ceased their activities or refused to participate in the life of the Movement. As a result of these expulsions, since 2007, Emmaus no longer has a single branch in Japan, Korea or Canada. In contrast, several groups in Switzerland have remained members.

The case of Harlem is different in that the Harlem group left the Movement at a later stage. Furthermore, the reasons for its desertion were not connected to its relationship with politics, but with religion. The group, led by Father David Kirk, a former friend of Martin Luther King, spearheaded a huge initiative in aid of the homeless, in particular those living with AIDS (providing meals, accommodation, support facilities for alcohol and drug addiction, vocational training, and literacy courses). This work meant that throughout the 1980s and 90s, Emmaus Harlem was "the largest organisation for the homeless in the USA after Covenant House",[34] with forty apartments for those living with AIDS and its sixty-three members of staff. The Community also worked to raise awareness within the political sphere of the problems at hand: in 1994–5, a widespread campaign against the re-election of a Mafia family saw it ousted from power and replaced by a defender of the poor. However, problems of financial management led both Emmaus and the city council to call for the departure of Father Kirk. This followed Emmaus' realisation that "the case of Harlem should serve as an example to our Movement: if we continue to function on charisma and generosity alone, with brilliant people at our helm, we will always end up in a state of gridlock. We must ensure that within each of our groups, there are checks and balances and people who maintain stability."[35] The Community opted to abandon the Movement and refocus its attentions on the religious aspect of its work. In 2005, it officially left Emmaus.

## Defending human rights: Africa and Eastern Europe

While Emmaus disappeared from Japan, Korea and Canada, it began to grow in Africa and eastern Europe. In addition to its Rwandan branch, the organisation gradually began to take root in Africa throughout the 1980s by providing support to existing groups, chiefly through networks of missionaries. It helped a diocese in Burkina to build primary schools, a monk in Senegal to dig wells and build market gardens, assisted the organisation *Amis de Sœur Emmanuelle* in Sudan, and so forth. Following the Verona assembly, new importance was attached to the criteria relating to fostering democracy and the defence of human rights when the locations of new Emmaus branches were chosen; consequently, Benin, Rwanda and Zaire were the new sites of choice along with eastern Europe, with the Balkans chosen to play host to Emmaus.

## Benin, economic innovation and the defence of democracy

In Benin, the turning point came in 1988 when Albert Tévoédjre discovered Emmaus. Born to a modest family from Dahomey (now Benin), Tévoédjre completed his university studies in Toulouse, became leader of the Federation of Students from Black Africa in France and joined the anti-colonialist struggle. In 1957 he published *Africa in Revolt*. Following the book's publication, he became Minister for Information before being appointed secretary-general of the African and Malagasy Union. In protest against the government's neo-colonialist policy, he chose to leave Africa and went into exile in Geneva, became the deputy director of the International Labour Organisation (ILO) and was later appointed the director of the International Labour Bureau (ILB). He first came into contact with Abbé Pierre in 1978, when the founder of Emmaus asked him for permission to reprint an extract of his work, *Poverty, the Wealth of the People*, the preface of which had been written by Dom Helder Camara, in *Faim et Soif*. He was later asked to speak at Emmaus' world general assembly in 1984.

In 1988, Tévoédjre founded the Pan-African Centre for Social Prospects (CPPS), whose work involved collecting and sorting the waste which cluttered the streets (an initiative for the improvement of public health) and the production of compost by young people who were out of work and in danger of falling into a life of crime (this was an economic initiative in that it created jobs and fertilised poor-quality land). He requested that his association be allowed to join Emmaus. At the same time, the Archbishop of Cotonou, Monseigneurde Souza, who was also the director of the diocesan service for development and charity, a close friend of Tévoédjre and a man who to become more familiar with Emmaus by undertaking a work-experience placement in a Community, called upon Emmaus International to help him launch a Community farm. The Movement responded to the call and the Association for the Development of Village Initiatives (ASSODIV) became a place where fruit and vegetables were produced and livestock reared, as well as a place providing practical training to villagers and legal advice to landless farmers.

These initiatives were instigated against the backdrop of a catastrophic economic and political situation. Independent since 1960, the country experienced major political instability and then, in 1972, was the victim of a coup d'état which saw a Marxist-Leninist dictatorship come to power. As a result, the 1970s and 80s saw years of food shortages and the frequent non-payment of wages, a single political party, a single school of thought, arbitrary arrests, cases of torture and political assassinations. And yet, in the summer of 1989, Tévoédjre was also the driving force behind the revival of democracy in Benin, together with the Council of Europe and the Organisation of African Unity. In late 1989, the single-party state renounced the values and institutions of Marxism, then in early 1990, a High Council of the Republic was created and its presidency placed in the hands of Monseigneur de Souza: a multi-party system was adopted, prisoners of conscience were rehabilitated and a time-frame for new elections was established. Tévoédjre and de Souza called upon their European partners to organise a lobbying campaign in order to raise awareness of and bolster this revival of democracy.

Initially, Emmaus International and the CCFD supported the initiative, providing both funding and assistance with communication: the democratic transition in Benin was viewed as an example of non-violent revolution which the whole of the African continent could follow. Things became complicated when Tévoédjre decided to stand for president: while it appeared impossible for Emmaus, as an apolitical organisation, to support the campaign, it was nevertheless clear that only with financial support from European organisations would it be possible to stage the campaign at all. Emmaus consequently elected to support the campaign indirectly, by asking other organisations to get involved.

This episode was an important one: the two key figures of Emmaus in Benin were also those of democracy and non-violent revolution, and the country became a model for Africa. After the Verona assembly, at which the Movement undertook to become politically involved, it allowed Emmaus to move from theory to practice. However, in the 1990s, the groups in Benin also posed the problem of tutelary relations with political and religious bodies: from the mid-1990s onwards, the fact that Emmaus and Tévoédjre were hand in glove prompted the Movement to also extend its support to other initiatives, "in order to demonstrate that Emmaus [was] independent of any political initiatives".[36] At the same time, ASSODIV's dependence on the diocesan service of Monseigneur de Souza was also heavily criticised.

Since the 1990s, Emmaus has continued to grow in Benin. While the Cotonou project does not appear to have undergone significant development, the project which focuses on integrated organic farming and the training of young people has experienced a certain degree of success, with access to European co-funding, interest from ADEME, the World Bank and the UNDP, and plans to expand. New groups came into being: Emmaus-Solidarity Benin was created thanks to programmes whereby containers were sent from Europe filled with goods which were then resold when they reached the country (clothes, bric-à-brac); *Envie* was founded in 1997 (repairing domestic appliances and selling on second-hand goods, and offering paid vocational training); initiatives in favour of women and against child trafficking.

## Zaire, Rwanda and Burundi

Emmaus' involvement in the African Great Lake region followed a broadly similar process, with the Movement working closely with existing organisations and piquing the conscience of those in the political sphere. In 1992, a Community group, Avoben, was born in Kinshasa following the return of a young man from Zaire to his homeland, after having completed a work-experience placement with the Belgian branch of Emmaus. In 1993, at the invitation of a priest from Zaire who wished to break the wall of silence and misinformation surrounding ethnic violence, an Emmaus mission was sent to draw up a report on the political situation in Zaire and the massacres in Kivu. This report highlighted the role that Mobutu had played in bringing the democratic process to a standstill, in plunging the country into its catastrophic state (organised famines, looting, ethnic divisions) and, in collusion with France, which wished to hold on to its positions in the region, in the assassination of the ambassador Philippe Bernard. Following the interviews Abbé Pierre conducted with the French authorities, the report was sent to the

President of the Republic, the Prime Minister, MPs and French-speaking members of the European Parliament.

However, the report was submitted only a short while before the Rwandan genocide. As the executive committee of Emmaus International noted in May 1994, "In order to raise awareness in both the public and the press, who were focusing their attentions on Rwanda, we need to find a link between the two."[37] The Movement quickly learned that all the members of the Rwandan group who, since the death of the founder in 1982 had been looked after by *Les Frères de la Charité*, and thus made more distant from Emmaus, had been victims of the genocide. The news prompted Emmaus International and Abbé Pierre to take action in favour of a united Rwanda through a collective including the CCFD, CIMADE and *Médecins du monde*. Their work also involved supporting local groups in their efforts to rebuild the country and foster national reconciliation: CAJED in Goma, which took care of street children; Avoben, which attempted to reform; ADLP in Bujumbura (Burundi), which fought against crime and poverty by taking in children who were victims of war, and offering them literacy courses and vocational training.

The crisis in the Great Lakes region once again forced Emmaus to reconsider its role: though it was not an emergency aid association, it did not wish to sit back and do nothing in the face of such urgent cries for help. This desire to take action saw food parcels sent to the area on several occasions, up until the early 2000s. The Movement wasn't a political or human rights association, such as the Human Rights League of Amnesty International. That said, as the general assembly of 1996 observed, "the drama which is unfolding across the region in its entirety calls for action which is primarily of a political nature".[38] It was also agreed that the drama called for efforts to make public opinion aware of events, along with and initiatives that targeted decision makers. Such a response was made even more necessary by the fact that Emmaus, as a result of both its own fame and that of Abbé Pierre, could have a real impact. In spring 1996, a new letter sent to President Chirac and the Prime Minister made clear the importance Emmaus had placed upon this role, which was based on supporting the reconstruction process at local level.

### The Balkans

The other major humanitarian crisis of the decade was that of the Balkans. During the Croatian War (1991), Emmaus did not appear to take any specific steps to support the country apart from sending a delegate to the scene of the fighting. However, from October 1992 onwards (during the Bosnian War), Emmaus dispatched a constant stream of military convoys carrying food, medicines and equipment to the country. These convoys came from France and Italy in turn. Given that Emmaus initially had no base in the region, goods were mostly sent to the Red Cross and *Médecins du monde*. The branches which were subsequently opened in 1993 in Split (the Emmaus delivery and storage point on Croatian territory) and Gradačac (a distribution point set up in the war zone on Muslim territory) became the destinations to which the majority of the goods were dispatched. Following the signing of the Dayton Agreements, efforts to rebuild the region got under way: Emmaus supported hospitals, worked with Handicap International to support the production of prosthetic limbs and wheelchairs, and restored and furnished the homes of refugees. Initiatives also spread to northern Bosnia, and the town of Tuzla was notably given a twin. Between 1992 and 1996, around thirty convoys were dispatched to Bosnia; in 1997 alone, thirty-eight lorries and 2 million francs' worth of goods were sent to the country. During the Kosovo War (1998–9), Emmaus focused its attentions on creating refugee camps in Bosnia.

The campaign waged by Emmaus International was supplemented – or rather contradicted – by the efforts of Abbé Pierre himself. The first of Abbé Pierre's initiatives was an appeal launched on the current affairs programme "7 sur 7" in early 1994, which brought in 500,000 francs. In the summer of 1995, he then left to travel alongside Bernard Kouchner as a "human shield". Emmaus International supported his endeavours, even if they were often forced to jump on the bandwagon and even if the lack of cooperation between the Movement and the man was often a source of tension. Such was the case with the July 1995 appeal, when Abbé Pierre called for western states to stage a military intervention in order to defend the people of Bosnia-Herzegovina. Despite the fact that Emmaus International was quick to back the appeal, it was nevertheless fiercely criticised by the non-violent activists within the Movement.

Another problem produced by this conflict was paradoxically the size of the campaign launched, both in terms of the funds it swallowed and the number of Companions required: despite the fact that Emmaus International was not an emergency aid organisation, for several years, the donations sent to Bosnia represented two-thirds of the money spent on all international solidarity campaigns combined...

Alongside these organisations working to defend human rights, whether during a humanitarian crisis or a period of democratic transition, new and more traditional branches flying the Emmaus International flag opened in eastern Europe and Africa. Africa was the first of the two regions to see these new branches appear. The first opened its doors in 1984 in Burkina Faso, the age-old stamping ground of those working in the development sector, and today four Emmaus groups now running within the country (a training centre for young people in difficulty, an association for the reintegration of the handicapped, a group training farmers and one supporting women). Emmaus has also worked in Cameroon since the late 1980s (opening a centre for the promotion of physical and social well-being and a Community which survives by farming and rearing livestock) and, since the 2000s, the Ivory Coast, Madagascar and South Africa. However, outside Benin and Burkina Faso, these branches of the organisation have never moved far beyond the embryonic stages of development.

Following the collapse of the Soviet empire, Emmaus also sought a presence in eastern Europe. Several attempts were made to create independent and viable groups, but these often failed to bear fruit (the groups' activities focused too heavily on issuing handouts to those in need, they lacked financial independence or their members were too closely linked to the Catholic Church). Only three groups were admitted as members of Emmaus, two in Poland and one in Romania. These organisations, which were the result of either chance meetings between individuals or personal connections, also came up against linguistic and cultural barriers. As Emmaus International noted at its general assembly in 1999, "It is sometimes difficult to explain to eastern Europeans what the Emmaus Movement is about because

Community living and working as a cooperative are concepts which remind them too much of a communist kolkhoz."[39]

Finally, apart from the Balkans and the Great Lakes, the majority of the humanitarian crises which unfolded at the time gave rise to only moderate, somewhat lacklustre campaigns. The campaign in support of South Asian refugees fleeing Cambodia in 1979 was the last international campaign spearheaded by Abbé Pierre alone, who approached the President of the Republic in person, taking steps to see the launch of an "immediate, widespread campaign". The funds collected were chiefly earmarked for the initiative of Bernard Kouchner and *Médecins sans frontières* (the ship *Ile de lumière*, which trawled the coasts to save refugees) and to the French Red Cross (for the purchase of medicines). In aid of Ethiopia in 1986, at the invitation of the CCFD, Emmaus joined the collective *Espoir Ethiopie*. Palestine was also a source of concern for Emmaus and the subject of statements of principle (for peace, the recognition of the Palestine Liberation Organisation, etc.), but was dealt with more through Lebanon, where Emmaus had presence. Apart from issuing statements which condemned the two Gulf wars on principle, Emmaus did nothing specific to support those affected. In the case of natural disasters, funds were sometimes raised to help victims (€605,000 were collected following the tsunami in South Asia) and Emmaus mainly provided support during the rebuilding phase.

## The survival and renewal of old groups

While some of Emmaus' main founding members deserted the Movement, and while conversely it began to take root in new parts of the world, in other areas existing branches of Emmaus were enjoying a certain degree of longevity and standing the test of time. Activities in the Lebanon, a country which since the 1970s had been brought to its knees by the Israeli–Arab conflicts and the civil war, carried on through thick and thin. Though *l'Oasis de l'espérance*, a Community created in Beirut in 1959, was ultimately forced to close its doors in 1988, a Professional Welfare Association was launched in 1984, offering low-interest loans to poor families to help them go into business as farmers or craftsmen. In 1999, 300 loans, or $1.2 million, were being paid back and the recovery rate stood at 73%. Between 1986 and the early 1990s, Emmaus also lent its support to the Lebanese Social Movement, created by Archbishop Grégoire Haddad and which worked to build centres providing medical and social care.

In the USA, the organisation set up in Maine in 1970 by a Carmelite nun, sister Lucy Poulin, continued to grow. It comprised both a Community for battered women and children, homeless families and the elderly, and later a home to widows, orphans and Native Americans. It became a large complex which gradually came to serve a whole variety of purposes (it was first a centre where handcrafted goods were manufactured and sold. In the 1980s it housed a series of homeless shelters, a centre building small rooms for poor families, a teaching centre and a crèche; and from the 1990s onwards it acted as a soup kitchen and a food bank, two free clinics, a car-repair firm, workshops for "personal development" and debate, etc.)

As far as Asia was concerned, it was in India where Emmaus remained most heavily present. The Movement worked mostly with the Untouchables, making them aware of their rights and providing them with training, and with lepers, women and children at work. It also focused on access to drinking water, living and working conditions, housing, gender equality, organic farming, microcredit and fair trade. Emmaus took root in Bangladesh too, with a health centre for the working classes opening its doors in Savar in 1972. The centre comprised a hospital, a laboratory for the production of antibiotics, and facilities to train paramedics. Other activities subsequently began to take shape, including family planning, fish farms, the production and sale of handcrafted goods, fair trade, organic farming, the promotion of women's rights, the defence of the landless, and activities which sought to increase access to drinking water. In addition, a new group opened its doors in Indonesia in 1980, specialising in the production of teak furniture and the provision of vocational training.

Latin America remained the key Emmaus stronghold outside Europe: Emmaus was present in almost all the countries on the continent. The Community of Companions collecting and recycling waste, known locally as a *trapería*, was a concept that spread considerably following the Verona assembly which, in addition to political action, advocated independence through work. Some groups focused more on making a living from the land (cattle farms and greenhouses of vegetables in Bolivia), while others preferred to survive by selling handcrafted goods (woollen clothing was made and sold, also in Bolivia), by fishing (with the help of co-funding from Europe in Colombia) or by providing services (Community bakeries). In addition to the initiatives designed to meet urgent needs, or provide education or healthcare, in the early 1990s centres offering vocational training were set up and activities initiated that aimed to support women. Furthermore, other groups organised political action: in Chile, Emmaus supported farmers' unions and the Mapuche Indians; and in Uruguay the Movement supported the people as they fought for their rights. Relations with the groups in the Northern hemisphere were transformed, with new importance attached to the operations sending containers southwards from Europe from 1987 onwards (clothes, small pieces of equipment, etc.) and the development of twinning schemes, particularly with UCC Communities. Religion continued to heavily influence the Movement in Latin America, both in terms of where groups were set up and the people chosen to lead them (in Argentina, Father José María Llorens was appointed leader, followed by Father Rogelio Urquiza, an Argentinian Jesuit and former university professor; in Bolivia, Father Daniel Stretch was at the helm; in Brazil, Father João Benevides managed the group, and so on) and sometimes in terms of the partners which these groups chose (the archdiocese in Santa Fe; the Catholic "New Evangelisation" movement in Rosario). Finally, the period was marked by the economic and political crises which rocked the majority of Latin American countries, with Colombia the most seriously affected. From the 1990s onwards, the country walked a tightrope between life and death, with drug dealing, death squads and kidnappings all commonplace).

However, it was Europe which remained, by far, the main bastion of Emmaus' activities: in 2007, of the 310 groups within the Movement, 253 were European and 171 of these were French. In northern Europe, the organisation had a strong foothold and was marked by the presence of the group *Les Hirondelles*: Norway was paired with Peru, Denmark with India and Bangladesh, and Finland with

Bangladesh and Latin America. Another feature which remained present within the Movement in this region, and which even became more marked, was the importance accorded to politics: from the 1970s onwards, and even more so following the Verona assembly, fair trade and awareness-raising initiatives became two lynchpins of the Movement's work. In the early 1980s, the Finnish branch of *Les Hirondelles* was heavily involved in the Percentage movement (a movement which encouraged people to donate 1% of their salary to help the Third World). Meanwhile, Sweden stood out on account of the fact it supported the Polisario Front (the movement for the liberation of the Sahraoui people) from very early on, joining the cause in 1978. Its support of this movement was such that by the late 1990s, it had managed to get the whole of Emmaus on board. Traditionally, other countries continued to adopt a more charity-based approach to helping those in need (Switzerland, Holland). In Italy, Emmaus experienced rapid growth from the 1990s onwards. However, it was in the UK that the expansion of Emmaus was most dramatic: built entirely from scratch in 1990, the UK branch of the Movement in 2008 comprised twenty-five groups, focused on helping young people, while others supported women or the homeless.

In conclusion, the fate of the organisation SOS-Milk Cartons will be briefly reviewed. Despite the fact that up until the 1970s, Emmaus had been the impressively fertile womb from which many new groups had emerged, both in Metropolitan France (CGL, ATD Fourth-World) and internationally (IRAMM, *Artisans du monde*, UCOJUCO), this period conversely hailed the end of expansion and the shrinking of the Movement. Only the small organisation SOS-Milk Cartons remained in the Emmaus bosom, relying on donations from Emmaus groups to cover 90% of its running costs. By 2005, the association supported twenty-three clinics, all located in Africa with the exception of two in India, and a third of which were Catholic mission centres. Its work, which was decidedly charitable in nature, appeared increasingly out of step with the rest of the Movement, given that it involved sending cartons of milk (concentrated, powdered or that which acted as a food supplement) to clinics in developing countries in order to help under- or malnourished children. Additionally, more than a third of its budget, which stood at 250,000 francs in 1993 and €55,000 in 2004, was eaten up by exorbitant shipping costs. Nevertheless, it embodied, as did to a certain extent the work of Association Emmaus with the homeless, the Movement's desire not to shirk its responsibility to respond to urgent need, a responsibility which Abbé Pierre himself had advised them to shoulder: "In the face of any human suffering, as far as you can, work not only to provide relief without delay but to destroy its causes. Work not only to destroy its causes, but to provide relief without delay."

It is clear then, that the Verona general assembly of 1988 constituted a turning point of fundamental importance. Despite the fact that religion appeared to re-emerge, it was in fact politics which came to the fore, and which has remained present within the Movement to this day. However, the process whereby politics was integrated into the work of Emmaus was a slow and uneven one, and saw some groups lose members and caused massive upheaval for many others. As Emmaus International noted at its executive committee of June 1994, "Little by little, we are slowly turning into a movement which speaks out against the status quo, and we are not used to behaving in such a manner."[40] The period, during which the Movement adopted a definitive stance on major issues, having passed, the challenge it now faced was incorporating this into its work and putting it into practice on the ground.

While few groups openly declared themselves opposed to globalisation, the ways in which Emmaus supported those in need had nevertheless been profoundly altered by this more political approach to North–South relations. Firstly, the operations dispatching containers to developing countries, practically non-existent until the mid-1980s, were now standard practice. Sent to Latin America and Africa, these containers allowed the Movement to supply the southern groups with clothes and small pieces of equipment, and created both jobs and wealth. However, while these operations redefined North–South relations by increasing each region's knowledge of the other, they also carried with them the risk that groups would come to rely on the containers for their survival and that competition would develop between those for whom they were intended. As part of an approach very similar to that advocated by Abbé Pierre following the tragedy in Bangladesh in 1971 ("cooperation-development"), twinning initiatives also became increasingly widespread throughout the 1990s, to such an extent that groups would sometimes bypass Emmaus International completely. The fair-trade dream became a reality. Finally, from 1993 onwards, Emmaus organised almost every year, and in France almost always in June, a large "solidarity sale", the profits from which were used to fund the Movement's work abroad.

The fact nevertheless remains that, due to the very organisation of the Movement itself, the North–South balance is ambiguous: In 2008, western Europe accounted for 82% of Emmaus groups with 55% in France alone. Given that each group is required to hand over a proportion of its budget to Emmaus, and given that these European groups are not only greater in number, but also the richest of them all, they provide an overwhelming share of the money at Emmaus' disposal, despite the fact that they have fewer votes within the organisation. Even discounting Abbé Pierre, all the presidents of Emmaus International have also always been European: a Swiss, a Dutchman, two Italians and today, a French citizen. Therefore, the challenge that Emmaus must continue to meet is that of constantly listening to needs and views of the South, in order that this part of the world might be actively involved in shaping its own destiny.

# *Chapter 12* / EMMAUS FRANCE THE DEVELOPMENT OF A POLITICAL DISCOURSE

Emmaus has existed as an association since 1954. Its various member organisations were initially brought together under an organisation which centralised operations, and which had a simple and logical name: Association Emmaus. Against the backdrop of the troubles that unfolded from 1956–8 and of the general desire – albeit for different reasons – to put an end to such centralisation, so as to make the various viable organisations independent, this Association quickly found itself devoid of any substance. From then on, and until the mid-1980s, there was no longer a body in place to bring together and regulate the various Emmaus organisations operating within France. By virtue of the freedom which each group jealously guarded, and against the backdrop of a conception which the founder had long held dear, according to which excessive organisation stifled action, the process favouring independence and fragmentation prevailed. Abbé Pierre alone was both the protector of the Movement and the glue which held it together.

In the late 1980s and early 1990s, two factors turned things on their head. Abbé Pierre himself was the first to spark change. Born in 1912, he was aware that he was not getting any younger. Furthermore, the rising economic and social crisis, of which the "new poor" became iconic, led both the media and the authorities to seek out spokespersons. And yet Emmaus could offer nothing more than a tangled mess of fragmented organisations, which were neither united in their vision nor their discourse. Consequently, in order to develop the Movement, the work of Emmaus France, a new umbrella organisation which brought together all of the French associations that were members of Emmaus, involved setting up an organisation which would be accepted by all, guarantee the respect of the Movement's values and communicate with the outside world. It would act as a spokesperson, able to replace the discourse of an ageing founder with that of a democratic organisation, and the cacophony of individual voices with one official line.

This official discourse itself evolved: barely audible until the mid-1990s, as it was constantly drowned out by that of the founder, it gradually became more public and then political. As we have seen, the 1980s was a decade during which Emmaus International became visibly political. During the same period, the majority of the Emmaus groups in France continued to focus on charitable initiatives in order to manage the increasing number of "new poor" as quickly as possible. In 1990, however, Abbé Pierre brought a strong political stance to the table made up largely of audacious statements in support of the homeless, reminiscent of those issued in 1954. Initially sparking a wave of opposition within Emmaus, the Movement adopted this political discourse from 1996 onwards.

## From Abbé Pierre to Emmaus France (1980–1996)

### The creation of Emmaus France (1970-1985)

Despite the fact that UCC and UACE continued to be the Movement's indomitable pair of warring brothers, the construction of Emmaus International meant they were forced to establish contact for the first time. On 22 May 1971, the first meeting bringing together all the Communities and Committees of Friends in France was held, in order to prepare for the world assembly in Montreal. The meeting, organised by the UCC, "was felt by all to have been extremely fruitful". It was decided that participants would come together again in October for a meeting that would this time be prepared by UACE. The meeting was to "examine the possibility of setting up a confederation which would guarantee that the many different forms of action launched would all be able to thrive, that the service provided was as efficient as possible and that the Movement would be represented by a single organisation when tackling the authorities."[1] Abbé Pierre encouraged this line of action: "It is a great source of comfort for me to see you working together to develop both the organisation and the unity necessary to ensure that everybody's endeavours stand the test of time, and the respect of the different personalities within the Movement required to ensure that we remain as open as possible to all individuals of good faith who are determined and acting on their convictions."[2]

However, the Movement had amassed a weighty catalogue of failures, and while everybody believed that such meetings ought to continue, the idea of a confederation appeared premature. UACE demanded that "concrete initiatives"[3] should first be developed: joint leader training sessions, debates on common problems, information exchange... After a number of tangible and successful joint ventures in 1973, which were open to other groups within Emmaus (common positions on conscientious objection and racism; an agreement in principle that UCC would train interns from other federations), the years 1974–7 saw relations cool once more.

In 1977, Abbé Pierre tried again and pushed UACE "to make progress with the creation of Emmaus France". At a meeting on 5 October 1977, the Federation once again agreed on "the need to look at each other differently, to accept that we are all different and, while according each other due respect, to clarify the bones of contention, and to iron out the misunderstandings created by rumours and hearsay,"[4] to stop "competing with each other as we do and to ensure instead that our work complements that underway elsewhere in the Movement."[5] However, the founder rejected any idea of a federation, viewing it as contrary to his vision of Emmaus. As he stated at a UACE meeting in January 1978: "We cannot aspire to standardise everything we do, because to do that would see us produce people with nothing unique about them, who had had their individuality 'maimed'."[6] Emmaus International continued to encourage the rapprochement of the different bodies within the French branch of the Movement: in early 1978, the executive committee demanded that France, which accounted for the lion's share of manpower and funding within Emmaus, be present on the board of directors, and appointed its representatives. In 1979, in a bid to develop local dialogue, six Emmaus regions were created in France for the first time, modelled on those created by the FNARS.[7] Then, two years later, a committee was set up which brought together those who represented the regions and those who represented the various Emmaus organisations (Communities, Committees of Friends and youth camps).

Soon afterwards, the economic and social crisis acted as a catalyst in the construction of Emmaus France. In January 1983, Emmaus was called upon to advise the Ministry for Social Affairs, and then the Elysée, together with *Secours catholique*, ATD Fourth-World, The Salvation Army, *Secours populaire*, the PACT (organisations campaigning for slum clearance), the FNARS (accommodation centres) and the National Committee of Social Welfare Offices. All of these organisations discussed the fact that insecurity in its various forms had worsened since 1980, and the idea of a guaranteed minimum wage was tabled.[8] A few days later, the Council of Ministers launched a first action plan to counter poverty and insecurity. In late 1983, the Emmaus France provisional committee devoted its founding meeting to the increasing insecurity across the country, and Abbé Pierre raised the alarm in the form of a press release. In the meantime, realising that awareness of Emmaus was now low, UCC launched a poster campaign in the metro during the summer of 1983. On the posters was a drawing by the humanist illustrator Piem with the phrase, "Don't throw your heart in the bin, it can always help somebody." The campaign aroused a certain degree of interest at UACE. Abbé Pierre was showing signs of fatigue: profoundly affected by the death of Lucie Coutaz in 1982, shortly afterwards he was diagnosed with Parkinson's disease and stepped down from his post as editor of *Faim et Soif.* He took on a new personal secretary, Father Jacques Perotti, whom he had met in 1954 as a young seminarian on work experience in Neuilly-Plaisance.

The structuring of Emmaus France was finally accelerated by the celebration of the thirtieth anniversary of the 1954 appeal. In the Paris region, UCC was the driving force behind an Awareness Week, the organisation's presence at the Paris trade fair, *La Foire de Paris*, and a press conference. Abbé Pierre launched a fresh appeal on the "new poor" and the anniversary spawned an abundance of local initiatives. From January to March 1984, both the Communities and Association Emmaus organised a vast night soup run. The anniversary coincided with the second stage of the government's fight against poverty: in October 1984, Abbé Pierre was invited to visit the Prime Minister and an extensive action plan was published. It was also in the autumn of

1984 that at the request of Association Emmaus, Abbé Pierre launched food banks, together with *Secours catholique*, the welfare organisation *l'Entraide protestante* and the Salvation Army. Finally, in December, in collaboration with Paris City Council, the newspaper *France Soir* and the Association of Variety Artists, Emmaus organised "Abbé Pierre's Christmas", a large-scale appeal for donations of money and goods which increased awareness of poverty and insecurity among both the public and the authorities, and triggered "an avalanche of calls for help". The operation raised a total of more than 10 million francs, which were ultimately used to purchase a building in Quai de Valmy, in Paris. The building was converted into a centre providing support and assistance with social reintegration, a restaurant for those on low incomes and a place where people could receive basic training in restoring and recycling waste items. Throughout the whole of 1984, the image conveyed of Emmaus France was one of a deeply charitable organisation, with its Ragpickers, soup runs and fundraising endeavours. While this image allowed the organisation to return to centre stage, it also sparked fierce criticism from certain quarters. At a meeting in December 1984, one member of the Emmaus France provisional committee asked, "What about our role as an agitator? [...] in forgetting that, we've gone backwards."[9]

The years 1983–4 can thus be considered a turning point which sealed the return of both Abbé Pierre and Emmaus to the media spotlight and the political arena. The actions undertaken allowed the Movement to realise that internal rapprochement was not only possible, but desirable and necessary in order for any large-scale initiative to take place. It was against this backdrop that in October 1984, Emmaus France decided to take the plunge as far as organisation was concerned and shift from "having an authority built around charismatic figures to one that was legal and officially instituted". Emmaus France was born on 25 November 1985 in the form of a confederation, "a place where things could be shared and information provided, where people could cooperate and work together." It was not, however, a decision-making body which had authority over its members. Its first president was Raymond Etienne, born in 1940 and the leader of a UCC Community in Metz. He arrived at

Emmaus in 1967 and was involved in the development of Emmaus France from 1978 onwards.

## Emmaus France takes root (1985–1996)

The new organisation took root gradually. From 1986 onwards, it took over the editing of *Faim et Soif.* In 1987, it hired a permanent member of staff – a part-time secretary and accountant provided by UCC. It also adopted a logo of a blue square with a sun in the top right-hand corner: the sun symbolised joy, human warmth, light and its radiance and dynamism, and the sun's six rays symbolised the six regions of Emmaus France. The blue square represented a window, calm, the protected space offered by Emmaus; and the sun lit up the area inside the square while at the same time symbolically opening up to the outside world.[10] In 1988, Emmaus France acquired headquarters in Paris, in the Passage Saint-Sébastien. At the same time, Abbé Pierre, who in February had been promoted to the rank of Commander of the Legion of Honour, announced that he would no longer visit Communities, except in exceptional cases. Speaking at the Emmaus France general assembly in December 1989 he declared, "It is important to be able to grow old, to take a step back, to be a grandfather. You know, [the monastery at] Saint-Wandrille is not very far away at all; if you need to, you can always come and see me while I still have some strength left, but it's good that it's now up to you to shoulder your own responsibilities."[11] In 1990, Emmaus France recruited its first full-time member of staff, and then moved the following year to the ground floor of a building in the Quai de Valmy, onto the site of a former restaurant for those on a low income, whose operating deficit had forced it to close.

The new organisation also sought to establish itself as the body representing the views of the Movement as a whole. The year 1987 was largely devoted to debates on "business charity", following the decision taken in 1984 by both Abbé Pierre and the Movement on the path to be followed in the future and, above all, following the publication of Bernard Kouchner's book[12] and a large number of newspaper articles. Indeed, 1984–7 were the years in which charity became show business and in which the world of entertainment became heavily involved in the charitable sector: *SOS-Drogue* was launched by singer Régine in 1984; comedian Coluche founded *Les Restos du cœur* in October 1985; singer Jean-Luc Lahaye set up a foundation for orphaned children in 1986; a media campaign in aid of Ethiopia was launched in spring 1985, with singer/songwriter Renaud notably on board;[13] and 1987 saw the launch of the televised fundraising event *Téléthon*. Conversely, the 1988 Emmaus International assembly in Verona encouraged the organisation to develop a new combative and proactive relationship with the political sphere, and Emmaus France opted to enact this principle, declaring in 1989 its wish to stand henceforth as a "conscience outraged and appalled by the extreme injustice and misfortune affecting the poorest members of society".[14] The task of Emmaus France was to orchestrate the transition from a message conveyed by Abbé Pierre to a discourse unique and common to the entire organisation, and to develop the capacity "to generate a definitive stance on the crucial and urgent problems of the moment".[15] In addition, the organisation focused on achieving real independence. During a meeting held in 1989, it declared, "While the Father is the founder of the Movement, when he states his position on an issue, he does so in his own name, and does not speak for Emmaus. He does so despite the fact this could be seen to go against the spirit of public opinion and even of the Movement itself. To counter this behaviour, Emmaus France must today adopt a strong and clearly recognised discourse, possibly by distancing itself from that of the Father."[16]

While the celebration of Emmaus' fortieth anniversary in 1989 was well and truly anchored in the Movement's new political, rather than charity-based approach, undoubtedly facilitated by the fact that the celebrations coincided with the bicentenary of the Revolution widely commemorated across France,[17] in contrast, Emmaus France was struggling to establish itself, and Abbé Pierre was continuing to monopolise the organisation's discourse. The fortieth anniversary celebrations began in late 1988 with a poster campaign that ran throughout 1989: the Movement put pressure on candidates running in the municipal elections; Abbé Pierre gave several interviews in May and June; a photography exhibition, *A Chronicle of Ordinary Poverty*, was held; and November saw the release of the film *Winter of '54:*

*Father Pierre* with Lambert Wilson, which was once again accompanied by a large number of interviews with the Abbé himself (he appeared on the current affairs programme "7 sur 7" fronted by Anne Sinclair, on a special edition of Michel Drucker's variety show "Champs Elysées", etc.).

Between 1991 and 1994, despite the fact he had just announced he was to retire to a monastery, Abbé Pierre continued, more than ever before, to monopolise the organisation's political discourse and to ensure he captivated the attention of the media, by adopting highly radical positions which the Movement itself did not always wish to follow.[18] The only initiative which emerged was the Emmaus France campaign within the collective Alert, put together by the poverty-insecurity commission of the UNIOPSS[19] after it had been declared a "major national cause" in 1994. In March 1995, as a result of the campaign, a "pact against poverty and exclusion" in the form of awareness-raising activities and a good-practice guide was put to citizens, associations, the media, businesses, regional authorities and the state, "to help us proceed from solidarity borne out of the distress we experience when faced with suffering to solidarity whose aim is to bring about justice. The time for organising handouts or making a show of solidarity has passed. There is a problem regarding the citizenship of those excluded from society which needs to be dealt with."

This realisation prompted Emmaus France to remain, until the mid-1990s, a place where structure was gradually imposed: it was a body of conciliation, revitalising the Emmaus regions, responsible for coordination and communication and for providing the authorities with information, guidance and a link to Emmaus. Meanwhile, political issues passed over their heads and beyond making statements of intent, the organisation had little interest in really grappling with those on the table. Debates focused primarily on internal relations (particularly problematic where new arrivals, including the Abbé Pierre Foundation, were concerned) and the power bases, regions or groups attached to the organisation. Indeed, certain members saw the future of Emmaus France as being in the regions, which allowed people from across the spectrum to come together and facilitated the gradual breakdown of ideological divisions from the bottom up.

Others, however, advocated a process whereby the organisation would be structured from the top down (with affiliated groups), believing that melting down the many different identities which had historically shaped the organisation until it became a homogenous mass "would sow the seeds of death for Emmaus France, causing it to fade into the background."[20] Of course, these two scenarios masked fierce power struggles, and the second option ultimately emerged victorious, becoming enshrined in the 1991 statutes and the organisation's guiding principles of 1995.

## 1990–1995: the homeless and illegal immigrants – Abbé Pierre introduces a political discourse

For Abbé Pierre, the early 1990s were, more than any other period before, a time of politics. Indeed, between 1990 and 1994, he was involved in all the demonstrations organised by the Committee of the Inadequately Housed (CML), and then with the organisation Right to Housing (DAL) playing a key role in the securing them media attention.[21]

The CML was created following four fires which in late 1986 had devastated hotels for the homeless in Paris' 20th arrondissement – Jean-Marie le Pen's new fiefdom – and the hotel residents' subsequent decision to occupy a building in the Rue des Vignoles. From the outset, the Community in Neuilly-Plaisance, at the time run by Joseph Cojean, was involved in the support committee set up to campaign for the rehousing of those affected by the fires and for an arson investigation to be launched. In early May 1990, the Rue des Vignoles squat was cleared on the Prefect's orders. The families consequently decided to occupy the neighbouring square, Place de la Réunion, and the Neuilly-Plaisance Community provided tents and mattresses. From the very beginning, Abbé Pierre also fought shoulder to shoulder with the families, encouraging a "discourse based essentially on a humanitarian rhetoric"[22] and making extensive use of the media. The Place de la Réunion camp functioned as a veritable "catalyst in bringing the forces of the left together".[23] These included political parties (the Greens, the Communist Party PCF, the Revolutionary Communist League LCR) and unions (CFDT, CGT, FEN, etc.) and also associations

(GISTI,[24] FASTI,[25] *SOS-Racisme*, Emmaus, *Secours catholique*, *Médecins du monde*, LDH, the Salvation Army, etc.). The Abbé Pierre Foundation then rallied behind the campaign, co-signing a telegram with its eponymous founder which was sent to political leaders. The telegram condemned the eviction, demanded "the immediate requisition of empty homes in order to permanently rehouse the families concerned", "the immediate implementation of the decrees of 30 March on the housing of the poorest members of society", and the construction in Paris of hotels for the socially disadvantaged. Association Emmaus also published its own communiqué calling for an end to evictions where those affected were not rehoused and for the enforcement of the right to requisition,[26] and took part in the post-crisis management operation (working with the authorities to rehouse the families affected).

The DAL was created following the members' decision to break away from the CML, and in early 1991 it campaigned against the draft reform of the law on civil eviction procedures,[27] supported both by Abbé Pierre and the Foundation. Action continued in June on Quai de la Gare: African families, whose papers were in order and debt repayments on track but who had nevertheless been evicted from their homes, came to camp on the site of what would later become the *Grande Bibliothèque*. Called in by the DAL, Abbé Pierre once again used his influence with the media to further the cause by witnessing the camp's set-up in order to stop it being evacuated. The strategy was to let families flock to the camp, and the original thirty-seven families soon became 500 people, half of whom were children. Just as it had done in 1990, the Neuilly-Plaisance Community provided the tents and Emmaus was thought to have funded the camp almost entirely from its own pocket during the four months it remained in place.[28] It was Abbé Pierre who suggested that an association be created to insure legal proceedings against the organisation and to avoid a situation whereby the families in the camp would be forced to cover the periodic penalty payment.[29] It was Abbé Pierre again who went as far as fasting for several days alongside the illegal immigrants on hunger strike, and those whose claims for asylum had been thrown out of court, and it was Abbé Pierre who then went on to become a member of the monitoring committee appointed by the Ministry. The Abbé Pierre Foundation, Association Emmaus, Emmaus HLM and its subsidiary organisation Housing for All all took action to ensure the families in the camp were rehoused: the Foundation did so by negotiating a contract containing rehousing targets which had to be met; Association Emmaus did so by agreeing to manage a building for a three-year period where thirty-three families were temporarily rehoused; and Emmaus HLM and Housing for All did so by building one hundred of the 600 houses for which plans had been drawn up. In contrast, Emmaus France remained distant and circumspect. At a meeting held in September 1991, one member noted, "The case is a very difficult one, due to the fact that the matter has become political, due to the open conflict between the council and the state over the site intended for the Grande Bibliothèque,[30] and due to the inexperience of the association DAL, which has allowed itself to become overwhelmed by and embroiled in a situation which no longer allows any acceptable short-term solutions, and which tends to force Emmaus to act as a mere channel for communication."[31]

In May 1992, this time on their own initiative, eight and, very soon, 300 African families set up camp on the esplanade of the Château de Vincennes. Once again, Abbé Pierre supported the DAL campaign, going as far as to decline his new promotion at the Legion of Honour in solidarity with those living in inadequate housing. In 1993, he once again supported squatters, this time on Avenue René-Coty; when in late September he announced that he would be moving in with the families, he was immediately invited to Matignon, the Prime Minister's official residence in Paris.[32]

Finally, in December 1994, DAL launched a squat in a building in Rue du Dragon, Paris. On that very same day, Abbé Pierre flew in by helicopter to support the movement and was – again – immediately invited to Matignon. Jacques Chirac endorsed his efforts by calling for the right to requisition to be enforced. Once again, the case flagged up a divide within Emmaus. On one side, Abbé Pierre and his Foundation supported DAL and the group signed common appeals, sometimes published under the name "Emmaus" (a name which was vague and usurped, since it did not in fact refer to any specific organisation), backed also by the LCR, the Communist Party PCF, and PS, its Socialist counterpart. On the other, Emmaus France and Association Emmaus kept their distance. In January 1995, the Association even went as far as to state that it "disagree[d] entirely with the name Emmaus being used in that way: such generalisation only serves to perpetuate confusion", and insisted "that Emmaus France distance itself from the positions adopted by [its] founder."[33] Nevertheless, the Foundation and the Association did involve themselves respectively in the rehousing of families and, together with the authorities, in the management of temporary accommodation blocks.

It is clear, then, that these highly political episodes were the cause, as much as the reflection, of a clear and growing chasm within Emmaus; between Abbé Pierre and his Foundation on the one hand, and the rest of the Movement on the other. The episodes are noteworthy for several reasons. While officially in retirement from Emmaus, in the first half of the 1990s, Abbé Pierre returned to the centre of the French political and social arena, more dominant than ever before, and this time in his own name; he was a leader and not waiting for Emmaus to follow. Pledging his support to DAL, a symbol of the "new social movement", the old man returned to the struggles that echoed 1954; defending housing and squats, launching commando-style initiatives and devising a political discourse which was sharp and critical. Once again the battle of rights versus the law was played out, when Abbé Pierre fought to defend the homeless and later, illegal immigrants.

By contrast, Emmaus' longest established organisations argued that the Movement should remain clearly focused on making compromises and achieving results. They also roundly condemned the distribution of roles made necessary by the positions which Abbé Pierre had publicly adopted: DAL was in charge of keeping the Movement in the spotlight and issuing political statements, while Emmaus was responsible for after-sales service, namely for launching tangible initiatives and the difficult, underground task of supporting and rehousing families. Finally, they rose up in vehement protest against campaigns which ultimately did not always work in favour of the families in need, because, as Emmaus France noted, "there was a danger that they would lead to a temporary housing situation that was more insecure than it originally had been":[34] the organisation spoke of the "moral imperative not to confuse healthy provocation with the exploitation of families living on the street as means to an end."[35]

It has become clear, then, that during this period Abbé Pierre escaped the clutches of Emmaus to place both his historic and media personas at the disposal of a nascent DAL in need of support. Initially, "the movement did not follow his lead";[36] overwhelmed by and at a loss to understand the new direction it was to take, Emmaus France spoke of "the need to give Abbé Pierre free rein but to avoid, above all, a situation whereby groups adopt an opposing stance to that taken by Abbé Pierre."[37] Hostility towards the Abbé was later more clearly expressed, particularly when it came to the issue of Abbé Pierre demonstrating alongside the DAL, an act which sparked "serious misgivings"[38] within Emmaus. These were years of deep divide; between founder who was elderly but very radical in the stances he adopted in public, and a movement with a largely underdeveloped political identity, overwhelmed by the gaping ideological chasm between its base and founder, a movement busy inserting structure wherever possible and, more than anything, seeking to become an institution.

## The Garaudy Affair: the fall of an icon

It was ultimately through the Garaudy Affair, an event as embarrassing as it was unexpected, that Emmaus managed to regain the upper hand. In addition to regularly expressing his views on the case in public, Abbé Pierre had already waged more personal struggles, as was the case in 1982 and 1984, to defend the Italian academic Vanni Mulinaris.[39] In 1996, Roger Garaudy, an old friend from the Abbé's time on the benches of the *Assemblée nationale*, asked him to support his book *The Founding Myths of Israeli Politics*. Out of friendship and in order to voice his opinion "on the issue, which he viewed as pernicious, of Israel's identification with the Bible's Promised Land",[40] the Abbé spoke out in support of the book, which he later confessed to having only leafed through, maintaining that "around [him], a number of people who had both high expectations and a great many talents, and who had read it in its entirety, attested to [its] importance."[41]

However, in the book the author defended Holocaust-denial theories and became the object of a widespread campaign launched to condemn his work. Consequently, Abbé Pierre found that he too was under attack. Following the fierce reaction of the media, the Abbé published his first communiqué condemning Holocaust denial and revisionism, but supporting Garaudy's work as that of an historian. He reaffirmed that "everything which he knew of the life and works of Roger Garaudy left [... him] in no doubt that to liken them to "denial" or "revisionist' works [...] would be to make a mistake or deceive the public."[42]

From that point on, the controversy escalated. On 29 April, the newspaper *Libération* accused Abbé Pierre of being "anti-Jewish" and "anti-Israeli", while the French episcopate published a communiqué making it clear that "in the eyes of the public, the moral guarantee which Abbé Pierre represents, the authority which he has acquired through his words and his actions, extend to the Church of France. It cannot allow itself to be compromised in this way." The following day, after having been interviewed by the chief rabbi and the president of the Central Consistory of the Jews in France, the Abbé stated once again that he fully acknowledged the Holocaust and condemned all forms of revisionism. He added, however, that he would only cease to back Garaudy if the author refused to acknowledge his "mistake".[43]

This semi-retraction finally prompted Emmaus to intervene, in order to distance itself from the ideological stances being defended while continuing to support both the founder as a man and his achievements in the humanitarian sector. A first communiqué, co-signed by Emmaus France and Emmaus International, appeared on 1 May, condemning the theories put forward by Garaudy in only two lines and devoting twenty-three lines to declaring its support for the founder. The disproportion was blatant and UCC threatened to publish its own text. A new common communiqué finally appeared on 8 May "to make vital corrections" and was this time devoted entirely to condemning revisionist theories.

Attacked from all sides, distressed and overwhelmed by the storm he had unleashed, Abbé Pierre spent some time away from the Movement in a monastery in Italy. He then left for Switzerland, but revived the debate by stating in an Italian newspaper, *Il Corriere de la Sera*, that the attacks of which he had been the victim had in fact been perpetrated by an "international Zionist lobby..."

Consequently, despite the fact that the creation of Emmaus France was intended to mark the beginning of the "post-Abbé Pierre period", the years 1985–96 became, on the contrary, the era of Abbé Pierre. A legally independent organisation until the mid-1990s, Emmaus France struggled to establish itself in the face of a founder who was more charismatic and omnipresent than ever.

## Emmaus France Today (1996–2008)

### A long age of reform

By historical accident, it was also in 1996, in the midst of the Garaudy affair, that Emmaus France changed president for the first time since its inception. One UCC Community leader made way for another – Jean Rousseau, who held the post from 1996 to 2002. Rousseau was born in 1955, had studied business and marketing, and had been the leader of the Angers Community since its creation in 1982. The arrival of Martin Hirsch (president from 2002 to 2007), placed the organisation in altogether different hands. Hirsch was a graduate of both ENS and ENA, two prestigious French higher-education establishments, a former chief executive of the Central Pharmacy of the Paris Hospitals, the former right-hand man of Bernard Kouchner, a former director of the French Agency for Food Safety, the Master of Requests and Secretary-General of the French Council of State and had entered Emmaus in 1995 as the president of UCC (1995–2002). With several end goals in mind, these two presidents concentrated their efforts on continuing to structure the organisation and on continuing the internal reorganisation process already under way.

The first goal was to turn Emmaus France into a more stable authority: in 1995, the structure in place was still minimal, with only two paid employees and, as we have seen, little political clout. The organisation's first step was to hire two representatives responsible for communication and the coordination of activities, an assistant manager and a part-time accountant. In 1996, the post of secretary-general was created, and the following year he was supported by a deputy. By 2007, Emmaus France had around fifteen permanent members of staff.

The second goal was to overhaul the Movement's press. After having been the mouthpiece of Abbé Pierre and Emmaus International for thirty years, in the mid-1980s it instead became that of Emmaus France, but its output was highly amateur and, most importantly, made a huge loss. In 1991, Bayard Presse took over the production and distribution of the newspaper *Faim et Soif.* In 1993, the number of pages in each issue was reduced. However, its circulation remained restricted, its readership was small and no definitive decision was ever taken as to whether the publication's target audience was internal or external. By late 1996, the deficit was such that the organisation finally decided to call time on *Faim et Soif.* In early 2001, *The Emmaus France Letter* was finally launched, as a smaller but more frequent publication which targeted a more explicitly external audience.

Most importantly, a long and far-reaching process of reform was undertaken in order to unite and render accessible a movement which was an amalgam of heterogeneous and independent or pro-independence organisations, and to meet the criteria required if Emmaus was to be declared a movement serving the public interest. The idea which first took root was one of an organisation with two "branches": the "Community" and the "non-Community". While the second branch clearly constituted a clumsy blanket solution designed to accommodate any Emmaus group, creating a more coherent, united second branch was no easy task, given that Communities had been built historically on a series of disagreements and disputes that saw members break away from the Movement and set up on their own. In the 1990s, the rapprochement of UCC and UACE allowed Emmaus to lay the foundations of this new model, and the partnership between these two warring brothers became the driving force behind the reconciliation process. The new statutes stipulated that no group was to remain isolated from the rest of the Movement. Consequently, a lengthy campaign then began to persuade the organisations in the north, with a very loose, regionally based organisation, to form a genuine Federation. In 2000, the idea of a third "branch" was floated, and given more concrete form the following year. Once all three "branches" were in place, the Movement's organisation was as follows: branch 1, the "Community" branch comprised the Emmaus Communities; branch 2, "social action and housing", was made up of the Abbé Pierre Foundation, Association Emmaus, Emmaus-Habitat, *SOS-Familles* and two local organisations, Roofs of Hope and Emmaus-Alternatives; and branch 3, "solidarity economy and integration", comprised the organisations for social integration, *Le Relais* and the Committees of Friends. It was also in the year 2000 that Emmaus France established itself as a "union of a federal nature," possessing significant powers (representing the Movement, expelling members and protecting the Emmaus identity), but these were balanced out by the organisation's respect of local diversity and the powers each of the three branches and the regions kept for themselves.

In 2002, the arrival of Martin Hirsch accelerated the process of internal reform. But this process, occasionally conducted with forceps and the intention of centralising powers to a considerable extent, turned the Movement on its head and became the source of serious tension. Very specifically, it was the issue of the power surrendered to Emmaus France which was at stake: should it publicly adopt a stance on housing issues on behalf of the Movement as a whole, or was that the responsibility of the Abbé Pierre Foundation? Should it come up with a stance on acute social exclusion or did this task now fall within the remit of Association Emmaus? In other words, should the Movement favour the principle of subsidiarity and first-hand knowledge of Emmaus, or have a single body that would liaise with the media and the authorities?

2005–6 marked the start of the crisis between Emmaus France and the Movement's major organisations, which ultimately succeeded in retaining their independence where issuing statements and launching initiatives were concerned. However, this mandate was subject to the condition that the "Community branch" merged with the rest of the Movement (disappearing with the merging of the Federations and the "families" which the Movement had historically comprised). The agreement whereby the permanent national level employees of these bodies would join Emmaus France came into effect in 2008, and the total number of staff within the organisation doubled. In a more peaceful, less drastic move, branch 3 acquired a permanent employee and became a truly unified body, while common headquarters, of which Emmaus France had dreamed of since 1999, were finally opened in Montreuil in 2008 – even if the Abbé Pierre Foundation, Emmaus-Habitat and Association Emmaus, three very large organisations, kept their respective headquarters.

## Emmaus France – the new spokesman for public and political matters

Besides the internal organisational issues, the other major common issue, first emerging in 1996, was that of public and political speech. Indeed, up until that point, Emmaus France appeared more focused on its internal development than on spreading its influence externally. This inward focus was the consequence of the enormous task which lay ahead, of having a founder who was never out of the headlines and, conversely, a president who at the time was less inclined to devote attention to political speech. However, from 1996 onwards, the Garaudy Affair and the Abbé's age combined with the change of president at Emmaus France and the major progress already made on organisational matters prompted the body to take up the torch of its founder once again. Once more, a distinction can be drawn between these two periods, the presidency of Jean Rousseau and that of Martin Hirsch.

Under Jean Rousseau, Emmaus devoted a particularly significant amount of time and energy to the preparation of the law on exclusion: the arrival in power of the Jospin government opened up an opportunity for dialogue, and Association Emmaus, the Abbé Pierre Foundation, *SOS-Familles* and Emmaus France all made a sizeable contribution to the Movement's efforts, each working within his own area of expertise. In 1999, Emmaus was invited to sit on the National Committee Combating Exclusion. Following the example set by Emmaus International, Emmaus France also became involved in the anti-globalisation movement. It participated in the G7 counter-summit held in

Lyons in 1996 and both joined the collective "Let's cancel the debt" and the group ATTAC in 2000. Finally, since 1999 Emmaus France has also supported the International Prison Observatory (OIP). However, the most salient feature of the Movement's work remained its fight alongside illegal immigrants, which was spurred on by the new campaigns of 1996 in Pajol, Saint-Ambroise and later in Saint-Bernard. In late 1995, Emmaus France had voted in favour of providing financial support to GISTI and of doing the same for FASTI on a temporary basis, in exchange for training in how to deal with foreign nationals. During the first stage of the 1996 campaigns (a squat was set up in the Pajol warehouse), it was announced that the Tobin Law had been passed and that a new bill was in the pipeline which would force those from abroad to meet much stricter conditions in order to obtain a residency permit. The announcement caused the associations to organise large-scale rallies, in which Emmaus France and the Abbé Pierre Foundation participated separately. In April 1996, each organisation signed a different statement calling for the legalisation of illegal immigrants. The text signed by Emmaus France, and also by the Franco-Belgian Chamber of Commerce (CCFB), focused on condemning French immigration policy, denouncing "the single-minded focus on closing the borders", "the myth of zero immigration" and the danger to democracy inherent in presenting the foreign national as the person responsible for all of society's ills. The statement signed by the Foundation was co-signed chiefly by the unions (CGT, FSU) and political organisations (LCR, Revolutionary Left), and aimed to demonstrate that "these foreign nationals are not attempting to slip under the radar. They are people without papers who, in every possible legal way, have tried countless times to obtain the residency and work permits to which they are humanly and often legally entitled." However, both texts had been signed by members of the main organisations spearheading the campaign: *Droits devant*,[44] FASTI, GISTI, LDH,[45] MRAP[46] and CIMADE.[47]

From 1996 onwards, opening up the borders and supporting immigrants became one of the major political causes championed by Emmaus France. Laws and bills on the matter regularly sparked fierce criticism in the name of welcoming immigrants unconditionally, a principle that had underpinned the work of Emmaus since its very beginning. However, the Movement also vehemently criticised such legislation in defence of human rights and solidarity, and of the distinction, which since the 1950s Abbé Pierre had recommended, that could be drawn between the respect of human rights and the respect of the law (Emmaus only respects laws which are just[48]). As Emmaus France declared on 28 November 1997, "Our Movement rejects an elitist ideology separating 'good' foreign nationals who, according to a market-driven approach to society, France allegedly needs, from 'bad' foreign nationals, allegedly from backgrounds which are both intellectually and economically poorer."[49] Emmaus France also expressed its disapproval of double jeopardy, where immigrants were concerned and of the increasing number of temporary, rather than permanent, residency permits being granted. Their partnership with GISTI deepened. Such statements and actions were a direct result of the fact that, in addition to issuing petitions out of principle, many Emmaus organisations (chiefly Communities, Association Emmaus and the boutiques) were confronted with the problem on a daily basis, and were anxious for tools which would help them address it. Indeed, in addition to the groups in the north, which were close to the refugee holding centre Sangatte, and therefore particularly active, while the authorities turned a blind eye, more than half of the Communities and all of the boutiques took in illegal immigrants in 1999. On 3 November 1999, Emmaus France remarked, "As regards the risks incurred when taking in illegal immigrants, the Ministry recently stated that it would allow associations helping these people to carry out their work."[50]

In the 2002 the political climate changed when the Right returned to power. This coincided with Martin Hirsch's appointment to the presidency of Emmaus France. It was at this point that Association Emmaus declared: "Every single measure taken by the government moves in the same direction. The rationale behind them is dubious and they seek to cast the poor from society. This is why associations have spoken out and said, 'It is poverty, not the poor, which we need to attack'."[51] This stance was the fruit of a mentality according to which war had to be waged: not against prostitutes but against prostitution; not against squatters but against those who did not comply with the SRU law on providing decent, sustainable accommodation in a diverse, democratic environment; not against travelling people but against those who did not comply with the law which made it compulsory to provide them with designated sites, and so on. The time had now come to criticise, through the proper channels, the social policy of the new Minister of the Interior, Nicolas Sarkozy, and a veritable front of associations began to form (Emmaus France, ATD Fourth-World, *Entraide protestante*, the Salvation Army, *Secours catholique*, *Médecins du monde*, etc.).

While Martin Hirsch's internal reforms were controversial, his contribution in terms of bringing the organisation into the media spotlight and by increasing its celebrity was incontrovertibly positive. A skilled communicator, with a solid network of contacts, he enabled Emmaus to become a highly visible presence on a number of battlefronts: the petition in favour of providing a decent welcome to foreign nationals and the communiqué issued to criticise the reform of the right to asylum (2002); the criticism of the bill on the *Revenu minimum d'activité*, the minimum wage which gave the unemployed a temporary, part-time contract (2003); the outward condemnation, alongside the International Prison Observatory (OIP), *Secours catholique*, FNARS and the Red Cross, of "the endless circle" which saw people move between social exclusion and the prison environment (2004); raising citizens' awareness of the draft European Constitution and the proposal to make an amendment relating to textiles in the 2005 Budget; participation in the parliamentary assembly on conditions in prison (2006), and so on. As far as the increasingly sensitive issue of immigration was concerned, Emmaus worked with collectives (GISTI, CIMADE), but also carried out its own initiatives, notably to condemn the fact that Companions without legal documents were arrested even within the Communities themselves. These arrests saw the 2003 general assembly decide that "if providing support to immigrants in a way which is in line with the values of Emmaus leads to individuals (presidents, friends or leaders) being brought before the courts, Emmaus France will publicly request that it be charged as a legal person."[52] The situation became increasingly paradoxical in view of the fact that "at the same time, the public services were sending those in administrative limbo to Emmaus", in particular "foreign families with children who had been excluded from the CADA"[53] and had been informed that their application for asylum had been rejected...[54]

Christophe Deltombe, who was appointed the new president of Emmaus France in 2007, continued along these lines. In October 2007, spearheading a large-scale campaign that brought together a plethora of associations, Emmaus France notably succeeded in getting article 21 removed from the law on controlling immigration, integration and asylum, which called into question the principle of providing a place for every immigrant in an accommodation centre, whatever their circumstances.

Finally, in its anniversary celebrations, Emmaus hesitated and alternated between organising internal events and expressing a desire to open up to the world outside.

In 1999, for its fiftieth anniversary, the slogan adopted – "At Emmaus, you can remake the world" – was at the crossroads between the Movement's daily work and its vision for the future, between the utopian ideal which formed the stuff of members' dreams and the fight against globalisation. The sponsorship committee was a highly prestigious body comprising political figures and politically active thinkers, both religious and of no particular faith: Isabel Allende, civil servant and activist François Bloch-Lainé, United Nations Secretary General Boutros Boutros-Ghali, Brazilian Archbishop Dom Helder Câmara, filmmaker Costa-Gavras, politician Jacques Delors, Cardinal Etchegaray, UNESCO director Federico Mayor, philosopher Edgar Morin, scientist Hubert Reeves and sociologist Alain Touraine, to name but a few. However, aside from the launch of a postage stamp and a photography exhibition, the events organised were few, far between and did little to clearly broadcast the Movement's message.

By contrast, the fiftieth anniversary of the 1954 appeal in February 2004 focused on the outside world, just like the appeal it marked. Designed to act as a "trigger" to bring back memories of 1954, the anniversary consisted of a one-off event in the presence of Abbé Pierre in Paris' Place du Trocadéro, and another, longer-lasting event – an interactive exhibition on poverty at the *Musée de l'homme*, which Emmaus' partner associations were invited to attend (*Secours populaire*,

*Secours catholique*, ATD, *Médecins du monde*, etc.). A "time bank" was also created and broadcast by France 2, with appeals for donations not of money, but of time to be given as a volunteer. The Abbé Pierre Foundation published a special report on inadequate housing and Association Emmaus organised a poster campaign in the Paris metro. The goal pursued by each and every one of these organisations was to change the way society looked at its poorest members and to encourage citizens to take action.

In conclusion, the birth of Emmaus France was delayed, lengthy and painful. The organisation's history clearly explains many things that seem either incongruous, the work of inexperienced beginners, such as the small size of the organisation (it had around thirty paid employees in 2008, while Association Emmaus had 430 and the Abbé Pierre Foundation more than eighty), or of an authority struggling to assert itself and always easily challenged. However, after a process of organisation and reform lasting no less than twenty years, it has succeeded in becoming an body effective body in both in terms of word and deed, a moral guarantor and a place where common positions are established, while always ultimately respecting the principle of subsidiarity.

Furthermore, the relationship between politics and Emmaus France has evolved considerably. After the 1980s, which focused heavily on promoting the image of the organisation as a charitable body with its Ragpickers and night soup runs, not forgetting the vast fundraising operations organised as part of "Abbé Pierre's Christmas", the 1990s were intensely political. This change was initially due to the Movement's founder, and then to the new presidents who followed. In this regard, Emmaus embraced the general trend, with French political activism in the 1980s symbolised by *Les Restos du cœur* and in the 1990s by the fight to enforce the right to housing and the anti-globalisation movement. And yet, in both cases, Abbé Pierre was decisively involved, having emerged from his silence of 1983–4 to support the "new poor" before becoming heavily involved in the campaign to see the right to housing enforced. These changes in identity, which were a difficult pill for the summit to swallow, troubled those at the bottom of the organisation to an even greater extent. At Emmaus France, the Abbé Pierre Foundation, Association Emmaus or within the Communities, the defence of illegal immigrants remained a controversial issue at local level, and the Foundation itself confessed to doing little to promote the work in aid of those from abroad "for fear of losing donors", despite the fact that "when Abbé Pierre did so, his popularity rating did not decrease".[55] This historic malleability, which has been wholly responsible for the enigma surrounding, but also for the popularity of, the figure of Abbé Pierre, is what makes the Emmaus Movement so rich: by ultimately bestowing upon it an identity assuming many different forms and never being set in stone.

# Conclusion

## Politics and Religion in the Humanitarian Field

We are often inclined to present humanitarianism as a neutral or neutralised ideology, a response to the contemporary crisis both in politics and of the old ideologies or "grand narratives" which structured society (communism, Christianity). Instead, the historical approach invites us to view the development of society as a process during which these ideologies have in fact taken on new forms, forms that both break away from and continue with the past.

While Emmaus has never been a religious organisation, its history allows us to conclude that it drew heavily upon the tenets of an ideology from whose womb modern humanitarianism emerged: Catholicism. The organisation focused initially on metropolitan France, against the backdrop of an acute housing crisis and society's increasing awareness of the extent of social exclusion. Until the 1970s, three types of activists were chiefly responsible for driving the organisation forward: ex-convicts and broken men, members of the clergy and men from the middle classes, often Catholics themselves. Emmaus then began to go international, thanks to the celebrity it acquired in the winter of 1954, and straightaway entered the major pontifical encyclicals of the 1960s on development. Catholics – both priests and laymen – were thus everywhere in the Movement at grass-roots and management level. While Catholic activists remained heavily involved in Emmaus' international activities until the 1990s, they increasingly withdrew from initiatives on French soil from the 1970s onwards.

Emmaus' changing relationship with the ideology that gave it life is in no way unusual, and was a phenomenon common to the majority of the other organisations within the sector. A previous study on the history of *Secours populaire*[1] allowed readers to understand the processes by which the Communists entered the humanitarian field and the goals they sought to achieve in so doing. The decision to enter this field appears to have been driven initially by the pragmatic desire, during the Spanish Civil War, to help civilian victims of political conflict. The aid provided was in no small way directly responsible for prolonging the resistance against fascism. From the mid-1950s onwards, the decision to remain within the humanitarian sector was motivated by the desire to widen the support base of the organisation. This desire prompted the organisation to openly develop initiatives which provided indiscriminate support to those in need (disaster victims, disadvantaged children, the sick, the elderly, etc.) and to adopt non-political discourse. Its efforts bore fruit and *Secours populaire*, which had up until that point been a mass communist organisation, gradually attracted non-Communists and women. In the years 1986–9, the extensive media coverage of the Biafra tragedy saw the organisation change direction and provide emergency humanitarian aid. Then, following the drought and famine that plagued the Sahel in 1973, the organisation became involved in the humanitarian-development movement. At the same time, its desire to adapt to the post-1968 context allowed its demographics to change as young people arrived and breathed new life into an old body. Lastly, since the 1980s and the economic crisis, the association has largely begun to focus once more on metropolitan France, and the majority of its volunteers are people who have retired young and who have joined out of a desire to take action to improve social welfare. Such changes have meant that since then *Secours populaire* has retained from its history an identity which, to a certain extent, has two distinct facets. For on the one hand, its non-political nature is seen as an integral part of its identity and is widely documented in the media. This is embodied namely in the two major campaigns organised every year: the *journées des oubliés des vacances* where children whose families cannot afford a holiday are taken on a day trip, and the Christmas campaign *Pères Noël verts.* On the other hand, however, and despite the fact the organisation has undoubtedly become increasingly professional, it continues to be led by activists who have risen up through the ranks and who remain faithful to communist values.

Thus, while a parallel can be drawn between Emmaus and *Secours populaire* in that both their original identities have been watered down but remain present in the background to a greater or lesser extent, the development of each association's relationship to politics appears to have followed a contrasting pattern. Indeed, unlike *Secours populaire*, which sought to avoid both adopting stances that set East against West and the fight against the causes of poverty, strategically choosing to focus solely on the consequences of social tragedies, Emmaus' development-orientated approach saw it gradually move towards revealing and targeting the causes of poverty in its international work. Such efforts bear traces of Abbé Pierre's successful battle to improve access to housing, waged since the beginning of the 1950s. In the words of Emmaus International: "When you meet a man who is suffering and hungry – and Abbé Pierre expressed this idea magnificently and on a thousand separate occasions – and when you can ease this suffering and this hunger, you must do so, it's as simple as that. That's one thing. But at the same time, you must understand what has caused this suffering; who has thrown this man out on to the street?; who has stripped him of his dignity?; who has potentially consigned him to the underclasses of society?; and who is keeping him there? You must understand this system of power and control, try to describe it and try to create another world in its place."[2]

The reasons for this contrasting development are twofold. First, as a result of the ideology which had shaped it from birth, *Secours populaire* was a member of the school of thought whose approach to social problems set the East against the West. As France moved into the 1960s, this approach was no longer able to provide an astute insight into society's problems and, as communism was discredited, it was increasingly stigmatised in the 1970s and 80s. At the same time, Emmaus remained rooted exclusively in an approach that set the North against the South. This was an approach which, conversely, was held in increasingly high esteem, both from a sociological and ideological perspective. Later, while *Secours populaire* sought to cast off its original status as a mass organisation and embarked on a process which saw it cast off its previous identity, Emmaus International continued to develop along the same lines with the same founder at the helm, whose reputation across French society was, above all, the result of the way he "raised hell" when combating social ills and his role as a prophet.

However, until the 1980s, the development of Emmaus' relationship to politics remained stifled by the charitable convictions and latent anti-communism of many of its leaders. In Metropolitan France, the Movement's role in the early days as an advocate for those in need, which involved defending human rights over and above upholding the law or publicly challenging the Minister for Housing, was erased by the 1954 appeal which adopted a primarily charitable approach. It focused on appeals for donations and volunteers, opening emergency shelters and rounding up the victims of the harsh winter temperatures, giving them a place in the warm. As the housing crisis was gradually resolved and Abbé Pierre slowly moved out of the public arena, the Movement ceased to play this role. As a result, from that point on, Emmaus was no longer associated so much with the image of the homeless person as with that of the Ragpicker. There is no doubt that the 1970s constituted a specific, unique phase in the history of Emmaus, with the arrival of activists who were drawn to the Movement by the socio-political revival of the communitarian utopia. However, when both Abbé Pierre and Emmaus returned to centre stage in the early 1980s to champion the cause of the "new poor", it was as a result of nightly soup runs and fundraising efforts. Involvement in the political sphere was also stifled on an international level, where the compromise which had to be maintained between those who advocated politicisation and those who favoured charity halted the expression of political beliefs in any area, where the Movement was at risk of becoming affiliated to a specific party or organisation. It was not until 1988 on an international level (at the Verona assembly) and 1990 in France (in the speeches Abbé Pierre made alongside the so-called "new" social movements) that the Abbé and finally Emmaus France returned to the aggressive political discourse of old, with a centre of gravity comprising leaders who were more deeply anchored in left-wing ideals. The development of activism within Emmaus thus mirrored the contemporary metamorphosis of Catholic activism taking place during the age of "political modernity". This process saw Emmaus move from charitable initiatives to worker-priests before going on to champion development with a humanitarian focus. It then adopted a pro-Third-World approach before finally evolving into networked activism, a form of militancy appearing in the 1990s. It did so in cooperation with DAL or GISTI, organisations whose own leadership was largely Christian. However, from the 1980s onwards, the number of atheists grew both at the base and at the summit of the Emmaus pyramid, while the Catholic beliefs of activists and leaders came to be heavily veiled. In the words of Bénédicte Havard-Duclos and Sandrine Nicourd: "as a result of the fact that they allowed people to come face to face with the misfortune and the difficulties of the 'weakest' members of society, the associations acted both as places where people could test out the concept of faith in action and places where the religious ideal of taking in, sharing with and listening to others could assume tangible form. [They] allowed people to prioritise actions over words, and if there was a mission to convert non-believers to Christianity, it involved recounting real-life experiences and displaying an appropriate attitude towards those in need."[3]

This attempt to weaken the ties with religion, which went hand in hand with the organisation's move to reassert the value of politics, was clearly visible in the speeches made by both Emmaus and its leaders. However, this process was not reflected to quite the same extent at the bottom of the Movement. Laurent Desmard has remarked, "it is perhaps true that those in power within Emmaus are closer to the left of the political spectrum than they are to the right, but at the bottom there are a huge number of people with right-wing beliefs. A huge number. And they are more than comfortable with a discourse in support of the underprivileged members of society which isn't too left-wing."[4] As soon as what's being said comes across as too left-wing or too subversive, as was the case with the speeches advocating supporting illegal immigrants, it sparks fierce disagreement, whether this is tacit or openly expressed. Thus it would appear that at Emmaus, like at *Secours populaire*, the lines dividing the Movement run, in part, from top to bottom: the summit of the pyramid, being more involved and therefore more "militant", is also more political and further to the left than its base.

## Managing Diversity

However, Emmaus is much more internally diverse than the majority of humanitarian associations. This is a direct result of the fact that for a long time the international branch of the Movement developed independently from the French branch: Abbé Pierre, who from 1958 to the early 1980s was relatively isolated from the French movement, left to found Emmaus across the globe and played at being one of the missionaries which, as a child, he had dreamed of becoming. The rationale behind the development of the French branch was itself twofold. On the one hand, to respond to the problems linked to poverty (hunger, accommodation, lack of protection, isolation, etc.), which sparked an increase in activities; and on the other, in the absence of a centre and with the founder's encouragement, to foster independence as part of a markedly outward-looking approach which produced an abundance of initiatives, each different from the other and each aiming to function as an independent body. In the words of Jacques Loch, "Abbé Pierre was able to sense the vision, the charisma of each individual, and attempted to find a place where this vision could become a reality, at the risk of subdividing his own movement."[5] This attempt ultimately resulted in the development of an organisation whose internal structure was impossible for the uninitiated to decipher, but of an organisation which delved deep beneath the surface of and took a holistic approach to dealing with the problems linked to exclusion. Abbé Pierre's endeavours are also responsible for the fact that today the Emmaus groups in France together constitute the second largest French NGO in terms of the budget they manage, and the largest strictly non-governmental organisation. Furthermore, several other organisations, which started life in the bosom of Emmaus, have broken away from the Movement and become independent: CGL, IRAMM, ATD Fourth-World, *Artisans du monde* and UCOJUCO/*Peuples solidaires*.

Consequently, Emmaus today represents an astonishing range of activities: initiatives in aid of the homeless, sustainable development, fair trade, cooperatives, social and solidarity-based economies, access to credit, access to citizenship and the enjoyment of human rights, the fight against illiteracy, training, etc. The multifaceted nature of the organisation raises the question of its identity: besides Abbé Pierre, who is no longer alive, what are the cornerstones which make the Movement a solid, cohesive whole? For a long time, the concept of independence through work was one such cornerstone, but it often appeared impossible to put into practice in both the southern countries and in France itself, given that the three largest Emmaus organisations did not, strictly speaking, live off their work – Association Emmaus was heavily dependent on subsidies, Emmaus-Habitat on funding from the state and heads of business and the Abbé Pierre Foundation on donations. Emmaus worked both to prevent poverty and alleviate its symptoms, and provided both emergency assistance and longer-term development aid. The fundamental principle "serve first he who suffers most" is not peculiar to Emmaus, but could be said to characterise the majority of associations in the solidarity sector.

Thus, over the last twenty years, Emmaus has been forced to continually reinvent its identity. Abbé Pierre was the first to be challenged on the issue of Emmaus' national fundraising initiatives – "it was pointed out to him that the Movement was gradually adopting two lines, each of which contradicted the other, and that this was giving rise to confusion. On the one hand, Abbé Pierre would say: 'Emmaus asks for nothing, it lives off its work', and on the other, Abbé Pierre himself was asking for money"[6] – and on the issue of the creation of the Foundation which bore his name. ("Given that the Foundation was created to live off donations and not off the fruits of its own labour, Abbé Pierre was asked whether there was not in fact a paradox between these two attitudes. Abbé Pierre reminded those challenging him that the Foundation was in its early days and therefore requested that critics be as lenient as humanly possible.")[7] In 1992, Emmaus International began to conduct a far-reaching debate on the criteria which had to be fulfilled before an organisation could join the Movement. However, once again the Abbé urged members to be flexible. At a meeting of the Emmaus International executive committee on 27–28 September 1995, he declared, "let us avoid drawing up a rigid code, because we cannot anticipate every scenario that will be asked to consider."[8]

It would in fact appear that the three principles shared by the largest number of the Movement's members, and which together could thus be termed the cornerstone of the Emmaus identity, are: "getting men back on their feet" to make them self-sufficient and dignified beings, whether this be achieved through work or raising awareness of and/or allowing them to enjoy their rights; acting as "the voice of those whose who have no voice", because "poverty is dumb and power is blind"; and striving to ensure that the fight against the causes of poverty is never separated from the battle waged against its consequences.

## Challenges for the Future

One of the questions posed today, both within and outside Emmaus, relates to whether or the not the Movement will be able to continue developing without its charismatic founder. It is a legitimate question: in addition to the fact that he was without a doubt, one form of cement that held Emmaus together, Abbé Pierre, who was for a long time France's best-loved son, could say (almost) anything and remain (almost) untouchable, considered as he was to be an historic figure whose presence on the front line of every new battle was a source of amazement, a prophet of modern times and a national conscience. However, at an organisational level since the 1980s, whatever the legitimate concerns regularly reappearing, the Movement has been independent of its founder and firmly anchored by those at the bottom of the pyramid. It is an unshakeable body even if it must still digest the reforms currently under way: the disappearance of the seven "families" of communities was a defining moment in the Movement's history which, in the space of only a few years, made the organisation generated by fifty years of disputes and diversity into a homogeneous entity, with no rucks in its fabric. The centre of gravity, which had previously been firmly rooted in the world of the communities (today [2008] known as branch 1), has shifted spectacularly in two decades towards branch 2 (social action and housing), while the development of branch 3 (the solidarity-based economy and social integration) has gathered pace.

In terms of its relationship to the outside world, the challenge facing Emmaus, which since the late 1980s has adopted a deeply political identity, is to remain an "outraged conscience" at the forefront of new struggles without becoming overwhelmed by them, combative while remaining clear-sighted, and capable, beyond making political statements and unmasking the causes of poverty, of managing its consequences. Artfully meeting all of these challenges was undoubtedly what made Emmaus' positioning during the DAL rallies of the 1990s and those organised by *Les Enfants de Don Quichotte* in the 2000s so subtle. The strength of Emmaus in this regard lies in the fact that it has always succeeded in combining its criticism of the causes of social problems with proposed solutions that are viable, because they have been tested before being brought to the table. In this sense, Emmaus' politics echo those of *Secours catholique* which seeks to "trigger a process whereby legislation will be adapted to the problems currently facing society", and to be "an enquiring mind which [...] puts in place and tests out new solutions to global poverty": because "the charity of today, is the politics of tomorrow".[9]

However, while Emmaus has never played at being an idealistic reformer with Utopian visions of the future, or a campaigner denouncing anything and everything, the converse risk is that of blurring the lines between the "humanitarian" and "political" domains, despite the fact that since the late 1990s the former clearly appears to have become entirely independent from the latter.[10] In our view, this is a possible interpretation of the presidency of Martin Hirsch, who was able to catapult Emmaus to media stardom and ensure it was fully acknowledged in the books detailing the mysterious workings and legends of institutional history, while at the same time using it as a springboard and a lever to encourage experimentation in the fight against poverty. Having moved into the political sphere, chiefly in support of a president whose policies on immigration and the fight against exclusion made him an object of loathing so far as the Movement was concerned, he was inevitably partly disowned.

Finally, Emmaus faces two very specific challenges for the future; namely in the waste-collection and recycling sector. While the Movement was born through the collection of waste items of little interest to anybody, since the 1990s this has become a veritable economic market that is regulated and highly competitive. While since the early days of Emmaus, and even before the invention of the concept, the communities were a perfect example of the social and solidarity-based economy, today [2008] the Movement's economic hub, which allows social welfare to become a living, breathing reality, is increasingly under threat. Nevertheless, taking in and supporting those in need is more than ever the most important of Emmaus' principles, a philosophy of the Movement and by extension, a philosophy of society. As Jacques Loch once remarked in interview: "You know, when Abbé Pierre said, 'We need to say I need you to companions', he was like us, he didn't need the new companion who arrived on the doorstep; he was no more in need of the new faces that arrived every day than we were. OK, sometimes we were short of blokes to help us, drivers... but most of the time, we were fine. But the Abbé's 'I need you' was philosophical. It meant: 'I am happy to be forced to need you in order to live; you are useful, we will find the place which will be yours, the place where you will be happy to be.' And so far as I'm concerned, that's the sort of society, the sort of life, I want."

## Appendix 1: Emmaus implodes (1954-1961)

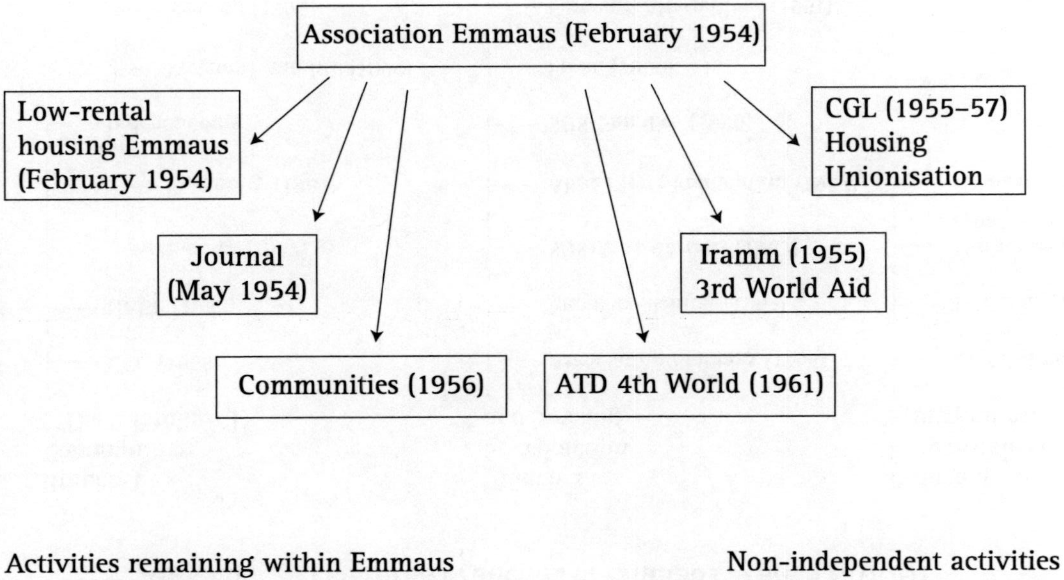

## Appendix 2: The three branches of Emmaus France (2008)

**Branch 1**
**Communities**
**("The 7 families")**

- UCC (1958)
- UACE (1962)
  - Liberty (1977)
  - Fraternity (1982)
- Independents
  - Welcome and life (1994)
  - Sharing (1995)
  - Nord-Pas-de-Calais (2002)

**Branch 2**
**Social action**
**and housing**

- Association Emmaus (1954)
- Emmaus-Habitat (1964)
- SOS-Milk Cartons (1963)
- Abbé Pierre Foundation (1987)
- SOS-Families (1990)
- Freha (1990)
- Emmaus-Alternatives (1991)

**Branch 3**
**Responsible economy**
**+ integration**

- CNAE (Friends Committees, 1980)
- Le Relais (1984)
- "Structures d'insertion" (1980–90)
- "Plates-formes textile" (1990)

# Notes

## INTRODUCTION

1. The so-called DALO law was finally passed on 5 March 2007.

2. See the Bibliography at the end of this book.

3. Survey: "Notoriété spontanée des ONG." 10 most frequently mentioned NGOs in descending order (1990): the Red Cross (55%), *Médecins sans frontières* (37%), *Les Restos du cœur* (32%), *Secours catholique* (24%), *Médecins du monde* (20%), UNICEF (18%) *Association de la recherche contre le cancer* (18%), Salvation Army (16%), *Secours populaire français* (14%), Amnesty International (13%).

4. In terms of 2005 budget, the Red Cross was far and away the largest organisation. Receiving extensive financial support, it had €910 million at its disposal. Emmaus was second (269 million), followed by *Secours catholique* (€130 million). All the other "large" humanitarian organisations (*MSF, CCFD, MDM, Secours populaire, ATD quart-monde, Cimade, Petits Frères des Pauvres...*) had an annual budget of less than €100 million.

5. These families which have historically made up Emmaus are currently being dissolved and merged into one "community branch."

6. See also Appendix 2 which depicts the major developments of the Emmaus organisation chart.

7. The only documents held at the *Centre des archives du monde du travail* (national archives) in Roubaix are the archives of Abbé Pierre (correspondence, activity reports of certain periods and certain bodies, photographs) and the Emmaus International archives up until 1988.

8. The opening of the *ATD quart-monde* archives, currently under way, should give fresh impetus to research in this area.

9. See the Bibliography at end of this book.

10. von Bueltzingloewen, Isabelle and Pelletier, Denis (eds), *La Charité en pratique. Chrétiens français et allemands sur le terrain social, XIXe–XXe siècle*, Strasbourg, Presses universitaires de Strasbourg, 1999; Gueslin, André et Guillaume, Pierre (eds), *De la charité médiévale à la sécurité sociale; l'économie de la protection sociale du Moyen Âge à l'époque contemporaine*, actes de colloque, Paris, Les Éditions ouvrières, 1992; Bec, Colette, Duprat, Catherine, Luc, Jean-Noël and Petit, Jacques-Guy (eds), *Philanthropes et politiques sociales en Europe, XVIIIe–XXe siècle*, Paris, Anthropos, 1994.

11. Gueslin, André, *Les Gens de rien. Histoire de la grande pauvreté dans la France du XXe siècle*, Paris, Fayard, 2004.

12. Paugam, Serge (ed.), *L'Exclusion. L'état des savoirs*, Paris, La Découverte, 1996 and Paugam, Serge, *La Société française et ses pauvres*, Paris, PUF, 1993; Thomas, Hélène, *La Production des exclus*, Paris, PUF, 1997; Bec, Colette, *L'Assistance en démocratie. Les politiques assistantielles dans la France des* XIX^e^ *et* XX^e^ *siècles*, Paris, Belin, 1998; Damon, Julien, *La Question SDF. Critique d'une action publique*, Paris, PUF, 2002 and *Vagabondage et mendicité*, Flammarion, coll. "Dominos", 1998; Merrien, François-Xavier, *Face à la pauvreté*, Paris, Les Éditions de l'Atelier/Les Éditions ouvrières, 1994; Vincent, Gilbert (ed.), *La Place des œuvres et des acteurs religieux dans les dispositifs de protection sociale. De la charité à la solidarité*, Paris, L'Harmattan, 1997.

13. Brodiez, Axelle, *Le Secours populaire français, 1945–2000: du communisme à l'humanitaire*, Paris, Presses de Sciences Po, 2006; Dubrulle, Luc, *Mgr Rodhain et le Secours catholique: une figure sociale de la charité*, doctoral thesis in the history of religions, religious anthropology and theology, Paris, Institut catholique de Paris, February 2007 (thesis published under the title *Monseigneur Rodhain et la charité*, Paris, Desclée de Brouwer, 2008).

14. Fourastié, Jean, *Le Trente Glorieuses, ou la Révolution invisible de 1946 à 1975*, Paris, Fayard, 1979.

15. *Les Exclus. Un Français sur dix*, Paris, Seuil, 1974.

16. See in particular the works of Jean Labbens published in the 1960s.

17. Interview with Abbé Pierre in *Convergence* (monthly magazine of *Secours populaire*), October 1991.

18. *Le Quart-Monde. La condition sous-prolétarienne*, Paris, Éditions Science et service, 1969, p. 273.

19. Chartier, Roger, "La pauvreté à l'âge moderne (XVI^e^–XVIII^e^ siècles). Définitions, représentations, institutions", in Fracassi, Alain, Marquès, Marie-France and Walter, Jacques (eds), *La Pauvreté, une approche plurielle*, Paris, Éditions ESF, 1985, p. 26.

20. *Histoire sociale: exclusions et solidarité*. Inaugural lecture at the Collège de France, Paris, Éditions du Collège de France, 1993, p. 15.

21. Blandenier, Jacques, *Les Pauvres avec nous. La lutte contre la pauvreté selon la Bible et l'histoire de l'Église*, Éditions LLB, 2006.

22. Gospel according to Luke XVI:19–31.

23. Gospel according to Luke VI:20–6; Gospel according to Matthew V:1–12 and XXV:31–46.

24. Leviticus XIX:18; Gospel according to Matthew XIX:19 and XXII:39; Gospel according to Mark XII:31 and XII:33; Gospel according to Luke X:27.

25. This differs from the Protestant interpretation, where faith is the only source of salvation.

26. Bernard Chevallier interview with Abbé Pierre, *Emmaüs ou venger l'homme*, Paris, Le Centurion, 1979, p. 35.

27. *Ibid.*, p. 30.

28. Quoted Desmard, Laurent in Abbé Pierre. *Images d'une vie*, Paris, Hoëbeke, 2006, p. 83.

29. Founder and first Secretary-General of *Secours catholique*.

30. Dubrulle, Luc, *Mgr Rodhain et le Secours catholique: une figure sociale de la charité*, thesis referenced.

31. "The social figure includes the actors, their practices and their representations, as well as the social image of the group which together these form [...]. We see the figure as comprising both the individual act of a person and the action of a group as whole", in Dubrulle, Luc, thesis referenced.

32. Integralism can be defined as "Catholicism's desire to provide an answer to all human questions, its desire to sow the seeds of and inspire all aspects of the life of societies and the existence each individual"; intransigentism can be defined as "Catholic philosophy's unequivocal rejection of the founding principles and values of modern thought" (Donegani, Jean-Marie, *La Liberté de choisir. Pluralisme religieux et pluralisme politique dans le catholicisme français contemporain*, Paris, Presses de Sciences Po, 1993, p. 173). These concepts were an integral part of the historiography of Catholicism in the 1970s and 1980s.

33. Dubrulle, Luc, thesis referenced, p. 298.

34. Roubaix, CAMT, 2000 050 1104, GA, 2–4 July 1971.

35. *Faim et Soif*, supplement to issue 19, January/February 1972.

36. A Catholic authority which functions as a watchdog, a place for debate and a body coordinating initiatives in aid of the poor. It was created in 1989 by the bishops of France and includes the *CCFD, les Petits Frères des Pauvres, le Secours catholique* and *St. Vincent de Paul Conferences*, among others.

37. Barles, Sabine, *L'Invention des déchets urbains, France: 1790–1970*, Seyssel, Champ Vallon, 2005 and de Silguy, Catherine, *Histoire des hommes et de leurs ordures du Moyen Âge à nos jours*, Paris, Le Cherche Midi, 1996.

38. Sylvie Bretel-Deluze, "De la décharge au tri à la source: évolution de la gestion des déchets municipaux", in Bertrand, Jean-René (ed.), *De la décharge à la déchetterie. Questions de géographie des déchets*, Rennes, Presses universitaires de Rennes, 2003, p. 59–87.

39. Seveso in 1976, l'Amoco-Cadiz in 1978, Chernobyl in 1986...

## CHAPTER 1

1. Violet, Bernard, *L'Abbé Pierre*, Paris, Fayard, 2004, p. 251.

2. Bernard Chevallier interview with Abbé Pierre, *Emmaüs ou venger l'homme*, Paris, Le Centurion, 1979, p. 46–7.

3. Chevallier, Bernard, *Emmaüs ou venger l'homme, op. cit.*, p. 15–16.

4. Formed from the merger of the *Société des hospitaliers*, created in 1763, and the *Société des veilleurs*, created in 1830, this association which worked at parish level tended to both the medical and spiritual needs of the sick in hospices and parishes. It also looked after those who were both sick and poor in their homes. On Sundays, it handed out tobacco, bread and clothes to the destitute and provided them with care.

5. Chevallier, Bernard, *op. cit.*, p. 14.

6. Gospel according to Matthew XXV:35–6.

7. *Ibid.*, XIX:30; see also Luke XIII:30.

8. Gospel according to Luke VI:20–6; see also Matthew V:1–12.

9. Chevallier Bernard, *op. cit.*, p. 43: "It is quite extraordinary to think how realistic this name was and just how accurate a glimpse it gave in to the future, when you consider that I was to spend so much of my life building, and so much of my life meditating."

10. *Op. cit.*, p. 44.

11. Chevallier Bernard, *op. cit.*, p. 25.

12. *Ibid.*, p. 26–7.

13. *Ibid.*, p. 27.

14. Violet, Bernard, *op. cit.*

15. Bernard Chevallier, *op. cit.*, p. 50.

16. *Ibid.*, p. 52.

17. On this and the following paragraphs, see the Diocesan Archives of Grenoble, attestation paper from the military government of Lyon dated 15 January 1945, attesting to Abbé Pierre's involvement in the Resistance.

18. Compulsory Work Service.

19. Diocesan Archives of Grenoble, attestation paper from the military government of Lyon dated 15 January 1945, attesting to Abbé Pierre's involvement in the Resistance.

20. On Lucie Coutaz, see *Faim et Soif*, 66, September 1982.

21. Diocesan Archives of Grenoble, attestation paper from the military government of Lyon dated 15 January 1945, attesting to Abbé Pierre's involvement in the Resistance.

22. Abbé Pierre, in Chevallier, Bernard, *op. cit.*, p. 78.

23. Title of a conference given by Abbé Pierre at Le Palais de Chaillot, 1945.

24. *Faim et Soif*, 66, September 1982.

25. Desmard, Laurent, *Abbé Pierre, images d'une vie*, Paris, Hoëbeke, 2006, p. 28.

26. Chevallier, Bernard, *op. cit.*, p. 159.

27. *Jeunesse ouvrière chrétienne (JOC)* and *Jeunesse étudiante catholique (JEC)*.

28. This is according to Boris Simon, *Les Chiffonniers d'Emmaüs*, Paris, Seuil, 1954. However, according to other sources this status was granted in Easter 1950.

29. Abbé Pierre, quoted in Montalbetti, Marcel, *Historique de la communauté Emmaüs de Cernay, 1955–1982*, Emmaüs-Cernay, 2004, p. 7.

30. It would appear that the most reliable source is the earliest one available: *Message des compagnons et des amis des commmunautés, de l'Auberge et des cités, 1, April 1953* (referenced by Balista, José, *Emmaüs et l'Abbé Pierre. Mythe, utopie et emprise charismatique*, thesis in sociology, EHESS, 1976, p. 68). Therefore, the work of Boris Simon which refers to spring must be revised, along with that of Pierre Lunel which mentions before August, that

of Laurent Desmard which refers to September and that of Bernard Violet which mentions November.

31. *Faim et Soif*, 69, 1966, p. 17.

32. *Op. cit.*, p. 163–4.

33. *Ibid.*, p. 166.

34. Interview with Henri Camus.

35. *La Grande Aventure d'Emmaüs*, Paris, Grasset, 1969, p. 24–5.

36. 23 and 29 December according to Boris Simon; two consecutive days according to Laurent Desmard. He is thought to have begged first on Boulevard Saint-Germain, and then on Boulevard Saint-Denis (Desmard, Laurent, *op. cit.*, p. 31).

37. Baron Empain declared that were the association to dissolve, the house was to remain the property of the Church; a new association allowing *Secours catholique* to come on board was consequently created, after consultation with Cardinal Feltin and Mgr Rodhain, who would assist *Secours catholique* with its (abortive) attempts to infiltrate Emmaus and poach its recruits.

38. On the key figures and day-to-day life within Emmaus at the time, cf. Lunel, Pierre, *L'Abbé Pierre, l'insurgé de Dieu*, Paris, Stock, 1989.

39. *L'Abbé Pierre, l'insurgé..., op. cit.*, p. 261–2.

40. Information letter, 59, December 1987, p. 28.

41. *Ibid.*

42. Lunel, Pierre, *L'Abbé Pierre, l'insurgé..., op. cit.*, p. 94–5.

43. *Ibid.*, p. 90.

44. *Ibid.*, p. 91.

45. Chevallier, Bernard, *op. cit.*, p. 174.

46. The tents distributed by *Médecins du monde* since summer 2006, those erected by *Les Enfants de Don Quichotte* in winter 2006 and those set up by the DAL since the early 1990s appear to have their precedent...

47. *Les Chiffonniers..., op. cit.*, p. 66–7.

48. *La Grande Aventure d'Emmaüs, op. cit.*, p. 26.

49. The community model is in no way uncharacteristic of the history of Christianity, on the contrary: "the community utopia is commonplace throughout the modern history of Catholicism, since the Catholic faith viewed it as a model which challenged the dominant order" (Pelletier, Denis, *La Crise catholique. Religion, société, politique en France (1965–1978)*, Paris, Payot, 2002, p. 121). Nevertheless, since the early 1950s, the model has only rarely been used.

50. Reports by Gérard Marin, published 4 January 1954.

51. *L'Abbé Pierre, l'insurgé..., op. cit.*, p. 135–6.

52. Around €17,800.

53. On the circumstances under which the appeal was developed, see Georges Verpraet, "L'histoire oubliée de l'appel de 1954", *La Croix*, 31 January 2004, article reprinted in *La Croix*, 23 January 2007.

54. The Abbé read out the half of the text which he had written, and Georges Verpraet his part. Due to the urgent need for a statement, each man had worked on a section of the text and each was only able to decipher his own handwriting. (*Fêtes et Saisons*, special issue, 1955, p. 7.)

55. This is the end of the section written by the Abbé. It is immediately followed by the section penned by Georges Verpraet (see the facsimile printed in *Faim et Soif*, 1 May 1954).

56. *La Souffrance à distance. Morale humanitaire, médias et politique*, Paris, Métailié, 1993, p. 42.

57. Bazar de l'hôtel de ville, opposite the town hall in Paris.

58. Saint-Martin, Liège, Rennes, Champ de Mars.

59. 176 million in today's euros.

60. Balista, José, *Emmaüs et l'abbé Pierre. Mythe, utopie et emprise charismatique*, thesis referenced.

61. 5 billion according to Bernard Violet; 2,408 million according to Sabine Effosse, *L'Invention du logement aidé en France. L'immobilier au temps des Trente Glorieuses*, Paris, Comité pour l'histoire économique et financière de la France, 2003. However, it appears that the accurate figures are those given by Marin and Bonnet (2.2 billion).

62. Viet, Vincent and Guerrand, Roger-Henri, *Sociétés anonymes d'HLM depuis 1853. Une certaine philosophie de l'action privée pour une mission d'intérêt général*, Paris, Fédération nationale des sociétés anonymes et fondations HLM, 1997.

63. According to Marin and Bonnet, *op. cit.*, Chapter 6.

64. Interview with Henri Camus.

65. *Fêtes et saisons*, special issue, 1955, p. 10.

66. *Op. cit.*, p. 5.

67. Barthes, Roland, "Iconographie de l'abbé Pierre," in *Mythologies*, Paris, Seuil, 1957, p. 54.

68. Barthes, Roland, "Iconographie de l'abbé Pierre," in *Mythologies*, *op. cit.*, p. 55.

69. Such was the case with his walking stick, which he never used to walk. Originally, he used it for one thing only; defending himself against the violent outburst from the Companions... He later kept it as a symbol.

70. Chabaud, Céline, *Hiver 1954: l'apparition de l'abbé Pierre et d'Emmaüs dans la conscience sociale française*, Master's thesis, Université Paris-X Nanterre, 1998.

71. *Op. cit.*, p. 55–6.

72. *Faim et Soif*, 4 December 1954.

73. The film is based on the book *Les Chiffonniers d'Emmaüs*, by Boris Simon (author of teen fiction), following several periods of time he spent in the Neuilly-Plaisance community in 1952–3. The work, which was published in January 1954, narrates community life in the early days of Emmaus by referring to accounts given in secret by Companions and making them anonymous.

In the film, the role of Abbé Pierre is played by André Reybaz and Gaby Morlay plays Lucie Coutaz, to a soundtrack written by Joseph Kosma.

74. €2.6 million.

75. €7 million.

76. €17.6 million.

77. *Op. cit.*, p. 192, 195.

## CHAPTER 2

1. Article for *Faim et Soif*, March 1957.

2. Gérard Marin and Roland Bonnet, *op. cit.*, p. 250–2.

3. Born in 1913, former lawyer Guy Houist was representative at the Ministry for Reconstruction and Town Planning (1947–8), then assistant private secretary at the Ministry of the Merchant Navy (1949) and private secretary at the Ministry for Work and Social Security (1950). He later left the ministries to take up posts in various associations: President of the *Committee of Housing of the National Union of Families* (1950–), delegate of the *International Union of Family Organizations to the European Organisation of Economic Cooperation* (1953–6). Member of the board of directors at Association Emmaus from 1954 to the 1960, at the same time he was the president of the *Federation of Family Holiday Homes* (1955–), co-founder of the *National Union of Hostels for Young Workers* (1955) and founding member of the first board of directors of the *Compagnons Bâtisseurs* (1957). See Arnaud Loustalot, thesis in history on associations in the construction sector which is currently under way.

4. The building still exists and continues to house the headquarters of Association Emmaus archives. Today, the Association Agora is next door in the same building, providing support to the homeless.

5. Association Emmaus archives, CA, 27 October 1956.

6. See below.

7. See the following chapter.

8. Michel Mouillart, "Le logement comme catégorie éonomique," in Ségaud, Marion, Bonvalet, Catherine and Brun, Jacques (eds), *Logement et habitat. L'état des savoirs*, Paris, la Découverte, 1998, p. 59–67.

9. Michel Mouillart, "Le logement comme catégorie éonomique," in Ségaud, Marion, Bonvalet, Catherine and Brun, Jacques (eds), *Logement et habitat. L'état des savoirs*, *op. cit.*

10. Bosvieux, Jean, "Besoins et demande de logement," in Ségaud, Marion, Bonvalet, Catherine and Brun, Jacques, (eds), *Logement et habitat. L'état des savoirs*, *op. cit.*, p. 86–93. These figures differ slightly from those which appear in Viet, Vincent and Guerrand, Roger-Henri, *Sociétés anonymes d'HLM depuis 1853. Une certaine philosophie de l'action privée pour une mission d'intérêt général*, *op. cit.*, 1997. According to this work, 457,000 homes were destroyed and 719,000 were damaged.

11. Effosse, Sabine, *L'Invention du logement aidé en France. L'immobilier au temps des Trente Glorieuses, op. cit.*

12. This decree made the system of voluntary contributions towards housing which some employers' unions had introduced mandatory. It forced all firms with more than ten employees to contribute 1% of their wage bill to housing. Employers could choose how to make this contribution from a wide variety of options open to them. They could partially fund their own building projects or contribute to those carried out by a property company in which it could take out shares. It could also make payments to organisations authorised to collect funds for housing and grant subsidies or direct loans to the employees themselves in order to supplement those issued by the mortgage bank *Crédit foncier.*

13. Mouillart, Michel, "Le logement comme catégorie économique," article referenced, p. 64.

14. Bosvieux, Jean, "Besoins et demande de logements," article referenced.

15. Viet, Vincent and Guerrand, Roger-Henri, *op. cit.*

16. Emmaus-Habitat archives, GA, 26 June 1956.

17. Issue 9, October 1955.

18. €88, €150 and €17.6 million, respectively.

19. Association Emmaus archives, CA, 23 July 1954.

20. Simon, Boris, *Les Chiffonniers d'Emmaüs, op. cit.*

21. Emmaus-Habitat archives, GA, 26 June 1958.

22. The equivalents of €375,000 and €114,000, respectively.

23. Emmaus-Habitat archives, CA, 5 November 1957.

24. *Ibid.*

25. *Faim et Soif,* 17, March 1957.

26. *Faim et Soif,* 46, second quarter 1977.

27. Note referenced in Montalbetti, Marcel, *Historique de la communauté Emmaüs de Cernay, 1955–1982, op. cit.*, 2004.

28. *Faim et Soif,* 46, second quarter 1977.

29. Association Emmaus archives, CA, 2 February 1955.

30. *Faim et Soif,* 22 February 1958.

31. Emmaus International information letter, 66, November 1989, Father Barral's story, p. 30.

32. Association Emmaus archives, CA, 2 February 1955.

33. *L'Abbé Pierre, l'insurgé..., op. cit.*, p. 222.

34. Association Emmaus archives, CA, 27 October 1956.

35. See above.

36. Lunel, Pierre, *Abbé Pierre. Mes images de bonheur, de misère et d'amour,* Paris, Fixot, 1994.

37. Emmaus International information letter, 66, November 1989, "Jules' story," p. 37.

38. Gérard Marin and Roland Bonnet, *La Grande Aventure d'Emmaüs, op. cit.*, p. 289.

39. €2.7 million.

40. *L'Abbé Pierre, Quarante ans d'amour*, Paris, Éditions n° 1, 1992, p. 475.

41. *L'Abbé Pierre, Quarante ans d'amour, op. cit.*, p. 112.

42. Interview with Yves Godard: "He was my guru."

43. *L'Abbé Pierre. Mes images..., op. cit.*, p. 115.

44. Weber, Max, *L'Éthique protestante et l'esprit du capitalisme*, Paris, Plon, 1964. See the following chapter.

45. *Faim et Soif*, 2, August 1954.

46. de la Gorce, Francine, *L'Espoir gronde. Noisy-le-Grand, 1956–1962*, Paris, Éditions ATD quart-monde, 1992.

47. *L'Espoir gronde. Noisy-le-Grand, 1956–1962, op. cit.*, p. 38.

48. de la Gorce, Francine, *L'Espoir gronde. Noisy-le-Grand, op. cit.*, p. 87.

49. *Ibid.*, p. 102.

50. Emmaus-Habitat archives, CA, 8 January 1959.

51. de la Gorce, Francine, *L'Espoir gronde. Noisy-le-Grand, op. cit.*

52. Paris-presse, *L'Intransigeant*, 18 April 1959.

53. The concept of "the right to housing" was explicitly enshrined in law for the first time in 1990 (Besson Law).

54. On the history of the squat, see in particular Péchu, Cécile, *Droit au logement. Génèse et sociologie d'une mobilisation*, Paris, Dalloz, 2006, Chapter 5; "Dans le combat ouvrier, Le Mouvement Populaire des families dans les Bouches-du-Rhône, 1941–1951," Cahiers du GRMF, 13, 2004.

55. Lunel, Pierre, *L'Abbé Pierre, Quarante ans..., op. cit.*

56. Recorded account from Abbé Pierre, "L'abbé Pierre infiniment," CD 2, produced jointly by Emmaus International, Pierre Lunel and Edition Escale.

57. This camp was also reminiscent, of course, of the DAL camps and of those set up by *Enfants de Don Quichotte* today.

58. Lunel, Pierre, *L'Abbé Pierre, Quarante ans..., op. cit.*

59. On the chronological development of the squats, see Raillard, Alain, *Chronologie de la CGL.*

60. Second UNASL congress, 27 November 1955.

61. Statement by Roger Dauphin at the November 1955 congress, quoted in *Faim et Soif*, 10, December 1955.

62. *Ibid.*

63. *Faim et Soif*, 16, December 1956.

64. *Faim et Soif*, 28, March 1959.

65. *Faim et Soif*, 23, April 1958.

66. *Faim et Soif*, 16, December 1956.

67. *Faim et Soif*, 20, September 1957.

68. *Faim et Soif*, 6, April 1955, on Nantes; 7, June 1955, on Marseilles; 8, September 1955, on Saint-Étienne; 13, June 1956, on Brest; 14, August 1956, on Lyon; 15, September 1956, on Limoges; 17, March 1957, on Dijon, etc.

69. Pelletier, Denis, *"Économie et humanisme". De l'utopie communautaire au combat pour le Tiers-monde*, Paris, Éditions du Cerf, 1996.

70. Mabille, François, *Approches de l'internationalisme catholique*, Paris, L'Harmattan, 2001.

71. Mabille, François, *op. cit.*

72. On Father Lebret and "Economics and humanism" see Pelletier, Denis *"Économie et humanisme"...*, *op. cit.*

73. International Bank for Reconstruction and Development.

74. *Faim et Soif*, 29, September–October 1973, p. 21.

75. *Faim et Soif*, 20, September 1957, p. 27.

76. *Faim et Soif*, 16, December 1956.

77. *Défection et prise de parole. Théories et applications*, Paris, Fayard, 1995.

## CHAPTER 3

1. Chevallier, Bernard *op. cit.*, p. 153–4.

2. Marin, Gérard Marin and Bonnet, *op. cit.*, p. 193.

3. Here, the original text uses terminology coined by Max Weber in *L'Éthique protestante et l'esprit du capitalisme*, Paris, Plon, 1964.

4. Association Emmaus archives, CA, 2 February 1955.

5. Dubrulle, Luc, *op. cit.*, p. 330.

6. Dubrulle, Luc, *op. cit.*, p. 333.

7. Abbé Pierre's private file, minutes of the meeting at Rives-de-Prangins, 30 December 1957.

8. Lunel, Pierre, *L'Abbé Pierre, Quarante ans...*, *op. cit.*, p. 248–9.

9. "In December 1957, Abbé Pierre was ordered by his superiors to go into a Swiss clinic and follow the instructions of the surgeon general...." An extract from Balista, José, thesis referenced, p. 150.

10. Decision of 30 December 1957 (Abbé Pierre's private file, minutes of the meeting held 30 December 1957 at Rives-de-Prangins).

11. Abbé Pierre with Lenoir, Frédéric, *Mon Dieu... pourquoi? Petites méditations sur la foi chrétienne et le sens de la vie*, Paris, Plon, 2005, p. 26.

12. *Op. cit.*, p. 240.

13. *L'Abbé Pierre, Quarante ans...*, *op. cit.*, p. 214.

14. *Op. cit.*, p. 26.

15. According to Olivier Gorce, this expression is thought to have been coined by Abbé Pierre and used only at that time. *L'Abbé Pierre. Le missionnaire de l'impossible*, Geps, coll. "Les dessous de l'histoire," hors série, 3, p. 78.

16. Association Emmaus, CA, 23 July 1954.

17. No history of the Rives-de-Prangins clinic has thus far been produced. However, we do know that this private clinic for mental health problems, created by Dr Oscar Forel, himself the son of the famous Swiss psychiatrist Auguste Forel, was opened in 1930 and located on the banks of Lake Geneva. Famous and very exclusive, it came to be attended by famous figures who came from across Europe. Oscar Foret was interested in all available treatments and sought to modernise psychiatric care. In 1946, he offered the position of clinic director/doctor to Dr Charles Durand, a French neuropsychiatrist who up until that point had been the head of clinic at Sainte-Anne psychiatric hospital (Paris). Dr Durand would care for Abbé Pierre. Having decided very early on to go into psychoanalysis, he was known among the psychiatric profession as an open man. Information very kindly provided by Catherine Fussinger, a historian specialising in the history of psychiatry and the head of research at the University Institute of the History of Medicine and Health in Lausanne, Switzerland.

18. The private file of Abbé Pierre, minutes of the meeting held on 30 December 1957 at Rives-de-Prangins: Decision "1) Abbé Pierre will return to his usual environment in Paris until formally given permission to do so by the doctor responsible for his care; 2) Until he returns, Abbé Pierre will live in a place decided upon by this doctor in the company of both an associate and his secretary, Miss Coutaz (59 years of age); 3) In order to fill this post of temporary associate, the Church hierarchy will be called upon to appoint a qualified member of the clergy. In view of the fact that this person will be asked to work closely with the doctor, the appointment will be made with the doctor's agreement; 4) Whilst this person is being appointed, we call upon Reverend Father Monnier (who has for some months now had the permission of his Province to dedicate a significant amount of his time to Emmaus) to kindly take up the post on a temporary basis; 5) During this period, the doctor treating Abbé Pierre will remain solely responsible for deciding which activities the Abbé will be allowed to undertake. In making such decisions, he will evaluate which activities are compatible with and useful for the treatment process; 6) this system can only be altered or terminated when the doctor deems it necessary and after a meeting identical to the one held today."

19. Letter from Dr Durand to Abbé Pierre dated 12 January 1958 (Abbé Pierre's private file), followed by a letter from Dr Durand to Mgr Fougerat dated 14 January 1958 (quoted by Lunel, Pierre, *L'Abbé Pierre, Quarante ans... op. cit.*, p. 348).

20. Letter from Abbé Pierre to Dr Durand dated 21 January 1958 (quoted by Lunel, Pierre, *L'Abbé Pierre, Quarante ans...*, *op. cit.*, p. 353).

21. Letter from Abbé Pierre (draft?) undated and no addressee, but seemingly written to Jean Bouchy in early July 1958 (Abbé Pierre's private file).

22. Letter from Abbé Pierre to Abbé Zundel, undated but seemingly written mid-April 1958 (Abbé Pierre's private file).

23. *L'Abbé Pierre, Quarante ans...*, *op. cit.*, p. 357–8.

24. Association Emmaus archives.

25. Association Emmaus archives, private note to the board from Yves Gousault dated 20 September 1958.

26. *Ibid.*

27. Abbé Pierre's private file, letters from Abbé Zundel to Abbé Pierre, undated but can be dated back to mid-April 1958.

28. Abbé Pierre's private file, letter from Abbé Pierre (draft?) undated and no addressee, seemingly written to Jean Bouchy in early July 1958.

29. The private letter to the board from Yves Goussault provided clarification on a very important point regarding the financial mechanisms adopted during the General Assembly held on 1 March: "It was after much hesitation that some of us ultimately accepted the responsibility which they were asked to shoulder. Namely, that of ensuring that the association's activities received the practical resources and moral support necessary to continue [...]. Their decision to accept this responsibility was based on a fundamental clause, clearly stated and understood: through the figure of his friend, Mr Bouchy, Abbé Pierre was to give the board total power of attorney and temporarily surrender any of the financial or practical responsibilities involved in managing Emmaus. [...]. It was also made clear that the power of attorney in question related to Abbé Pierre's bank account and even his personal correspondence. This sensitive clause in no way constituted a bullying tactic designed to facilitate some sort of humiliating and useless 'checks', but was made necessary by the fact that Abbé Pierre had ensured that he and the Movement were almost one and the same, that new activities continued to develop which bore the founder's name, a system which Emmaus voluntarily kept in place. The large cheques which continued (and continue) to be sent to the organisation are almost always made out to Abbé Pierre himself."

30. Thesis referenced, p. 151.

31. Association Emmaus archives, GA, 25 October 1958.

32. Association Emmaus archives, CA, 6 October 1959.

33. These terms were coined by Antoine Sueur, former leader of the Caen community and national secretary of the UCC. Today he is the leader of the "community branch."

34. *L'Abbé Pierre. Quarante ans...*, *op. cit.*, p. 362.

35. *Op. cit.*, p. 255.

36. Association Emmaus archives, letter from Georges Lillaz to Jean Bouchy, dated 12 February 1959.

37. See in particular Olivier Gorce: "in summer, Miss Coutaz was stripped of her duties within the Association and thrown out onto the streets," *op. cit.*, p. 87.

38. Private note from Yves Goussault to the Emmaus board, dated 20 September 1958.

## CHAPTER 4

1. Initially, the Movement operated in Seine, Seine-et-Oise and Seine-et-Marne. After the electoral districts were redrawn on 10 July 1964, the

Movement was active in the administrative departments currently known as Paris, Seine-Saint-Denis, Val-de-Marne, Hauts-de-Seine, Essonne, Yvelines, Val-d'Oise and Seine-et-Marne.

2. Emmaus-Habitat archives, CA, 15 June 1960.

3. Emmaus-Habitat archives, GA, 22 June 1967.

4. de la Gorce, Francine, *Un peuple se lève (1963–1968)*, Paris, Éditions ATD quart-monde, 1995.

5. de la Gorce, Francine, *Un peuple se lève, op. cit.*

6. Between 1954 and 1963, the percentage of residents under the age of ten went from 50% to 40%, whilst the percentage of teenagers increased from 15% to 28% (Labbens, Jean, *La Condition sous-prolétarienne.* L'héritage du passé, Paris, Éditions ATD quart-monde, 1965).

7. De la Gorce, Francine, *Un people se lève, op. cit.*

8. *Ibid.*

9. Labbens, Jean, *La Condition sous-prolétarienne..., op. cit.*

10. *Op. cit.*, p. 136.

11. *Op. cit.*, p. 169–71.

12. *Op. cit.*, p. 198–9.

13. €430,000.

14. Emmaus-Habitat archives, CA, 18 May 1972.

15. Emmaus-Habitat archives, CA, 19 December 1972.

16. On this issue, see in particular the work of Marie-Claude Blanc-Chaléard.

17. Paugam, Serge, *La Société française et ses pauvres. L'expérience du revenu minimum d'insertion*, Paris, PUF, 2002 [1st edition 1993], p. 48.

18. Bosvieux, Jean "Besoins et demande de logement," article referenced.

19. Clanché, François and Fribourg, Anne-Marie, "Grandes évolutions du parc et des ménages depuis 1950," in Ségaud, Marion, Bonvallet, Catherine and Brun, Jacques (eds), *Logement et habitat, op. cit.*, p. 77–85.

20. *Faim et Soif*, 56, January–February 1964.

21. GA, 27 June 1968.

22. Emmaus-Habitat archives, CA, 6 February 1962.

23. *Ibid.*

24. Emmaus-Habitat archives, CA, 6 May 1971.

25. Emmaus-Habitat archives, CA, 5 March 1970.

26. Emmaus-Habitat archives, GA, 11 June 1970.

27. Office Central Interprofessionnel du Logement.

28. Emmaus-Habitat archives, CA, 19 December 1973.

29. Danièle Voldman, "Le toit," in Rioux, Jean-Pierre and Sirinelli, Jean-François Sirinelli (eds), *La France d'un siècle à l'autre. 1914–2000. Dictionnaire critique*, Paris, Hachette, 1999, p. 307.

30. Stébé, Jean-Marc, *Le Logement social en France*, Paris, PUF, 1998.

31. Emmaus-Habitat archives, CA, 20 May 1975.

32. *Ibid.*

33. UACE archives, speech given by Abbé Pierre during the Friends-Leaders meeting, 5 September 1975.

34. The Paris Chamber of Commerce and Industry, EDF, *Polymécanique* and *Sudaviation* (later renamed *Aérospatiale*).

35. APEC, Cilvama, Paris region branch of CIL and UGIP.

36. Not including the unknown figures for Xavier Colas des Francs and Pierre Join-Lambert.

37. This more exclusive accommodation took the form of both HLM (*Habitations à loyers modérés*) – and ILN – (*Immeubles à loyers normaux*.)

38. Emmaus-Habitat archives, CA, 19 December 1973.

39. Association Emmaus archives, GA, 22 May 1964.

40. CA, 23 April 1964.

## CHAPTER 5

1. Whilst the administrative headquarters were from the very beginning at Rue des Bourdonnais, from an administrative perspective the social headquarters remained at Neuilly-Plaisance until late 1961.

2. UCC archives, GA, 7 March 1959.

3. UCC archives, GA, 7 March 1959.

4. This was the view expressed at the Leaders meeting held in Limoges on 11 and 12 May 1956.

5. UCC archives, GA, November 1976, report on the housing conditions of UCC employees.

6. Interview.

7. Board of directors, 26 and 27 January 1974.

8. UCC archives, GA, 1962.

9. UCC archives, GA, 7 March 1959.

10. UCC archives, 1974 general assembly.

11. The FNCHRS was renamed the FNARS in 1977 (National Federation of Associations for Support and Social Reintegration.)

12. Which would later move to Berne.

13. UCC archives, subject of the national meeting held in April 1973.

14. Printed in *Faim et Soif*, 32, March–April 1974.

15. UCC archives, GA, 27–28 April 1968.

16. UACE archives, Friends-Leaders meeting, 25 January 1978. The two extracts in italics are capitalised in the original text.

17. Who later became secretary, president and treasurer, respectively.

18. See Chapter 7.

19. *Faim et Soif*, 24, November–December 1972.

20. See Chapter 2, "L'aventure des itinérantes de Normandie."

21. UACE archives, Friends-Leaders meeting.

22. UACE archives, Friends-Leaders meeting, 31 March 1977.

23. UACE archives, bureau meeting, 27 July 1972.

24. UACE archives, committee meeting, 18 March 1972.

25. Emmaus International information letter, 59, December 1987, p. 29.

26. Gérard Marin and Roland Bonnet, *op. cit.*, Chapter 8.

27. *Faim et Soif*, supplement, 19, January–February 1972.

28. *Faim et Soif*, 1974.

29. UACE archives, Friends-Leaders meeting.

30. *Défection et prise de parole. Théorie et applications*, Paris, Fayard, 1995 [original edition: *Exit, Voice and Loyalty. Responses to Decline in Firms, Organizations and States*, Cambridge, MA, Harvard University Press, 1970).

31. Roubaix, CAMT, 2000 050 0469 (Raimbeaucourt).

32. *Ibid.*

33. Interview with Pierre Duponchel.

34. 35–36, September–December 1974.

35. In 1965, the Catholic Church authorised the reintroduction of worker-priests.

36. *Chemins d'Emmaüs*, Paris, Cerf, 1988, p. 84.

37. UACE archives, GA, 5 December 1978.

38. Emmaus-Liberté, manifesto, 1979.

39. Henri le Bouriscaud, Communautés d'Emmaüs, Marquain (Belgique), Éditions Jules Hovine, 1984.

40. In the usual sense of the word, not in the sense that it was given by Abbé Pierre.

41. All quotations which follow are also taken from an interview with Yves Godard.

42. The term "Federation" is used to refer to the groups which, legally speaking, are Associations (UCC, UACE) and the term "Family" is used for the others.

43. Hatzfeld, Hélène, *Faire de la politique autrement. Les expériences inachevées des années 1970*, Rennes, PUR, 2005.

44. Lacroix, Bernard, *L'Utopie communautaire. Mai 68, histoire sociale d'une révolte*, Paris, PUF, 1981.

45. Pelletier, Denis, *Économie et Humanisme..., op. cit.*

46. On liberation theology, see Chapter 7.

47. Hatzfeld, Hélène, *Faire de la politique autrement. Les expériences inachevées des années 1970, op. cit.*

48. Pelletier, Denis, *La Crise catholique..., op. cit.*

49. Emmaus-Liberté, manifesto, 12 September 1979.

50. UACE archives, CA, 18 March 1982, provisional charter of Emmaus-Fraternité

51. Laurent Desmard would go on to become a UCC Community leader and later the private secetary of Abbé Pierre.

52. UCC archives, GA, 2 December 1973.

53. Interview.

54. *Ibid.*

55. *Ibid.*

56. *Faim et Soif*, 24, November–December 1972, minutes of the UCC West regional meeting.

57. UCC archives, GA, November 1976.

58. *Ibid.*

59. Interview with Laurent Desmard.

## CHAPTER 6

1. UACE archives, Régis Thimoreau, “Regard sur les communautés de l'UACE”, 1 July 1977.

2. Standard practice within Emmaus.

3. Quoted by Gérard Marin and Roland Bonnet, *op. cit.*, p. 135.

4. Association Emmaus archives on the Prost home.

5. For the source of these figures, see Marcel Montalbetti, *op. cit.*

6. Association Emmaus archives on the Prost home, survey referenced.

7. Association Emmaus archives on the Prost home, survey referenced.

8. *Ibid.*

9. This figure appears high when compared with the divorce rate of the time. What is also surprising is that this figure pertains to a rural area.

10. Association Emmaus archives on the Prost home.

11. Abbé Pierre, “Coutumier”, *Servir*, 31 August 1956.

12. Account in Marcel Montalbetti, *op. cit.*, p. 260–1.

13. CAMT, 2000 050 0947, Le Maillon, 1971.

14. Account from Bernard Eidenschenk in Marcel Montalbetti, *op. cit.*, p. 263.

15. Equivalent to €12.85 in 1960, and €9.7 in 1968 (in real terms).

16. Equivalent to €23.6.

17. Interview with Hervé Le Ru.

18. Account from Bernard Eidenschenk in Marcel Montalbetti, *op. cit.*, p. 260.

19. Averages calculated based on results collected between 1975 and 1978.

20. UACE archives, GA, 31 March 1977.

21. UACE archives, UACE, CA, 4 September 1977.

22. *Ibid.*

23. Goffman, Erwin, *Asiles. Études sur la condition sociale des maladies mentaux et autres reclus*, Paris, Minuit, 1968.

24. Lacroix, Bernard, *L'Utopie communautaire...*, *op. cit.*

25. Lacroix, Bernard, *L'Utopie communautaire..., op. cit.*, p. 57.

26. UACE archives, Friends-Leaders meeting, 20 March 1981.

27. In Alsace, the term *gendarme* also describes a smoked beef dish.

28. Account from Bernard Eidenschenk in Marcel Montalbetti, *op. cit.*, p. 251.

29. *Ibid.*

30. Marin, Gérard and Bonnet, Roland, *op. cit.*, p. 134.

31. UACE archives, Régis Thimoreau, "Regard sur les communautés de l'UACE," 1 July 1977.

32. Account from Bernard Eidenschenk in Marcel Montalbetti, *op. cit.*

33. UACE archives, meeting of the leaders of settled communities, 23 March 1973.

34. *Faim et Soif*, 1–2, March–April 1969.

35. Coutumier in *Servir*, 31 August 1956, p. 29.

36. Coutumier in *Et les Autres*, September 1957, p. 29.

37. UACE archives, bureau meeting, 27 July 1972, statement by Abbé Pierre.

38. UACE archives, Leaders meeting, 6 June 1979, statement by Abbé Pierre.

39. Coutumier, p. 29, quoting an article from *Et les Autres* published in September 1957.

40. A female Companion speaking at an evening organised in honour of Abbé Pierre, Bercy, 25 January 2007.

41. UCC archives, GA, 23–24 April 1966.

42. Brodiez, Axelle, *Le Secours populaire français*, *op. cit.*

43. See the following section.

44. Brochure, June 1970.

45. Prost home archives, meeting, 16 November 1964.

## CHAPTER 7

1. Thévenin, Étienne and Follereau, Raoul, *Hier et aujourd'hui*, Paris, Fayard, 1992.

2. Rodet, Anne-Sophie, *Naissance et fonctionnement d'Emmaüs International (1949–1988). Un rassemblement d'initiatives autour de l'esprit d'Emmaüs*, Master's thesis, Paris, Université Paris-IV Sorbonne, June 2003.

3. "Ten years before the events of May 1968 and the revolts of young people across the world who were wealthy to a greater or lesser extent, the man who created the Ragpicker-builders had put his finger on the wound, diagnosed the disease that was eating away at our consumer societies: it was called boredom, saturation, the slow death of faith, of all faiths. Those youngsters were slowly dying of no longer believing in anything, of bathing in unnecessary excess at twenty years of age, of being prematurely jaded. They are unhappy at being too happy. What's more, they had the means to survive: they were lacking reasons to live," in Gérard Marin and Roland Bonnet, *op. cit.*, p. 323. Then quoting the speech given by Abbé Pierre: "The cure for this

disease is to use your courage, your health and your studies to take yourself by the hand once you have finished preparing for life and to take your strength and your will to those who suffer, not as masters but as brothers," *op. cit.*, p. 324.

4. Information letter 60, March 1988.

5. Rodet, Anne-Sophie, *Naissance et fonctionnement d'Emmaüs International (1949–1988)*, thesis referenced.

6. *Histoire du christianisme*, t. XIII "Crises et renouveau (de 1958 à nos jours)," p. 658.

7. On the transition from missionary work to humanitarian development, see in particular Prudhomme, Claude, "De la mission aux ONG de solidarité internationale: quelle continuité?," in Duriez, Bruno, Mabille, François and Rousselet, Kathy (eds), *Les ONG confessionnelles. Religions et action internationale*, Paris, L'Harmattan, 2007, p. 55–69.

8. On the development of Emmaus in Japan, see *Faim et Soif*, 19, July 1957; *Faim et Soif*, 11, October–November 1970; 26, March–April 1973; 29, September–October 1973; 42, second quarter 1976; 47, third quarter 1977; Six, Anne-Sophie, *Le Mouvement d'Emmaüs en Asie (implantation, développement et difficulties (années 1950–1990)*, Master's thesis, Lille, Université Lille-III, June 2003; Glynn, Paul, *Satoko San, une femme chez les chiffonniers*, Hunters Hills, Marists Fathers Books, 1992.

9. Issue 11, October–November 1970.

10. Marin, Gérard and Bonnet, Roland, *op. cit.*, and Six, Anne-Sophie, thesis referenced.

11. *Faim et Soif*, 30, August 1959.

12. Marin, Gérard Marin and Bonnet, Roland *op. cit.*

13. *Faim et Soif*, 23, September–October 1972, p. 18.

14. *Faim et Soif*, 30, August 1959.

15. On Emmaus in Peru, see *Faim et Soif*, 44, January–February 1962; 47, July–August 1962; 59, late 1964; 76, 1967; *Faim et Soif*, 5, November 1969; 8, June–July 1970; 34, July–August 1974; 48, Christmas 1977.

16. On Dom Helder Camara, see in particular Löwy, Michael, *La Guerre des dieux, Religion et politique en Amérique Latine*, Paris, Éditions du Félin, 1998 and Toulat, Jean, *Dom Helder Camara*, Paris, Le Centurion, 1989.

17. *Faim et Soif*, 51, third quarter 1978.

18. On Emmaus in Rwanda, see in particular *Faim et Soif*, 14, March–April 1971, and 33, May–June 1974.

19. Roubaix, CAMT, 2000 0501 102, general inaugural assembly of Emmaus International, 27 November 1957.

20. *Faim et Soif*, 1–2, March–April 1969.

21. *Faim et Soif*, 44, Christmas 1976.

22. Roubaix, CAMT, 2000 050 1106, administrative commission, 7–8 October 1978.

23. Toscer, Sylvie, *Les Catholiques allemands à la conquête du développement*, Paris, L'Harmattan, 1997.

24. Issue 53.

25. Extract quoted in issue 72.

26. CAMT, 2000 0501105, Emmaus International GA, September 1974, "Emmaüs et son engagement."

27. *Faim et Soif*, 51, March–April 1963.

28. *Faim et Soif*, 68, 1966.

29. The fifth General Latin American Episcopal Conference, held in Medellín from 26 August to 6 September 1968, was a turning point. Denouncing the structures in place based on injustice, the violation of fundamental rights and institutionalised violence, the conference affirmed the Church's solidarity with the aspirations of the people "to be free of servitude" and acknowledged that, in certain circumstances, revolutionary action was legitimate. See in particular Compagnon, Olivier, "L'Amérique Latine," in Mayeur, Jean-Marie, Piétri, Charles and Luce, Vauchez, André and Venard, Marc (eds), *Histoire du christianisme*, Paris, Desclée, 2000, t. XIII, p. 509–77 and Vayssière, Pierre, *Les Révolutions d'Amérique Latine*, Paris, Seuil, 1991.

30. *Faim et Soif*, 79, Summer 1968.

31. Löwy, Michael, *La Guerre des dieux*, *op. cit.*, p. 55: the term "Liberation Christianity" is used to refer to the very broad social movement which began to develop in the early 1960s, and whose key figures were in no way theologians; and more specifically "liberation theology" was the term used to describe "the spiritual product of this social movement" which itself began to develop in the 1970s.

32. This was undoubtedly for reasons just as closely linked to the county's political situation as to the sociological principles specific to the group led by J.-Y. Olichon.

33. Roubaix, CAMT, 2000 050 1103, GA, 24–25 May 1969.

34. *Ibid.*

35. Liberation theology first appeared in 1971, moulded by two priests, Gustavo Gutiérrez and Leonardo Boff. After a decade of Christian initiatives in Latin America from activists whose aim was to improve social welfare, and after several years of debate among progressive theologians, this form of theology stated that the poor man should not wait for salvation from on high, he should not receive pity or charity, but should be the architect of his own liberation. As a result, Liberation theology advocated the wholesale destruction of the system through social revolution. See Lowy, Michaël, *op. cit.* and Compagnon, Olivier, article referenced.

36. *Faim et Soif*, 28, July–August 1973, p. 12–13.

37. CAMT, 2000 0501111, quoted in the meeting of the Administrative Commission, 13 September 1974.

38. Roubaix, CAMT, 2000 0501103, GA, 24–25 May 1969.

39. Issue 8, June–July 1970.

40. Pelletier, Denis, *La Crise catholique, Religion, société, politique en France (1965–1978)*, Paris, Payot, 2002 and Rousseau, Sabine, "Les cathos de gauche: l'engagement dans les luttes politiques," in Artières, Philippe and Zancarini-Fournel, Michelle (eds), *68. Une histoire collective [1962–1981]*, Paris, La Découverte, 2008, p. 634–41. On the Catholic pro-Third World approach, see also Denis Pelletier, "Tiers-mondisme catholique: un héritage incertain," in Bruno Duriez, François Mabille and Kathy Rousselet (eds), *Les ONG confessionnelles, op. cit.*, p. 71–84.

41. Roubaix, CAMT 2000 0501106, meeting of the Administrative Commission, 7–8 October, text unanimously adopted.

42. *Faim et Soif*, 38, late 1960.

43. With the 1947 partition, the British and the Indians created a secular state, India, and a Muslim state, Pakistan, which was itself divided into two parts separated by India. East Pakistan (Bengal), economically underdeveloped and politically controlled by West Pakistan, was first a victim of the slow reaction on the part of the Western Pakistanis to the huge floods, and then to the cyclone which caused devastation in 1970. During the elections in late 1970, East Pakistan reacted by awarding the Bengalis a resounding victory. In March 1971, Bengal declared its independence, but its leader was arrested, causing an influx of between 7 and 10 million Bengali refugees to flow into neighbouring India. India's military intervention in December finally resolved the crisis, and Bangladesh became independent.

44. Issue 17, September–October 1971.

45. Roubaix, CAMT, 2000 050 0497, speech made by Abbé Pierre on the occasion of the creation of UCOJUCO, July 1972: italicised in the original text.

46. *Faim et Soif*, 48, Christmas 1977.

## CHAPTER 8

1. On the General Confederation of Housing (CGL), see Chapter 2.

2. Damon, Julien, *Vagabondage et Mendicité*, Paris, Flammarion, 1998.

3. The collective eventually comprised all the major associations in the sector, almost all of which had religious roots: *Association Emmaus*, the Salvation Army, *Secours catholique*, FNARS, *Centre d'action sociale protestant, Équipes Saint-Vincent* and *Société Saint-Vincent-de-Paul, Fonds social juif unifié, Petits Frères des Pauvres, Œuvres de la mie de pain*, ATD Fourth-World, etc.

4. Damon, Julien, *La Question SDF. Critique d'une action publique*, Paris, PUF, 2002.

5. Founded in 1956, the *Fédération des centres d'hébergement* changed its name several times before becoming the *Fédération nationale des associations d'accueil et de réinsertion sociale* (FNARS) in 1999.

6. Damon, Julien, *La Question SDF, op. cit.*; Emmanuelli, Xavier and Frémontier, Clémentine, *La Fracture sociale*, PUF, 2002.

7. The remaining percentage was split between the Salvation Army (7%), the *Centre d'action sociale de la ville de Paris* (7%) and the association *La Halte des amis de la rue* (3%).

8. Damon, Julien, *La Question SDF, op. cit.*

9. *Grande pauvreté économique sociale*, report submitted by Mr Joseph Wresinski to the Economic and Social Council, at its session of 11 and 12 February 1987, *Journal official de la République française*, 28 February 1987.

10. The Departmental Integration Council (CDI) was responsible for preparing the integration programme for its administrative department. They met twice a year to evaluate needs and take stock of the work under way.

11. The Local Integration Committee (CLI) was responsible for drawing up integration contracts with those receiving support.

12. According to estimates, it is necessary to multiply the amount of time spent on the street by between five and ten in order to calculate the time needed for a homeless person to reintegrate into society with support.

13. See the following chapter.

14. At the time, the RATP was carrying out works underneath Rue des Bourdonnais to build Châtelet station on line 14, and also became involved with a policy in aid of the homeless, who were heavily present in the metro.

15. *Direction de l'action sociale, de l'enfance et de la santé* (a specific branch of the Paris social affairs department which deals with social welfare, childhood and health). The department was created in 1985 as part of the decentralisation process.

16. Association Emmaus archives, GA, 16 June 1998.

17. *Août secours alimentaire, les Sœurs missionnaires de la Charité, La Lumière dans la rue, le Cœur des halles, le Centre Beaudricourt du CASP (Centre d'action sociale protestant), les Orphelins apprentis d'Auteuil, la Fraternité Notre-Dame, Association Emmaüs.*

18. For a summary of the history of these organisations, see in particular Gueslin, André, *Gens pauvres, pauvres gens dans la France du XIXe siècle*, Paris, Aubier, 1998, Chapter 8.

19. Today known as FNARS.

20. This was later changed to "reintegration."

21. Emmanuelli, Xavier and Frémontier, Clémentine, *La Fracture sociale, op. cit.*

22. Damon, Julien, *La Question SDF, op. cit.*

23. Association Emmaus archives, CA, 12 February 1992.

24. On the Quai de Valmy building, see also Chapter 12.

25. Association Emmaus archives, GA, 28 June 1994.

26. In both the apartments and supported apartments, each resident received APL, a housing benefit awarded to those paying rent or a mortgage, the length of stay was adapted to their individual situation, and there was no maximum length of stay. These housing facilities offered social support and group activities.

27. Tenants paid the rent on these properties while being actively monitored by the Association.

28. The social residences were small facilities, where residents were able to receive APL (see note 26 above). The maximum length of stay was two years and limited social support was provided.

29. See the eloquent account in Prolongeau, Hubert, *Sans domicile fixe*, Paris, Hachette, 1993.

30. French Office for the Protection of Refugees and Stateless Persons.

31. Association Emmaus archives, GA, 28 May 2002.

32. *Ibid.*

33. Association Emmaus archives, GA, 28 May 2002.

34. Each individual was given a place until an alternative housing solution was found.

35. Association Emmaus archives, GA, 13 May 2008 and Abbé Pierre Foundation, *Rapport mal-logement 2008.*

36. Association Emmaus archives, CA, 15 December 1998.

37. Association Emmaus archives, GA, 14 September 1988.

38. Association Emmaus archives, CA, 12 September 1995.

39. Association Emmaus archives, GA, 29 May 2001.

40. Association Emmaus archives, CA 11 April 1995.

41. Association Emmaus archives, CA, 28 June 2005.

42. Association Emmaus archives, CA, 7 February 1995.

43. On IRAMM, see Chapter 2.

44. Association Emmaus archives, CA, 17 December 1996.

45. Association Emmaus archives, CA, 2 March 2004.

## CHAPTER 9

1. Stébé, Jean-Marc, *Le Logement social en France, op. cit.*

2. Emmaus-Habitat archives, GA, 21 June 1978.

3. Horenfeld, Gilles, "L'univers des HLM," in Ségaud, Marion, Bonvallet, Catherine and Brun, Jacques (eds), *Logement et habitat, op. cit.*, p. 136–46.

4. Emmaus-Habitat archives, CA, 14 December 1983.

5. *Prêts locatifs aidés*, subsidised housing loans, also created in 1977 to diversify and extend the social housing supply.

6. Simon, Patrick, "Le logement et l'intégration des immigrés," in Ségaud, Marion Bonvallet, Catherine and Brun, Jacques (eds), *Logement et habitat, op. cit.*, p. 327–35.

7. Chaline, Claude, *Les Politiques de la ville*, Paris, PUF, 1997 (4th edition 2006), p. 22.

8. As a percentage of the primary residences in the commune.

9. Emmaus-Habitat archives, GA, 24 June 1999.

10. Emmaus-Habitat archives, CA, 2 October 1981.

11. The following quotation is also taken from an interview with Claude Néry.

12. *Comité Interprofessionnel pour le logement.* A Not-for-Profit organisation designed to collect the money which employers were legally obliged to contribute to social housing (1% of the total wage bill for employers with ten or more employees.)

13. Interview with Claude Néry.

14. *Faim et Soif*, 87, January 1988.

15. Emmaus France, CA, 6–7 January 1989.

16. Interview with Claude Néry.

17. *Ibid.*

18. Originally, this group comprised one representative from the Ministry of Social Affairs, one from the Ministry of Home Affairs, one from the Ministry for Works and one from the European Commission.

19. Abbé Pierre Foundation archives, bureau meeting, 15 February 1989.

20. Abbé Pierre Foundation archives, 1996 activity report.

21. Abbé Pierre Foundation archives.

22. Abbé Pierre Foundation archives, CA, 13 December 2000.

23. Abbé Pierre Foundation archives, 1997 activity report.

24. To make the text easier to read, the term "Foundation" is used here. However, this is an anachronism as the organisation officially remained an association until 1992.

25. For a general overview of these campaigns, see Barthélémy, Martine, *Associations: un nouvel âge de la participation?*, Paris, Presses de Sciences Po, 2000.

26. See Chapter 12.

27. Abbé Pierre Foundation archives, telegram to Minister Louis Besson, 14 March 1991.

28. Letter dated 24 February 1993.

29. *Union nationale des organisations privées sanitaires et sociales.* Union representing private organisations working with vulnerable sectors of the population.

30. *Fédération nationale des associations d'accueil et de réinsertion sociale.* Federation of bodies and association offering a bed, support and assistance with social reintegration to those in serious difficulty.

31. This figure included 800,000 people who were struggling to acquire a decent, legal dwelling, 1.9 million living in conditions which did not meet official comfort and hygiene standards and 600,000 people living in critically overcrowded accommodation.

32. Abbé Pierre Foundation archives, bureau meeting, 9 May 1989.

33. The Foundation was also given free publicity on six national networks and twelve local radio stations, in seventy-seven titles in the written press across 325 towns and thirty-four departmental councils and six free slots on

M6. Commercial and promotional inserts were broadcast or printed at a discount price on TF1, France 2 and France 3, France inter, Radion bleue; *Télérama, La Vie, Témoignage chrétien, La Croix, Le Pèlerin, L'Express, Le Point, Notre Temps, Télé Z, Télé poche, Le Figaro* and *Le Monde*; 300 posters were put up in places owned by railway company SNCF in the Paris region, 284 in the major cities outside the capital and 600 in the metro. Records show that the Foundation broadcast fifty-four messages on television, 821 on the radio, placed fifty-seven advertisements in the written press, fifty-five in magazines and put up a total of 22,500 posters of all shapes and sizes.

34. Abbé Pierre Foundation archives, CA, 23 February 1994.

35. Abbé Pierre Foundation archives, CA, 10 July 1996.

36. IFOP survey, February 1997: 12% of those interviewed knew of the Foundation.

37. IFOP survey, January 1998: 14% of those interviewed knew of the Foundation.

38. These comprised households who had filled in an in-depth questionnaire on consumption habits and behavioural patterns.

39. Abbé Pierre Foundation archives, CA, 16 June 2004.

40. Boltanski, Luc, *La Souffrance à distance, op. cit.*

41. Abbé Pierre Foundation archives.

42. Abbé Pierre Foundation archives, CA, 20 June 2001.

43. This poster was innovative in comparison with those previously produced by the Foundation. Nevertheless, its composition, the techniques used and its ability to challenge the viewer made it heavily evocative of the poster produced by the agency Magnum for the Secours populaire campaign "grande cause nationale."

44. Those who have made a donation in the last 24 months.

## CHAPTER 10

1. UACE archives, Friends-Leaders meeting.

2. UACE archives, Friends-Leaders meeting, 25 September 1981.

3. See in particular the speeches by Abbé Pierre at the first two general assemblies of CNAE (8 June 1980 and 13 June 1981).

4. We have combed through the economic and social records of UCC (1980s and 1990s), of all of the UACE communities throughout the 1990s and of all of the French communities for the years 2000–3. In view of the fact that community members constantly switched from one community to another, we will view these three sources as comparable.

5. The limitations of conducting a sociological analysis using a synchronic graph thus become clear: in his thesis, Betrand Bergier calculates that the average for 1988–9 stood at 11.6% (Bergier, Bertrand, *Compagnons d'Emmaus, Sociologie du quotidien communautaire*, Paris, Les Éditions ouvrières, 1992,

p. 46). He compares this to 1964–5. However, had he been looking at any other year, he could well have produced very different results.

6. Damon, Julien, *La Question SDF, op. cit.*

7. At the time, these were mainly businesses for social integration working in construction, restoration, the creation of green spaces, etc.

8. Created in 1983, les *Travaux d'utilité* collective were part-time work-experience placements completed by young people looking for work. They were paid half the SMIC (*Salaire minimum interprofessionnel de croissance*).

9. Created in 1990, the *Contrats emploi-solidarité* were part-time contracts for a maximum of 12 months, designed for people of all ages. They were paid at half the SMIC rate and funded by the state.

10. *Contrats emploi consolidé.* Designed for the long-term unemployed over the age of 50.

11. CNAE archives, GA, 29–30 October 1988.

12. *Contrat initiative emploi.* Designed to allow those experiencing serious difficulty in finding a job to find secure, long-term employment.

13. Source for 1988–9: Bergier, Bertrand, *Emmaüs: les droits de succession. Contribution à une systémisation de l'intentionnel et de l'inintentionnel à Emmaüs*, doctoral thesis in sociology, Université Paris-7, November 1990.

14. Bergier, Bertrand, *Emmaüs: les droits de succession..., op. cit.*

15. UACE archives, Friends-Leaders meeting, 14 June 1984.

16. Limagne, Paul, *Quelle retraite pour les compagnons d'Emmaüs?*, DESS thesis, Grenoble, Université Pierre-Mendès France, 1995: 42% of the Companions surveyed at the time wished to spend their retirement living independently, 20% wished to live in a house specially designed for the elderly and a further 12% wished to live in a home.

17. In the sociological sense of the word, even though for some, it is not inappropriate to use it in the professional sense.

18. Limagne, Paul, *Quelle retraite pour les compagnons d'Emmaüs?,* thesis referenced.

19. de Silguy, Catherine, *Histoire des hommes et de leurs ordures, op. cit.*, p. 169.

20. Emmaus France Emmaus, CA, 18–19 June 1993.

21. This was the result of new competition from the private sector (large firms), but also from the public sector (the emergence of plants which repaired and recycled waste). It was also the result of the boom in attic sales, bric-à-brac stalls, flea markets and the development of recycling websites.

22. Balet, Jean-Michel, *Gestion des déchets*, Paris, Dunod, 2005: Bardes, Sabine, *L'Invention des déchets urbains, op. cit.*

23. Contributions at the symposium *Récupération des textiles à l'heure des choix: détruire ou créer des emplois?*, organised by Emmaus France, 23 March 2006, contribution from Serge Sztarkman, president of the National Recycling Union (*Syndicat national du recyclage*), p. 13.

24. Emmaus France archives, CA, 26 April 2002.

25. Unable to afford new, 85% of the population in developing countries dressed themselves in second-hand clothes. The delivery of these European containers also created jobs. Workers were needed to unload the containers, do business, run small workshops, etc.

26. These platforms were created following the realisation that only 40% of the textiles which the Communities and Committees of Friends received had been treated, compared with 60% of those which went to those collecting unwanted items or which were sent to incinerators.

27. The "WEEE" can be broken down into four categories: large domestic appliances (washing machines, dishwashers, electric ovens, microwaves...), "cold" appliances (refrigerators and freezers), screens (television or computer screens...) and small, miscellaneous items (hi-fi systems, computer equipment other than screens, radios, toasters, hairdryers, lamps, electric power tools, etc.).

28. UACE archives, Friends-Leaders meeting, 20 March 1981.

29. UACE archives, Friends-Leaders meeting, 16 June 1983.

30. UCC archives GA, 8–9 June 1991.

31. Ion, Jacques, *La Fin des militants?*, Paris, Les Éditions de l'Atelier, 1997. There will be no further discussion of these thesis. They have already been extensively debated in several articles and in our most recent work.

32. UACE archives, GA, 17 June 1983.

33. CNAE archives, GA, 23–24 April 2005.

34. UCC archives, Credoc report, 2001 survey.

35. UACE archives, Friends-Leaders meeting, 15–16 September 1983.

36. See above.

37. Pelletier, Denis, *La Crise catholique*, *op. cit.*

38. Interview with Hervé Le Ru.

39. UCC archives, GA, 29–30 November 1974.

## CHAPTER 11

1. The expression of Danièle Hervieu-Léger used to describe the change seen in religious ideologies: Hervieu-Léger, Danièle, *Le Pélerin et le converti. La religion en movement*, Paris, Flammarion, 1999.

2. Agrikoliansky, Eric, Fillieule, Olivier et Mayer, Nonna eds, *L'Altermondialisme en France. La longue histoire d'une nouvelle cause*, Paris, Flammarion, 2005.

3. Roubaix, CAMT, 2000 0501111, CA, 14–16 October 1987.

4. Roubaix, CAMT, 2000 0501111, executive committee, 5–6 June 1986.

5. Emmaus International information letter, 61, June 1988.

6. Mayeur, Jean-Marie, "L'enseignement sociale de l'Église catholique," in *Histoire de christianisme*, *op. cit.*, 2nd part, Chapters 6 and 7, p. 320–31.

7. Roubaix, CAMT, 2000 0501108, GA, 21–23 September 1988, working document.

8. Roubaix, CAMT, 2000 0501111, executive committee, 26–27 January 1988.

9. *Ibid.*

10. *Ibid.*

11. Boff, Leonardo and Elizondo, Virgil, *Une théologie partant de l'optique des pauvres*, Concilium, 207, 1986, p. 7–10, reprinted in full in the Emmaus International information letter, 61, June 1988.

12. *Ibid.*

13. Emmaus International information letter, 64, March 1989, transcription of the speech by Juan Manuel Hurtado at the general assembly.

14. Emmaus International information letter, 63, December 1988, opening speech by Franco Bettoli.

15. Common Ethical Investment Fund. Invested in development aid associations at a rate higher than inflation.

16. See Löwy, Michael, *La Guerre des dieux*, *op. cit.*: the term "liberation Christianity" is used to refer to the very broad social movement which began to develop in the early 1960. The key figures of this movement were by no means theologians. The more specific term "liberation theology" refers to "the spiritual product of this social movement" (p. 55) which began to develop in 1970.

17. Agrikoliansky, Éric, "Du tiers-mondisme à l'altermondialisme: genèse(s) d'une nouvelle cause," in Agrikolansky, Éric, Fillieule, Olivier and Mayer, Nonna (eds), *op. cit.*, p. 70.

18. Emmaus International information letter, 65, October 1989.

19. Agrikoliansky, Éric, "Du tiers-mondisme à l'altermondialisme: genèse(s) d'une nouvelle cause", article referenced.

20. The Other Economic Summit.

21. Alfortville, Emmaus International archives, GA, 1992, speech by Pepe Aravena (Chile).

22. EFTA (European Fair Trade Association) was founded in 1988. IFTA (International Fair Trade Federation) followed in 1989.

23. Emmaus International information letter, 80, May 1993.

24. See following chapter.

25. *Centre de recherche et d'information pour le développement* (a collective of associations).

26. Signed in USA in July 1994, the Bretton Woods agreements sketched out the post-war international economic and financial system, and famously created the IMF and IBRD.

27. Professor of Political Economics at Université catholique de Louvain, and a key figure of the anti-globalisation movement.

28. Alfortville, Emmaus International archives, GA, 9–12 September 1996.

29. "Introduction: aux origines de l'altermondialisme français," in Agrikoliansky, Éric Fillieule, Olivier and Mayer, Nonna (eds), *op. cit.*, p. 31.

30. *Ibid.*, p. 36.

31. See below.

32. DG5 is the European Directorate General responsible for employment, social affairs and education. The federation is EAPN (European Anti-Poverty Network).

33. Alfortville, Emmaus International archives, executive committee, 19 June 1990.

34. Alfortville, Emmaus International archives, CA, 21–23 November 2000.

35. Alfortville, Emmaus International archives, GA, 24–25 September 1999.

36. Alfortville, Emmaus International archives, executive committee, 13–14 February 1995.

37. Alfortville, Emmaus International archives, executive committee, 25–26 May 1994.

38. Alfortville, Emmaus International archives, GA, 9–12 September 1996.

39. Alfortville, Emmaus International archives, GA, 24–26 September 1999.

40. Alfortville, Emmaus International archives, executive committee, 21–24 June 1994.

## CHAPTER 12

1. *Faim et Soif*, 17, September–October 1971.

2. *Ibid.*

3. UACE archives, GA, 23 April 1972.

4. UACE archives.

5. UACE archives, Friends-Leaders meeting, 6 October 1977.

6. UACE archives, 25 January 1978.

7. *Fédération nationale des associations d'accueil et de réinsertion sociale.*

8. Emmaus France archives, minutes of the meeting held at L'Élysée on 24 January 1983.

9. Emmaus France archives, meeting of the provisional committee, 12 December 1984.

10. Letter written in preparation for the 40th anniversary celebrations.

11. Emmaus France archives, GA, 8–9 December 1989.

12. *Charité business*, Paris, Le Pré aux clercs, 1986.

13. Marquès, Marie-France, "Spectacle, don et travail social," Projet, 204, March–April 1987, p. 7–22.

14. Emmaus France archives, GA, 8–9 December 1989.

15. Emmaus France archives, CA, 27–28 May 1988.

16. Emmaus France archives, CA, 9–10 June 1989.

17. On the celebrations to mark the bicentenary, see Garcia, Patrick, *Le Bicentenaire de la Révolution française. Pratiques sociales d'une commémoration*, Paris, CNRS Éditions, 2000. As far as the resurgence of political expression on the part of the associations around the bicentenary was concerned, it has

been demonstrated elsewhere that the bicentenary also caused this association to adopt more political forms of expression. This was seen despite the fact that the entire history of *Secours populaire* since the early 1960s can be read as the slow rejection of affiliation to a particular political cause in favour of a charitable approach.

18. See below.

19. *Union nationale interfédérale des œuvres privées sanitaires et sociales*. Has since become *Union nationale interfédérale des œuvres et organismes privés sanitaires et sociaux*. Union which brings together private-sector organisations supporting vulnerable groups of the population.

20. UCC archives, GA, 1990.

21. On these two organisations and on the demonstrations over housing which took place between 1987 and 1994, see Péchu, Cécile, *Droit au logement, Genèse et sociologie d'une mobilisation*, Paris, Dalloz, 2006.

22. Péchu, Cécile, *op. cit.*, p. 243.

23. Péchu, Cécile, *op. cit.*

24. The Association made such demands underlining that at the time, 4,000 council houses and around 1,00,000 private homes were unoccupied in the Paris area.

25. This reform provided for the abolition of the ban on evicting squatters during winter.

26. Péchu, Cécile, *op. cit.*, p. 445.

27. Emmaus France archives, CA, 21 September 1991, speech by Abbé Pierre.

28. Not wishing to give land to the state, and not helping to rehouse those who had been evicted either, Paris Town Council tended to play for time when it came to dealing with squatters.

29. Emmaus France archives, CA, 20 September 1991.

30. Péchu, Cécile, *op. cit.*

31. Association Emmaus archives, CA, 17 January 1995.

32. Emmaus France archives, CA, 7–8 April 1995.

33. Emmaus France archives, GA, 5–6 May 1995.

34. Emmaus France archives, CA, 30–31 July 1992.

35. *Ibid.*

36. Emmaus France archives, CA, 7–8 April 1995.

37. Mulinaris lives in France and is married to one of Abbé Pierre's nieces. In late 1981 he was arrested and imprisoned in Italy as part of the fight against the Red Brigades. Abbé Pierre took charge of the fight to secure his release: a file of evidence was compiled to disprove the accusations, the case was brought before the European Court of Human Rights, and pressure was placed on the French Ministry of Home Affairs and the General Intelligence Department, amongst others. In 1984, Abbé Pierre even went as far as fasting for a week, supported by the Cardinals of Turin and Milan, the Pope's entourage and the Archbishop of Udine. Mulinaris was eventually released and cleared.

38. Emmaus France archives, CA, 26–27 April 1996.

39. "Letter to Roger Garaudy", dated 15 April 1996.

40. First press release, dated 24 April 1996.

41. Second press release, dated 30 April 1996.

42. GISTI, formerly known as *Groupe d'information et de soutien aux travailleurs immigrés*, is an association founded in 1972 which today supports immigrants chiefly by providing them with legal support.

43. FASTI (*Fédération des associations de solidarité avec les travailleurs immigrés*) was created in the 1960s as a response to the working conditions and treatment of immigrants, and fights for equal rights.

44. *Droits Devant* is an association for the protection of illegal immigrants created in the early 1990s.

45. *La Ligue des droits de l'homme* was founded in 1898 during the Dreyfus affair. It combats human rights violations.

46. Le MRAP (*Mouvement contre le racisme et l'amitié entre les peuples*), was founded during the war and officially relaunched in 1949. It fights racism and aims to foster friendship between people of different countries.

47. *La Cimade* (*Comité intermouvement auprès des évacués*) was founded in October 1939. Originally a Protestant organisation, since the late 1970s it has been particularly active in supporting immigrants.

48. Emmaus France archives, meeting of the Immigration Commission, 3 November 1999.

49. Emmaus France archives, CA.

50. Emmaus France, meeting of the Immigration Commission.

51. Association Emmaus archives, CA, 22 October 2002.

52. Emmaus France archives, CA, 27 June 2003.

53. *Centre d'accueil pour demandeurs d'asile.* Association providing support to asylum seekers.

54. Emmaus France archives, CA, 18 November 2005.

55. Abbé Pierre Foundation archives, CA, 20 June 2001.

## CONCLUSION

1. Brodiez, Axelle, *Le Secours populaire français, op. cit.*

2. Emmaus International information letter, 64, March 1989, speech by Jean Ziegler at the 1988 general assembly.

3. *Pourquoi s'engager? Bénévoles et militants dans les associations de solidarité*, Paris, Payot, 2005, p. 108.

4. Interview.

5. Interview.

6. Emmaus France archives, CA, 9–10 June 1989.

7. Emmaus France archives, CA, 6–7 October 1989.

8. Emmaus International archives.

9. Dubrulle, Luc thesis referenced, p. 339, 342.

10. Péchu, Cécile, *op. cit.* In her text, Péchu uses the term "*champ associatif*" which has been translated in this text as "humanitarian domain." Péchu's term is relevant to her argument. It is, however, a controversial term, given that the world of humanitarian associations is not sufficiently uniform to create a genuine "champ" or domain, as it appears in this translation. (cf. Andrieu, Claire, le Béguec, Gilles and Tartakowsky, Danielle 'eds), *Associations et champ politique*, Paris, Publications la Sorbonne, 2001).

Mise en page : Corlet Imprimeur